Kant's Moral and Legal Philosophy

Kant's Moral and Legal Philosophy brings to English readers the finest postwar German-language scholarship on Kant's moral and legal philosophy. Examining Kant's relation to predecessors such as Hutcheson, Wolff, and Baumgarten, it clarifies the central issues in each of Kant's major works in practical philosophy, including *The Groundwork of the Metaphysics of Morals, The Critique of Practical Reason,* and *The Metaphysics of Morals.* It also examines the relation of Kant's philosophy to politics.

Collectively, the essays in this volume provide English readers with a direct view of the way leading contemporary German philosophers now look at Kant's revolutionary practical philosophy – one of the outstanding achievements of German thought.

Karl Ameriks is McMahon-Hank Professor of Philosophy at the University of Notre Dame. A recipient of fellowships from the Humboldt Foundation, the National Endowment for the Humanities, the American Council of Learned Societies, and the Earhart Foundation, he is the author of several books, including *Kant's Theory of Mind* and *Kant and the Fate of Autonomy,* and editor of *The Cambridge Companion to German Idealism.* He is also coeditor of the series Cambridge Texts in the History of Philosophy.

Otfried Höffe is Professor of Philosophy at the University of Tübingen and permanent visiting Professor of the Philosophy of Law at the University of St. Gallen. He is also Doctor Honoris Causa of the University of Porto Allegre (PUCRS), Fellow of the Heidelberger Akademie der Wissenschaften, and Fellow of The German Academy of Sciences Leopoldina. He is the author of *Immanuel Kant, Political Justice, Categorical Principles of Law, Aristotle, Kant's Cosmopolitian Theory of Law and Peace: Democracy in an Age of Globalisation,* and many other books in German. He has coedited *Hegel on Ethics and Politics,* edited *Lexikon der Ethik* and *Lesebuch zur Ethik,* and is editor of *Zeitschrift für philosophische Forschung,* the series Denker, and Klassiker Auslegen. With Robert Pippin, he is coeditor of the Cambridge series The German Philosophical Tradition.

The German Philosophical Tradition

This series makes available in English for the first time important recent work by German philosophers on major figures in the German philosophical tradition. The volumes provide critical perspectives on philosophers of great significance to the Anglo-American philosophical community, perspectives that have been largely ignored except by a handful of writers of German philosophy. The dissemination of this work will be of enormous value to Anglophone students and scholars of German philosophy.

Otfried Höffe is Professor of Philosophy at the University of Tübingen.

Robert B. Pippin is Evelyn Stefansson Nef Distinguished Service Professor in the Committee on Social Thought, Department of Philosophy, and the College, University of Chicago.

Kant's Moral and Legal Philosophy

Edited by

Karl Ameriks
University of Notre Dame

Otfried Höffe
University of Tübingen

Translated by
Nicholas Walker

CAMBRIDGE
UNIVERSITY PRESS

CAMBRIDGE UNIVERSITY PRESS
Cambridge, New York, Melbourne, Madrid, Cape Town, Singapore, São Paulo, Delhi

Cambridge University Press
32 Avenue of the Americas, New York, NY 10013–2473, USA

www.cambridge.org
Information on this title: www.cambridge.org/9780521898713

First published 2009

Printed in the United States of America

A catalog record for this publication is available from the British Library.

Library of Congress Cataloging in Publication data
Kant's moral and legal philosophy / edited by Karl Ameriks, Otfried Höffe
    p.   cm. – (The German philosophical tradition)
Includes bibliographical references and index.
ISBN 978-0-521-89871-3 hardback
    1. Kant, Immanuel, 1724–1804. 2. Ethics. 3. Law–Philosophy. I. Ameriks, Karl, 1947–
II. Höffe, Otfried, 1943– III. Title. IV. Series.
B2799 E8K39 2009
170.92–dc22   2008045086

ISBN 978-0-521-89871-3 (hardback)

Contents

Acknowledgments

This collection brings together in translation the finest postwar German-language scholarship on Kant's moral and legal philosophy, including considerations of politics. All of the essays appear in English here for the first time. The editors acknowledge the original publishers and publications with thanks.

Dieter Henrich, "Hutcheson und Kant," *Kant-Studien* 49 (1957/58): 49–69.

Clemens Schwaiger, "Zur Theorie der Verbindlichkeit bei Wolff, Baumgarten und dem frühen Kant," Italian version in *La filosofia practica tra metafisica e antropologia nell'età di Wolff e Vico*, ed. G. Cacciatore et al. (Naples, 1999), pp. 323–340.

Ludwig Siep, "Wozu Metaphysik der Sitten? Bemerkungen zur Vorrede der *Grundlegung*," in *Grundlegung zur Metaphysik der Sitten. Ein kooperativer Kommentar*, ed. O. Höffe (Frankfurt, 1989), pp. 31–44.

Dieter Schönecker, "Gemeine sittliche und philosophische Vernunfterkenntnis. Zum ersten Übergang in Kants *Grundlegung*," *Kant-Studien* 88 (1997): 311–333.

Gerold Prauss, "Für sich selber praktische Vernunft," in *Grundlegung zur Metaphysik der Sitten. Ein kooperativer Kommentar*, ed. O. Höffe (Frankfurt, 1989), pp. 253–263.

Michael Albrecht, "Kants Maximenethik und ihre Begründung," in *Kant-Studien* 85 (1994): 129–146.

Otfried Höffe, "Die Form der Maximen als Bestimmungsgrund (§§ 4–6, 27–30)," in *Immanuel Kant/Kritik der praktischen Vernunft*, ed. O. Höffe (Berlin, 2002), pp. 63–80.

Annemarie Pieper, "Zweites Hauptstück (57–71)," in *Immanuel Kant/Kritik der praktischen Vernunft*, ed. O. Höffe (Berlin, 2002), pp. 115–133.

Eckart Förster, "Die Dialektik der praktischen Vernunft (107–121)," in *Immanuel Kant/Kritik der praktischen Vernunft*, ed. O. Höffe (Berlin, 2002), pp. 173–186.

Friedo Ricken, "Die Postulate der reinen praktischen Vernunft (122–148)," in *Immanuel Kant/Kritik der praktischen Vernunft*, ed. O. Höffe (Berlin, 2002), pp. 187–202.

Kristian Kühl, "Von der Art, etwas Äußeres zu erwerben, insbesondere vom
Sachenrecht," in *Immanuel Kant/Metaphysische Anfangsgründe der
Rechtslehre*, ed. O. Höffe (Berlin, 1999), pp. 117–132.

Wolfgang Kersting, "'Die bürgerliche Verfassung in jedem Staate soll republi-
kanisch sein,'" in *Immanuel Kant/Zum ewigen Frieden*, ed. O. Höffe (Berlin,
1995), pp. 87–108.

Bernd Ludwig, "Kommentar zum Staatsrecht (II) §§ 51–52; Allgemeine
Anmerkung A; Anhang, Beschluss," in *Immanuel Kant Metaphysische
Anfangsgründe der Rechtslehre*, ed. O. Höffe (Berlin, 2000), pp. 173–194.

Volker Gerhardt, "Der Thronverzicht der Philosophie. Über das moderne
Verhältnis von Philosophie und Politik bei Kant," in *Immanuel Kant/Zum
ewigen Frieden*, ed. O. Höffe (Berlin, 1995), pp. 171–193.

We thank the Fritz-Thyssen-Stifung for its generous financial support,
which has been a major factor in making possible the volumes in this
series.

For extensive assistance with the editorial preparation of this volume,
including matters such as correspondence, review of the translation, and
preparation of the bibliography and index, we thank Ina Goy, Thomas
Mulherin, and Nico Scarano.

And we thank Beatrice Rehl, our editor at Cambridge University Press,
for her support and encouragement for this project and for bringing it
into the series; Nicholas Walker, for his superb translation of the essays
from the original German; and Ronald Cohen, for editing the manuscript
thoughtfully and with respect for the contributors' work.

Contributors

Michael Albrecht is Professor of Philosophy at the University of Trier. His publications include *Kants Antinomie der praktischen Vernunft* (1978) and *Christian Wolff, Oratio de Sinarum philosophica practica/Rede über die praktische Philosophie der Chinesen* (1985). He has coedited *Moses Mendelssohn im Spannungsfeld der Aufklärung* (2000).

Eckart Förster is Professor of Philosophy at Johns Hopkins University. His publications include *Kant's Final Synthesis* (2000). He edited *Kant's Transcendental Deductions* (1989) and coedited *Immanuel Kant, Opus postumum* (1993), and the series *Studies in Kant and German Idealism*.

Volker Gerhardt is Professor of Philosophy at Humboldt University Berlin. His publications include *Vernunft und Interesse* (1976); *Immanuel Kant* (1989, with F. Kaulbach); *Pathos und Distanz* (1989); *Der Begriff der Politik* (1990); *Vom Willen zur Macht* (1995); and *Eine Theorie der Politik* (1995). He is editor of the yearbook *Politisches Denken*.

Dieter Henrich is Professor Emeritus of Philosophy at Ludwig-Maximilians University Munich. His publications include *Der ontologische Gottesbeweis: Sein Problem und seine Geschichte in der Neuzeit* (1960); *Identität und Objektivität. Eine Untersuchung über Kants transzendentale Deduktion* (1976); *Fluchtlinien* (1982); *Bewußtes Leben. Untersuchung zum Verhältnis von Subjektivität und Metaphysik* (1999); and *Between Kant and Hegel. Lectures on German Idealism* (2003).

Otfried Höffe is Professor of Philosophy at the University of Tübingen. His publications include *Strategien der Humanität* (1975, 2nd ed. 1985); *Ethik und Politik* (1979, 3rd ed. 1987); *Sittlich-politische Diskurse* (1981); *Immanuel Kant* (1983, 6th ed. 2004, English 1994); *Politische Gerechtigkeit* (1987, 3rd ed. 2002); *Der Staat braucht selbst ein Volk von Teufeln* (1988); *Kategorische Rechtsprinzipien* (1990, 2nd ed. 1993, English 2001); *Moral als Preis der Moderne* (1993, 4th ed. 2000); *Aristoteles* (1996, 2nd ed.

1999); *Vernunft und Recht* (1996); *Gibt es ein interkulturelles Strafrecht?* (1999), *Demokratie im Zeitalter der Globalisierung* (1999), *"Königliche Völker."* *Zu Kants kosmopolitischer Rechts- und Friedenstheorie* (2001, English 2006); *Kleine Geschichte der Philosophie* (2001); and *"Kants Kritik der reinen Vernunft. Die Grundlegung der modernen Philosophie"* (2003, 4th ed. 2004). He edited *Lexikon der Ethik* (1977, 6th ed. 2002); *Lesebuch zur Ethik* (1998); and *Zeitschrift für philosophische Forschung*, and he edits the series *Denker* and *Klassiker Auslegen*.

Wolfgang Kersting is Professor of Philosophy at the University of Kiel. His publications include *Wohlgeordnete Freiheit. Immanuel Kants Rechts- und Staatsphilosophie* (1984); *Niccolo Machiavelli* (1988), *Thomas Hobbes* (1992); *John Rawls* (1993); and *Die politische Philosophie des Gesellschaftsvertrags* (1994).

Kristian Kühl is Professor of Law at the University of Tübingen. His publications include *Die Beendigung des vorsätzlichen Begehungsdelikts* (1974); *Unschuldsvermutung, Freispruch und Einstellung* (1983); *Eigentumsordnung als Freiheitsordnung – Zur Aktualität der Kantischen Rechts- und Eigentumslehre* (1984); and *Die Bedeutung der Rechtsphilosophie für das Strafrecht. Würzburger Vorträge zur Rechtsphilsophie*, Heft 28 (2001).

Bernd Ludwig is Professor of Philosophy at the University of Göttingen. His publications include *Kants Rechtslehre* (1988) and *Die Wiederentdeckung des Epikurischen Naturrechts. Zu Hobbes' philoso- phischer Entwicklung im Pariser Exil* (1998). He edited *Immanuel Kant, Metaphysische Anfangsgründe der Rechtslehre* (1986, 2nd ed. 1998) and *Tugendlehre* (1990).

Annemarie Pieper is Professor Emeritus of Philosophy at the University of Basel. Her publications include *Sprachanalytische Ethik und praktische Freiheit* (1973); *Albert Camus* (1984); *Ein Seil geknüpft zwischen Tier und Übermensch. Nietzsches erster Zarathustra* (1990); *Einführung in die Ethik* (1991, 4th ed. 2000); *Selber denken* (1997); *Gut und Böse* (1997); *Gibt es eine feministische Ethik?* (1998); *Søren Kierkegaard* (2000); *Glückssache. Die Kunst, gut zu leben* (2001). She edited *Geschichte der neueren Ethik* (2 vols., 1992) and *Philosophische Disziplinen. Ein Handbuch* (1998) and coedited *Angewandte Ethik. Eine Einführung* (1998).

Gerold Prauss is Professor Emeritus of Philosophy at the University of Freiburg. His publications include *Platon und der logische Eleatismus* (1966); *Erscheinung bei Kant. Ein Problem der "Kritik der reinen Vernunft"*

(1971); *Kant und das Problem der Dinge an sich* (1974, 2nd ed. 1977); *Kant über Freiheit als Autonomie* (1983), and *Die Welt und wir* (1990 ff.).

Friedo Ricken is Professor of History of Philosophy and Ethics at Hochschule für Philosophie München. His publications include *Der Lustbegriff in der Nikomachischen Ethik des Aristoteles* (1976); *Allgemeine Ethik* (1983, 3rd ed. 1998); *Philosophie der Antike* (1988, 3rd ed. 2000); and *Antike Skeptiker* (1994). He edited *Lexikon der Erkenntnistheorie und Metaphysik* (1984) and *Klassische Gottesbeweise in der Sicht der gegenwärtigen Logik und Wissenschaftstheorie* (1991, 2nd ed. 1998) and coedited *Kant über Religion* (1992) and *Philosophen der Antike* (2 vols., 1996).

Dieter Schönecker is Professor of Philosophy at the University of Siegen. His publications include *Kant: Grundlegung III. Die Deduktion des kategorischen Imperativs* (1999); *Immanuel Kant: "Grundlegung zur Metaphysik der Sitten. Ein einführender Kommentar"* (2002, 2nd ed. 2004 with A. W. Wood) and *Kants Begriff transzendentaler und praktischer Freiheit. Eine entwicklungsgeschichtliche Studie* (2005). He coedited *Kant verstehen. Understanding Kant. Über die Interpretation philosophischer Texte* (2001, 2nd ed. 2004); *Der moralische Status menschlicher Embryonen* (2003); and *Einführungen in die Philosophie* (2002 ff.).

Clemens Schwaiger is Professor of Philosophy at Philosophisch-Theologische Hochschule der Salesianer Don Boscos Benediktbeuern. His publications include *Das Problem des Glücks im Denken Christian Wolffs. Eine quellen-, begriffs- und entwicklungsgeschichtliche Studie zu den Schlüsselbegriffen seiner Ethik* (1995); *Kategorische und andere Imperative. Zur Entwicklung von Kants praktische Philosophie bis 1785* (1999); and *Wie glücklich ist der Mensch? Zur Aufnahme und Verarbeitung antiker Glückstheorien bei Thomas von Aquin* (1999). He is coeditor of the series *Forschungen und Materialien zur deutschen Aufklärung*.

Ludwig Siep is Professor of Philosophy at Westfälische Wilhelms-Universität Münster. His publications include *Hegels Fichtekritik und die Wissenschaftslehre von 1804* (1970); *Anerkennung als Prinzip praktischer Philosophie. Untersuchungen zu Hegels Jenaer Philosophie des Geistes* (1979); *Der Weg der Phänomenologie des Geistes. Ein einführender Kommentar zu Hegels "Differenzschrift" und "Phänomenologie des Geistes"* (2000, 2nd ed. 2001); and *Konkrete Ethik. Grundlagen der Natur- und Kulturethik* (2004). He coedited *Das genetische Wissen um die Zukunft des Menschen* (2003) and *Hegels Erbe* (2004).

Works by Kant

The standard critical edition is the Academy edition, or *Akademieausgabe* (= AA), originally edited by the Royal Prussian Academy of Sciences (Berlin, 1900 ff.). Individual works here are listed by their original title and Academy edition volume and page number, followed by an English edition, if available. In the essays in this volume, Kant's works are sometimes referred to by the abbreviations given to the left of the titles.

Anthropology *Anthropologie in pragmatischer Hinsicht*, in AA 7: 117–334. *Anthropology from a Pragmatic Point of View*, trans. Mary J. Gregor. The Hague, 1974.

Anweisung zur Menschen- und Welterkenntnis, ed. Friedrich Christian Starke. Leipzig 1831, 2nd ed. Quedlinburg, 1883, reprint. Hildesheim, 1976.

Observations *Beobachtungen über das Gefühl des Schönen und des Erhabenen*, in AA 2: 205–256. *Observations on the Feeling of the Beautiful and Sublime*, trans. John T. Goldthwait. Berkeley and Los Angeles, 1960.

"Bemerkungen zu den Beobachtungen über das Gefühl des Schönen und Erhabenen," in AA 20: 1–192.

Das Ende aller Dinge, in AA 8: 325–340. "The End of All Things," trans. Robert Anchor. In *On History*, ed. Lewis White Beck. Indianapolis and New York, 1963, 69–84.

Dissertation *De mundi sensibilis atque intelligibilis forma et principiis*, in AA 2: 385–420. *Concerning the Forms and Principles of the Sensible and Intelligible World*, trans. David Walford. In *Theoretical Philosophy, 1755–1780*, ed. David Walford. Cambridge, 1992, 377–416.

Der Streit der Fakultäten, in AA 7: 1–116. *The Conflict of the Faculties*, trans. Mary J. Gregor. New York, 1979.

MM *Die Metaphysik der Sitten*, in AA 6: 203–493 [includes *Tugendlehre* (*Doctrine of Virtue*) and *Rechtslehre* (*Doctrine of Right*)]. *Metaphysics of Morals*, ed. and trans. Mary J. Gregor. Cambridge, 1997.

DohnaWundlaken *Die philosophischen Hauptvorlesungen Immanuel Kants. Nach den neu aufgefundenen Kollegheften des Grafen Heinrich zu*

Dohna-Wundlacken, ed. Arnold Kowalewski. Munich and Leipzig, 1924, reprint. Hildesheim, 1965.

Religion *Die Religion innerhalb der Grenzen der bloßen Vernunft*, in AA 6: 1–202. *Religion within the Limits of Reason Alone*, trans. George di Giovanni. In *Religion within the Boundaries of Mere Reason and Other Writings*, ed. and trans. Allen W. Wood and George di Giovanni. Cambridge, 1998, 29–215.

Eine Vorlesung Kants über Ethik, ed. Paul Menzer. Berlin, 1924. *Lectures on Ethics*, trans. Louis Infield. London, 1930, reprint. New York, 1963.

Gr *Grundlegung zur Metaphysik der Sitten*, in AA 4: 385–463. *Groundwork of the Metaphysics of Morals*, ed. and trans. Mary J. Gregor. Cambridge, 1996.

Idee zu einer allgemeinen Geschichte in weltbürgerlicher Absicht, in AA 8: 15–31. "Idea for a Universal History from a Cosmopolitan Point of View," trans. Lewis White Beck. In *On History*, ed. Lewis White Beck. Indianapolis and New York, 1963,11–26.

Jäsche Logic *Immanuel Kant's Logik. Ein Handbuch zu Vorlesungen*, ed. Gottlieb Benjamin Jäsche, in AA 9: 1–150. Logic, trans. Robert Hartmann and Wolfgang Schwarz. Indianapolis and New York, 1974.

Kants Briefwechsel, in AA 10–12 (2nd ed. 1922). *Correspondence*, ed. and trans. Arnulf Zweig. Cambridge, 1999.

CPrR *Kritik der praktischen Vernunft*, in AA 5: 1–163. *Critique of Practical Reason*, ed. and trans. Mary J. Gregor. Cambridge, 1996.

CPR *Kritik der reinen Vernunft*, B edition in AA 3: 1–552, A edition in AA 4: 1–252. *Critique of Pure Reason*, ed. and trans. Paul Guyer and Allen W. Wood. Cambridge, 1998.

CPJ *Kritik der Urteilskraft*, in AA 5: 165–485. *Critique of the Power of Judgment*, ed. Paul Guyer, trans. Paul Guyer and Eric Matthews. Cambridge, 2000.

Lose Blätter zu den Fortschritten der Metaphysik, in AA 20: 333–551. [In part in:] *Notes and Fragments*, ed. Paul Guyer, trans. Curtis Bowman, Paul Guyer, and Frederick Rauscher. Cambridge, 2005.

Menschenkunde oder philosophische Anthropologie. Nach handschriftlichen Vorlesungen, ed. Friedrich Christian Starke. Leipzig, 1831, 2nd ed. Quedlinburg. 1883, reprint. Hildesheim, 1976.

Metaphysische Anfangsgründe der Naturwissenschaft, in AA 4: 465–565. *Metaphysical Foundations of Natural Science*, ed. and trans. Michael Friedman. Cambridge, 2004.

"Mutmasslicher Anfang der Menschengeschichte," in AA 8: 107–123. "Conjectural Beginning of Human History," trans. Emil Fackenheim. In *On History*, ed. Lewis White Beck. Indianapolis and New York, 1963, 53–68.

Nachricht von der Einrichtung seiner Vorlesungen in dem Winterhalbjahre von 1765–1766, in AA 2: 303–313. *Announcement of the Programme for his Lectures for the Winter Semester 1765–6*, trans. David Walford. In *Theoretical Philosophy, 1755–1780*, ed. David Walford. Cambridge, 1992, 287–300.

Opus postumum, in AA 21: 1–645, 22: 1–824. *Opus postumum*, ed. Eckart Förster, trans. Eckart Förster and Michael Rosen. Cambridge, 1993.

Prol. *Prolegomena zu einer jeden künftigen Metaphysik, die als Wissenschaft wird auftreten können*, in AA 4: 253–384. *Prolegomena to Any Future Metaphysics, with selections from the* Critique of Pure Reason, ed. and trans. Gary Hatfield. Cambridge, 2nd ed., 2004.

Refl. [by number, RR] Reflexionen, in AA 14–19. [in part in:] *Notes and Fragments*, ed. Paul Guyer, trans. Curtis Bowman, Paul Guyer, and Frederick Rauscher. Cambridge, 2005.

Träume eines Geistersehers, erläutert durch die Träume der Metaphysik, in AA 2: 315–373. *Dreams of a Ghost-Seer*, trans. David Walford. In *Theoretical Philosophy*, 1755–1780, ed. David Walford. Cambridge, 1992, 301–359.

"Über den Gemeinspruch: Das mag in der Theorie richtig sein, taugt aber nicht für die Praxis," in AA 8: 273–314. "On the Common Saying: That May Be Correct in Theory, but It Is of No Use in Practice," trans. Mary J. Gregor. In *Practical Philosophy*, ed. and trans. Mary J. Gregor. Cambridge, 1996, 273–309.

Prize Essay 1791 "Über die von der Königl. Akademie zu Berlin für das Jahr 1791 ausgesetzte Preisfrage: Welches sind die wirklichen Fortschritte, die die Metaphysik seit Leibnizens und Wolffs Zeiten in Deutschland gemacht hat?" ed. Friedrich Theodor Rink, in AA 20: 253–332. *What Real Progress Has Metaphysics Made in Germany since the Time of Leibniz and Wolff?* trans. Ted Humphrey. New York, 1983.

Prize Essay 1764 *Untersuchung über die Deutlichkeit der Grundsätze der natürlichen Theologie und Moral*, in AA 2: 273–302. *Enquiry Concerning the Distinctness of the Principles of NaturalTheology and Morality (Prize Essay) 1764*, trans. David Walford. In *Theoretical Philosophy*, 1755–1780, ed. David Walford. Cambridge, 1992, 243–275 [written in 1762 for the 1763 competition].

"Verkündigung des nahen Abschlusses eines Tractats zum ewigen Frieden in der Philosophie," in AA 8: 411–422. "Proclamation of the Imminent Conclusion of a Treaty of Perpetual Peace in Philosophy," trans. Peter Heath. In *Theoretical Philosophy* after 1781, ed. Henry E. Allison and Peter Heath. Cambridge, 2002, 451–460.

"Vorarbeiten und Nachträge," in AA 23: 1–545. Includes "Zu *Die Metaphysik der Sitten. Erster Teil. Metaphysische Anfangsgründe der Rechtslehre*," in AA 207–370; "zu *Zum ewigen Frieden*," in AA 153–192; "*zum Streit der Fakultäten*," in AA 421–464.

Vorlesungen über Moralphilosophie. Includes "Praktische Philosophie Herder," in AA 27/1: 1–89; "Moralphilosophie Collins," in AA 27/1: 237–471; "Moral Mrongovius," in AA 27/2.2: 1395–1581. [In part in:] *Lectures on Ethics*, trans. Peter Heath, ed. Peter Heath and J.B. Schneewind. Cambridge, 1997.

Moral M II "Moral Mrongovius II," in AA 29: 593–642. In *Lectures on Ethics*, trans. Peter Heath, ed. Peter Heath and J.B. Schneewind. Cambridge, 1997, 225–248.

Vorlesungen über Metaphysik und Rationaltheologie. Includes "Metaphysik
  Dohna," in AA 28/2.1: 611–704; "Metaphysik Mrongovius," in AA 29/1.2.
  [In part in:] *Lectures on Metaphysics,* ed. and trans. Karl Ameriks and Steve
  Naragon. Cambridge, 1997.
Pädagogik *Vorlesungen zur Pädagogik,* ed. Friedrich Theodor Rink, in AA 9:
  437–500. *Kant on Education,* trans. Annette Churton. London, 1899; reprint.
  Ann Arbor, 1960.
Zum ewigen Frieden, in AA 8: 341–386. *Perpetual Peace,* trans. Lewis White
  Beck. Indianapolis and New York, 1957.

Introduction

Karl Ameriks and Otfried Höffe

I. Background

The widespread influence of Immanuel Kant's moral and legal philosophy is a striking exception to the division that can often be found between the approaches of modern European philosophy and the Anglophone analytic tradition. Although Kant's system as a whole exhibits a deeply cosmopolitan orientation even in its general foundations, his philosophy has become especially relevant in our time primarily because of the numerous practical implications of its central ideal of autonomy, which still determines the dominant liberal views of history, law, and politics.[1]

The international reception of Kant's practical philosophy has become so enthusiastic that it has tended to stand in the way of an appreciation of the distinctive contributions of contemporary German Kant scholarship. This development is in one sense a compliment to the openness of German scholars to the outstanding achievements of earlier Anglophone Kantians such as H. J. Paton, Lewis White Beck, and John Rawls. In another sense, however, it may also be a testimony to the perplexing fact that for more than two centuries, Kant's ethics has often been displaced from a central position within Germany itself – even though, from the outside, it

---

[1] See, for example, *Rechtsphilosophie der Aufklärung*, ed. R. Brandt (Berlin, 1982); *Autonomy and Community: Readings in Contemporary Kantian Social Philosophy*, eds. J. Kneller and S. Axinn (Albany, 1998); and Katerina Deligiorgi, *Kant and the Culture of the Enlightenment* (Albany, 2005).

can appear to be nothing less than the obvious shining glory of German thought.[2]

Even though Kant's views had an enormous influence on figures such as Schiller, Fichte, Hegel, Jean-Paul, and Kleist, these views were also quickly regarded as surpassed by the avant-garde in his homeland.[3] Most of the first German idealists, positivists, and naturalists mocked Kant's ethics even as they borrowed from and radicalized his stress on human autonomy. The development of neo-Kantianism at the end of the nineteenth century and the beginning of the twentieth century did not bring about a fundamental reversal of this tendency. Whatever the intrinsic distinction of their work, the influence of first-rank neo-Kantians such as Hermann Cohen and Ernst Cassirer was minimized by the distressing (to say the least) developments that led to the fall of the Weimar republic. Isolated works on Kant's ethics by figures such as Leonard Nelson, Julius Ebbinghaus, Gerhard Krüger, and Hans Reiner are interesting exceptions that only prove the rule of the marginal status of Kantianism in mid-twentieth-century Germany.[4] In the bestselling works of Nietzsche, Heidegger, and the other influential thinkers of the era, the main features of Kant's thought – when they were highly influential – became more often a target of criticism than a model to be followed. For decades even after World War II, Kantianism was eclipsed in many circles by movements such as critical theory, existentialism, philosophy of language, hermeneutics, structuralism, and revivals of later idealist approaches.

In the Continental tradition in general (in contrast, still, with much work in the analytic tradition), Kant's ethics is not treated in isolation but tends to

---

[2] There are, of course, exceptions. In addition to the authors in this volume, see, for example, Hermann Krings, *System und Freiheit: Gesammelte Aufsätze* (Freiburg, 1980) and, more recently, the series of "cooperative commentaries" on Kant's main works in practical philosophy, ed. by O. Höffe: *Grundlegung zur Metaphysik der Sitten* (Frankfurt, 1989); *Zum Ewigen Frieden* (Berlin, 1995); *Metaphysische Anfangsgründe der Rechtslehre* (Berlin, 1999); and *Kritik der praktischen Vernunft* (Berlin, 2002).

[3] Matters got worse later on. One of the Nazis' first decisions in power was to eliminate the state of Prussia. This act, combined with the Cold War and the situation of "Kaliningrad" (Kant's renamed birthplace in an isolated part of present-day Russia), has left Kant without even a German chamber of commerce that can provide him with the usual local institutions for preserving the memory of a first-rank historical figure.

[4] Leonard Nelson, *Critique of Practical Reason* (Scarsdale, NY, 1957); Julius Ebbinghaus, *Gesammelte Aufsätze, Vorträge, und Reden* (Darmstadt, 1956); Gerhard Krüger, *Philosophie und Moral in der kantischen Ethik* (Tübingen, 1931, 2nd ed. 1969); Hans Reiner, *Duty and Inclination: The Fundamentals of Morality Discussed and Redefined with Special Regard to Kant and Schiller* (Hingham, MA, 1983). (If a German book has an English translation, the translated edition is the one listed in this Introduction.)

be approached from the outset as a component of his Critical Philosophy as a whole and as a culmination of the mainstream of modern philosophy after Descartes. Although leading exponents of this tradition take note of Kant's idea that there is a "primacy of the practical," they are sensitive to the way in which Kant's ethics remains embedded in a very complex epistemological and metaphysical system. They also stress the fact that Kant's views arise in a historical context that involves an appropriation of ideas from earlier viewpoints such as stoicism, rationalism, pietism, the Newtonian revolution, and the Rousseauian enlightenment. All this understanding of the background of Kant's position does not necessarily lead, however, to a widespread advocacy of it; on the contrary, its entanglements with the philosophical tradition have often been a cause of its rejection. For a long time, Continental philosophy was dominated by figures who were sharply critical of Kant precisely to the extent that his work appeared to epitomize the character of earlier modern philosophy in general. These figures approached Kant's systematic views through the lens of their own allegiance to one of the main schools that followed in the wake of the Critical Philosophy and that aimed at reversing the overall trajectory of the modern "Cartesian" approach. Followers of Hegel, Romanticism, Marx, Nietzsche, phenomenology, and pragmatism all became well-known for their outright rejection of many of the general features most commonly associated with Kant's thought such as formalism, rigorism, and anti-naturalism. The common presumption of these followers was that Kant's own ethical position – that we should will only in accordance with maxims whose form is consistent with "pure" practical rationality – was so clearly wrong-headed that the only question remaining was exactly what kind of "material" alternative should be developed in opposition to it. For this reason, not only Nietzsche and Heidegger, but also such diverse leading thinkers as Max Scheler, Nicolai Hartmann, Theodor Adorno, Hans-Georg Gadamer, and Jürgen Habermas all argued vigorously that a fundamentally new starting point was needed in practical philosophy, one that would overcome what they took to be severe limitations in Kant's own moral theory.

In more recent German philosophy, as throughout philosophy in the rest of the world, anti-Kantian tendencies have remained popular, flourishing in a variety of guises such as broadly Aristotelian virtue theory, broadly Humean "quasi-realism," and broadly Nietzshean "anti-theory" approaches.[5] At the same time, however, a steady stream of significant

---

[5] See, for example, Ernst Tugendhat, *Vorlesungen über Ethik* (Frankfurt, 1993); Ursula Wolf, *Die Philosophie und die Frage nach dem guten Leben* (Hamburg, 1999); Rüdiger Bittner, *Doing Things for Reasons* (Oxford, 2001).

new Kant scholarship has been produced by contemporary German philosophers who appreciate the systematic and stylistic advances of analytic approaches even as they manifest the historical and interpretive skills that are distinctive of the Continental tradition. While maintaining a broadly sympathetic attitude toward much of the Critical Philosophy, the scholars of this era have focused on developing extremely careful interpretations of Kant's arguments in a way that does not shrink from offering significant criticisms of his theory. Instead of trying to resurrect a unified "neo-Kantian" school, or orienting themselves in terms of a traditional post-Kantian movement, they have concentrated on particulars and on the fact that many of the crucial elements of the background and logical structure of Kant's main arguments still deserve much closer analysis.[6] In addition, German scholars have made significant progress recently in publishing new material concerning lectures by Kant on ethics, law, and anthropology.[7] This development is especially relevant for practical philosophy in general now that leading Anglophone ethicists have also placed a new emphasis on understanding contemporary arguments against the background of little-known details in the development of modern ethical thought.[8]

The continuing relevance of Kant's work, and hence of the latest German scholarship on it, thus rests on a wide variety of tendencies. Philosophers who are oriented toward close conceptual analysis, or at least to the challenge of a rigorous system that aims to parallel the achievement of modern science, cannot help but be intrigued by Kant's classical texts – their striking innovations as well as their bold architectonic. Similarly, philosophers who have taken a "historical" turn, or are interested primarily in phenomenology, hermeneutics, or politics, cannot help but be interested in the rich data provided by Kant's system and its

[6] An exception is the strong interest in Rawlsian ideas. See *Zu Idee des politischen Liberalismus: John Rawls in der Diskussion,* ed. W. Hinsch (Frankfurt, 1997); Otfried Höffe, *Politische Gerechtigkeit. Grundlegung einer kritischen Philosophie von Recht und Staat* (Frankfurt, 2002, 3rd ed.); and *Kants Ethik,* eds. K. Ameriks and D. Sturma (Paderborn, 2004).

[7] See Reinhard Brandt, *Kritischer Kommentar zu Kants Anthropologie in pragmatischer Hinsicht: 1798* (Hamburg, 1999); G. Felicitas Munzel, *Kant's Conception of Moral Character: The Critical Link of Morality, Anthropology, and Reflective Judgment* (Chicago, 1999); Manfred Kuehn, *Kant: A Biography* (New York, 2001); and *Essays on Kant's Anthropology,* eds. B. Jacobs and P. Kain (Cambridge, 2003). See also n. 10.

[8] See, for example, Jerome Schneewind, *The Invention of Autonomy* (Cambridge, 1998), and the contributions – all in English and several on historical issues – by Anglophone and German scholars in *Kant's Metaphysics of Morals: Interpretive Essays,* ed. M. Timmons (Oxford, 2002).

widespread impact. Despite its detractors, Kant's persuasive stress on the deep interconnections between autonomy-oriented concepts such as reason, lawfulness, duty, respect, rights, and self-determination has made his ethics a central and irreversible feature of modernity.

II. Kant's Moral Philosophy

The contributions in this volume fall into four parts. They have been selected with the aim of covering central but relatively unexplored themes in Kant's major works while providing a representative, but by no means comprehensive, sampling of works from both older and newer generations of scholarship.

Part I contains two essays illuminating the historical background of Kant's ethics and the fact that, years before he had taken his Critical turn, Kant was already trying to develop a unique synthesis of the most valuable ideas in the practical philosophies of his empiricist and rationalist predecessors.

Part II contains four essays on Kant's best known text in this area, the *Groundwork of the Metaphysics of Morals* (1785), presented in approximately the same order as the four-part structure of the *Groundwork*, which contains a preface and three main sections. These essays take up themes that tend to be neglected in the Anglophone literature on Kant's ethics, which has concentrated primarily on issues such as the various formulations of the Categorical Imperative in the *Groundwork*'s second section.

Part III contains four essays devoted to the *Critique of Practical Reason* (1788) and themes that also have not been the main focus of typical analytic work, such as the dialectic and the postulates of pure practical reason. Part II and III also each contain an essay on Kant's central notion of a maxim, and these contributions illustrate the wide range of opinion that is typical of current literature on this controversial subject.

Part IV contains four essays that explore some of the main themes of works from Kant's practical philosophy that go beyond his two best-known texts. This part concerns the broader sphere covered by the German term *Recht*, which includes not only legal "duties of justice" (in contrast to "duties of virtue," the topic of the other half of Kant's most extensive work in ethics, the two-part *Metaphysics of Morals*, 1797), but also the whole range of social considerations bearing on economic and political relations within and between modern states. Unfortunately, there is not enough space to include samples of work on the significant value implications of important texts by Kant that focus on related areas such as religion, history, and aesthetics.

Chapter 1 in this collection is the first English version of one of Dieter Henrich's seminal early essays on Kant. Among postwar specialists, Henrich is recognized as the leading expert on classical German philosophy in general. In recent years, he has become especially well-known for his research on developments in philosophy immediately after Kant,[9] but his interpretation of this period in many ways presupposes the broad and nuanced perspective that he developed on Kant's practical philosophy in earlier essays such as this treatment of Hutcheson and Kant. Henrich's discussions typically have a complex systematic structure combined with an original and subtle historical hypothesis. In this essay, he distinguishes four basic themes in Kant's ethics, all intended to have a pure meaning rather than an empirical meaning: "universality," "binding character,"[10] "transcendental grounding," and "the content of ethical consciousness."

These themes correspond, in order, to what could also be called Kant's answers to the fundamental questions of the content, authority, possibility, and motivation of morality. The issue of "possibility," or "transcendental grounding," involves the metaphysical question of how it is that Kantian morality, especially with its strong features of normativity and freedom, can be thought of coherently at all. Kant's eventual answer to this question rests largely on his doctrine of transcendental idealism.[11] This question is a major concern in all of Kant's Critical ethics, especially the final section of the *Groundwork*, and it is a principal theme of some of Henrich's most extensive and significant later work on Kant.[12] In Kant's early reflections on ethics, however, and especially with respect to the

<hr/>

[9] See, for example, Dieter Henrich, *Between Kant and Hegel: Lectures on German Idealism* (Cambridge, MA, 2003).

[10] Henrich thus claims that already by the 1760s, Kant had grasped the notion of the categorical character of morality. See, however, *Immanuel Kant: Vorlesung zur Moralphilosophie*, ed. W. Stark, with an Introduction by Manfred Kuehn (Berlin, 2004). Kuehn's Introduction disputes whether at this point Kant had yet clearly settled on the view that we need an imperative that goes beyond our sensory interests altogether.

[11] Under this heading, Henrich also discusses some motivational issues that are entangled in Hutcheson's peculiar teleological account of how God governs our affections; these discussions might also be placed under the heading of Henrich's fourth concern, the proper determination of "ethical consciousness."

[12] See, especially, Henrich, *The Unity of Reason: Essays on Kant's Philosophy*, ed. R. Velkley (Cambridge, MA, 1994); and "The Deduction of the Moral Law: The Reasons for the Obscurity of the Final Sections of the Groundwork of the Metaphysics of Morals," in *Kant's Groundwork of the Metaphysics of Morals: Critical Essays*, ed. P. Guyer (Lanham, MD, 1998), pp. 303–341.

relationship to Hutcheson that Henrich emphasizes, Kant's discussion focuses instead on the issue of motivation and moral consciousness: how can we explain the peculiar fact that even though morality essentially requires a clear recognition of what is right and wrong, this merely judgmental attitude is not by itself sufficient for moral commitment?

Kant calls this problem the "philosopher's stone," the mystery of explaining how it is that we might "know" what is right and still not have the kind of distinctive action-guiding "insight" that occurs in a moral consciousness genuinely willing to act for the sake of duty. Henrich argues that the posthumously published "Reflections" reveal that a consideration of Hutcheson's position played a key role in Kant's coming to an appreciation of the great difficulty of this problem. Kant did not take over Hutcheson's notion of moral sense, but he did take over Hutcheson's point that genuine moral consciousness requires more than mere "kind affection." It requires a distinctive second-level attitude of approval, which is rooted in something that can be found even in the "humblest" uneducated person, and is based in something other than mere theoretical reason and an abstract recognition of the difference between right and wrong. It is not difficult to see that these reflections prefigure Kant's later doctrine of the distinctive feeling of moral respect and his Critical account of the non-reducible "interest" that reason, as pure will, has in morality.

Henrich also stresses that even in this early context, Kant's work already reveals an overriding concern with the value of justice (as opposed to mere benevolence) and with the need to find a more complex moral psychology and theory of subjectivity than that provided by the empiricist tradition.[13] Hutcheson went so far as to argue that intellect alone is not enough for morality, but although he called the extra factor that was needed "will," he still tended, as did others in the British tradition, to conflate this factor with the domain of "feeling" or "drive" rather than recognizing it as an irreducible third faculty.

In his early period, Kant studied not only the empiricists but also (as Henrich notes) the rationalists, and it is well-known that he also contested Wolff's idea that moral consciousness can be explained through the intellectual representation of perfection. Clemens Schwaiger's essay (Chapter 2) picks up on this point and then goes so far as to argue that the

---

[13] Henrich's thought that Kant "developed his own specific conception of morality in terms of the rational structure of the will" and as a "kind of self-relation" corresponds to a theme of Prauss's essay, Ch.5 in the present volume.

early Kant might be best understood in terms of his reaction to the rationalists in general. Schwaiger shows how Kant's early teaching was strongly influenced by discussions of obligation in Pufendorf, Leibniz, Wolff, and Baumgarten. He argues that these figures, rather than any British thinkers, or pietists such as Crusius, are the key to Kant's special emphasis on duty as the fundamental notion of ethics. Wolff took a first step by following Leibniz and insisting, against Pufendorf, that acts are moral only when they are acknowledged as intrinsically right (that is, involving a "natural" obligation and not merely a "civil" obligation) and not merely commanded by an external authority. Wolff also went on to argue that a genuine sense of obligation requires not mere passive obedience but an active process of acceptance on our part. Baumgarten, whose texts Kant always used as a basis for his own ethics lectures, took a further step by defining morality entirely in terms of obligation, and placing discussions of happiness under the heading of religion. In addition, Baumgarten was innovative in stressing that morality involves not only necessity but also necessitation – that is, the constraint of the human will because it, unlike the divine will, is not intrinsically in accord with reason. Precisely because of this complex combination of religious concerns and pure moral considerations regarding obligation, Schwaiger concludes that it is best to understand Kant's ethical teaching as being indebted to Baumgarten above all (even if Kant also departed from Baumgarten in many ways). At the very least, Schwaiger establishes the premise that anyone trying to understand the origins of Kant's practical philosophy must pay close attention to the extensive "scholastic" sources that are documented here.

Ludwig Siep's essay (Chapter 3) focuses critically on Kant's argument in the preface of the *Groundwork* that ethics requires a purely metaphysical foundation. Siep notes that the pre-Critical reflections of the 1760s already show that Kant was committed to the view that the highest practical principle must be *a priori*. Given that the first *Critique* (1781) and the *Metaphysical Foundations of Natural Science* (1786) remain transcendental even while making use of general empirical features, such as the fact of dynamic motion, it might seem that there could also be a Critical ethics that begins by incorporating so-called "anthropological" but still very general features, such as the existence of a dynamic plurality of dependent and embodied persons. The works of the Critical era, however, clearly emphasize the need to develop a metaphysics of morals that is completely independent of anthropological considerations.[14]

---

[14] This point is noted (with regret) in Kuehn's "Introduction"; cf. the essays in Jacobs and Kain (2003).

Siep argues that although the *Groundwork*'s preface offers both "speculative" and "practical" arguments for this project, they are not clearly convincing. The speculative considerations focus on the possibility of establishing a basic principle that is valid for a rational will as such and that ignores factors specific to the human will. Kant often employs this kind of general and stipulative notion of a pure core meaning to "morality" even in his later work,[15] but it is striking that he hardly keeps to it even within the *Groundwork* itself. As Siep notes, the preface glosses over the fact that a central part of morality consists of legal duties of right, which necessarily involve external relations of human beings, and examples from this realm (for example, concerning a bank deposit) play a central role in the *Groundwork*'s arguments. Even the notion of "virtue" is defined by Kant in terms of the constraints and difficulties that a finite will like ours must face, and so it does not fit the notion of metaphysics in its purest sense. This is also true of the "imperatival" aspect of the Categorical Imperative, for although the moral law as such can be stated in purely rational terms that make no mention of the inclinations of a finite will, an imperative is something directed toward beings who need to overcome tendencies to be less than fully rational.

All of this suggests that Kant's call for a pure metaphysics of morals should be understood in terms of a number of different meanings,[16] and that Kant's main concern may not always be absolute purity, but at times simply a perspective that at least is not dependent on variable and highly contingent features of the human situation. This position may seem to be all that is required by Kant's own "practical" arguments for a metaphysics of morals, which stress that moral life requires certainty, stability, and strict obligation. These features correspond to the claims about authority, motivation, and content that were noted earlier as central to Kant's rationalist ethics. As Siep notes, however, what is striking about the preface and the beginning of the first section of the *Groundwork* is that Kant contends not only that the practical perspective of "everyday" moral consciousness acknowledges the need for these features, but also that these features demand an unconditional grounding of their possibility in the pure metaphysical notion of a rational will. Siep argues that even if one grants the internal consistency of Kant's project, there may

---

[15] See, for example, Kant's *Religion*, preface to the first edition, "since its maxims bind through the mere form of universal lawfulness…morality…needs no end" (6: 3f). Translation from *Religion within the Boundaries of Mere Reason*, eds. A. Wood and G. di Giovanni, with an Introduction by Robert M. Adams (Cambridge, 1998).

[16] See Dieter Schönecker's essay, ch. 4 in the present volume.

be theories that are not purely metaphysical in Kant's strict sense and can nonetheless undergird an ethics with commands that are universal in content, motivated by a respect for freedom, and rest on an authority rooted in rationality. In other words, an adequately demanding morality might exist without being independent of human nature altogether and without being focused entirely on the concepts of pure lawfulness and unconditional value that Kant stresses.[17]

Dieter Schönecker's contribution (Chapter 4) provides a detailed analysis of the logical relationship between the first two sections of the *Groundwork* and the endpoints of the "transitions" between them. At first sight, it can certainly seem that in accord with the three-part title, *Groundwork of the Metaphysics of Morals*, Section I is concerned with ordinary moral consciousness, Section II with the philosophical or "metaphysical" determination of the formula of its supreme principle, and Section III with the grounding of the possibility of this kind of morality in an account of transcendental freedom. Matters are complicated, however, by the fact that Kant makes not only transitions between these sections but also within them, and that the end point of an earlier transition need not be exactly the same as the starting point of the next transition. In particular, Section I moves from "common rational" to "philosophical rational moral knowledge," whereas Section II moves from "popular moral thought (that is, philosophy) to the metaphysics of morals." In other words, the "philosophical rational" knowledge at the end of Section I is not quite the same as the "popular moral thought" at the beginning of Section II.

Schönecker shows how this distinction is by no means trivial, but reveals the very different concerns of the two sections. Section I starts at a popular and sound level, and in revealing the concept of good will and duty, it reaches a sound philosophical position, albeit one that still has to be developed much further. Section II can then be understood as beginning from a standpoint that is already philosophical but "popular" in a mixed and unsound sense because it is based on heteronomous principles, and these principles create an obstacle to our holding true to the sound notion of duty that has just been made explicit. Kant's criticism of these principles reflects his long-term concern with the history of ethical theory as well as his belief that these principles arise from a common and corrupt

---

[17] It may be that Kant could acknowledge this point by distinguishing between unconditional and conditional goods within his own system; see Prauss's essay, ch. 5 in the present volume.

source in ordinary consciousness – and hence that, left uncriticized, they can come to infect the sound moral consciousness that Kant accepts as the proper starting point of the *Groundwork*.

Schönecker's microscopic analysis reveals how even some of the most basic features of a key Kant text can have eluded the eyes of leading scholars. His analysis also has numerous substantive implications, one of which is a reminder of the importance of understanding Kant's thought properly in relation to common sense and the debates concerning it in his era. Kant saw his philosophy as not only a constructive systematic enterprise but also as an apologetic and intensely practical project, one aimed at using philosophy itself to save the deep truths of the "common people" (and to be "truly popular" in that sense) from the "rationalizing" snares of forms of philosophy that are "popular" in only a de facto, crude, and ultimately corrupting sense.[18]

Gerold Prauss's essay (Chapter 5) is a concise sample of work by one of the most systematic and challenging writers in contemporary German philosophy. Although Prauss has written several classic books of Kant scholarship, his ultimate aim is to use Kant's most basic ideas to develop an even more radical and adequate account of the most fundamental features of subjectivity.[19] Prauss's discussion of "reason practical in its own right" begins with an analysis of how Kant's use of the term "own" (*eigen*) must be understood. This term is crucial to the extremely difficult argument of the notorious third and final section of the *Groundwork*, which aims to show that the Categorical Imperative, which is revealed as the highest principle of morality in Section II, is not a mere "figment of the brain." Kant's argument turns on a consideration of the idea of having one's "own will" (4: 448). Prauss argues that here the crucial term "own" must be meant by Kant in a reflexive and not merely possessive sense. The key feature of our will is not merely that we have one – for there are many things that we have – but that this will can be and is directed to itself, and hence is capable of the self-determination and self-legislation that is central to Kant's ethics.

---

[18] On the relation of Kant's philosophy to common sense, see Manfred Kuehn, *Scottish Common Sense in Germany, 1768–1800* (Kingston and Montreal, 1987); Karl Ameriks, "Introduction," in Karl Leonhard Reinhold, *Letters on the Kantian Philosophy,* ed. K. Ameriks (Cambridge, 2005), ix–xxxv; and Karl Ameriks, "A Commonsense Kant?" *Proceedings and Addresses of the American Philosophical Association* 79 (2005), 19–43.
[19] See, for example, Gerold Prauss, *Erscheinung bei Kant* (Berlin, 1971), and *Einführung in die Erkenntnistheorie* (Darmstadt, 1980); see Karl Ameriks, "Contemporary German Epistemology: The Significance of Gerold Prauss," *Inquiry* 25(1982), 125–138.

Kant's main project in Section III is to demonstrate that we cannot rationally deny that we have a will of this kind, and that it is free in the radical transcendental sense that is essential to the Categorical Imperative (and thus the concern that it is a mere "figment" can be dismissed). Such a demonstration is by no means easy. Prauss follows those who read Kant as having recognized that his *Groundwork* argument did not succeed and as having then opted in the second *Critique* for the weaker fall back strategy of relying on a "fact of reason." Prauss notes that this kind of fall back procedure can seem very odd in view of the fact that Kant, in his theoretical works, continues to speak without qualification of a "free synthesis" that subjectivity carries out in all of its basic intentional acts (A 221, B 269). Kant repeatedly speaks of an "absolute spontaneity" of our understanding, a spontaneity that he sometimes even describes as "autonomous." To the objection that this kind of theoretical spontaneity cannot be relevant to the practical freedom that is the concern of the *Groundwork*, Prauss replies that the very centrality of spontaneity to Kant's theoretical philosophy shows that (even if Kant himself did not fully recognize this) this notion cannot be a "merely" theoretical one. Since the notion of spontaneity is introduced by Kant precisely to account for the way we can be successfully theoretical at all, it must be more basic than the common conception of theoretical intentionality that it is explaining. Hence it can be taken to be indicative of a "reason that is practical in its own right" – that is, in a way that can also have a bearing in practical contexts, where the issue is the relation of the will to itself.

Prauss sees this kind of relation as central to the most remarkable claim about value in the *Groundwork* – the contention that the good will alone can be "unconditionally good." Prauss notes that it is the notion of the unconditional that is central here, not goodness, for clearly there can also be an evil will, and only an evil will can be unconditionally evil. The unconditionality of moral value here cannot be a matter of quantity; it appears to depend rather on the unique self-relatedness of the will. All other moral goods are matters that are used or developed by the will (and hence are conditional on it), but the will itself, in its relation to itself, cannot "use" itself – it can only be itself, and as such it must always be in some form of self-relation that is not conditioned in the way that other morally valuable items are. Because of the way that this relation determines itself, Prauss takes it to exhibit how the will as such, even before it is directed in a specifically moral way, has the kind of absolute self-determination that is Kant's ultimate concern.[20]

---

[20] One might still ask, if the fact that something is in a spontaneous self-relation has to exclude the possibility that it is nonetheless also externally determined. Leibniz's

Michael Albrecht's contribution (Chapter 6) offers a detailed treatment of Kant's notion of a maxim. This term is especially important in Section II of the *Groundwork*, which stresses that maxims are what determine moral worth, and must be tested by the various formulations of the Categorical Imperative. No wonder the term "maxim" takes on a central role in all of Kant's other main works in practical philosophy and that it has become a standard focus of current discussions of Kantian ethics.[21] Albrecht critically reviews recent interpretations of the term and contrasts them with his own provocative reading of a maxim as a "fundamental practical subjective principle." It is not controversial that maxims are meant to be "practical" in the sense of action-guiding. The "subjective" nature of maxims is more complex; like Prauss, Albrecht stresses that the will's maxims involve a self-imposed relation to one's self. For Albrecht, this implies that maxims express principles that are "important" to the subject, "intentionally persist" in its life, reflect "ends" the agent is interested in as an individual, and involve a "plurality" of concerns that need to be harmonized. Albrecht's most striking claim is that the "fundamental" character of Kantian maxims lies in their having a form that is not only general (for example, "live as independently as possible," "smoke no more than once a day") but that also reflects a commitment to govern oneself by principles as such. On this interpretation, maxims require a level of deliberateness that perhaps only a few individuals reach. There are admittedly many passages in Kant, especially in works such as the *Anthropology*, that use this highly demanding conception of a maxim, something that not many interpreters apart from Albrecht have emphasized. But there are also understandable reasons why other interpreters have understood maxims as simply reflecting general ways in which "we lead our lives as a whole," and thus as something that can be present even in persons who are not very reflective at all.

Albrecht also departs from other interpreters by arguing that maxims should be understood as being tested primarily not in retrospect but in the very process in which they are being formulated, in the fact that rational agents always have the moral law present to themselves in some way, and

---

philosophy – and, more recently, Wilfrid Sellars' – would be sources for this concern. See also Gerold Prauss, *Kant über Freiheit als Autonomie* (Frankfurt, 1983); and Karl Ameriks, *Kant and the Fate of Autonomy* (Cambridge, 2000), and *Interpreting Kant's Critiques* (Oxford, 2003).

[21] See, especially, Onora O'Neill, *Acting on Principle: An Essay on Kantian Ethics* (New York, 1975), and *Constructions of Reason: Explorations of Kant's Practical Philosophy* (Cambridge, 1989).

thus have the opportunity to develop a principled character (which on this view is tantamount to having a character at all). Maxims may be good, but they can also be evil, as in the case of Sulla, whom Kant speaks of as condemnable and yet also worthy of consideration simply insofar as his character shows how resolute persons can be. Albrecht believes that one reason why Kant makes maxims the locus of moral evaluation is that he holds that virtue and moral perfection require the kind of long-term commitment found only in principles that have a "fundamental" nature and are definitive of character. This point is, at the very least, a helpful corrective to analyses that try to understand Kantian practical principles directly in terms of very specific acts and limited aspects of one's life.[22] It may also be true, however, that there are a number of different ways in which Kant, like many of us, uses terms such as "maxim" and "character," and there can be advantages to understanding these terms in a way that allows their instances to be relatively common and non-deliberate rather than only very deliberate and rare.

Precisely this kind of approach to maxims is developed in Otfried Höffe's opening essay (Chapter 7) in Section III of this volume on the *Critique of Practical Reason*. Höffe's treatment of maxims is embedded in a close analysis of Book I, Chapter I (§§4–6) of the "Analytic of Pure Practical Reason," in which, after introducing the notion of an objective practical principle (that is, law), Kant argues step by step that such a principle must be grounded in "pure form," "universal legislation," and "transcendental freedom." To illustrate how the pure form of universalizability functions as the criterion for the morality of maxims, Kant discusses the example of being entrusted with a bank deposit "whose owner has died without leaving any record" (5: 27). Kant has already argued that a "pure" will, in being guided by the form of universal lawgiving, must exclude all particular "material" content as its determining ground. Kant now insists that any such content, whether it concerns lower-level sensations or higher-level "delights," would make the "rule of the will" – that is, its maxim – determined by an "empirical condition" – namely, a desire for pleasure in an object, and therefore not (as it should be for a "pure will") by the mere form of "a practical law" (5:27). To help us understand what Kant means by a maxim here, Höffe proposes that one should focus not on a mere particular purpose – for example, "to relieve one's anger" – but on a general policy – for example, "to relieve one's anger by any means." Once

---

[22] See Karl Ameriks, "Kant on the Good Will," in *Grundlegung zur Metaphysik der Sitten: Ein kooperativer Kommentar,* ed. O. Höffe (Frankfurt, 1989), pp. 45–65.

a maxim is understood in this way, one can see fairly easily (Kant believes) whether it manifests a concern for univeral lawfulness as such. The universality here is not a matter of merely effecting an unrestricted range of objects, but of adopting (at least implicitly) a character defining rule that can hold consistently for every rational agent as such.

Another important (but often overlooked) feature of Kant's discussion of the example of the bank deposit is that its main concern is not with a particular external good, such as property, but rather with an agent's character and general attitude toward deception. Kant is describing an agent who is willing to violate an act of trust with another person (which concerns a "perfect duty") through the maxim of gaining wealth "by any means" to satisfy the "cold" and culturally acquired passion of avarice (5: 27–8). When Kant speaks of the deceiver's maxim here as "self-annihilating," Höffe argues that this should be understood not in terms of a consequentialist argument that the institution of deposits could not survive in a situation where deposits are not completely secure, but rather in terms of a point about the "intrinsically self-contradictory" will of an agent committed to a policy of taking something as another's entrusted property while also denying it this status. This overriding concern with having a rationally coherent internal attitude also explains why Kant argues here that hedonism is a policy that leads to conflicts with oneself as well as with other agents, for it lacks necessary consistency and thus is not even "fit for inner legislation" (5: 28). Moreover, in thereby linking freedom in the 'strictest sense" (5: 29) to the concern for necessary lawfulness that is central to the maxims of a rational will as such, Kant is already anticipating his own doctrine of autonomy. The notion of a genuine pure will involves more than simply avoiding determination by merely material and contingent grounds; it also involves accepting "unconditional" positive imperatives that respect what rational law demands for its own sake (§§7f.). The very experience of understanding moral principles and adopting them as such thus provides both an awareness of the moral law as well as our only access to the "fact" of reason as free will. For Kant, this experience tends to be most vivid in cases that concern the temptation of deception, and, as Höffe points out, examples of such cases can be found throughout Kant's work. It is no accident, then, that this section of the *Critique* ends by stressing the famous claim that we can "without hesitation" see that (we believe that) it is always "possible" for us to reject the policy of giving "false testimony" – even when this policy seems to be the only way of saving our own "happiness" (5:30).

Annemarie Pieper's contribution (Chapter 8) covers the main features of the second chapter of the second *Critique*'s Analytic. Pieper stresses two difficult and relatively overlooked topics of this text: Kant's notions of categories of practical reason, and his discussion of the role of judgment in mediating between the moral law and specific actions. Kant discusses the categories in this context as ways of determining the "object" of practical reason, which is defined in terms of the concepts of good and evil. Here, unlike the first *Critique*, the categories apply not to empirical things but rather to items of moral evaluation, which for Kant are always ways of determining oneself freely. In this context, the categories are not to be understood in terms of the theoretical principles underlying the laws of nature. Instead, they are now understood in terms of the moral law and the basic *a priori* normative ways in which free good and evil items can be determined – for example, quantitatively as principles that can be either individual, collective, or universal, and qualitatively as principles that are to be performed, omitted, or allowing of exemption. Most significant is Kant's characterization of moral personality in terms of the three relational categories: a person is an agent that is defined not in terms of bodily characteristics but as having a causality that is free and moral, rather than natural, and includes a sense of reciprocal duties to other persons as such.

Perhaps the most striking part of Pieper's analysis is her emphasis on Kant's understanding of the need for a special practical use of the faculty of judgment. In theoretical judgment, particulars are "determined" by being subsumed under general laws, or universals are sought by "reflection" that starts from present particulars. In practical judgment, something universal is present from the start – namely, the moral law – but there are no laws of nature that determine its application. Instead, practical judgment uses the notion of lawfulness as such as a "type" for evaluating the moral status of relevant maxims (5: 69), a procedure that contemporary Kantians are familiar with through John Rawls' idea of considering what would happen in a world where the laws of nature are "socially adjusted" by the attempt to universalize one's maxims.[23] Pieper stresses ways in which Kant's notion of practical judgment cannot rely on either the notion of a spatiotemporal schema or the principle of purposiveness, which are the main features of his discussion of our capacity to make judgments in the other two *Critiques*. Perhaps judgment in the practical realm is related most closely to what Kant at one point calls a "peculiar talent" (A 133/B 172) to see what is relevant[24] and thus to have a sense for

---

[23] See John Rawls, *Lectures on the History of Moral Philosophy*, ed. B. Herman (Cambridge, MA 2000), p. 169.
[24] See especially nn. 7 and 8 in Pieper's essay, Ch. 8 in the present volume.

what Barbara Herman has discussed under the heading of appreciating what is "morally salient."[25]

Eckart Förster's essay (Chapter 9) on the second *Critique*'s dialectic stresses ways in which this section of the text cannot be an exact parallel to the dialectic of the *Critique of Pure Reason*. In the first *Critique*, Kant had suggested that practical reason would not be subject to dialectical illusions (A 795f). Förster contends that a 1782 review forced Kant to reflect further on how morality is often strongly disputed, and hence by the time of the *Groundwork*, Kant had acknowledged a "natural dialectic" in the practical realm in our tendency to "rationalize" situations in order to try to escape the moral law (4: 405). By the time of the second *Critique*, however, Kant had come to focus on a kind of dialectic that more closely resembles the first *Critique* insofar as it involves conflicting ideas concerning the notion of the unconditioned. In particular, practical reason's notion of the highest good – a realm in which full happiness is obtained in proportion to virtue – introduces the thought of something of unconditioned value that can seem at once both possible and impossible. Our sense of an obligation to strive for the highest good gives us the thought that this goal is possible; but we can be led to think that it is not possible once we realize that (given the deeply unjust world that we appear to inhabit) we alone do not at all appear able to bring about this good. The solution is to see that we need not go so far as to assert that the highest good is impossible, given the first *Critique*'s arguments against asserting the transcendental reality of spatiotemporality (5: 115). How this possibility is to be positively understood is not entirely clear. Förster notes that in the first *Critique*, Kant suggests that the solution involves a "life beyond this one" (A 811, A 813), whereas in the second *Critique* (5: 124), he speaks of a "harmony of nature," which may suggest that we can believe that God could eventually make possible a highest good in "this" world.[26] Förster concludes by noting that although Kant speaks of a "primacy of practical reason," he also sees that the existence of God, which is introduced to make intelligible the possible realization of the highest good, concerns a "theoretical proposition," albeit one whose justification for us rests essentially on pure practical considerations. For some readers, this may leave Kant with an appropriately balanced system,[27]

[25] Barbara Herman, *The Practice of Moral Judgment* (Cambridge, 1993).
[26] Förster cites a passage from Kant that speaks of "happiness in this life" (5: 115); Ricken's essay in the present volume (Ch. 10) offers an alternative reading.
[27] See John Hare, *The Moral Gap: Kantian Ethics, Human Limits, and God's Assistance* (Oxford, 1996).

but as Förster's own work on the *Opus postumum* has demonstrated,[28] even Kant himself eventually became interested in seeking a more unified theory, one that might not need to rely on introducing transcendent entities at all.

Friedo Ricken's contribution (Chapter 10) directly analyzes the second *Critique*'s arguments for the "postulates of pure practical reason": the existence of God and the immortality of the soul.[29] Ricken stresses that Kant's position here is very closely connected with his sympathy for "even the most ordinary understanding" (A 831/B 859), the need for philosophy to rely on cognitions that reflect "universal human interests" and "approach popularity" (cf. 5: 10). In the first *Critique*, Kant had tied religion closely to the plight of humanity's frail nature by suggesting that the idea of God is necessary for human beings to appreciate the "obligatory" power of morality (A 633/ B 661) and to have sufficient motivation to hold to the moral law. In the second *Critique*, this point is expressed in terms of the thought that there could be a way that the idea of God can be used to save us from thinking that the highest good is "impossible" and the moral law "is itself false" (5: 114).[30] Ricken notes that Kant's discussion parallels ideas already introduced in the first *Critique*'s notion of matters that can be objects of proper "belief" even if they are not strictly speaking of items of "knowledge" because they do not rest entirely on "objective" that is, theoretical grounds as opposed to practical grounds (A 822/B 850). Hence, even in the second *Critique*, Kant's postulate arguments are offered only for those who already accept the moral law and the commitment to seek the highest good (5: 143). Nonetheless, Kant holds that the conclusions of the postulates rest on practical interests of reason that supposedly no normal agent ought to reject.

As Ricken shows, Kant's discussion in the second *Critique* can be read as a more developed version of a view that he had already hinted at in the first *Critique*'s reference to viewing oneself "as in a world of grace" (A 812/B 840), and that also parallels arguments given in other works such as *Religion within the Limits of Reason Alone* (1793) (see 6: 5). On this reading, the Critical Philosophy clearly has substantive noumenal

---

[28] Eckart Förster, "Die Wandlungen in Kants Gotteslehre," *Zeitschrift für philosophische Forschung* 52 (1998), 341–362.

[29] In a sense, our transcendental freedom is also a postulate, but its assertion does not involve the extra premises that the other postulates of pure practical reason need.

[30] Because the notions of the moral law and the highest good are not the same, one might wonder what Kant means here. One explanation is that he is imagining an opponent who holds to the impossibility of the highest good because of a doctrine of transcendental realism – for it does seem that such a doctrine would in turn make the law "false," given Kant's understanding of it as requiring non-natural freedom.

commitments. In affirming God as not only the "sovereign of the kingdom of ends" (4: 439) but also as the cause of nature (5: 125), Kant brings the realms of freedom and nature together under a single transcendent spiritual power. Ricken contends that when Kant speaks of God as a cause of "all nature, distinct from nature" (5: 125), he is revealing a deep ambiguity in his terminology that can only be resolved by saying that there is a broadest notion of nature that embraces sensible nature as well as the noumenal realm.

Kant's doctrine of immortality involves similar ambiguities; it is not easy to say whether it is meant to concern an endless existence within time or rather some kind of existence beyond time altogether. In either case, Ricken takes the postulate of immortality to mean not relying on the full doctrine of the highest good, because the postulate itself does not require happiness but only that one have a chance to improve one's will "endlessly" (5: 122). Ricken cites a passage from Kant's *The End of All Things* (1794), which speaks of a continuing existence "wholly incomparable with time" (7: 327), but this is surely one of Kant's most opaque sayings. One cannot help but wonder why more time is needed to improve the will if the will is, "from the start," timeless in itself. Here, more than anywhere else, it may be the case that Kant's primary aim is not to argue for new speculative conclusions but to present an apology for common beliefs – supposedly essential to the interests of reason – by contending that such beliefs they are at least not clearly impossible. This may also suggest another way to read the passage on God from the third *Critique* that Ricken ends with (5: 477) – namely, as meaning that what the experience of purposiveness gives us is not exactly new evidence for God but rather an appropriate and vivid way of reinforcing a "conviction" that (supposedly) "everyone feels most deeply."

III.   Kant's Legal and Political Philosophy

Kant is generally recognised, and this far beyond the confines of professional philosophy, as a thinker who basically destroyed the inherited "fundamental philosophy" of the Western tradition – metaphysics – by the radical application of transcendental "critique," and thereby effectively erected a new type of fundamental philosophy over the ruins of the old. Kant is also essentially recognised as a moral philosopher, and here pre-eminently as the theorist of the Categorical Imperative and the autonomy of the will. And, further, fundamental aspects of his philosophical aesthetics continue to exercise an influence on theoretical discussions of the nature of art and literature. Yet there is still little general awareness or appreciation, on the other hand, of Kant's significance as a legal and political thinker.

And for a long time, this has also been true in the context of the professional academic discussion of the Critical Philosophy. As far as Kant's practical philosophy was concerned, it was essentially his moral philosophy in the narrow sense, and particularly the *Groundwork of the Metaphysics of Morals* and its basic themes, that occupied the centre of attention. It is true that the *Critique of Practical Reason*, Kant's second series of "prolegomena" to moral philosophy, was also subsequently drawn into the discussion. But few authors took pains to study Kant's contribution to political philosophy and the philosophy of law. One reason for this certainly lay in the enormous influence long exercised in this area by the Hegelian School. This neglect was subsequently reinforced even further by an increasing loss of interest in the fields of political philosophy and the philosophy of law in general, although for very different reasons, on the part of philosophers and jurists alike. And this has unfortunately resulted in a substantial narrowing of perspective as far as the overall reception of Kant is concerned. This is all the more surprising given that Kant's systematic exposition of his theory of morality – the two-part *Metaphysics of Morals* (1797) – contains a distinct philosophy of law and of the state that is fully developed in the first part of the book, the "Metaphysical First Principles of the Doctrine of Right," the part that has undoubtedly proved the most important with regard to the effective history of Kantian thought.

But Kant's brief essay on the philosophy of history, his "Idea for a Universal History from a Cosmopolitan Point of View," published more than a decade earlier in 1784, is also highly significant from the perspective of the philosophy of law insofar as it attempts to determine the progress of humanity explicitly in terms of relevant concepts of law and right. And the attentive reader will already discover fundamental juridical concepts deployed throughout the *Critique of Pure Reason*, such as that of the condition of nature and its overcoming through the condition of right or of perpetual peace (B 779f.), as well as other important references to the Platonic concept of a republic (B 372–374) and the concept of civil legislation (B 358, 372 ff.). In addition, the very term "critique," and the method connected with it, are clearly derived from the domain of law and mutual contestation, along with a plethora of other associated concepts and metaphors: arena, feud, private justice, deduction, antinomy, title (in the sense of documented legal entitlement), public trial, tribunal, legislation, the government of reason, and so forth. Indeed, the essential idea behind Kant's philosophy of law can already be clearly discerned at the heart of the first *Critique*. Ever since his early period of study with Martin Knutzen, himself a pupil of the important Enlightenment thinker Christian Wolff, Kant had frequented lectures on "natural law," as the philosophy of right and law was still traditionally known. The evidence from his personal library indicates that Kant was studying a number of works on jurisprudence and the philosophy of right between 1762 and 1764, and by 1788 he had lectured no less than twelve times on "natural law" (the philosophy of right). Kant, the engaged intellectual who followed the political developments of his own time so closely, the penetrating thinker who established philosophy on the new basis of the critical transcendental method, was already in a position to formulate his basic claims concerning law and the state in 1781 in the first edition of the *Critique of Pure Reason*, even before he turned explicitly to the two great domains of nature and freedom in the practical context (from the personal and political perspective): "A constitution allowing the greatest possible human freedom in accordance with laws which by which the freedom of each is made to be consistent with that of others – I do not speak of the greatest happiness, for this will follow of itself – is at any rate a necessary idea, which must be taken as fundamental not only in first projecting a constitution but in all its laws" (A 316/B 373).

In the intervening period between the first *Critique* and the "Idea for a Universal History," on the one hand, and the "Doctrine of Right," on the other, Kant published three other important works that are also crucially concerned with issues in the philosophy of law and the state. The title of his book *Religion within the Boundaries of Mere Reason* (1793) clearly indicates the drift and content of this work. But the third part of the book "Concerning the victory of the good over the evil principle" also goes on to discuss, as the full title specifies, the idea of the "founding of the Kingdom of God on earth." Even if this kingdom is grounded in uncoerced "laws of virtue" rather than in legally enforceable "laws of right," concepts that are central to the philosophy of right, such as the (ethical) concept of the condition of nature and the commonwealth, play a significant role here as well. For the ethical commonwealth, as Kant attempts to show, itself presupposes the concept of the rightful community.

Kant's essay "On the Common Saying: That May be Correct in Theory, But It Is of No Use in Practice," published in the same year as the book on religion (1793), devotes two of its chapters to questions of the philosophy of right: "II: On the relation of theory to practice in the right of the state (against Hobbes)" and "III: On the relation of theory to practice in the right of nations considered from a universally philanthropic, that is, cosmopolitan point of view (against Moses Mendelssohn)."

Two years later, Kant published what must still be regarded as the most important and substantial theoretical contribution ever penned by a philosopher on the question of peace: *Toward Perpetual Peace: A Philosophical Sketch* (1795). Finally, Kant's essay on *The Conflict of Faculties* (1798), published after the "Doctrine of Right," is also a significant text for the philosophy of law and right. For the second section of the essay, "The Conflict between the Philosophical and the Juridical Faculty," in taking up once again the old question of "Whether the human race is constantly progressing towards the better," also attempts to assess the significance of the French Revolution as the most important contemporary historical event with fundamental implications for the philosophy of right and of the state.

For some time now, all of these writings, have been commanding increased attention in the German-speaking world, and this, given their subject matter, not merely from professional philosophers in the narrower sense, but also from jurists and even political scientists. In accordance with their intrinsic importance within the Kantian corpus, it is the theory of right and the essay on peace that have attracted by far the most discussion. From amongst the many contributions in this area, the present volume includes essays by four of the most important recent interpreters of Kant's philosophy of right and the state: the philosophers Volker Gerhardt (Berlin), Wolfgang Kersting (Kiel), Bernd Ludwig (Göttingen), and the legal philosopher and specialist in penal law Kristian Kühl. Otfried Höffe, the coeditor of the present volume, has not contributed an essay to the final section here since his work is already represented in part III, and he has also published two monographs on Kant's philosophy of right and a general book on Kant, in English translation.[31]

The contributions in this volume by these four Kant interpreters are presented in accordance with the systematic structure of Kant's philosophy of right rather than in the chronological order of their original publication: first a discussion of private right, then two contributions on issues

[31] See Otfried Höffe, *Immanuel Kant* (Albany, 1994; Munich 1983, 6th German ed. 2004), *"Königliche Völker": zu Kants kosmopolitischer Rechts- und Friedenstheorie* (Frankfurt, 2001), and *Categorical Principles of Law: A Counterpoint to Modernity* (University Park, PA, 2002; Frankfurt 1990, 3rd German ed. 1995).

of public right, and finally an essay on the relationship between politics and philosophy.

Kant's doctrine of property has never received much attention, either in the context of theories of property in general or in that of Kant research and scholarship in particular. And even when this aspect of Kant's thought has been directly discussed, it has often been subjected to particularly harsh criticism. Thus Schopenhauer, for example, accused Kant of simply defending the rights of the stronger in a way that deprives property of any real moral foundation, and allegedly falls behind Rousseau and even the arch-liberal Locke. Ever since his dissertation on *Property as Freedom: The Contemporary Significance of Kant's Theory of Right and Property* (Heidelberg 1983; published 1984), Kristian Kühl has emphatically contested this reading of Kant's philosophy of property. Kühl's contribution to the present volume (Chapter 11) analyses the second chapter of Part I of Kant's "Doctrine of Right," and specifically the first section (§§ 10–17). As in the first chapter of his discussion, Kant is concerned in the second chapter with clarifying the difference between what is inwardly mine and yours, an innate human right, and what is externally mine and yours. After developing in the first chapter what it means to "have" things as externally mine and yours, Kant turns in the second chapter to the way in which something can be "acquired" in the first place. As a skilled jurist, Kühl proceeds with characteristic exegetical care, and with occasional reference to current law, to expound Kant's argument paragraph by paragraph, examining in turn the general principle of external acquisition (§10), the details of the principle as presented in the first section, "On Property Right," which is essentially concerned with what is "mine and yours in relation to a corporeal thing": what is this right? (§11); what is the only thing (land) that can be acquired first? (§12); and how is it acquired "originally" (§13) through a process of "taking control," which must, remarkably enough, be treated as a rightful act"? (§14). With regard to §11, Kühl effectively highlights Kant's definition of property right and the way in which it legitimately contradicts its currently prevailing definition in civil law: property right does not relate directly to the thing in question and relates only indirectly to the idea of an unrightful possessor. Properly speaking, it represents a direct right against a possessor to refrain from use of the thing. On the other hand, Kühl criticises the discussion in §§ 12–13 for overestimating the significance of land in relation to "moveable things," a treatment that, he argues, reveals the "historical limitation of parts of Kant's theory of property." As far as §§15 and 17 are concerned, Kühl shows how they are thematically interconnected and really belong together at the end of the discussion of property right insofar as they already deal with the transition from provisional private right to public conclusive acquisition. In opposition to many other interpreters of Kant, but on good internal Kantian grounds, Kühl finally defends the idea that "the state has an obligation to promote a fairer distribution of opportunities with regard to freedom and property."

Wolfgang Kersting is not only a leading interpreter of Kant, but also an important political philosopher in his own right, equally familiar with Plato, Machiavelli, and Hobbes, and with the work of Rawls and other contemporary social contract theories. His dissertation on *Organised Freedom: Immanuel Kant's Philosophy of Right and the State* (published in an expanded form in 1984) has already become a standard work on this subject. In his contribution to the present volume (Chapter 12), Kersting analyses the "first definitive article" of Kant's essay *Towards Perpetual Peace*. He begins by clarifying the theoretical background of Kant's conception of peace: the initial absence of war is characterised in Kant's preliminary articles as a condition of nature; the concept of right itself necessarily demands the overcoming of this condition in favour of an explicit condition of peace; and the three definitive articles articulate positive conditions of right that define a condition of peace that is far more ambitious and comprehensive than that envisaged by Hobbes. The first definitive article presents a twofold thesis with regard to the condition of peace as Kant envisages it: (1) there is a fundamental connection between the constitution of a particular state and the state's readiness to maintain peace or to undertake war; (2) the republican constitution, for internal reasons, essentially tends to favour the condition of peace that is intrinsically demanded by reason. Kersting then presents an extremely illuminating interpretation of Kant's concept of a truly republican constitution: a constitution of political self-determination that elevates the otherwise subordinate subject to the level of a genuine citizen. Kersting discusses Kant's positive concept of peace, in critical comparison with the conceptions of Friedrich von Gentz and Hegel, and examines the way in which Kant slightly modifies Aristotle's analysis and distinguishes between the three morally indifferent forms of sovereignty (*formae imperei*) – autocracy, aristocracy, and monarchy – and the two morally relevant forms of government (*formae regiminis*) – republicanism and despotism. Kersting emphasises the anti-Rousseauean implications of Kant's specifically rights-based theory of contract, and concludes by showing how in "an essentially reformist spirit Kant mediates the conflict between the purely rational conception of a republic and existing historical forms of political authority by appealling to a deliberate and ongoing realisation of a free and law-governed order of social life."

Bernd Ludwig is already a familiar name to interpreters of Kant's philosophy of right by virtue of his new edition of "Doctrine of Right," which introduced a number of changes with regard to the precise organisation of the text (Hanburg 1986, 1998). And it is indeed true that the original published version of Kant's "Doctrine of Right" reveals some problematic features as far as the order of the text is concerned. There remains some controversy about whether all of the suggested changes are fully justified, but the majority of them are entirely convincing. In his contribution to this collection (Chapter 13), Ludwig carefully analyses §§51–52 of the "Doctrine of Right," together with the "General Remark" (A) that follows, "Appendix," and "Conclusion" to the text. He is principally concerned here with two themes. The first concerns an aspect of Kant's teaching that clearly shows, although it has seldom been read this way, that Kant is a pre-eminently political philosopher. For in §§51 and 52,Kant reflects explicitly upon the normative, indeed specifically moral, task of mediating between a rights-based ideal of the political state and the concrete political domain itself. The key issue here concerns the person of the "head of state," a concept that Kant elucidates through his important distinction between the "idea" of the head of state as such and the "physical person" who "allows this idea to act upon the will of the people." Ludwig explicates the significance of this distinction, suggests some of its applications to the preceding sections of the "Doctrine of Virtue," and emphasises the fundamental difference between Kant and Rousseau in this context: "autocracy, aristocracy and democracy are not therefore, as they are for Rousseau, forms of executive power which are subordinate to the sovereign will of the people, but rather specifically organised forms of sovereignty itself." Above all, Ludwig locates and identifies the methodological significance of the question concerning the nature of "despotism," something that can only be clarified by reference to the "idea" or eternal norm of the state. This has the politically important consequence that the theory of despotism is effectively detached from the theory of the different forms of the state: "A polity which, irrespective of its external form as autocracy, aristocracy or democracy, is governed in such a way that the head of state treats the legislative will as his own private will stands closer to the 'ideal of despotism' than it does to the ideal of a republic." Finally, Ludwig also rejects attempts to claim that Kant's theory implicitly involves a theory of direct democracy.

The second theme that Ludwig addresses is Kant's notorious rejection of the right of rebellion. Ludwig carefully distinguishes between three types of the alleged right to resistance or rebellion: that of the people as such, that of the individual citizen, and that of redress against the state. He clarifies Kant's specific arguments, and concludes by observing that Kant's categorical repudiation of revolution, like that of Hobbes, also involves "the categorical demand to obey a revolutionary government once it has established itself."

In the final essay in this collection (Chapter 14), the political philosopher Volker Gerhardt, who has also made significant contributions to the interpretation of Kant and Nietzsche, analyses the "secret article" that Kant appended in an ironical spirit to the text of the second edition of his essay *Towards Perpetual Peace*. Gerhardt emphasises the irony and wit behind Kant's brief article, which actually constitutes a fundamental reflection the relationship between philosophy and politics. With judicious reference to other Kantian texts and to relevant classical contributions from Cicero and, especially, from Plato, Gerhardt brings out the substantial philosophical content of the "secret article": the critique of the allegedly privileged status of philosophy, the venerable idea of philosopher rule, and the authentically practical character of relevant philosophical knowledge, along with the two criteria that properly distinguish the philosopher from the statesman and the appropriate division of labour that follows from this distinction. Gerhardt concludes that Kant's "new alternative model is based upon his emphatic confidence in both the *critical* and *grounding* function of *philosophy*. But it also presupposes a new confidence in the domain of *politics*. In both cases, this confidence is sustained by the essentially mediating role of the *public sphere*, where individuals can communicate openly without forfeiting their own independence."

I

EARLY CONCEPTIONS

I

Hutcheson and Kant

Dieter Henrich

When a new epoch opens up in the history of philosophical thought, it often transpires that the very thinkers who first helped to encourage and prepare the way for this development themselves fall into almost immediate oblivion. There are therefore a host of figures who were once considered significant participants in the philosophical debates of the past and proved effective and tenacious opponents of now celebrated philosophers, but who are now only familiar to us from the assessment they have received in the works of the philosophers in question. One purpose of historical research in the philosophical field must be to reveal a proper and fuller picture of the thought of such figures behind the faded image of them, which is generally communicated to us by the great and now-established names of subsequent philosophy. Only then shall we find ourselves in position, with independent judgement of our own, to evaluate the real significance of such figures for the emergence of a genuinely new line of philosophical thought. As far as classical Greek philosophy is concerned, there are particular difficulties facing this task insofar as the only texts now surviving from the time of the original manuscript's creation are those that were judged to be the most significant at the time. But even in much later periods, when the lineage of the relevant materials was completely secure, there are still places where a new idea suddenly emerges without any surrounding clarity concerning the conditions and circumstances of this development.

Thus, those earlier systematic approaches and attempts that Kant himself regarded as a concentrated expression of previous philosophical achievement were already, with the exception of the thought of Hume, largely unfamiliar or unknown to the subsequent thinkers of speculative idealism. The true intentions and concrete development of the investigations of Christian Wolff, for example, 'the greatest of all the dogmatic philosophers,'[1] have effectively remained concealed to this day behind the schematic picture of his system as presented by Kant, even though this account was merely intended briefly to recall Wolff's position to contemporaries, who had themselves already read the philosopher, and within a specific polemically determined perspective of his own. A similar fate has likewise befallen the ethics of Francis Hutcheson. Although Hutcheson, along with Hume, had long been 'exceptionally important' for Kant,[2] any further independent interest in Hutcheson's work has effectively been hampered by the objections raised against his position in Kant's own critical writings, where he is repudiated as one of those who failed to grasp that the commandment of duty is categorically necessary and independent of any interest in pleasure or satisfaction (*Groundwork*: 4:442 note). Through subsequent and unconditional identification with the position articulated in the mature Critical Philosophy, readers have tended, in Wolff's case, to find Kant's respectful remarks hard to understand at all, and, Hutcheson's case, to assume a certain radical change in Kant's moral philosophy around 1770 that allegedly reversed his original estimation of Hutcheson's ethical thought.

In fact, historical research concerning the development of Kant's philosophy has long since shown just how continuous the progress of his thinking with regard to the fundamental questions of ethics really was. Förster[3] and Menzer[4] were fully aware of the independent character of Kant's early position and the consistent way in which he undertook to develop it. And it must be said that P. E. Schilpp's objections, principally directed against Menzer in this connection, are largely unfounded.[5] But this consensus amongst those who have closely examined the development of Kant's ethics has never penetrated the standard manuals and

[1] *The Critique of Pure Reason*, B xxxvi. Kant's works are cited in accordance with the usual abbreviations and conventions. Kant's posthumously published 'Reflections' are cited as (Refl.).
[2] L. E. Borowski, *Darstellung des Leben und Charakters Immanuel Kants*, Königsberg 1804. Cited from the 1912 edition, Deutsche Bibliothek, Berlin, p. 78.
[3] Friedrich Wilhelm Förster, *Der Entwicklungsgang der Kantischen Ethik*, Berlin 1893.
[4] "Der Entwicklungsgang der kantischen Ethik in den Jahren 1760 bis 1785," *Kant-Studien* 2 (1898), 290–322, and 3(1899), 41–104.
[5] Paul Arthur Schilpp, *Kant's Pre-Critical Ethics*, Evanston Northwestern University Studies No. 2, 1938.

handbooks and has failed to affect the general outlook of the broader circle of readers interested in the field of moral philosophy. The few relevant remarks in Kant's writings between 1760 and 1770 do seem to support the idea of a major shift of position during this period, particularly because of the quite different assessments of the tradition of British moral philosophy that Kant offers us. Whereas between 1763 and 1765, Kant is often ready to cite Shaftesbury and Hutcheson in a positive vein, in 1770 he feels 'fully justified in censuring' the latter explicitly (*Dissertation* §9), though on both occasions for the same reason – for having assumed some sort of 'sensus moralis.' Given this undeniable discrepancy of judgement, which any further analysis must take as its point of departure, those who have emphasised the continuous evolution of Kant's thought must undertake to render the positive acknowledgement and the repudiation of his predecessors equally intelligible within the context of that thought. This would of course require a close examination of Hutcheson's writings and an attempt to specify precisely which doctrines Kant was able to learn from and the reasons why he could regard them so highly in the first place.

All previous interpreters have avoided the real difficulty presented by Kant's entirely different judgements in this connection by attempting to separate the early Kant as much as possible from Hutcheson from the start. But even if it is quite true that Kant was never satisfied with the assumption of 'a particular moral sense,' it is a rather feeble explanation of Kant's praise for Hutcheson simply to say that he was indebted to the latter for drawing his attention to the 'emotional factor' in our ethical consciousness.[6] This interpretation of the relationship between Kant and Hutcheson, and likewise that of Menzer as well, merely reveals the lack of any independent acquaintance of this Scottish thinker. Hutcheson's work has only been acknowledged in terms of its results with a view to clarifying an interpretation already taken over from Kant, rather than in terms of the immanent movement of thought that yielded those results in the first place. But specifically within the context of Hutcheson's work itself, this conceptual movement far exceeds the significance of the results that have subsequently been taken up on their own account. Just as scepticism, for example, which can represent a comfortable prejudice, can equally be the product of highly sophisticated and intelligent reflection, so too Hutcheson's 'moral sense' is not merely the expression of an enthusiastic literary trend following on in the wake of Shaftesbury, but a final and

---

[6] Schilpp, op. cit., p. 39.

considered response to a question concerning the theoretical clarification of fundamental dimensions of ethical experience, and one that was posed and sustained in terms of extremely penetrating analyses and observations. We must therefore allow the concrete features of Hutcheson's genuine work to emerge from out of Kant's own grey-on-grey depiction of heteronomous moral principles. Only then will we be in a position to understand in what sense the problem posed by Kant was also that of Hutcheson, even if the latter was unable to bring that problem to a satisfactory resolution.

The following discussion is intended, in the first place, to present the concrete form and full range of Kant's critique of Hutcheson. This is something that can only be determined in the context of Kant's posthumously published 'Reflections,' which clearly show how important it was for Kant to clarify his own position with regard to the principle of 'moral sense.' Then we shall be able to understand precisely how and to what extent we must credit Hutcheson with exercising a significant influence on Kant's thought. The trajectory of Kant's philosophy as expressed in his own writings must itself serve to explain why Kant himself, despite his repeated criticisms of Hutcheson, could still describe the basis of ethical consciousness as a *sensus moralis*, and that at a time when he had already discovered the formula of the Categorical Imperative.

I. Kant's Criticism of Hutcheson's Conclusions[7]

Hutcheson's interpretation of ethical consciousness appears extremely impoverished if we consider only the 'results' of his investigations. His approach appears to be completely entangled in the Stoic tradition of

---

[7] The relevant works of Hutcheson are cited as follows (listed here in chronological order of original publication in English and Latin):
  A. *An Inquiry into the Original of Our Ideas of Beauty and Virtue* (London, 1725); *Untersuchung unserer Begriffe von Schönheit und Tugend* (cited as Bea.), translated by Merk, Frankfurt and Leipzig, 1762.
  B. *An Essay on the Nature and Conduct of the Passions and Affections, with Illustrations on the Moral Sense* (London, 1728); *Abhandlung über die Natur und Beherrschung der Leidenschaften* (cited as Aff.), translated anonymously, Leipzig 1760.
  C. *Synopsis Metaphysicae Ontologiam et Pneumatologiam complectens* (cited as Syn.), in an edition of 1771.
  D. *A System of Moral Philosophy*, 2 vols. (cited as Mor.), posthumously published in London, 1755. A German translation appeared in Leipzig in 1756.

moral thought, which had been repeatedly renewed in the West through the continuing welcome reception of Cicero's writings.

For Hutcheson, judging the good essentially involves the joint action of three dimensions of subjectivity: Firstly, the unselfish or 'kind affections,' which enable us to take an immediate interest in and actively promote the well-being of others. These affections are spontaneously directed towards assisting others in their distress, and express a sense of pleasure, unmixed with envy, at the happiness and good fortune of our fellow human beings. (Aff., pp. 18, Mor. I, p. 43, p. 228). Secondly, these affections do not, of themselves, produce the act of moral approval or judgement. The 'benevolence' (Bea., p. 138f., p. 172) that finds expression here is simply experienced by us as a natural need. The action of a person ready and eager to help another expresses an inner tendency of the human being, and involves no reflection on ethical norms or demands. The fact that we value this capacity in ourselves, regard it as something unquestionably good, and interpret the pleasure involved as a form of approval or what Hutcheson calls 'complacence' (Bea., p. 138) – all this derives from the operation of another subjective capacity that Hutcheson calls 'the moral sense.' And it is through this alone that the word 'good' acquires real significance in the specifically moral context. All acts that spring from 'benevolence,' and thus specifically benevolence itself as a form and feature of human character,[8] come to be evaluated from a pure perspective in and through the moral sense, something that is clearly quite different from the original spontaneous tendency itself (Mor. I., p. 53). And third, reason also has a role to play in the interaction of these capacities. The 'kind affections' embrace all those who are within their capacities with active benevolence. But they depend upon finding relevant objects for the

---

[For the translation of this essay, all quotations and page references have been adjusted to match Hutcheson's own original editions. The editors of the present volume are indebted to Ina Goy and Eric Watkins for helping to check passages in the eighteenth-century texts, and have added translations of brief passages from Kant's Latin.]

The numerous translations of Hutcheson that appeared in such rapid succession amply document the enormous significance of his thought for German philosophy in the eighteenth century. Not even Hume was so enthusiastically translated into German during this period. The fact that even today we still have to refer to these early translations that are naturally difficult to access clearly indicates the almost total oblivion into which Hutcheson has now fallen.

[8] On the difficulty of deciding whether this approval attaches essentially to actions or to character, see William Robert Scott, *Francis Hutcheson*, Cambridge 1900, pp. 182 ff. See also the somewhat less illuminating study by Thomas Fowler, *Shaftesbury and Hutcheson*, London 1882.

exercise of their 'kindness.' In themselves, these affections are blind, only a reaction to those possibilities for activation with which they are presented. Hence they may also promote the interests of the unworthy, and they may exert and concentrate all of their strength on an extremely small circle of persons, like that of the family, without regard for, and even to the express detriment of, some larger whole that would itself be capable of inciting like benevolence if only it were perceived and apprehended clearly enough. This circumstance therefore also gives rise to the further task of clarifying and extending the expression of benevolence with respect to broader and more universal perspectives. Reason offers an ultimate aim and end to the 'kind affections' that love alone, entangled in its own internal conflicts, can never provide: the general happiness and well-being of humanity itself. The highest degree of approval the moral sense can bestow falls therefore to the calm, considered, dispassionate and active exercise of benevolence with regard to humanity as a whole (Mor. I, p. 59, and many other instances).

In relation to these final ethical 'conclusions' of Hutcheson's theory, which are indebted to the tradition, Kant's critical objections are clearly very convincing. There are four issues above all that Kant raised in rebuttal of Hutcheson from the beginning. These concern the universality, the binding character, the transcendental grounding, and the content of ethical consciousness. According to Kant, none of these questions was properly addressed or even acknowledged by Hutcheson. It soon becomes obvious that Kant's most important objection concerns the necessary universality of judgement with regard to the morally good. For Kant, the feature of universality incontestably requires us to seek the origin of the ethical, and the form of insight that it involves, in reason itself.

1. The entire semantic horizon of the word 'feeling,' which refers us to the insistently felt experience of something objectively given to the sense of touch, already indicates that the subject's experience here lacks transparency and consistency. The immediate evidence provided by a feeling is therefore always something peculiarly 'mine' in each particular case, something that I cannot expect to be perpetually binding on all others, or even on myself at different times. Feelings merely possess a 'private validity,' as Kant puts it (Refl. 541). Since they are by nature variable in their degree of intensity and 'differ infinitely from one another,' they cannot furnish any 'uniform standard of good or evil' (Gr: 4:442). And since feeling always represents a particular experience of a purely individual subject, we cannot merely appeal to it in matters of moral judgement

without undermining the possibility of meaningful argument and discussion with other people. Such an appeal would simply promote a 'division of general outlook' and destroy 'possibilities of agreement' (Refl. 241). To cling obstinately to feeling thus contradicts the idea of humanity, which always seeks a common view with regard to what essentially belongs to all human beings as such. Thus Kant perceives a certain tyrannical element in the sometimes zealous philanthropy of the British thinkers, and in something they share with the sort of ethical theory that appeals to some special revelation from God, or to that kind of 'enthusiastic' conviction of the good that Kant dubs 'intellectual intuition.' Kant identifies this element more precisely when he draws attention to a further implication of the concept of 'feeling.' For we always also judge feelings with respect to the degree of agreeableness they involve. Indeed, the measure of this agreeableness seems identical with the degree of intensity of the feeling in question. 'If there were such a thing as a moral feeling, we would reckon it a means for procuring pleasure for ourselves, it would be an additional sense through which to procure pleasure' (Refl. 6755). The intentional character of feeling is also directly related to the particular subject and its state of well-being. Kant does not of course claim that these implications of the theory would be recognised or endorsed by Hutcheson himself. Indeed, he regarded Hutcheson so highly precisely because Hutcheson had at least attempted to expel 'everything merely pragmatic' from the moral domain (Refl. 6841). But this cannot properly be done by an appeal to any moral sense, to any merely felt certainty of the good.

2. This can be seen even more clearly from the fact that the doctrine of moral feeling makes it impossible to acknowledge the unconditional demand that attaches intrinsically to the character of the good. Feelings are not forms of knowing. They merely represent forms of the state of the individual subject as it finds itself in fact. Hence they can claim no authentically binding validity. Their actual character consists simply in their real intensity. Feeling as such contains no ground that transcends the specific character of a particular act. But knowledge involves more than a factual process or psychological event. We must therefore regard moral experience as a form of knowing, and thus as an accomplishment of reason, precisely because its actual character does not depend on the intensity with which it affects human beings. If two feelings conflict with one another, we simply follow the stronger or more persistent one. The conflict here is resolved by comparing both feelings on the level of their actual strength and intensity. If moral experience were a matter of moral feeling, then the unconditional character of such experience would be grounded in the

specific strength of the feeling in question. But that could not possibly do justice to the characteristic demand of moral experience. 'The subjective ground of the moral feeling, if it were conceived as stronger than anything else, would explain how something particularly comes to pass. But only reason can prescribe the ought' (Refl. 7253). However powerful we might imagine the strength of such a moral feeling to be, it could still never properly explain the kind of demand the good effectively makes upon us. The intelligible and unconditioned character of this demand is not quantitatively, but rather qualitatively, different from anything grounded in mere feelings.

It is also quite inaccurate to characterise moral consciousness through this appeal to a certain strength of feeling. Moral consciousness does not actually possess an 'intensity' that overcomes any other feeling or passion. 'We can even approve or disapprove of something without any perceptible feeling on our part, and we can experience [*empfinden*] abhorrent actions as worthy ones' (Refl. 6760). 'Morally good actions do not procure us the highest gratification, but we regard this gratification as the highest thing there is – that is, we judge that this gratification itself merits the greatest approval' (Refl. 6749). Even when our knowledge of what is genuinely good is weakened or distorted, relegated perhaps to some tiny corner of consciousness where it fails to influence our general conduct, the good nonetheless announces itself in a decisive and unconditioned manner, even if we actually fail to respond to it. With regard to its influence upon action, the good is perhaps the weakest of all motives. But it still leads us to judge that 'it should properly outweigh all other motives' (Refl. 6623). It does not indeed drive us to perform certain acts, but it does make them binding on us. No theory based upon an appeal to moral sense can possibly explain this phenomenon of binding obligation and the universality that that necessarily involves. Such theories thus fail with respect to the very idea that Kant had already identified in 1763 as the basic concept and fundamental problem of ethics, the idea that would continue to guide all of Kant's subsequent attempts to articulate a convincing moral philosophy.

3. There is a third point of criticism, that Kant only expresses in some brief and rather obscure 'reflections,' In deriving his 'moral sense' from a creative act of God himself, Hutcheson once again contradicts that essentially unconditional character of the good that reveals itself only to knowledge. For Hutcheson, the three independent faculties of the soul (feeling, inclination, and reason) are nonetheless intimately connected with one another where moral consciousness is concerned. Since it is impossible

to explain internally why 'affections' are required precisely to realise the rational idea of general welfare, and why we express our approval for the latter precisely in terms of feeling, we must assume some ground external to the subject for this 'fashioning' of our faculties. Hutcheson claims that we are 'befooled into a public interest against our will' (Aff. , p. 35). 'It was reasonable for the general good that we should in some degree be subjected [to affections]; ... with the most benign counsel our minds are so constituted that we value them [these affections] upon calm reflection in proportion to their importance to the happiness of the whole system' (Mor. I., pp. 137–8). This intersubjective teleology of the faculties is therefore ultimately grounded in God's purpose in effectively willing everything for the best of his creatures. The 'mind' is fashioned by God in such a way as to promote acts that are advantageous to the 'entire system.' But since our moral approval attaches solely to the 'kind affections,' and not to the general good or advantage as such, it would appear that moral judgement, in approving the means rather than the end, is nothing but a deliberately created illusion. It would simply serve God's purpose in enabling his creatures to preserve their own existence and promote their own interests. But that would deprive the human judgement of certain acts are good 'per se' under any circumstances of all real meaning.

If we examine Hutcheson's theory in more detail, this teleological construction of the good also appears as one of its weakest aspects. And Hutcheson himself could never fully entertain the view that moral consciousness is simply an artificial arrangement for preserving and promoting the existence of the human race. He evades this conclusion by asking the proper question: why should God show such persistent concern for the well-being of his creatures in the first place? The only possible answer is that God himself, through such 'kind affections' on his part, also desires the happiness of human beings. The divinity must have known that the 'kind affections' implanted in man contributed to the happiness of his creatures. And this implies a 'kind of affection or benevolence in the deity' (Aff., p. 240). Hutcheson believes that natural theology can demonstrate the goodness of the Almighty from the mere fact of such moral feelings (Bea., p. 303, Aff., p. 280). God's ultimate purpose, one that he desires 'without any farther view or reason' (Aff., p. 239 note), is not simply the preservation, but also the happiness, of his creatures. This transcendent grounding of moral consciousness therefore manages to avoid any straightforward utilitarianism. But the decisive Kantian objection remains unaffected: Hutcheson still understands human moral judgement as originating in a merely factual 'arrangement' of the soul's faculties on the part of God.

If this is indeed so, then moral judgement is essentially limited and defined by its origin. For we cannot then seriously describe the 'kind affections' of God, which gave rise to the human faculty of moral judgement in the first place, as actually good in themselves. Their force remains purely factical in character.

We do therefore bestow our moral approval upon these kind affections, yet Hutcheson demands the impossible when he expects moral reflection to grasp how the possibility of this act is itself grounded in a divine attribute to which our approval is only subsequently related. The act of approval is not merely ungrounded in its own right, but serves essentially as a means for something else – namely, the kind affections. The object of approval appears as the ground of the existence of the approval itself. This is an absurdity because moral approval necessarily makes an unconditional claim in its own right. Hutcheson's attempt to legitimate moral judgements by grounding them in God is therefore a complete theoretical failure. And the reason lies in the elementary deficiency of his basic principle: it inevitably turns moral insight, which must be grounded within itself if it is to count as knowledge, into something merely factical. Even in God, the 'kind affections' are still described as something merely real or actual. They can therefore never properly elucidate the essentially shared and common character of that moral insight in which both God and his creatures clearly perceive the unconditioned character of the good.

Such considerations as these surely prompted Kant to a remark like the following: 'If moral feeling is to determine our judgement, then it is all an arbitrary arrangement on the part of God, and we cannot know whether something is good or not' (Refl. 6798; cf. 6803). The philosophy of moral sense eliminates the proper field of the human understanding and 'might just as well make appeal to divine creation' (Refl. 241).[9]

In the second place, Kant also criticises Hutcheson's method of analysis, which he had effectively derived from the psychology of Locke. This method is all too ready simply to assume a particular faculty in order to explain the specific capacities of human subjectivity, and is quite content to leave it at that. It is true that Kant himself rejects the psychological monism of Wolff, who had attempted to derive all the capacities of the soul a priori from one fundamental power or faculty. But he also conceded

---

[9] I also refer the reader briefly to Kant's letter to M. Herz of 21.2.1772, for another example of Kant's attempt to interpret moral sense as a form of intellectual intuition.

that Wolff's attempt was at least 'undertaken in a philosophical spirit' and
in accordance with the 'maxim of reason' that encourages us to seek for
unity in all our principles.[10] We must regard 'the principle of Hutcheson,'
on the other hand, as 'unphilosophical insofar as it introduces a new feeling as a ground of explanation' (Refl. 6634).

As we shall see, however, Hutcheson did not simply proceed care-
lessly in this respect or without first closely examining other alternative
attempts at explanation. And since Kant himself had also grasped the
original and irreducible character of the consciousness of the good, it was
certainly not this claim itself, but rather the introduction of a new and
specific 'feeling' here, that motivated his criticisms. 'The moral feeling
is no original feeling' (Refl. 6598). The absolutely binding claim of the
good reveals that some power or accomplishment of reason, that insight
or knowledge, is essentially implied here. And as P. E. Schilpp rightly saw,
this was something that had always been clear to Kant. After 1769, Kant
even identified the 'vitium subreptionis generaliter' in the fact that 'we
treat the judgement of the understanding as appearance [*Erscheinung*]
and reflection as intuition [*Intuition*]' (Refl. 280).

4. The Kantian objections we have discussed so far essentially concern
the formal dimension of the idea of the good. If Hutcheson's conclusions
in this respect already fail in Kant's eyes to do justice to the authentic character of moral experience, it is clear that Kant was even less satisfied with
the substantive determination of the good provided by the moral sense theory of morality. He was particularly suspicious of the way in which the
theory relates the moral sense in question to the 'kind affections.' For it
merely serves to distract our attention from the virtue that seemed to Kant
to be the first amongst all virtues – that of justice. 'People talk the whole
time of goodness [*Gütigkeit*] and benevolence [*Wohltat*], which is just a
fabled hobby-horse. Hutcheson belongs here too.'[11] And this objection is
not entirely unjustified. It is quite true that Hutcheson in his last book had
also explicitly related the act of approval bestowed by the 'moral sense' to
the striving to possess virtue. The will to make oneself a good human being
is also something fundamentally good. But the goodness after which such
a will strives is exclusively that characterised by the 'kind affections'. In the
last analysis, therefore, the good is defined here solely in terms of our duties
to others. Thus the injunction against lying and overindulgence can only be

---

[10] Dohna-Wundlaken, *Die philosophischen Hauptvorlesungen Immanuel Kants,
Metaphysik*, p. 144.
[11] *Eine Vorlesung Kants über Ethik*, ed. Paul Menzer, Berlin 1924, p. 146.

grounded by an appeal to the fact that they do harm to others or reduce our own capacities to help others (Bea., p. 196).

Nor is it really as easy to understand, as Hutcheson thinks it is, just how, on the basis of his system, this striving for benevolent dispositions and affections is also something emphatically good. How can one and the same moral 'sense' recognise with the same delight and approval something like love for one's fellow human beings and the entirely different kind of respect and love that we bestow on moral excellence? Consideration of the phenomena themselves here inevitably introduces a real tension into an otherwise unified theory, a tension that Kant formulates in terms of the following alternative: 'We must ask whether we do in fact take an immediate delight in the well-being of others, or whether the pleasure here really lies in the possible application of our powers to promote that well-being. Both are quite possible, but which is actual? As far as the sympathising instincts of compassion and benevolence are concerned, we have reason to believe that they are merely strong impulses to ameliorate the distress of others that derive from the soul's own approval [*Selbstbilligung*] of the soul and produce these sensations within us' (20:144). It is quite true that this passage is not directly concerned with Hutcheson, and does not precisely capture his position on the matter. But it clearly shows how Kant, early on in his development, was already seeking, in express contrast to Hutcheson's principle, to locate the subjective ground of our moral capacities and achievements in subjectivity conceived explicitly as a kind of self-relation. Kant is therefore forced to interpret the love that human beings have for one another, which he still treated as an ultimately self-evident 'perfection' in the Prize Essay of 1764 (2: 299), as a form of rational self-activity.

The more Kant concretely developed his own specific conception of morality in terms of the rational structure of the will, the more emphatic his critique of Hutcheson inevitably became insofar as the latter conceptualised the essence of the good in terms of a relationship to something other than itself. It is quite true for Hutcheson that reason itself extends this relationship to the well-being of mankind as a whole. But Kant still cannot properly regard even this totality of our fellow human beings as the authentic object of morality. For human morality is grounded upon our 'capacity to judge the particular solely through the universal' – that is, upon a rational self-relation on the part of the singular self. The 'kind affections' (and Shaftesbury's 'sympathy') are 'something entirely different and are concerned merely with the particular, albeit the particular in relation to others. Here we do not rise to the idea of the whole, but

assume the position of another individual' (Refl. 782). Hutcheson's philanthropic ideal involves material universality, whereas the Kantian ideal
of the rational will involves formal universality. There is no possible point
of mediation between these two approaches.

II. The Productive Aspects of Hutcheson's Argument

The full range and extent of Kant's critique of Hutcheson has really only
been revealed with the posthumous publication of Kant's remaining literary works. The works that Kant published in his own lifetime give confi-
dent expression to a position that he had already developed over decades
of constant reflection. Kant therefore felt no special need to examine in
any further detail positions he believed he had effectively transcended.
But close consideration of the fuller and more detailed arguments that
he developed in his earlier period forces us to acknowledge a greater distance between Kant and Hutcheson than might initially appear. And the
idea that our two thinkers shared a broadly similar standpoint during
the period to which the relevant 'Reflections' can be dated appears to
be quite indefensible. It is true that for the majority of the passages we
have cited this would actually be the period immediately after 1770, and
they might therefore have resulted from a change in Kant's conception of
moral philosophy. But some of them certainly go much further back than
this, and date from the time when his few published remarks first confirm Kant's 'particular esteem' for Hutcheson. And even in 1778, Kant
still certainly did not deny that Hutcheson, despite failing to recognise
our duties towards ourselves, was a thinker of 'considerable philosophical spirit' (Menzer, op. cit., p. 146). It is far from obvious, therefore, that
the difficulties with Hutcheson's ethics that Kant had already identified
according to his lecture announcement for 1765 (2: 311) are necessarily quite different to those that find expression in the posthumously published 'Reflections.'

But in that case, what were the positive features of Hutcheson's thought
that led Kant to esteem him so highly in the first place? He certainly did
not need Hutcheson's assistance to draw his attention to the emotional
dimension of the moral life for the first time. If this had been necessary,
the work of Cicero, or of edifying pietistic literature, or of other Scottish
moral philosophers could easily have performed the same function. But
the Prize Essay of 1764 clearly shows that it was Hutcheson's interpretation of moral consciousness in terms of 'moral sense' that had made a

distinct impression on Kant. It simply remains to ask whether Kant initially lauded Hutcheson for the very thing that he later completely repudiated, or whether the combination of laudatory citation and radical critique can be rendered intelligible by reference to the concrete form of Kant's particular investigation of morality.

Kant's criticisms were directed exclusively against the specific form that the consequences of the theory of moral sense had assumed. In what follows, I will more affirmatively show that Hutcheson's own development of this conception reveals certain features that effectively transcend the significance of the moral sense theory itself. It is precisely these features that bring this particular representative of the Scottish School into a greater proximity to Kant than the concept of 'moral sense' itself would ever lead us to expect. And they can explain Kant's praise for Hutcheson and show us why Kant could still consider himself indebted to Hutcheson at a stage of his own development that would nonetheless lead consistently to his mature rationalist position on ethics.

The British moral philosophers of the seventeenth and eighteenth centuries were the leading ethical thinkers of their age. Hobbes and Bernard Mandeville had regarded self-love as the essential basis of moral consciousness and skilfully defended their hypothesis in terms of a carefully developed psychology. Those who remained unconvinced by this assault upon the Platonic and Stoic theory of the good as an intrinsic reality in itself were therefore forced to reflect much more deeply if they were to successfully ground their own conviction of the reality of the good in an age when empiricist philosophy was becoming increasingly dominant. Thus the writings of Samuel Clarke and William Wollaston, for example, already manifest a very high level of intellectual reflection. Both of them attempted to identify an objective principle of the good as an intrinsic ontological identity that is intelligible to reason and is violated by the immoral action of the will.

While Hutcheson shared Clarke's and Wollaston's opposition to the empiricist principle of self-love, he also criticised their approach because of the theoretical difficulties he had identified in their arguments. They effectively convinced him for the first time that the authentic character of moral consciousness cannot properly be grasped through reason itself, and thus encouraged him to introduce the concept of a specifically 'moral sense.'

The significance of Hutcheson's work lies in the way in which, and in the reasons for which, he insisted upon the undiminished reality of moral consciousness in its own right as against an inadequate interpretation of morality in terms of theoretical reason, even though he also acknowledged the intentions and achievements of Clarke and Wollaston themselves. Shaftesbury's appeal to 'emotion' and 'sympathy' was still grounded in an essentially aristocratic ideal of life eloquently defended with all the pathos of poetic art. Hutcheson, on the other hand, is not really concerned with promoting 'moral sense' on account of the profound feelings or passionate enthusiasm allegedly at work in our moral life. The prevailing tone of his writings is more scholastic, or at least cooler, in character, and is marked by a milder and more abstract sense of humanity that is solely concerned with evaluating the 'calmer affections' in relation to the good. He grounds morality in sensibility almost apologetically, and then for exclusively theoretical reasons, and only indulges in harsh polemics when the genuinely strong arguments of his philosophical opponents have to be countered. And it is his constantly re-elaborated and ever more refined refutations and analyses that are particularly instructive in this respect. For they clearly reveal the difficulties that attend all non-empirical attempts to ground morality in a convincing manner. And it is precisely these parts of Hutcheson's work that must have been especially significant for Kant.[12]

Any human act can be justified in two different ways: either as an appropriate means for the realisation of one of our ends, or as the actual realisation of our intention. We approve of something either for the sake of itself or for the sake of something else (Aff., pp. 227; Syn., pp. 20–1). Now Hutcheson shows that in neither case can the grounds of approval be derived from reason alone. We can only explain approval if we presuppose certain affections or inclinations that do not intrinsically belong to the faculty of thought itself. This is easy to see with regard to hypothetically justified acts. For they refer to something else for the sake of which they are performed, and thus ultimately, if a *progressus in infinitum* is to be avoided, to something that is intrinsically good. The question concerning the ultimate ground of any and every choice, including cases of moral decision, is concretely implicated in the question concerning the possibility of immediate approval and the role of reason in relation to it. Now

---

[12] Hutcheson's most compelling arguments and his deepest insights are to be found in his *Essay on the Nature and Conduct of the Passions and Affections*, which has never been examined by Kant scholars in the past. This work is dedicated to defending the position that Hutcheson had developed in the *Inquiry* and providing it with further psychological justification and support. Hutcheson's later system betrays distinctly pedagogical features and gives a much less vivid and convincing impression of Hutcheson's true originality.

spontaneity is a formal criterion of our moral approval. 'But [as for] the mighty reason we boast of above other animals, its processes are too slow, too full of doubt and hesitation, to serve us in every exigency to direct our actions ... without this moral sense' (Bea., p. 271). And since it is generally accepted that the moral character of a human being does not necessarily grow in proportion with the further development of his intellectual capacity, it is not at all clear why proper knowledge of the most essential features of things should be required in this respect. Just like Kant, who had learned from Rousseau 'how to honour' the ordinary and unlettered human being, so too Hutcheson demands that moral philosophy must not cast doubt upon the real and undiminished value of virtue as it is also encountered amongst those of even the humblest social estate (Bea., p. 195).[13]

But what if the experience of spontaneous moral approval were actually based upon a process of thought, albeit a wholly universal one, that operates so tacitly and readily that it is almost inevitably confused and conflated with an immediate feeling? We cannot absolutely rule out this possibility if the act of moral approval could plausibly be interpreted as a product of reason. Wollaston and Clarke appealed to two concepts of reason in their own attempts to ground morality deductively: the concept of perfection (intrinsic excellence) and that of the intrinsic truth of things. But it seems that an act of robbery or murder could also be executed to perfection. This criterion, which is also endorsed by Wolff, remains purely formal, and necessarily presupposes a specific concept of the morally good. Those who regard an evil or morally wrong act as a denial of truth, as a murderer might be said to deny the truth that his victim is a living human being the same as himself, fail to acknowledge that every act involves reference to innumerable such truths, and yet they only presuppose and demand absolute moral legitimation for some acts rather than others (Aff., p. 269). Furthermore, the morally wrong or evil will seems to admit of differences of degree, which is certainly not the case where theoretical truth is at issue. If it is equally true in the relevant sense that three pennies are worth something, and that a person is a living human being like oneself, then the thoughtless disposal of pennies must be considered just as reprehensible as an act of murder, and that is clearly absurd.

In the third place, we find Richard Cumberland and others defending the promotion of the best universal good as an ethical postulate of reason

---

[13] There are numerous other specific ideas in Hutcheson that closely correspond to Kant's own view of moral experience, such as the Scottish thinker's explanation of evil in terms of a 'sophistry of the passions' (Mor. I., p. 126; cf. *Groundwork*: 4: 405).

itself. But Hutcheson, who also regards this principle as the authentic ideal of real morality, also decisively rejects the idea that it can be grounded or rendered intelligible in terms of reason. For on what basis do we actually bestow our approval upon a state of universal happiness? Because it is 'the best'?

'But here I ask again: what is the meaning of 'best.' Is this a moral or a natural 'best'? If we claim the first, we reason in a vicious circle and merely describe the same word in terms of itself. If we claim the latter, holding the happiest state to be that in which all are happy, then I further ask, for whom is it the happiest state, for the whole or for the individual members of the whole? If happiest for the whole, then what causes us to approve the happiness of the whole? Here again we appeal to a feeling or to the kind affections. If happiest for individual members, then the orientation to particular happiness is not based upon the rational character of action' (Aff., p. 228). It is clear that we can indeed form the idea of the common good without reference to moral feeling, but one could only desire it for the sake of one's own private advantage (Bea., p. 221). It might then be objected that it is surely 'more rational' to promote universal happiness even as we seek our own since this would involve 'more happiness' as a whole. But this is as absurd as encouraging a man who needs a single stone to gather a whole pile of them together just because it would contain even 'more stone' (Aff., p. 222–3).

All these arguments seem quite simple and plausible. Nonetheless, apart from some perceptive remarks by Joseph Butler,[14] Hutcheson was the first to marshal them in this way. They proved entirely convincing to many and did much to establish the dominant role of the Scottish School in the moral philosophy of the time. Hume repeats them in only slightly changed form in his *Treatise*, and we still find Adam Smith appealing to Hutcheson as an effectively classical source.[15] And Kant, too, when he was still thinking in terms of Wolff's 'Philosophia Practica,' was also inevitably impressed by these arguments as providing a further confirmation and extension of the criticisms that Crusius had already mounted against Wolff.

---

[14] On the importance of Butler's thought for Hutcheson, see Scott, op. cit., pp. 198ff. See also Leslie Stephen, *English Thought in the Eighteenth Century*, London 1876, vol. 2, pp. 50ff, and Friedrich Jodl, *Geschichte der Ethik*, Berlin 1906, pp. 366ff. For an important discussion of the Scottish School in its historical context, see G. V. Gizyeki, *Die Ethik Humes*, Boeslan 1878.

[15] See A. Smith, *Theory of Moral Sentiments*, Edinburgh 1759, part VII, section 3, chapter 8; *Theorie der ethischen Gefühle*, translated by Eckstein, Leipzig 1926, p. 534.

The conclusions that Hutcheson drew from his rejection of every attempt to deduce morality from reason are also instructive. Hutcheson shares Locke's view that reason is a purely logical faculty that allows us to relate and connect ideas (Bea., p. 237). Reason produces no original representations of its own, let alone ones that can function as an influence upon or as a determining ground for action. 'No opinion or judgement, can move us to an act where there is no prior desire of some end' (Mor. I., p. 38). The psychological doctrines of the moral rationalists have never succeeded in properly 'distinguishing the various sensations of the soul' (Mor. I., p. 48), and they have essentially been governed by the false assumption that all the powers of the soul can ultimately be traced back to a single principle (Mor. I., p. 6; Bea., p. 35). But, as Hutcheson points out, the psychological theory of Aristotle and his Scholastic successors had already identified, in addition to pure theoretical reason, another equally essential and equally original power: the will (*appetitus rationalis*) is the faculty of the soul 'for striving after something represented as good and for rejecting what is bad' (Aff., p. 30, p. 217). Despite the obvious impotence of pure theory with regard to action, the role of the will 'has in recent times been entirely forgotten and there are some who ascribe to the understanding not only the reflections of science, but also such things as choice, desire, love and continued striving' (Aff., p. 30 note).

For Hutcheson, the will is simply the overarching concept for all our feelings and affections, and he can find no intelligible sense in the idea that it is itself intrinsically rational. It is characterised on the contrary by all the features that already belong to what we call 'impulse' or 'affection' and cannot therefore originally be understood in terms of rational cognition. And even if rationalist ethics concurs with Christian doctrine in regarding love as a fundamental form of moral life, the former would have to 'be called an act of the understanding, contrary to all language' (Mor. I., p. 228). Hutcheson therefore regards it as incontrovertibly certain that the proper foundations of moral consciousness can only be found within the domain of feeling. And this is why he speaks of the 'moral sense' and the 'kind affections' in this connection. His own conception of subjectivity, oriented as it is to Locke's position, does not permit him any alternative to a purely theoretical understanding of reason.

But, as we have seen, it is already clear from Kant's criticisms of Hutcheson's conclusions that the phenomenon of moral experience, in its binding and universal character, cannot really be explained by appeal to actual or given feelings of any kind. The binding character of moral judgement, or the loving benevolence towards another person, are such intimate and essential features of subjectivity that we cannot distance ourselves from them in the way we always can do in relation to a mere feeling that I just happen to 'have' rather than to 'be.' For I am inwardly addressed by the claim that the good fundamentally makes upon me. To exempt myself from this claim by a process of reflection, to present it to myself in a neutral manner as something purely factical, is not to fulfil a fundamental possibility of reflective reason. It is rather a guilty act that is experienced as such.

Hutcheson himself, who had so clearly demonstrated the original character of moral consciousness and the impossibility of deriving it from self-love or reason alike, was by no means insensitive to this difference, which marks off so-called moral sense from all our other feelings. When he speaks of moral motivation as a feeling [or 'instinct'], as Hutcheson emphasises, he is not supposing that it 'belongs to that low kind of sensation dependent on bodily organs such as even the brutes have. It may be a constant settled determination of the soul itself, as much of our powers of judging and reasoning.' And here 'instinct' [*Trieb*] means nothing more than a capacity 'toward…action' (Mor. I., p. 58). Hutcheson says we can relinquish this off-putting word if we wish, although we should not take offence at it once it is properly defined (Aff., p. 286). Thus Hutcheson's argument leads him more than once to certain formulations that effectively remove any suggestion of 'sensuousness' from the concept of 'moral sense.' But the purely theoretical conception of reason he has inherited from Locke essentially prevents him from interpreting the phenomena, whose specific features he has clearly recognised, in a way that does proper conceptual justice to their inner and intrinsic character. The moral consciousness, as experienced through 'moral sense,' is said to represent, in contrast to our other merely external senses, 'the true perfection of our self' (Aff., p. 160; Mor. I., pp. 201–2). It is only in and through moral consciousness that we become what we ultimately are, that we collect ourselves in terms of our most authentic essence. But Hutcheson's almost Kantian terminology in this context is repeatedly undermined by the language of the Lockean approach, which cannot conceptualise the universality of moral sense as anything other than the universality of a law of nature. In this regard, the 'kind affections' are thus compared with the law of gravity (Aff., p. 279). As a result of this approach, Hutcheson is necessarily driven to formulate a misconceived and unintelligible critique of the concept of freedom (Syn., pp. 38–9; Aff., p. 280).

Hutcheson speaks of an 'appetitus rationalis,' identifies moral consciousness with the true self, and treats such consciousness as equally original with the 'power of reasoning.' All of this naturally suggests an essential relationship between moral sense and reason, but he nonetheless insists that 'reason can only direct to the means or compare two ends previously constituted by some other immediate powers' (Mor. I., p. 58). The good is the ultimate end, albeit one that can only be experienced through a certain 'sense,' however that particular sense is actually constituted.

Hutcheson's theoretical position thus finds expression in a question it would be utterly paradoxical to answer in a positive fashion: 'Is there nothing preferable, or eligible antecedently to all affections too? No certainly, unless there can be desire without affections, or superior desire, i.e. election antecedently to all desire' (Aff., p. 242). In adumbrating the concept of a choice free of all inclination (Aff., p. 215, pp. 286, 288), Hutcheson thus speaks like a prophet despite himself, unwittingly anticipating the morality of pure practical reason. This concept clearly reveals the problematic and unresolved tension between Hutcheson's own analyses of moral consciousness and his actual systematic conclusions. Once a philosophy arose that seriously attempted to grasp the decision that precedes all particular choice as a reality in its own right, then it could also properly regard itself as inheriting the authentic impulse, if not the official doctrine, of Hutcheson's ethical theory.

III. Kant's Concept of Rational Ethics and Hutcheson's Concept of Moral Sense[16]

It is now possible to understand why Kant found Hutcheson's thought to be so valuable and instructive, even at a time when he had already clarified and established his own basic standpoint. Hutcheson shared Kant's conviction concerning the categorical character of moral obligation, and the concept of 'moral sense' clearly posed and revealed the problem of providing a satisfactory theoretical grounding for moral philosophy. Hutcheson had demonstrated the absolute impossibility of deriving the idea of 'the good' in terms of hypothetical or deductive logical reasoning. If Hutcheson's positive proposals ultimately contradicted the ethical phenomena he had perceptively analysed, because his psychological notions

---

[16] For the original context of the ideas presented in the final section of this essay, see my post-doctoral dissertation, *Selbstbewusstsein und Sittlihkeit*, Heidelberg 1956, I, pp. 103–174.

concerning the structure of the subject proved to be fundamentally inadequate, then the pressing task is to develop a theory of subjectivity that is genuinely superior to Locke's and will not obscure the essentially internal and unconditional character of the idea of the good. The earliest remaining sources of Kant's developing moral thought already show him moving towards this goal. Kant here praises Hutcheson as a predecessor only in the sense we have now explained, and not as an advocate of the kind of moral sense theory that is discussed and then rejected in his later writings.

We can distinguish three phases of Kant's moral thought in the period between 1763 and 1766, and in each of these phases we find Kant interpreting and applying the concept of moral sense. The particular significance that Hutcheson came to acquire for Kant can be assessed by examining the development of his (Kant's) concerning the application of this concept.

As is well known, Kant cites Hutcheson in his Prize Essay, *Enquiry into the Distinctness of the Principles of Natural Theology and Morals*, when he attempts to show that specific self-evident material principles are also required in addition to the purely formal principle of the good in order to make determinate substantive moral demands intelligible (2: 300). This work reveals that Kant has already grasped the concept of the categorically binding character of morality with total clarity. But he has not yet succeeded in deducing the *principium diiudicationis* of morality from this concept itself. The highest formal rule still remains devoid of substantive content and must therefore be co-ordinated with further evident material principles derived from another source. Kant points out that it is 'only in recent times' that we have begun to realise that such principles cannot properly be derived, as Wolff had believed, from the objective concept of 'perfection' and its relevant application, but are subjectively disclosed through feeling. These material first principles satisfy an indispensable condition of authentic moral consciousness insofar as they are not grounded hypothetically in terms of something beyond themselves. On the contrary, they effectively formulate ultimate ends. And they are not simply a matter of theoretical cognition, but are essentially related, qua feelings, to the concrete self-actualising subjectivity itself.

Crusius had already repudiated Wolff's monistic position and sought a specific foundation for moral knowledge in the independent faculty of will belonging to the human soul.[17] One reason why Kant, who otherwise frequently echoes Crusius in the work under discussion, also appeals to Hutcheson in elaborating his own moral philosophy is precisely because the latter had clearly revealed the special character of moral experience, which, over and above being an act of judgement, always involves a reference to a certain kind of satisfaction, or 'complacence,' as Hutcheson describes it. The concept of moral sense properly captures this moment, although it certainly does not adequately explain it. Another reason lies in the fact that Hutcheson, unlike Crusius, made no appeal to the kind of theonomous moral principle that would once again effectively nullify his own insight into the special and original character of morality.

Every moral demand must possess a kind of immediate certainty. Some indemonstrable first principles are required here, even though 'we should generally be rather reluctant to regard things as beyond demonstration whether in practical or theoretical philosophy'. 'Under the name of moral feeling, Hutcheson and others have made a good beginning and provided some fine observations in this connection' (2: 300).

Of course the students of Kant's development have always recognised that such praise hardly signifies unqualified approval, and that his particular mode of expression here ('under the name of moral feeling') clearly implies an evident distancing on his part in relation to Hutcheson. But we understate the emphatically positive moment that this remark betrays if we fail to acknowledge the particular achievement of this Scottish thinker in identifying and defending the essentially internal and original character of morality over against any attempt to derive it from something else. What was the subject of Hutcheson's 'fine observations' in Kant's eyes? Certainly not that moral certainty is just 'a matter of feeling' (this bourgeois and sentimental notion of feeling is quite foreign to the language of Kant and Hutcheson, which was so strongly influenced by the tradition of theoretical psychology). Kant was clearly thinking of the kind of remarks already cited that attempted to reveal the necessity for independent principles of morality incapable of being derived from anything else.

Kant's demand for a deeper and more carefully articulated concept of feeling clearly indicates his dissatisfaction with Locke's psychology, and shows that he is already attempting to develop a much more adequate theory of subjectivity. But that does not prevent him from appreciating the genuinely productive moment in Hutcheson's thought for which

---

[17] See C. A. Crusius, *Entwurf der notwendigen Vernunftwahrheiten*, Leipzig 1745, §§446ff.

the 'moral sense' was no simple feeling, as that was usually understood either. And Kant himself, despite his demand for categorically binding principles, still felt unable to relinquish the term 'feeling' or to replace it with a more adequate analysis of the phenomenon to which it effectively pointed. He only succeeded in accomplishing the latter task in 1770, and then not through any revolutionary break with his earlier thought, but rather through a further rigorous and consistent development of the problem he had already explicitly posed in 1763. This further advance in Kant's thinking facilitated an emphatic critique of the kind of errors naturally encouraged by the concept of 'feeling.' Neither Hutcheson nor Kant in 1763 had actually committed these errors themselves, but they could not theoretically be ruled out as long as the authentic and original character of moral consciousness was described solely in terms of feeling. A radically transformed assessment of the principle of moral sense does not therefore necessarily imply a fundamental break in the development of Kant's thought, and it does not necessarily affect his relationship and attitude to Hutcheson's specific arguments in this connection.

This can be seen particularly clearly with respect to Kant's systematic thought in 1765. The Prize Essay did not succeed in adequately mediating the formal and material principles with one another. But shortly afterwards, Kant did indeed discover the formal principle that is both substantively fruitful and immediately applicable: the formula of the Categorical Imperative based on the universality of the will itself.

It was particularly unfortunate for Kant scholarship in general that the Latin annotations from his personal edition of the *Observations upon the Feeling of the Beautiful and the Sublime*, so important for a proper understanding of Kant's intellectual development, were only published in 1942.[18] On the textual basis of Schubert's incomplete work, which actually ignored the most important materials, neither Schilpp nor Menzer were able to form a really clear idea of the highly elaborated character of Kant's early ethical thought. For the published text of the *Observations* only serves to suggest that Kant showed no real interest at that time in the fundamental theoretical problems of moral philosophy. When considered against the background of the Latin annotations, however, the published essay reveals itself as an essentially popular work in the manner

---

[18] For the history of this important textual source, see Gerhard Lehmann's remarks in vol. 20 of the standard *Akademie* edition of Kant's works, from which the following citations are drawn.

of Rousseau that rather obscures the systematic thinker who is still strug-
gling to clarify and articulate his new principle.

For Kant now clearly grasps moral consciousness entirely in terms of the
essence of the will. The will is good when it can regard itself 'in consensus
with the universal will' (20:145). The origin of moral judgements derives
'a mentis humanae natura, per quam quid sit bonum categorice judicat
non ex privato commodo nec ex alieno, sed eandem actionem ponendo in
aliis si oritur oppositio et contrarietas displicet si harmonia et consensus
placet' (20:156) ['from the nature of the human mind, which appraises
that which is categorically good not according to private or external usefulness but by considering the action in others; if contradiction or conflict
arises, it displeases, and if harmony and unity arises, it pleases']. On pages
67 and 161, Kant applies this formula, in a way entirely analogous with his
own later procedure, in order to ground specific concrete duties. Thus it
is easier to understand why Kant, from the middle of the 1760s onwards,
could repeatedly entertain the imminent publication of a work explicitly
concerned with moral philosophy. For Kant is already essentially in possession of the theory he will subsequently present in the first two sections
of the *Groundwork of the Metaphysics of Morals*. He merely needs to
develop the requisite transcendental grounding of ethical knowledge to
his own satisfaction. And he must still adequately clarify the specific and
enigmatic relationship between the will and the emotional factors that
cannot be deduced from theoretical reason.

In order to explicate the genuinely independent character of morality, Kant continues to deploy Hutcheson's concept of moral sense. For
Hutcheson was the first thinker to formulate, with reference to this very
term, the problem concerning the true relationship between reason and
feeling. 'Necessitas categorica actionis tanti mon constat sed pescit solem
applicationem facti ad *sensum moralem*' (20:155, my emphasis). ['The
categorical necessity of an action is not so difficult to establish but only
requires applying moral feeling to the issue.'] The necessity of relating
the individual will to potential universality cannot simply be understood
on the basis of reason itself, although this relation necessarily involves
a process of rational reflection. The *fact* that we must relate the will to
universality in this way is consciously experienced in a specific way that
Kant can only follow Hutcheson in describing as a certain kind of feeling.
'Est enim sensus communis veri et falsi non nisi ratio humana generatim
tamquam criterium veri et falsi, et sensus boni vel mali communis criterium illius. Capita sibi opposita certitudinem logicam, corda moralem tol-
leret' (20:156). ['Human reason is of course nothing other than a common

sense for the true and the false, and a common sense for good and evil is the criterion for these.'] Although the content of moral obligation must be determined through reason, the actual force and power of morality remain something purely factical.

But Kant refuses to regard the *sensus* in question as simply an ultimate reality that could only be grounded in God rather than in human subjectivity. In its ultimate effective power moral, sense still remains a *qualitas occulta* in Kant's eyes. It must be regarded as a 'facultas animae cuius ratio ignoratur' (20:147) ['a faculty of the soul whose ground is unknown']. Kant's remarks here already make some attempt to identify and clarify the character of this *ratio*. He suggests that it must somehow be rooted in our own 'natura sociabilis' (20:156). In the *Dreams of a Ghost-Seer*, Kant had already tried to explain human sociability in terms of the powerful reciprocal influence that intellectual beings exercise upon one another. This effectively forms the third and last phase in the development of Kant's ethical thought when he still regarded the *sensus moralis* as the ultimate source and ground of moral approval.[19]

In his lecture announcement for the winter semester of 1765–66, Kant refers expressly to Hutcheson's efforts, as well as to Shaftesbury's and Hume's, because 'despite their defective and imperfect character, they have nonetheless penetrated furthest in the search for *the first principles of all morality*' (my emphasis).[20] As his Latin annotations show, Kant at this time had already developed a moral principle that strongly resembles his later formulation of the Categorical Imperative. But he continues to employ the conceptual means he has derived from Hutcheson in order to describe the peculiar compulsion we experience in conscious reflection on the universality of the will. We should therefore interpret these remarks in the lecture announcement to imply that the defective and imperfect character of the Scottish ethical theory consists essentially in its problematic *principium diudicatis* (in the concepts of general advantage and the kind

[19] As is generally recognised, the concept and the problem of moral feeling still retains a considerable, if naturally transformed, significance within the context of the later and definitive formulation of Kant's moral philosophy. This is only really intelligible if we also acknowledge the important role that the problem of moral feeling already played in the development of Kant's systematic thought.

[20] This remark is clearly not simply intended to emphasise the importance of empirical anthropology in Rousseau's sense for moral philosophy. This is of course subsequently acknowledged as far as the *Doctrine of Virtue* is concerned. But Kant is essentially praising the three British thinkers because of their achievements in the field of 'universal practical philosophy.' The distinction between these different disciplines derives from Wolff.

affections). Kant's lectures clearly intend to underline Hutcheson's particular service in convincingly demonstrating the authentic and original
character of moral consciousness.

There is a problematic passage in the *Metaphysics of Morals* that
only really becomes intelligible if it is interpreted as a specific allusion to
this earlier phase of his own moral thought. In the Preface to the second
part of that work (*The Doctrine of Virtue*), Kant explicitly defends the
necessity of providing a 'metaphysics' even for a moral philosophy that
is exclusively directed to the 'practical' domain. For in this sphere, a philosopher 'must seek out the first principles of the concept of duty since
otherwise neither certitude nor purity can be expected anywhere in the
doctrine of virtue' (6:376). And Kant then presents his own instructive
argument against appealing to feeling in this connection, and explicitly
criticises any conflation of the Categorical Imperative with the concept of
moral sense – namely, the kind of position that Kant himself had defended
between 1765 and 1769. For 'a popular teacher can indeed be content to
rely on a certain *feeling* that, because of the results expected from it, is
called *moral*, insofar as he insists that the following lesson be taken to
heart, as the touchstone for deciding whether or not something is a duty
of virtue: "How could a maxim such as yours harmonize with itself if
everyone, in every case, made it a universal law?" But if it were mere feeling that made it our duty even to use this proposition as the touchstone,
this duty would not be dictated by reason but would be taken to be a
duty only instinctively, and hence blindly' (6:377). As far as the 'popular
moral philosophy' presented in the second section of the *Groundwork
of the Metaphysics of Morals* is concerned, it is enough to appeal to a
certain feeling as the supposedly self-evident ground of the good. In this
sense, Kant's own standpoint in 1765 can be recognised as just such a
philosophy. And we can also recognise Hutcheson as Kant's predecessor
here precisely insofar as he defends the essentially immediate character of
moral consciousness over against any and every system that would seek to
explain such consciousness either on the basis of self-love or that of theoretical knowledge.

Thus Kant's sharp criticisms of Hutcheson's central principle do not contradict the fact that he continued to value Hutcheson's philosophy, even
if it is solely in a polemical context that Kant later alludes to. For there
was certainly shared ground between them in the way in which they
opposed traditional forms of moral philosophy and conceptualised the
theoretical problem of moral experience. But this problem effectively led
moral philosophy beyond the limits of a partial and particular discipline

and allowed it to pose a fundamental question concerning philosophy in general.

As a result of its intrinsically internal and apodictic character, moral knowledge represents a case of real insight, but it is not the kind of demonstrable cognition with which we are familiar in the sciences. It is rather, as Plato pointed out, a 'knowing which involves the whole soul.'[21] For it is precisely through such knowing that concrete subjectivity essentially understands the character of its own being. But this is something quite beyond the grasp of traditional psychology, with its repertoire of different powers and faculties, which defines thought in terms of abstractive theoretical reason and reduces the actuality of human life to a matter of feelings and sensations, of meaningless and purely factical acts. But moral consciousness essentially involves an apodictic insight that is always originally determined in a specific affective-emotional manner. This insight – whether in the form of approval, demand, satisfaction, or love – constitutes an inviolable unity of knowing and active reality. We cannot make sense of moral experience through any principle of reason that is essentially oriented to a mathematical ideal of science.

Kant always recognised that it was Hutcheson's undeniable merit – at a time when an inadequate concept of reason had effectively obscured the peculiar and original character of moral consciousness – to have drawn attention to the genuinely independent character of the idea of the good that Plato and Aristotle had already acknowledged in their own way. Hutcheson had raised a serious problem for every attempt to discover the real foundation of moral experience, but an instructive problem of quite fundamental significance. It is perfectly true that his concept of moral *sense* was incapable of capturing the cognitive character of the good as a form of knowing. But if we take Hutcheson's critique of rationalist and empiricist ethics together with Kant's critique of Hutcheson's concept of feeling we can clearly recognise the necessity of providing an entirely new foundation for our theory of morality. And the required unity of reason and emotion compels us to rethink the concept of knowledge and to ground the traditional definition of man as a rational being in a new and deeper form. Kant's own theory of a 'pure practical reason' thus represents a late response to the questions that Hutcheson had already raised.

And after a long period (1769–1783) of attempting to derive moral consciousness from his new subjective concept of thinking, Kant once again came close to Hutcheson in recognising the effective reality of the

[21] Plato, *The Laws*, 689a.

moral demand, which is more than a mere rule of judgement, as something beyond our comprehension – namely, as a 'fact of reason.' But this
'fact' possesses much greater significance than any easy assumption of a
specifically moral 'feeling.' This assumption merely revealed the extent to
which Hutcheson had remained beholden to traditional psychology and
thereby had failed to appreciate the full import of the problem he himself
had raised. Hutcheson did not really rethink the theory of subjectivity,
but merely enriched it by identifying a further and important element.
With this element clearly in view, Kant, on the other hand, essentially
transforms the fundamental philosophical discipline of ethics. Whereas
Hutcheson contents himself with simply assuming a certain kind of
'feeling,' Kant develops the 'fact of reason' in order to adumbrate a far-
reaching conception of the intelligible world. Thus Kant moves beyond
the merely factical dimension of moral sense, interprets morality in terms
of reason, and grounds it in the intelligible realm. But for all that he does
not deduce morality from any presupposed or given grounds. He simply
explicates its meaning as something that is not a matter of purely theoretical cognition. The concept of 'pure practical reason' denotes a kind
of knowing that certainly displays a rational structure, but nonetheless
possesses an underivable and original character of its own as a demand
essentially governing our conduct.

The thinkers of speculative idealism, it is true, soon resumed the
attempted deductions that Kant had repudiated. But here, too, Hutcheson's
intentions, partly mediated through Jacobi, once again make themselves
felt. The meaning of knowing in general is now ultimately defined and
determined in terms of moral consciousness itself. The theoretical contributions of Fichte and Hegel are always oriented towards the task of
properly describing and grasping the true essence of human ethical self-
understanding.

The Scottish School of ethics originally developed in an analogous
way. What Hutcheson had regarded as an underivable form of consciousness was now explained by Hume and Smith in terms of other powers
and faculties of the mind. But this reduction clearly marked the triumph
of the old psychology grounded upon the concept of self-love. The fundamental problem concerning the intrinsic character of the good thus fell
into oblivion once again. With Hutcheson, the Scottish School of ethical thought, indebted as it was to the empiricist tradition, formulated for
a while the kind of thought that would eventually inspire and encourage an entirely different kind of idealist philosophy. The actual results
of Hutcheson's thought, and especially the concept of moral sense, did

indeed imply a kind of psychologistic reductionism, and to that extent his British successors proved to be more effective and successful and than he was. But they certainly could not match those insights of Hutcheson's that would later earn Kant's particular commendation and respect. Hutcheson posed the question concerning the essence of moral consciousness with such clarity that he effectively revealed the very inadequacy of his own solution to the problem. The greater thinker who followed him was thereby challenged and provoked to a much deeper level of philosophical reflection that could do proper theoretical justice to the true objectivity and essentially internal character of the good. In this sense, Hutcheson is the Hume of Kantian ethics.

Now it may be quite true that is impossible to arrive at a real understanding of moral consciousness on the basis of philosophically justified insights into the essence of being or the human subject, and that our understanding of being and of ourselves can only ultimately be grasped in relation to the indubitable claims and demands of morality. H. J. Paton was the first to show that this is indeed Kant's well-grounded view of the matter[22]. But this only makes it all the more imperative to rescue the philosophical achievement of his great Scottish predecessor from the oblivion into which it has so unjustly fallen.

[22] H. J. Paton, *The Categorical Imperative*, London 1946, pp. 256ff.

2

The Theory of Obligation in Wolff, Baumgarten, and the Early Kant

Clemens Schwaiger

The 2,500-year history of Western philosophy has witnessed quite fundamental changes in the way that human conduct and action in general has
been evaluated and understood. Ernst Tugendhat has attempted to formulate the basic transformation that has transpired between the *via antiqua*
and the *via moderna* in the sharpest terms as follows: 'The question governing ancient ethics was: what is it that I truly desire for myself; that governing modern ethics is: how should I properly act in relation to others.,[1]
The general turn from a classical ethics essentially concerned with the
achievement of happiness towards a modern and specifically deontological ethics is usually traced back to the work of Kant. For it is here that
moral philosophy effectively seems to lose its earlier character as a theory
of happiness to become what is now pre-eminently a theory of duty and
obligation. But in fact this Kantian reorientation of practical philosophy,
fundamental as it is, is hardly something that simply fell unprepared from
the heavens, but one that actually possesses an interesting and significant
prehistory of its own. This prehistory has remained largely unexamined
and unclarified as far as previous research is concerned.[2]

---

[1] Ernst Tugendhat, *Antike und moderne Ethik*, in the same author's *Problema der Ethik*
(Stuttgart 1984), pp. 33–56, specifically p. 44; see also Hans Krämer, 'Antike und
moderne Ethik?' in *Zeitschrift für Theologie und Kirche* 80 (1983), pp. 184–203.
[2] For a significant exception in this respect see Stephen Darwall, *The British Moralists
and the Internal 'Ought': 1640–1740* (Cambridge 1995), although the discussion is concerned exclusively with the field of British moral philosophy.

I should like here to make some small contribution to exploring this important lacuna in our knowledge. Taking the general concept of 'obligation' as a guiding theme, I shall identify certain previously unconsidered features of the development of German Enlightenment thought that were taken up and further developed in the context of Kant's new approach to moral philosophy.

The following discussion falls into three parts: the first part clarifies the issue indirectly by identifying some of the possible sources for the concept of obligation as it is deployed in Kant's pre-Critical work. The examination of Kant's earliest systematic treatise on ethical principles, the so-called 'Prize Essay' of 1764, will reveal the previously obscured and largely unappreciated fact that it is Alexander Gottlieb Baumgarten who stands in the background here as both Kant's most important partner and opponent in the moral debate. The appropriate evaluation of this often misinterpreted thinker, who was also in fact the most important and most independently minded follower of Wolff in the field of moral philosophy, requires in turn a careful examination of Wolff's theory of obligation. For Wolff's thought on this question had itself undergone a number of significant changes, beginning from the standpoint of Pufendorf, and gradually developing, under the impact of Leibniz's criticism of the latter, into an original theoretical position. In the second part, drawing upon the earlier research of Mariano Campos, I reconstruct the developmental history of Wolff's theory of obligation. In the third part, I closely compare Wolff and Baumgarten and identify the innovations specifically introduced by Baumgarten that would in turn prove so significant and influential for Kant.[3]

1. New light on the old question concerning the context and sources for the 'Prize Essay'

It may come as a surprise to readers that in Kant's first systematic outline of moral philosophy, the *Enquiry into the Distinctness of the Principles of Natural Theology and Morals* of 1764, we already find him apostrophising

---

[3] If we refer without distinction to 'obligation' and 'obligatedness' [*Verbindlichkeit* or *Verpflichtung*] or occasionally simply 'duty' [*Pflicht*] in the following discussion, these are always intended as equivalent expressions for the Latin '*obligatio*.' In the eighteenth century, the Latin word was also sometimes rendered by other German terms such as '*Verbindung*' or '*Obliegenheit*,' though these are no longer, or only rarely, employed in a similar sense today.

the concept of 'duty.' The part of the work specifically dedicated to moral questions, which was composed in response to an essay competition organised under the auspices of the Berlin Academy of Sciences, begins with a powerful dramatic flourish. Kant intends, as he says at the begining, 'to show just how little the primary concept of obligation itself is still properly understood' (A 96).[4] It is thus worth asking in some detail precisely why the concept of obligation is already playing this kind of decisive role even in Kant's early moral philosophy. Who is Kant's real target here, when he is so intent on emphasising the lack of clarity that still attends the crucial concept of obligation?

Many commentators have claimed that this period marked the very height of Kant's 'empiricist' phase, when he was most sympathetic to the British philosophers of 'moral sense.'[5] Yet as far as the important trio of Shaftesbury, Hutcheson, and Hume are concerned, the question of moral obligation can hardly be said to form the heart of their reflections on moral philosophy. And the lack of attention accorded to this question was indeed already noted by British thinkers themselves around the middle of the eighteenth century. Thus Henry Home, in his *Essays on the Principles of Morality and Natural Religion* of 1751, openly criticised these afore-mentioned predecessors for not properly attempting to clarify the concepts of duty and obligation despite the obvious central importance of the latter for moral philosophy.[6] The unsparing analysis which this Scottish moral philosopher and aesthetic theorist provided in this respect reveals a striking affinity with Kant's pessimistic assessment of the state of the contemporary debate in his Prize Essay. If one may indeed speak of Kant's

---

[4] Kant's writings are cited here from the edition by Wilhelm Weischedel, *Werke in zehn Bänden* (Darmstadt 1983), with reference to the original pagination as reproduced there. A refers to the first edition and B to the second edition of Kant's works where relevant. Kant's correspondence, the *Nachlass*, and lecture transcripts are cited from the Prussian Academy Edition, *Kant's gesammelte Schriften* (Berlin 1900–), with volume and page number in Arabic numerals, and line number in subscript.

[5] See in the first instance Dieter Henrich's influential articles on Kant's development, especially: 'Hutcheson und Kant,' in *Kant-Studien* 49 (1957/58), pp. 49–69 (presented as Chapter 1 in present volume); for other relevant discussions, see the dissertations by Minghuei Lee, *Das Problem des moralischen Gefühls in der Entwicklung der Kantischen Ethik* (Taiwan 1994) and Chang-Goo Park, *Das moralische Gefühl in der britischen moral-senseSchule und bei Kant* (Tübingen 1995).

[6] See Henry Home, *Essays on the Principles of Morality and Natural Religion* (Edinburgh 1751; reprinted New York/London 1976), Part I, Essay II, Ch. 3, particularly p. 54: 'Tho' these terms [i.e. 'duty' and 'obligation'] are of the utmost importance in morals, I know not that any author has attempted to explain them.'

intellectual proximity to British thought at this time, then this is justified more in relation to Home's sober diagnosis of the central issues than in relation to any attempt to ground ethical obligation in a theory of moral sentiments.

In view of the rather marginal role generally played by the concept of obligation in the work of the 'moral sense' theorists, commentators have often been tempted to identify Christian August Crusius as the principal source for the ideas expressed in the portion of Kant's essay that concerns ethics. It is claimed that this Leipzig philosopher and theologian, in opposition to the prevailing tradition, already regarded duty rather than happiness as the central concept of moral philosophy. And this is why he exercised a deeper and more lasting influence on Kant than the British moralists, at least according to the now widely accepted argument first presented by Joseph Schmucker.[7] But this attempt to identify the relevant historical sources for Kant's early approach is highly problematic in view of the fact that Kant had always decisively rejected this kind of theological moral positivism that effectively sought to ground morality in the will of God. For there is absolutely no question that Crusius regarded duty and obligation as fundamentally rooted in 'that which drives subjects to obey the commands of their supreme lord and master [*Oberherrn*].'[8] For Crusius, the necessary character of moral demands is ultimately grounded in our obedience to God. Atheists, on the other hand, can acknowledge nothing beyond what Crusius calls a more or less attenuated 'obligation of prudence.'[9]

This conception of ethics, as developed by Crusius, was being expressly defended in public discourse by the university teacher Daniel Weymann in Königsberg at the very time that Kant was working on his essay. This ardent disciple of Crusius enjoyed considerable local prominence during this period, not least because he repeatedly sought open engagement with Kant's philosophical views on a range of issues.[10] In the Prize Essay, Kant

---

[7] See Joseph Schmucker, *Die Ursprünge der Ethik Kants in seinen vorkritischen Schriften und Reflektionen* [sic] (Meisenheim am Glan 1961), p. 85.

[8] Christian August Crusius, *Anweisung vernünftig zu leben* (Leipzig 1744); reprinted in C. A. Crusius, *Die philosophischen Hauptwerke*, eds. Giorgio Tonelli, Sonia Carboncini and Reinhard Finster, vol. 1 (Hildesheim 1969), §133, p. 161.

[9] See ibid., §176, p. 220; §347, p. 423.

[10] See Daniel Weymann, *De vero stabiliendo juris naturae et genium principio. Pars prima* [Disputation of June 12, 1762] (Königsberg 1762), especially §§10 and 12, pp. 21–23. The relevant texts by this earliest philosophical critic of Kant are: *Beantwortung des Versuchs einiger Betrachtungen über den Optimismus* (Königsberg 1759), and *Bedenklichkeiten über den einzig möglichen Beweisgrund des Herrn M. Kants zu einer*

explicitly counters all such attempts by Crusius, Weymann, and others to
ground morality in an essentially 'theonomous' manner. For the imperative that 'I should act in accordance with the will of God,' as the immediate
and supreme principle of morality, is 'entirely incapable of demonstration'
in itself and merely represents 'a formula of problematic skill, and not one
of obligation at all' (A 96f.).

There has been a widespread tendency in the scholarly literature to turn
the forty-year-old Kant, despite the obvious differences between the two
respective positions, into either a wavering philosopher of 'moral sense' or
a fully-fledged follower of Crusius. And this has merely served to obscure
the true significance of another possible source that lies much closer to
hand in this connection– namely, Alexander Gottlob Baumgarten, the
established author of philosophical compendia whom we know was so
highly regarded by Kant. According to the lecture notes taken by Herder,
Kant explicitly praised Baumgarten's work on philosophical ethics as his
'materially richest and perhaps his best book.'[11] The remarkable neglect
into which Baumgarten has fallen in the relevant secondary literature has
only been further reinforced by the premature tendency simply to identify his position in moral philosophy, as in other areas of philosophical
thought, with that of Wolff. Yet it is Wolff who accords the kind of central
role to the concept of 'perfection' in ethics that is so strongly contested by
Kant.[12] This itself has led commentators to overlook the fact that Wolff,
in the course of his own philosophical development, also introduced an
influential conceptual innovation into the theory of moral obligation.
For in Wolff, moral obligation is no longer interpreted in relation to the
external authority of a commanding legislator, but rather in terms of an
inner motivation to perform acts that are properly acknowledged as right.

Demonstration des Daseyns Gottes (Königsberg 1763 II, p. 461f and p. 470). For the
vigorous debate that surrounded the thought and work of Weymann, who proved a
most successful and vigorous defender of Crusius in the early 1760s, see Leben und
Abenteuer des Andrej Bolotow von ihm selbst für seine Nachkommen aufgeschrieben,
vol. 1, ed. Wolfgang Gruhn (Munich 1990), pp. 357f.
[11] Praktische Philosophie Herder (27:16$_{25-26}$). This complement to Baumgarten's Ethica
philosophica (Halle³ 1763; ¹1740) [reprinted in 27:871–1028] can probably also be
extended to his Initia philosophiae practicae primae (Halle 1760) [reprinted in 19:7–91],
the second compendium by Baumgarten that Kant used as a manual for his lectures on
ethics.
[12] See, for example, J. B. Schneewind, 'Kant and Natural Law Ethics,' in Ethics 104 (1993),
pp. 53–74, especially 56–58, who emphasises that Wolff, unlike the modern theorists
of natural law, understood human action primarily from the perspective of individual
'perfection' and regarded the question concerning 'obligation' merely as a secondary
issue.

Through a further radicalisation of this approach, Baumgarten became the first to interpret the whole of practical philosophy consistently and explicitly from the perspective of the concept of obligation, and in this sense he can be said to have decisively anticipated and contributed to Kant's orientation to the idea of duty in ethics.

2. Wolff's attempts to develop a new concept of obligation

a. Repudiation of his early Pufendorfian position under the impact of Leibniz's critique

Despite the now firmly established and apparently indestructible prejudice to the contrary, Wolff was not a precocious and monolithic philosopher whose thought was entirely immune to any real internal development. In fact, he gradually deepened his original position in significant ways, and indeed subjected it in part to fundamental transformation. A perfect example of this is provided in the realm of practical philosophy, as Wolff himself willingly concedes, precisely by the development of his concept of obligation.

In his first programmatic work, the *Philosophia practica universalis, mathematica methodo conscripta* of 1703, Wolff defends a positivistic concept of law and obligation that owes much to the thought of Samuel Pufendorf. This influential theorist of natural law was certainly one of the most avidly studied writers during the period when Wolff was studying in Jena and subsequently teaching in Leipzig.[13] In Pufendorf, the obligating power lies in the authority that lays down and determines legal punishment for the transgression of law, and is reflected in the obligated party as fear before the sanction of punishment. In the early position of Wolff, just as in Pufendorf, who was primarily here influenced by Hobbes, it is the commandment of a superior power that first establishes any binding or obligating law.[14]

[13] See *Christian Wolffs eigene Lebensbeschreibung*, ed. Heinrich Wuttke (Leipzig 1841); reprinted in Christian Wolff, *Gesammelte Werke*, ed. Jean École et al. [henceforth abbreviated as WW], Part 1, Vol. 10 (Hildesheim/New York 1980), p. 132; also Wolff's letter to Leibniz April 4, of 1705, in: *Briefwechsel zwischen Leibniz und Christian Wolff*, ed. C.I. Gebhardt (Halle 1860; reprinted Hildesheim/New York ²1971 ['1963]), p. 23.
[14] See Christian Wolff, *Philosophia practica universalis, mathematica methodo conscripta*, in *Meletemata mathematico-philosophica cum erudito orbe literarum commercio communicata* (Halle 1755; reprinted WW II. 35 Hildesheim/New York 1974),

Leibniz, who had long since shown himself to be an uncompromis-
ing opponent of Pufendorf's, emphatically rejected this entire approach
to the problem. In his first, and extremely important, letter to Wolff of
February 21, 1705, which contained a devastating critique of the latter's
Habilitationsschrift that precipitated a profound intellectual crisis for
Wolff, with long-lasting consequences for his thought, Leibniz expressly
defends the contrary claim: even without any higher divine power, and
therefore also in the case of atheists, obligation remains binding. This
sense of obligation cannot simply be derived from our fear of possible
punishment and our hope for future reward.[15] The idea that the true
source of obligation, as far as natural law is concerned, can only lie in
a principle of reason rather than in the arbitrary decision of a supreme
legislator is also strongly defended by Leibniz a little later in his famous
Monita quaedam ad Samuelis Pufendorfii principia, where he repudiates
Pufendorf's 'voluntaristic' grounding of duty and obligation.[16] We know

sect. II, p. 197, Def. 28: 'Obligatio duplici modo spectari potest, vel quatenus est aliquid
in obligante, vel quatenus aliquid importat in obligato. Priori modo obligatio est actus
superioris, quo poenam statuit transgressoribus legum harumque rationem reddit.
Posteriori autem est metus, quem sanctio poenalis, & reverentia erga superiorem, quam
expositio rationis legum producit'; ibid., Def. 29: 'Lex est jussus superioris inferiori pro-
mulgatus eumque obligans'; Samuel Pufendorf, De iure naturae et gentium (Frankfurt a.
M./Leipzig 1759) (Lund ¹1672; reprinted Frankfurt am Main 1967), Lib. 1, Cap. VI, §4,
p. 89: 'In genere autem lex commodissime videtur definiri per decretum, quo superior
sibi subiectum obligat, ut ad istius praescriptum actiones suas componat'; and similarly
again in *De officio hominis et civis juxta legem naturalem* (Lund 1673; reprinted in:
S. Pufendorf, *Gesammelte Werke*, vol. 2 (Berlin 1997), Ch. II, §2). Pufendorf's influence on the Wolffian concepts and terminology as discussed here is also emphasised by
Mariano Campo, *Cristiano Wolff e il razionalismo precritico* (Milan 1939; reprinted
in WW III.9 (Hildesheim/New York 1980), see p. 404 especially). Campo is the only
scholar who has hitherto explored Wolff's intellectual development in any real detail
(for this whole question, see ibid. pp. 399–435, 504–515 and 547–559). For a specific discussion of Pufendorf's conception of law and obligation in its intellectual and historical
context, see J.B. Schneewind, 'Pufendorf's Place in the History of Ethics,' in *Synthese*
72 (1987), pp. 123–155, especially pp. 128 and 143f.; and *Fiammetta Palladini, Samuel
Pufendorf discepolo di Hobbes. Per una reinterpretazione des giusnaturalismo moderno* (Bologna 1990), pp. 33–90.

[15] See Leibniz's letter to Wolff of April 21, 1705, in *Briefwechsel*, p. 19: 'Putem esse etiam
sine superiore obligationem, ut aliqua esset etiam apud Atheos obligatio [...]. Nolim
igitur obligationem unice a metu poenae et spe praemii peti, cum sit aliquod non merce-
narium recte faciendi studium.'

[16] See Gottfried Wilhelm Leibniz, *Monita quaedam ad Samuelis Pufendorfii principia,
Gerh. Wolth. Molano directa*, in G.W. Leibniz, *Opera omnia*, ed. Ludwig Dutens,
vol. IV, 3 (Geneva 1768; reprinted Hildesheim/New York 1989), pp. 275–283, especially p. 279. For further historical background to the publication, reception, and influence of this text, composed in 1706 but first published three years later, see Norberto
Bobbio, 'Leibniz e Pufendorf,' in *Rivista di Filosofia* 38 (1947), pp. 118–129; for further

that Wolff was familiar with this important text because he mentions it explicitly in his obituary eulogy of Leibniz, which he published in the *Acta Eruditorum*.[17] Wolff was fundamentally shaken by Leibniz's penetrating objections to the position defended in his first published work, as the thorough self-criticism that Wolff presented in the *Ratio praelectorum* of 1718 clearly reveals. Without actually mentioning Leibniz by name, Wolff admits here that, still under the influence of Pufendorf as he was, he had failed to distinguish properly between natural and civil obligation. Obligation itself derives from the very nature of the human spirit, and remains binding upon us even if we were to concede that God does not exist.[18] And Wolff will subsequently continue to attack Pufendorf and his followers for only recognising laws and obligations insofar as they are held to derive from the commanding will of a supreme lord and master. For Wolff, this approach effectively destroys the objective morality and the intrinsic goodness of our acts.[19] And further intellectual disputes in this regard

discussion of the celebrated debate between these two important theorists of natural law, see Fiammetta Palladini, 'Di una critica di Leibniz a Pufendorf' in the same author's *Percorsi della ricerca filosofica. Filosofie tra storia, linguaggio e politica* (Rome 1990), pp. 130–142; Detlef Döring, *Pufendorfstudien. Beiträge zur Biographie Samuel von Pufendorfs und zu seiner Entwicklung als Historiker und theologischer Schriftsteller* (Berlin 1992), pp. 130–142; J.B. Schneewind, 'Barbeyrac and Leibniz on Pufendorf,' in *Samuel von Pufendorf und die europäische Frühaufklärung. Werk und Einfluß eines deutschen Bürgers der Gelehrtenrepublik nach 300 Jahren (1694–1994)*, ed. by Fiammetta Palladini and Gerald Hartung (Berlin 1996), pp. 181–189.

[17] See Christian Wolff, *Elogium Godofredi Guilielmi Leibnitii*, in *Acta Eruditorum*, July 1717, p. 334, reprinted in *Meletemata*, Sect. I, p. 130, where he refers to the publication announcement of this text in the Leipzig review journal *Neuer Bücher-Saal der gelehrten Welt* for 1711.

[18] See Christian Wolff, *Ratio praelectionum Wolfianarum [in] mathesin et philosophiam universam* (Halle ²1735 [¹1718]; reprinted Hildesheim/New York 1972), WW II. 36, Sect. II, Ch. VI, §§4–14, pp. 192–196; see also Wolff's letter to Leibniz of May 4, 1715, in *Briefwechsel*, p. 167. There is little doubt in the secondary literature that Wolff's subsequent rejection of Pufendorf's theory of natural law transpired principally through the influence of Leibniz: see Campo, *Cristiano Wolff e il razionalismo precritico*, p. 504f; Marcel Thomann, 'Christian Wolff et le droit subjectif,' in *Archives de Philosophie du Droit* 9 (1964), pp. 153–174, especially p.162f. This development in Wolff's thought must also be linked to the early repudiation of Cartesian voluntarism, which was also encouraged by Leibniz.

[19] See Christian Wolff, *Oratio de Sinarum philosophia practica. Rede über die praktische Philosophie der Chinesen*, ed. by Michael Albrecht (Hamburg 1985), note 190, p. 250f; see also C. Wolff, *Ausführliche Nachricht von seinen eigenen Schrifften, die er in deutscher Sprache von den verschiedenen Theilen der Welt-Weißheit heraus gegeben* (Frankfurt a. M. ²1733 [¹1726]; reprinted Hildesheim/New York 1973, WW 1.9, §137, p. 392f); C. Wolff, *Philosophia practica universalis, methodo scientifica pertractata,*

would also soon be joined between the students and followers of Wolff
and Pufendorf.[20]

b. An alternative approach: The distinction between active and passive obligation

How then does Wolff positively attempt to counter the voluntaristic concept of obligation we have just outlined? It is here that Wolff shows his
genuinely creative and synthetic style of thought, which proved capable of
integrating earlier intellectual achievements even while developing them
further in an independent manner. On the one hand, he incorporates the
definition of obligation as moral necessity, itself entirely characteristic
of the modern natural law tradition, into the very heart of his systematic philosophy. On the other hand, he supplements this concept with a
second determination of his own that expressly concerns the connection
between the motivating ground and the act. Moral necessity is characterised as passive obligation, and the connection between the motivating
ground and act is characterised as active obligation – a terminological
and conceptual distinction that derives specifically from Wolff.[21]

Both Leibniz and Pufendorf had already interpreted 'obligatio' as
'necessitas moralis' rather than as the 'vinculum iuris' that was characteristic of Roman law. In this sense, they both conceived of obligation
as an ultimately ethical category and no longer as a purely juridical

---

vol. 1 (Frankfurt am Main/Leipzig 1738; reprinted Hildesheim/New York 1971, WW
II.10, §63 note, p. 57 and §131 note, p. 115); C. Wolff, *Philosophia moralis sive ethica,
methodo scientifica pertractata*, vol. 3 (Halle 1751; reprinted Hildesheim/New York
1970, WW II.14, §91 not., p. 181). In spite of these fundamental differences of opinion with Pufendorf, he refuses to hold the latter responsible for all potential effects of
'rabid consequentialism' that others might derive from his basic approach to the problem (see C. Wolff, *De peccato in philosophum*, in: *Horae subsecivae Marburgenses
Anni MDCCXXX, Trimestre aestivum* (Frankfurt a. M./Leipzig 1731; reprinted
Hildesheim/Zürich/New York 1983), WW II.34.2, §8, pp. 409–414.)

20 For contemporary reference to these polemical debates, see Johann Heinrich Zedler,
Grosses vollständiges Universal-Lexicon aller Wissenschafften und Künste, vol. 47
(Leipzig/Halle 1746; reprinted Graz 1962), the entry on the concept of 'obligation'
[*Verbindlichkeit*], columns 1555–1570, especially column 1561f.; also in this connection
see Johann Liborius Zimmermann, *De actionum humanarum moralitate nec non de
obligatione iuris, legibusque stricte dictis dissertatio philosophica, in qua celeberrimi
Prof. Wolffii principia nonnulla moralia examinantur* (Jena 1728).

21 For this claim, see Joachim Hruschka, *Das deontologische Sechseck bei Gottfried
Achenwall im Jahre 1767. Zur Geschichte der deontischen Grundbegriffe in der
Universaljurisprudenz zwischen Suarez und Kant* (Hamburg 1986), p. 52.

category.[22] Although Wolff shared this formal definition of obligation, he was also concerned to identify the ground upon which this moral necessity, governing the acts we should perform or refrain from performing, itself rests.[23] A passive state of being obliged presupposes an active process through which we become obliged. We can only be said to will an act as necessary where there is a motive for the act in question. It is thus the binding connection between the relevant act and its motivating ground that first constitutes the obligatory character of the latter.[24] Wolff regards this psychological rather than positivistic grounding of obligation, and rightly so, it seems to me, as an original philosophical contribution of his own. He believes he has thereby placed the concept of obligation in a quite new and hitherto unsuspected light.[25] Obligation consists in motivation:

[22] See Pufendorf, *De jure naturae et gentium*, Lib. I, Cap. I, §21, p. 21: 'Obligatio est, per quam quis praestare aut admittere vel pati quid necessitate morali tenetur'; G. W. Leibniz, the Preface to the *Codex iuris gentium diplomaticus* (Hanover 1693), in Leibniz, *Die philosophischen Schriften*, ed. C. I. Gebhardt, vol. 3 (Berlin 1887; reprinted Hildesheim 1960), p. 386: 'Est autem ... obligatio necessitas moralis'; for the fundamental difference between this Leibnizian conception and the concept of obligation in Roman law, see Axel Hägerström, *Recht, Pflicht und bindende Kraft des Vertrages nach römischer und naturrechtlicher Anschauung*, ed. Karl Olivecrona (Stockholm/Wiesbaden 1965), pp. 59–63; for this whole question, see also the particularly illuminating study by René Sève, *Leibniz et l'École moderne du droit naturel* (Paris 1989), especially pp. 102–122.

[23] See C. Wolff, *Theologia naturalis methodo scientifica pertractata*, vol. I.2 (Frankfurt a. M. – Leipzig ²1739 ['1736]; reprinted Hildesheim/New York 1978), WW II.7.2, §973, p. 942: 'Necessitas moralis agendi est id, quod uno nomine Obligatio, passiva scilicet, dici solet'; C. Wolff, *Philosophia practica universalis*, vol. I, §118, p. 103: 'Necessitas moralis agendi vel non agendi dicitur obligatio passiva.' In his German writings, Wolff does not refer to this traditional conceptual formulation; nor is there any reference there to the distinction between the concepts of active and passive obligation. This is a typical and fairly frequent example of the way in which the series of Latin writings represent a more carefully developed and elaborated stage of Wolff's thinking than do the German works.

[24] See C. Wolff, *Vernünfftige Gedancken von der Menschen Thun und Lassen, zu Beförderung ihrer Glückseeligkeit* [= *Deutsche Ethik*] (Frankfurt am Main/Leipzig ⁴1733 [Halle '1720]; reprinted Hildesheim/New York 1976), WW I.4, §8, p. 8: 'To obligate someone to perform something, or to refrain from so doing, is simply to connect a motivating ground for willing or not willing with regard to the act'; C. Wolff, *Theologia naturalis*, vol. I.2, §973, p. 942: 'obligatio activa non est nisi connexio motivi cum actione'; C. Wolff, *Philosophia practica universalis*, vol. I, §118, p. 103: 'Connexio autem motivi cum actione, sive positiva, sive privativa obligatio activa appelatur'; and finally, in precisely the same terms again in C. Wolff, *Institutiones juris naturae et gentium* (Halle 1750; reprinted Hildesheim 1969), WW II.26, §35, p. 18.

[25] See C. Wolff, *Deutsche Ethik*, preface to the second edition; C. Wolff, *Ausführliche Nachricht*, §137, p. 395; C. Wolff, *Theologia naturalis*, vol. I.2, §973 note, p. 942. Wolff's subjective turn in relation to the concept of obligation in Roman law is strongly emphasised by Marcel Thomann, *Christian Wolff et le droit subjectif*, p. 159.

this is effectively Wolff's new formulation of the question. Ethics should thus become a pragmatic rather than a purely theoretical science, – one that is now related explicitly to the realm of practice.[26] And Baumgarten also assumes the same psychological standpoint when he orients morality, even more strongly than Wolff himself, directly towards the nature of obligation and the problem of practical realisation.

3. Baumgarten's radicalisation of the problem of obligation

The further emphasis and significance that Baumgarten accords to the problem of obligation, by comparison with the Wolffian position, is already obvious even in purely external terms from the very structure of his practical philosophy. Whereas Wolff's *Philosophia practica universalis* had dealt with 'obligatio' merely in one section of a single chapter, Baumgarten's *Initia philosophiae practicae primae* organises its subject matter in terms of this concept.[27] The question of obligation constitutes the unifying, indeed sole, theme of the entire work.[28] Thus Baumgarten can define practical philosophy, and specifically ethics, as the science of those obligations that present themselves to man in the state of nature, and that can therefore be known to us without recourse to faith.[29] Wolff, on the other hand, interprets the practical disciplines of philosophy as sciences that are essentially concerned with the rules governing free acts, and does not therefore speak directly, let alone exclusively, of binding duties and obligations in this connection.[30]

[26] See Wolff's letter to an unknown recipient in London of December 7, 1750, printed as a supplement in Johann Christoph Gottsched, *Historische Lobschrift des weiland hoch- und wohl-gebohrnen Herrn Christians, des H. R. R. Freyherrn von Wolff* (Halle 1755; reprinted Hildesheim/New York 1980), WW I.10, p. 97.

[27] See the prospective summary of contents in C. Wolff, *Philosophia practica universalis*, vol. 1, p. 593; C. Wolff, *Philosophia practica universalis, methodo scientifica pertractata*, vol. 2 (Frankfurt am Main/Leipzig 1739; reprinted Hildesheim/New York 1979), WW II. 11, p. 809; A. G. Baumgarten *Initia*, p. XI (XIX, 8f.).

[28] As rightly pointed out by Susanna del Boca, *Kant e i moralisti tedeschi. Wolff, Baumgarten, Crusius* (Naples 1937), p. 29.

[29] See A. G. Baumgarten, *Initia*, § 1, p. I (XIX, 9_{18-20}): 'philosophia [...] practica est scientia obligationum hominis sine fide cognoscendarum'; A. G. Baumgarten, *Ethica*, §1, p. 5 (XXVII, 873_{3-5}): 'Ethica [...] est scientia obligationum hominis internarum in statu naturali'.

[30] See C. Wolff, *Philosophia rationalis sive logica, methodo scientifica pertractata*, vol. 1 (Frankfurt a.M./Leipzig ³1740 ['1728]; reprinted Hildesheim/Zürich/New York 1983), WW II 1.1, §64, p. 31: 'Ethicam definimus per scientiam dirigendi actiones liberas in statu naturalis, seu quatenus sui juris est homo, nulli alterius potestati subjectus';

It is quite true that Baumgarten's radicalisation of the problem of obligation also involves certain problems of its own. Thus it effectively neglects a whole range of thematic questions that were still central to the work of his predecessor Wolff. Above all, there is no real discussion of 'happiness' in the context of moral philosophy, an issue that was of decisive importance for Wolff. In Baumgarten's work the doctrine of human happiness, already conceptualised in a way that has little in common with Wolff, acquires an entirely different systematic position: it is displaced from the realm of morality into that of religion. For Wolff, the specifically philosophical kind of happiness that can be attained in this life constitutes a central question in relation to empirical psychology and also to the foundations of morality. For Baumgarten, on the other hand, the question of happiness is primarily a religious matter, which is why for him it is properly discussed in the context of rational psychology in relation to the 'last things.' In the domain of ethics itself, happiness is only mentioned in connection with our duties towards religion. Baumgarten even speaks explicitly of an obligation in relation to our happiness, something that would never even have occurred to Wolff.[31]

In his understanding of obligation, Baumgarten also introduces some characteristically new emphases of his own that serve to reinforce the authentically compelling character of practical prescriptions. Obligation is no longer simply defined, as it was in Leibniz and Wolff, as a moral 'necessity' (*necessitas*) but rather as a moral 'necessitation' (*necessitatio*).[32]

C. Wolff, *Philosophia practica universalis*, vol. 1, §3, p. 2: 'Philosophia practica universalis est scientia affectiva practica dirigendi actiones liberas per regulas generalissimas'; C. Wolff, *Philosophia moralis sive ethica, methodo scientifica pertractata*, vol. 1 (Halle 1750; reprinted Hildesheim/New York 1970), WW II. 12, §1, p. 1: 'Philosophia moralis, sive Ethica est scientia practica, docens modum, quo homo libere actiones suas ad legem naturae componere potest.'

[31] See C. Wolff, *Deutsche Ethik*, §§44–57, pp. 31–38; C. Wolff, *Psychologia empirica, methodo scientifica pertractata* (Frankfurt am Main/Leipzig ²1738 [¹1739]; reprinted Hildesheim 1968), WW II. 5, §§636–639, p. 477f.; A.G. Baumgarten, *Metaphysica* (Halle ⁴1757 [¹1739], §787, p. 321f. (XVII, 153f.): the paragraph in question forms part of the section concerning the 'status post mortem'; A.G. Baumgarten, *Ethica*, §13, p. 11 (XXVII, 875₂₅₋₂₇): 'obligaris ad tuam beatudinem tantam, quanta possibilis. [...] Obligaris ad tuam felicitatem.' For Wolff's conception of happiness, which he developed in an independent manner of his own even though it was essentially derived from Leibnizian sources, see the detailed discussion in my dissertation, *Das Problem des Glücks im Denken Christian Wolffs. Eine quellen-, begriffs- und entwicklungsgeschichtliche Studie zu Schlüsselbegriffen seiner Ethik* (Stuttgart/Bad Cannstatt 1995), pp. 161–188.

[32] See A.G. Baumgarten, *Metaphysica*, §723, p. 284 (XVII, 137₆): 'Necessitatio moralis est obligatio.'

The concept of 'necessitation' here implies the transformation of something contingent into something strictly necessary.[33] Thus Baumgarten,
who invented so many new Latin terms, here introduces another new and
highly influential neologism.[34] The contemporary Enlightenment debates
about the concept of freedom surely formed the relevant background to
these terminological proposals and innovations, given that the distinction between 'inclining' an agent to act ['geneigt machen'/'incliner'] as
opposed to 'necessitating' an agent to act ['nötigen'/'nécessiter'] had
already become common currency through the work of Leibniz.[35]

The significance of this new term of Baumgarten's for the moral philosophy of Kant can hardly be overestimated. In the *Groundwork of
the Metaphysics of Morals*, Kant explicitly refers back to Baumgarten's
conceptual coupling of 'necessity and 'necessitation' when he transforms
the word 'imperative' from a merely grammatical term to a specifically
ethical technical term, and thereby furnishes the decisive concept for all
modern deontological ethics. It is because the human will is not intrinsically or spontaneously entirely concordant with reason, but also remains
susceptible to the inclinations, that practical necessity [*Notwendigkeit*]
presents itself to our will, as distinct from the divine will, as a form of
necessitation [*Nötigung*]. The virtue ascribable to creatures is fundamentally different from the holiness ascribed to the creator precisely because
it is only for finite beings that a potential discrepancy between will and
duty can arise in the first place.[36] The seemingly self-evident thought that
we human beings must frequently be morally compelled or necessitated to
certain acts because we do not always spontaneously perform them of our
own accord was originally conceptualised by Baumgarten, even if it first
came effectively to dominate the field of practical philosophy only with
the work of Kant himself.

---

[33] See ibid., §701, p. 271 (XVII,131₅): 'Necessitatio (coactio) est mutatio alicuius ex con-
tingenti in necessarium'; for the concept of 'necessitas,' see ibid., §102, p. 29 (XVII, 48).
[34] The passage cited in note 33 is listed as the first recorded occurrence of the terms 'necessitatio' and 'Nötigung' in *Onomasticon philosophicum latinoteutonicum et teutonicolatinum*, eds. K. Aso, M. Kurosaki, T. Otabe and S. Yamauchi (Tokyo 1989), pp. 240,
627.
[35] See G. W. Leibniz, *Essais de Theodicée*, in Leibniz, *Die Philosophischen Schriften*, ed.
C.I. Gebhardt, vol. 6 (Berlin 1885; reprinted Hildesheim 1961), p. 381. Here we also
find Leibniz using the French term 'nécessitation' in a characteristic way of his own
(see *Leibniz Lexicon. A Dual Concordance to Leibniz's 'Philosophische Schriften,'*
compiled by R. Finster, G. Hunter, R.F. McRae, M. Miles, and W.M. Seager, Teil 2:
Konkordanz des vollständigen Vokabulars vom Typ Key-Word-In-Context [on 65
microfiches], Hildesheim/Zürich/New York 1988).
[36] See I. Kant, *Groundwork*, 4: 36–39.

There is also another respect, seemingly insignificant at first sight perhaps but ultimately highly influential, in which Baumgarten develops and extends the theory of obligation and ethical motivation beyond the parameters of Wolff's thought. For Wolff, as we have seen, an obligation exists when there is 'simply a connection to a motivating ground for willing or not willing.'[37] The weight accorded to the motive in question is entirely irrelevant to the existence of the obligation. For Baumgarten, on the other hand, we can only properly speak of obligation where *more powerful* motivating causes, outweighing all impulses to the contrary, are expressly related to action.[38] And it is this that first brings the question of the intensity and character of given motivating impulses or incentives into center stage. It is only then that we can first begin to address the problem concerning the actual variety and potential hierarchy of possible motives for action, the problem that Kant will subsequently resolve in a fundamental manner in affirming the absolute priority of specifically moral obligations over all pragmatic considerations.

In conclusion, we might also try to identify the relevant concrete factors in the actual historical background that will help to clarify the significant originality of Baumgarten's views in the domain of ethics. As I believe has already been emphatically revealed, we shall henceforth have to credit Baumgarten with developing Wolffian doctrines in a genuinely independent manner in his work as a moral philosopher, and not merely as the founder of aesthetics and as the rigorously epitomising metaphysician with whom we are all already familiar.[39] This successful author

---

[37] See C. Wolff, *Deutsche Ethik*, §8, p. 8.

[38] See A. G. Baumgarten, *Initia*, §15, p. 6 (XIX, 13_{35-37}): 'Obligatio tam activa [...] quam passiva [...] potest definiri per connexionem vel activam vel passivam causarum impulsivarum *potiorum* cum libera determinatione' (my emphasis). This radicalisation of the properly obligatory character of moral 'necessitation' in Baumgarten as compared with Wolff seems to have been overlooked in the previous literature. Thus Max Küenburg, *Ethische Grundfragen in der jüngst veröffentlichten Ethikvorlesung Kants. Studie zur Geschichte der Moralphilosophie* (Innsbruck 1925), p. 51, can claim, without further differentiation of their respective positions, that Baumgarten interprets obligation 'after the manner of his teacher Wolff as a connection between an action and its *preponderant* motive grounds' (my emphasis). A further difference with respect to Wolff can be seen from the fact that passive obligation is also explicitly included in the definition we have cited, whereas Wolff's Latin writings, as noted earlier, interpret the connection with motive causes solely in terms of active obligation. And indeed Baumgarten also defines the distinction between active and passive obligation in an entirely new way according to the bearer of obligation: the former belongs to the obligating person, whereas the latter belongs to the obligated person (cf. *Initia*, §10, p. 4 [XIX, 11_{32-34}]).

[39] For this, see the pioneering study by Mario Casula, *La metaphysica di A. G. Baumgarten* (Milan 1973), the important critical review of this work by Giorgio Tonelli

of philosophical compendia, who was so highly esteemed by Kant for
his penetrating analytical mind, was clearly no mere 'follower' of Wolff
in any significant area of philosophical thought. But what was the ultimate root and source for the far-reaching differences and decisive shifts
of emphasis that can, on careful examination, be seen to distinguish the
ethical approaches of these two thinkers, even though the relevant distinctions between them have hitherto been generally overlooked?[40].

The fact that Baumgarten emphasises obligation and its religious orientation more strongly than Wolff[41] may suggest that his original pietist
background was an important biographical factor here.[42] Baumgarten
was certainly strongly marked by his early education under Pietist influence in Halle. He never actually heard Wolff lecture, and probably never
met him personally in any other context either.[43] Even though we cannot deny that Baumgarten's discovery of Wolff's philosophy possessed
an almost fateful significance for his own intellectual development, it
would be rather surprising, under these circumstances, if he were ever to

in: *Kant-Studien* 66 (1975), p. 242f, and the author's response: 'A. G. Baumgarten entre
G. W. Leibniz et Christian Wolff,' in *Archives de Philosophie* 42 (1979), pp. 547–574.
Tonelli's rejection, on substantive internal grounds, of Casula's claim that Baumgarten
was more emphatically Leibnizian in perspective than Wolff also appears highly questionable from a biographical perspective. For unlike Baumgarten, Wolff certainly possessed, through both personal acquaintance and private correspondence, a privileged
knowledge of Leibniz's philosophy at a time when the latter was only very partially
accessible to the broader learned public.

[40] Dieter Henrich in particular is a rare exception here. He has performed an important
service in pointing out the significant differences between the ethical writings of the
two thinkers and drawing relevant conclusions for the general interpretation of Kant's
thought. See D. Henrich, 'Über Kants früheste Ethik. Versuch einer Rekonstruktion,'
in *Kant-Studien* 54 (1963), pp. 404–431, especially p. 422; D. Henrich, 'Über Kants
Entwicklungsgeschichte,' in *Philosophische Rundschau* 13 (1965), pp. 252–263, especially p. 258.

[41] Thus in his concrete exposition of ethics, Baumgarten once again assigns a primary
position to our duties towards God (see *Ethica*, Synopsis [XXVII, 742–744]), whereas
Wolff had treated these after the discussion of our duties towards ourselves (cf. *Deutsche
Ethik*, Table of Contents, pp. 711–712).

[42] This is certainly the view of Bernhard Poppe, *Alexander Gottlieb Baumgarten. Seine
Bedeutung und Stellung in der Leibniz-Wolffischen Philosophie und seine Beziehungen
zu Kant* (Borna/Leipzig 1907; reprinted Ann Arbor/London 1982), p. 32: '...the way in
which Baumgarten's ethics is presented is entirely different from Wolff. The ethics of
Baumgarten specifically reveals a strong influence from pietistic currents of thought.'

[43] See B. Poppe, op. cit., p. 15; M. Casula, *La metaphysica di A. G. Baumgarten*, pp. 14,18;
for the general intellectual and cultural climate at the University of Halle around the
middle of the century, see the Introduction by Axel Bühler and Luigi Cataldi Madonna
to their edition of Georg Friedrich Meyer, *Versuch einer allgemeinen Auslegungskunst*
(Hamburg 1996), pp. VII–XII.

defend a pure and entirely unmodified form of Wolffianism. We may well suppose that it was just this specific synthesis of ethical religiosity and a modern philosophical attitude in Baumgarten that particularly appealed to Kant and significantly affected his use of Baumgarten in compiling his compendia for teaching and lecturing purposes. For ever since the time of his own teachers Franz Albert Schultz and Martin Knutzen, the uneasy coexistence between Wolffianism and Pietism had typically formed an important aspect of the cultural and intellectual in Königsberg.[44] It was thus by building upon the work of one of the most original Wolffian philosophers of the age that Kant himself became an original thinker *par excellence*. As the founder of a new 'imperativist' ethical doctrine of his own, Kant remained nonetheless deeply indebted to the earlier innovations of his established 'Scholastic' predecessors.

[44] See the standard works by Benno Erdmann, *Martin Knutzen und seine Zeit. Ein Beitrag zur Geschichte der Wolfischen Schule und insbesondre zur Entwicklungsgeschichte Kants* (Leipzig 1876; reprinted Hildesheim 1973), and Erich Riedesel, *Pietismus und Orthodoxie in Ostpreussen. Auf Grund des Briefwechsels G.F. Rogalls und F.A. Schulz' mit den Halleschen Pietisten* (Königsberg/Berlin 1937).

II

GROUNDWORK OF THE METAPHYSICS OF MORALS

3

What Is the Purpose of a Metaphysics of Morals? Some Observations on the Preface to the *Groundwork of the Metaphysics of Morals*

Ludwig Siep

I

Kant's philosophy of ethics and his doctrine of right seem to reveal a double face. On the one hand, he presents a modest and 'minimalist', entirely formal, theory of morals that only rules out principles of action (maxims) that cannot be willed or conceived without contradiction as universal principles valid for every rational being. On the other, he offers an extremely ambitious ultimate metaphysical grounding for all moral and juridical duties (and for the only permissible motive of complying with them) in terms of pure reason conceived independently of any specifically human attributes and characteristics. Kant's interpreters, critics, and successors have generally opted for one of these two aspects of his thought, often by assigning a different degree of weight and importance to different texts in the Kantian corpus. Thus the late work *The Metaphysics of Morals* is often treated as a kind of retreat from the critical self-limitation to a purely formal ethics that characterises the *Groundwork of the Metaphysics of Morals*. And it is sometimes even claimed that the latter text itself is difficult to reconcile with the position articulated in the *Critique of Pure Reason*.[1]

But anyone attempting to elucidate the Preface to the *Groundwork* can hardly ignore the exceedingly strong metaphysical claim that is clearly

---

[1] Karl-Heinz Ilting, for example, speaks of persisting 'elements of a pre-Critical metaphysics' in Kant's theory of the moral law as formulated in the *Groundwork* and the second *Critique*. See Ilting 1972, p. 130.

presented there. The *Critique of Pure Reason* had already outlined the project of a metaphysics of morals, the principles of which must be established independently of any appeal to experience and therefore of any empirical knowledge of human beings (cf. A 841/B 869). And in some respects, even Kant's 'pre-Critical' moral philosophy had already suggested such an approach. As early as 1763,[2] it was clear to Kant that morality requires a highest formal principle of its own, and ever since his study of Rousseau and his own separation between the rational and the sensible worlds – about the mid 1760s – Kant had essentially decided that this principle can only be the rational and universal legislative will itself.[3] In the *Critique of Pure Reason*, therefore, Kant was already clearly attempting to integrate an *a priori* moral theory into the overall context of his new conception of philosophy – both in the treatment of 'Ideas in general' and of 'transcendental Ideas,' and in the resolution of the Third Antinomy, within the Transcendental Dialectic, and in the discussion of the Canon and the Architectonic of Pure Reason within the Doctrine of Method. But because Kant eventually decided for various reasons to separate the philosophy of practical reason from the treatment of transcendental philosophy as such (cf. A 15; A 841), he effectively contented himself with general indications concerning the implications of his transcendental grounding of philosophy in general for the domain of moral philosophy in particular. It is only with the *Groundwork to the Metaphysics of Morals*, therefore, that Kant properly undertakes the systematic 'integration' of moral philosophy within the context of the Critical Philosophy. In this connection, the *Groundwork* emphatically insists on the necessary 'independence' of a metaphysics of morals from anthropological considerations of any kind. The Introduction to the second edition of the *Critique of Pure Reason*, on the other hand, already suggests a somewhat weaker claim insofar as Kant there admits that anthropological elements must 'necessarily be drawn into the formulation of the system of pure ethics' (B 29). In the *Metaphysics of Morals* of 1797/8, this weaker claim also exerts an effect on the concept of metaphysics itself (cf. 6:216f.). I shall return to this question in the course of the following discussion.

The fact that the idea of a metaphysics of morals emerges directly from the way in which Kant 'adapts' his moral philosophy to the concept of philosophy articulated in the *Critique of Pure Reason* does not

---

[2] See, for example, Kant's *Investigation Concerning the Distinctness of the Principles of Natural Theology and Morals* of 1763 (2:299).
[3] In this connection, see Schmucker 1961, pp. 143 ff. and pp. 266 ff.

imply that this adaptation is a smoothly effected one. This holds for the question as to whether the *Groundwork* is actually capable of redeeming its transcendental claims.[4] But it also holds for the alternative question as to whether Kant's interpretation and grounding of the indisputable character of moral consciousness and its intrinsic demands really does provide a powerful additional argument for the Critical distinction between the intelligible and the phenomenal 'standpoint.' Kant's appeal to the understanding of moral demands that 'everyone' already shares, and the way in which he speaks of the 'transitions' that lead us on from our 'common rational ethical knowledge' through popular philosophy to an expressly Critical moral philosophy, might well suggest that the *Groundwork* – not unlike Hegel's *Phenomenology of Spirit* in this respect – is intended to lead us methodically from a neutral analysis and immanent critique of ordinary 'non-metaphysical' concepts of morality in the direction of a metaphysical, transcendentally grounded moral philosophy. But such an expectation is not forthcoming as soon as we read the *Groundwork* itself. For the phenomena of moral consciousness are here criticised and interpreted from the beginning in terms of Kant's own metaphysical and transcendental standpoint. Kant's approach corresponds rather to the method already frequently employed in Aristotle's ethics when he attempts to harmonise a philosophically more sophisticated standpoint with established and widely shared ethical views, and through this kind of 'descent' to lend additional weight to the philosophical standpoint.[5]

From a substantive point of view, of course, Kant's moral philosophy is possibly the clearest example in modern thought of a direct reversal of Aristotle's 'ethical' critique of Plato. In contradistinction to the highest forms of theoretical reason, it is precisely practical reason for Aristotle that is not governed by principles (ideas) that are separable from considerations concerning human nature. Knowledge concerning appropriate human

---

[4] In the Introduction to the first edition of the *Critique of Pure Reason*, Kant restricts 'transcendental philosophy' to the domain of 'purely speculative reason' precisely because empirical concepts 'must be presupposed' even in relation to the *a priori* principles of morality (A 15). But in the *Groundwork*, Kant explicitly draws a parallel between the metaphysics of morals as the science of the laws of the 'pure will determined entirely by *a priori* principles' and transcendental philosophy as the science of 'the particular acts and rules of pure thought' (Gr: 4:390). And the 'deduction of the concept of freedom from pure practical reason' that Kant provides in the third part of the *Groundwork* (Gr: 4:447) must of course also be treated as a 'transcendental' deduction.

[5] See, for example, *Nicomachean Ethics* I, 8 and 9. Naturally Aristotle also shows us examples of the opposite approach, which begins from prevailing ethical convictions and moves on to their philosophical analysis and interpretation.

conduct, in philosophy and action-governing reason, is directly related to man as *zoon*, as a living and affective being acting under characteristic but variable conditions of life and behaviour. For Kant, on the other hand, reason's intrinsic orientation to unconditioned and perfect principles (Ideas) is essentially connected with the practical 'use' of reason, whereas its theoretical use is confined to setting the ends and limits of the 'understanding' in relation to our empirical knowledge. In the *Critique of Pure Reason*, Kant himself made it quite clear that the idea of a metaphysics of morals essentially represents a Platonism of practical reason (A 314ff./B 371ff.). It is all the more remarkable, therefore, that Kant's arguments for such a metaphysics never really engage with the (properly formulated) Aristotelian objections to this approach. Kant sees his most obvious opponents in the defenders of Stoic and Epicurean ethics, and their followers in the 'popular philosophy' of Kant's own time – and not in a properly Aristotelian ethics of finite reason, an ethics that sought, like that of Kant himself, to unify virtue and happiness, to bring formality (the criterial dimension) together with the purposive character of the unconditioned good.

I shall specify the sense of these admittedly broad claims in the following discussion of the Preface and of one or two specific passages from the main text of the *Groundwork* that expressly pursue the argument in the Preface concerning the necessity for a 'metaphysics of morals.'[6] Kant himself divides his arguments into 'speculative' and 'practical.' The speculative arguments concern the systematic structure of philosophy and the articulated presentation of its relevant 'objects.' And we can find corresponding remarks in the *Critique of Pure Reason* and the main text of the *Metaphysics of Morals*. In this way, we shall be able to justify my earlier claim concerning the place and function of the *Groundwork* in the development of Kant's practical philosophy as a whole. The practical arguments, on the other hand, concern the way in which Kant's position is supposed to coincide with the understanding that 'everyone' already possesses concerning morality. I shall try to elucidate these arguments further and ultimately question whether it is really necessary to provide a metaphysical grounding of ethics at all.

II

The Preface begins by presenting a systematic outline of philosophy that largely corresponds to that already articulated in the 'Architectonic' of the

6 Above all, Gr: 4:404 f. and 408–412.

Critique of Pure Reason (A 84f./B 869f.). There, Kant had developed his systematic outline from the idea of philosophy as a 'possible science that is nowhere actually given *in concreto*' (A 838/B 866), whereas here in the *Groundwork* he merely claims to offer the general organisational principles that already underlay the 'ancient philosophy of the Greeks,' but were actually more characteristic of the Stoics. Since Kant in the *Groundwork* also includes 'logic' as part of philosophy, while the relevant parallel text of the first *Critique* appears to treat it simply as a *techne*, or an 'art of reason' (A 839/B 867), the *Groundwork* initially makes a methodological distinction between material knowledge, which is concerned with objects, and formal knowledge, which is merely concerned with the 'universal rules of thought in general without distinction of objects' (Gr: 4:387).

The text then makes a substantive distinction, as in the first *Critique*, with regard to 'objects and laws' (ibid.) that are accessible to rational knowledge – according to the *Groundwork*, to all rational knowledge; according to the first *Critique*, to the 'legislation of human reason (philosophy)' (A 840/B 868). Kant is thus concerned with two kinds of object and the kinds of laws that determine them in each case: with nature and freedom, with laws of nature and laws of morality. The overall argument here presupposes the entire analysis of the first *Critique* and above all the resolution of the problem of the antinomies in terms of the distinction between the phenomenal world and the intelligible world. For there can only be laws of freedom at all if freedom represents a specific kind of causality independent of the temporal succession of empirical events – a causality that is at least conceivable in accordance with Kant's resolution of the third antinomy. Kant underplays these presuppositions when he presents in both texts the difference between the 'is' and the 'ought' as evidence for the difference between the two kinds of law. In truth, for Kant it is only laws of *unconditional* obligation (categorical imperatives) that are properly laws of freedom.

The further and final organising principle he presents is once again methodological in character, and can also be found in both texts: this is the distinction between empirical philosophy on the one hand and pure philosophy or 'rational knowledge' on the other. Unlike 'logic,' with its purely formal rational knowledge, 'metaphysics' involves material rational knowledge 'purely on the basis of a priori principles.' In accordance with metaphysics respective kinds of object, it is therefore either a metaphysics of nature (rational physics) or a metaphysics of morals (rational ethics or morality).

The concept of 'morality' (Gr: 4:388), or 'pure morality' (A 841/B 869), clearly embraces the rational foundations of both the doctrine of virtue and the doctrine of right – although in the first *Critique* Kant expressly says that 'morality is the only code of laws applying to our actions that can be derived completely *a priori* from principles' (ibid.). And in the Preface to the *Groundwork*, it is also remarkable that Kant makes no reference whatsoever to the two kinds of ethical legislation, to inner and to 'possible' outer legislation. In the context of his practical arguments for the necessity of a metaphysics of morals, arguments I shall consider in the next section, Kant even explicitly restricts 'what is supposedly morally good' to actions undertaken for the sake of the moral law, whereas merely 'legal' actions, ones that simply 'conform' to the moral law, are said to rest upon 'a ground that is not moral' (Gr: 4:390). On the other hand, the *Groundwork* itself already includes examples concerning 'duties of right' (such as the case of the bank 'deposit'), and it is very difficult to believe that Kant in 1785 did not already think that it was possible to provide a rational grounding of the doctrine of right.[7]

The strict differentiation between the purely rational – the *a priori* – element and the empirical domain explicitly requires the exclusion of all 'anthropological' considerations from metaphysical moral philosophy or 'the rational part of ethics' (Gr: 4:388), and this holds for both the *Groundwork* and the first *Critique*. The metaphysics of morals 'borrows nothing whatsoever from our knowledge of human beings,' as Kant puts it in the *Groundwork*, and is certainly 'not grounded upon any anthropology (any empirical condition),' as he puts it in the first *Critique* (A 841/B 869). The concept of morality, or the concept of the ethical will, from which 'we must be able to derive practical rules for every rational being, and therefore also for human beings' (Gr: 4:410), must not contain any particular conditions of specifically human willing and acting (Gr: 4:390). On the contrary, a metaphysics of morals must proceed on the basis of the 'Idea of ethical perfection which reason itself projects *a priori*' (Gr: 4:409) – and which holds indeed for a rational will that can in principle be actualised in different 'natures.'

If, on the other hand, we consider the moral law in relation to the 'human will,' one that can be 'affected' by inclinations of one kind or another, and if we consider the moral law as determining how 'everything ought to transpire, but also along with those conditions under which it

---

[7] In the *Critique of Pure Reason* (A 316/B 373), Kant describes a 'constitution allowing the greatest possible freedom in accordance with laws by which the freedom of each is made to be consistent with that of all the others' as a 'necessary idea' which can be drawn from pure reason rather than 'derived from experience.' For the development of Kant's philosophy of right, see Ch. Ritter 1971 , W. Busch 1979, and H. Oberer 1973, 88ff.

often fails to do so,' then we already find ourselves occupied with the empirical part of ethics, with what Kant calls 'practical anthropology' (Gr: 4:387).

But if we take this differentiation seriously, we soon encounter problems with the way in which Kant himself structures the project of a metaphysics of morals. It seems to leave the *Groundwork* and the Analytic of the *Critique of Practical Reason*[8] as the only appropriate sources for elucidating such a programme insofar as, according to all Kant's relevant remarks between 1765 and 1798, the *Doctrine of Virtue* does at least relate the moral law directly to 'the nature of human beings' (2:311). Kant's definition of the concept of virtue in the *Metaphysical First Principles of the Doctrine of Virtue* of 1798 already involves this relation: virtue is 'the capacity and considered resolve' to resist 'what opposes the moral disposition within us,' those 'obstacles to the fulfilment of duty' that are encountered in human nature (6:380). In effect, the concept of duty itself already implies the concept of constraint 'which does not apply to rational beings as such (...) but rather to human beings as rational natural beings' (6:379). Nonetheless, Kant still continues to describe the *Doctrine of Virtue*, which now terminologically coincides with 'ethics,'[9] as 'metaphysical' in character – namely, as a 'system of the ends of pure practical reason' (6:381).

It does appear therefore that Kant's original demand for absolute 'purity' in the *Groundwork* has been moderated by the time of the later *Metaphysics of Morals*. In the Introduction to the first part of the later text, with regard to the 'idea of and the necessity for a metaphysics of morals,' Kant writes: 'But just as there must be principles in a metaphysics of nature for applying those highest universal principles of a nature in general to objects of experience, a metaphysics of morals cannot dispense with principles of application, and we shall often have to take as

---

[8] On the other hand, the concept of 'the highest good', which is so central to the 'Dialectic' of the *Critique of Practical Reason*, also involves, once further interpreted as the 'whole and complete good,' happiness as 'the object of the faculty of desire of rational finite beings' (5:510).

[9] In the Introduction to the *Doctrine of Virtue*, Kant clearly distinguishes between the concept of ethics represented 'in ancient times' by 'the doctrine of morals (*philosophia moralis*)' from the more recent use of 'ethics' to designate one specific part of moral philosophy. Ethics in the latter sense, as distinct from the 'doctrine of right,' is concerned only with 'those duties which do not come under external laws' (6:379), with those duties therefore which properly involve 'self-restraint' and not external coercion. Kant tells us that 'it was thought appropriate to call this, in German, the doctrine of virtue [*Tugendlehre*]' (6:379).

our object the particular *nature* of human beings, which is cognized only
by experience [...] a metaphysics of morals cannot be based upon anthropology but can still be applied to it' (6:216f.). Kant then distinguishes this
application, which properly belongs to the metaphysics of morals, from
'moral anthropology' itself, which 'would deal only with the subjective
conditions in human nature which hinder people or help them in *fulfilling*
the laws of a metaphysics of morals' – and precisely not as a doctrine of
virtue itself but as a pedagogics of morals (ibid.).

But the *Groundwork* does not yet address the question of such an
'internal application' within the metaphysical framework itself. On the
contrary, the metaphysics of morals must be systematically developed
in its entirety 'on the basis of the universal concept of a rational being
in general' (Gr: 4:411f.). In contradistinction to 'speculative philosophy'
proper, a metaphysics of morals is not permitted to appeal to anything
concerning the 'special nature of human reason' (ibid.). Even if morality
'requires recourse to anthropology with regard to its application to human
beings,' it must first be developed and grounded 'quite independently of
anthropology – namely, as pure philosophy, as metaphysics (as can certainly be done in this entirely separated domain of knowledge)' (ibid.).
It is doubtful whether metaphysics in this sense can properly include a
theory of virtue that already involves clearly anthropological concepts
such as 'inclination,' 'obstacles to duty,' 'happiness,' and so on amongst
its own 'metaphysical first principles.'

But what then constitutes the 'completeness' of 'pure philosophy' as a
metaphysics of morals grounded in terms of its own supreme principle?
There has been considerable argument concerning the idea of 'deriving'
all the imperatives of virtue 'from its own principle' (Gr: 4:421 – that is,
from the Categorical Imperative (see Krausser 1968 in particular). Kant
does not claim that the *Groundwork* itself has already provided a complete grounding for the distinction between perfect and imperfect duties
towards oneself and others that effectively underlies his concrete examples (ibid.). He only accomplishes this in the *Doctrine of Virtue* of 1798,
although that is a text, on my reading, that does permit reference to human
nature even in a metaphysical context. In the *Groundwork*, on the other
hand, Kant already claims that 'all duties, so far as the kind of obligation
(not the object of their action) is concerned, have by these examples been
set out completely in their dependence upon the one principle' (Gr: 4:424).

Now Kant's four classes of duty only involve two 'kinds of obligation' –
that attaching to perfect (or strict) duties and that attaching to our imperfect
(or meritorious) duties whose non-fulfilment is not strictly forbidden. In

effect, Kant explains this difference with respect to the traditional theory of virtue in relation to the different ways in which the Categorical Imperative is applied to maxims: perfect duties are those whose rejection cannot be *thought* without contradiction; imperfect duties are those whose rejection cannot be *willed* without contradiction. This distinction – or more precisely, this grounding of a traditional distinction – seems to be the only example of purely metaphysically grounded systematic moral philosophy on Kant's part. But we may well harbour doubts even here. For it follows neither from the difference between thinking and willing, nor from that between laws of thought and laws of action, that specific principles of action can be thought as law without contradiction (as a 'universal law of nature'), but not willed as such. This difference only emerges in relation to specific natural conditions of willing. With regard to Kant's own examples, these involve the fact that our physical and intellectual capacities need to be cultivated and developed, and the fact that we are dependent on the 'sympathy' of other human beings. But neither these nor any other natural conditions are themselves contained in the idea of a 'possible pure will' (Gr: 4:390). Essentially even Kant's formulation of the Categorical Imperative in terms of possible 'laws of nature' already goes beyond morality as an Idea of reason in order 'bring the latter closer to intuition (in accordance with a certain analogy) and thereby closer to feeling' (Gr: 4:436).

But if this distinction between the highest forms of duty, or 'kinds of obligation,' does not properly belong to pure metaphysics either, it would seem that all that remains to be done here is to 'seek out and identify' the moral law. But Kant explicitly distinguishes this 'preliminary labour' from the task of the metaphysics of morals proper (Gr: 4:391f.). We must therefore, still clarify, what is implied by the strictly metaphysical programme that the Preface of the *Groundwork* sets out so explicitly, and indeed with such polemical emphasis.

III

In addition to the 'speculative' arguments based on the system of transcendental philosophy and the nature of reason itself, the Preface also contains practical arguments in favour of a metaphysics of morals. These concern the obligatory nature of moral duties, the certainty of moral judgements, and the stability of character. Because the proper understanding of moral duties can only be 'metaphysical,' and because goodness of character in a sense depends upon such an understanding, Kant can quite consistently claim in his later *Metaphysics of Morals* that to possess such a metaphysics is 'itself a duty.' He is not referring here, of course, to an explicit and philosophically articulated metaphysics, but to a proper moral consciousness itself – and perhaps also to the kind of religion that genuinely promotes morality – insofar as 'every human being also has such a thing within himself, though usually only in an obscure way' (6:216). And although Kant does not explicitly say that a non-metaphysical moral philosophy is also morally reprehensible, or that such a philosophy somehow only really befits a bad character, the rhetorical and metaphorical language he employs in this context certainly suggests as much. Thus 'spotlessness' of disposition and firmness of character correspond to the 'purity' of metaphysics, whereas 'confusion' of moral judgement and instability of character correspond to the 'delusions' and the 'nauseating mishmash' of a philosophy that is solely based on our 'knowledge of human nature' (see Gr: 4:390; 490f.).

In the Preface, Kant claims that the strictly obligatory feature – the 'absolute necessity' of moral commands – already implies, even from the perspective of our everyday 'common' consciousness, that such commands be universally valid not only for human beings, but for all rational beings in general (see Gr: 4:389). Since the human being is merely one specific kind of rational being, a moral philosophy grounded only in terms of mankind could never contain any unconditionally valid moral propositions – that is ones that would not permit of exceptions or special cases.

Moral commands or prohibitions are obviously unconditional for Kant in a threefold sense:

(a) They are binding for every rational being possessed of a will;

(b) They are susceptible to 'ultimate grounding' – that is, we can answer the question as to why they are binding through recourse to a principle that cannot itself be put into question or meaningfully challenged.

(c) They can move or motivate the will insofar as they correspond to this grounding principle, and do so independently of and potentially in opposition to any other 'incentives.'

According to Kant, this threefold unconditional feature of moral commands presupposes a principle that is capable of grounding such commands theoretically and practically (that is, in terms of motive). If there is no such principle, then there simply are no unconditionally binding commands or unconditionally proper (true) moral judgements at all. But the highest moral principle in turn can only possess 'truth and a relation to any possible object' if 'its own law is of such wide-ranging significance that it is binding not only for human beings but for all rational beings in general' (Gr: 4:408).

In addition to this unrestricted 'range' and priority over all other rules, the principle must enjoy an incontestable ultimate grounding and a certain 'autarchy' with respect to the motivation of the will (acting 'for the sake of duty'). However, this does not mean that any attempt to contest the principle, theoretically or practically, would necessarily produce a purely logical or 'conceptual' contradiction. It is rather, according to Kant, that the acting subject would thereby involve itself in a kind of 'self-contradiction': the subject would here contradict its own essential definition and vocation as a rational will.

Given the conclusions of the first *Critique*, it is hardly surprising that Kant should demand such a principle, nor that it consists in reason's own 'demand for lawfulness' in relation to all maxims of conduct. Considered independently of those conclusions, however, it is highly questionable to claim that a moral philosophy lacking this principle is incapable of containing unconditionally binding moral propositions. And it is also questionable whether Kant effectively provides any further arguments for the claims of the first *Critique* when he comes to analyse moral consciousness.

It follows both from the concept of will expounded in the *Groundwork* and from the concept of reason presented in the first *Critique* that a rational will must be capable of subjecting its maxims to a supreme law of reason as the *principium diudicationis* and *executionis*. According to the *Groundwork*, the will is the 'capacity to act in accordance with the representation of laws, that is, in accordance with principles' (Gr: 4:412). In this connection, Kant is clearly conceiving the relationship between act and law by analogy with the traditional theory of the practical syllogism, to which indeed he also explicitly appeals in the *Doctrine of Right* when he is justifying the division of powers or authorities in the state (see 6:313). In the *Groundwork*, he writes: 'Since reason is required for the derivation of actions from laws, the will is nothing other than practical reason' (Gr: 4:412). Normally, of course, one would be more likely to interpret such 'derivation' as a process that advances from alternative possibilities of action through maxims to the moral law.

But this would not yet be 'rational' in the specifically Kantian sense if it failed to correspond to the 'nature' of reason, which requires us to advance to a truly unconditioned law (cf. A 323/B 330 ff.). Unconditioned

principles of reason (Ideas) are of course precisely those to which nothing
in experience can ever correspond. For knowledge based on experience
(knowledge through the understanding) can never be unconditioned, but
must in principle always allow for the identification and investigation of
further conditions. As far as theoretical reason is concerned, therefore,
every idea of the unconditioned necessarily remains 'a problem without
any solution' (A 328/B 384). The 'idea of practical reason,' on the other
hand, as the 'idea of the necessary unity of all possible ends,' already possesses reality and 'causality' insofar as it 'must as an original, and at least
restrictive condition, serve as standard in all that bears on the practical'
(A 328/B 385). It is easy to see how the concept of reason, as the demand
for the 'absolute completeness' of all conditions, leads in the practical
domain to the demand for the potential coherence of all proposed ends
and maxims with an ultimate law. But if we ignore the 'syllogistic character' of the will and the unconditional demand of reason, does Kant's claim
to provide the only possible explanation and grounding of the concept of
moral commands and of moral consciousness still prove convincing?

According to Kant, moral commands are commands (1) that are binding upon free beings that are conscious of their freedom, (2) that have to
be assumed as an unconditional obligation binding in all 'relevant' situations and in relation to all possible rational partners in action, and (3) that
demand to be obeyed for the sake of the 'rational' character that such
commands embody.

There seems to be no particular problem with the idea that moral commands are binding on free beings and require explicit, or at least potentially explicit, acknowledgement on the part of the agent that they exclude
the possibility of making special exceptions for us on the basis of self-
interest ('dodging the fare') and that they must also be capable of motivating us to act contrary to our given inclinations. But is it true that we can
only properly explain or ground the consciousness of freedom – the sense
of unconditional obligation or the notion of 'rational motivation' – by
appealing to a 'metaphysics' based upon the idea of a purely rational will
derived by abstraction from all particular characteristics of the *conditio
humana*?

Without examining Kant's theory of freedom in any detail here, I will
touch on the following objections.

1. It is certainly true that the problem of making appropriate moral
decisions only arises if we regard ourselves as beings that are not entirely
'determined' in relation to action, although I shall here leave aside the
question of whether it really is 'practically' possible to conceive ourselves

otherwise (see Strawson 1976). But the freedom of individuals to act in accordance with their own knowledge or understanding, to shape their behaviour by conscious reference to maxims or principles, does not itself imply that the latter must be grounded in a single supreme principle that is independent of all knowledge of nature. To say that our knowledge is conditioned by its objects is not the same as saying that our action is determined by the 'causality of nature.' Even if individuals only recognise their freedom because they are capable of acting on reasons of their own, this does not necessarily imply that a rational will in general can only be 'autonomous' if its principles are conceived without any reference whatsoever to 'nature.' If we disregard the theoretical conclusions concerning knowledge that Kant presents in the first *Critique* – and particularly the claim that all events in time, including the states and conditions of the 'empirical character,' are necessarily subject to causal 'determination' by preceding events (A 553/B 581) – then it is not at all obvious that human beings can only be said to be free if the rules and motivations underlying their actions are subject to the kind of law that would properly govern the actions of a rational will entirely independent of nature. It would make sense to take a will entirely free of natural ends, free of all and any representations of some specifically desirable state of the world, as the criterion for morally proper acts of willing, if human beings could conceive of themselves only as imperfectly capable of 'incorporating' an intrinsically perfect rationality. But the idea of a perfect rational will appears rather as an extension of the human consciousness of freedom. Or is Kant's claim that 'one cannot possibly conceive of a reason that would consciously receive direction from any other quarter with respect to its own judgements' (Gr: 4:448) really independent of human self-knowledge itself? How can we know that a non-human reason is possessed of consciousness anyway? How can we know that such a reason would will its own autonomy?

2. Kant's claim that the unconditional character of moral commands or prohibitions can only be legitimated through an explicitly metaphysical grounding is not immediately obvious either. On the one hand, it is questionable whether all our moral considerations, reasons, rules, and decisions can adequately be captured and assessed by reference to juridical terminology and the characteristic rhetoric of law, command, prohibition, permission and duty. Perhaps the difference between the domains of right and morality is really greater than Kant, or even Fichte, imagined. On the other hand, we may well ask ourselves if unconditionally binding moral judgements must really be referred back to a *single* principle that is unconditional in all three sense, as outlined earlier.

If the task of ethics is indeed to justify commands or prohibitions that are binding under all conditions and circumstances (and our ethical intuitions certainly suggest that there are always some such commands), then we shall have to examine whether we can successfully address this task with weaker claims than those advanced by Kant.

I will clarify this point with the following example: the unconditional moral repudiation of sadism – 'you should never under any circumstances inflict pain upon another human being for your own pleasure' – can be justified by appeal to two independent propositions that there are no 'good' arguments to challenge:

(a) A human being's claim to freedom from consciously inflicted bodily pain outweighs under all circumstances another human being's claim to physical or psychological pleasure.

(b) The human capacity for determining our actions in light of what is proper 'in itself,' and not merely in relation to our own interests, is an unreservedly valuable characteristic of human beings.

Of course, both of these propositions contain normative expressions ('claims,' 'valuable,' and so on) that seem to call in turn for an appropriate criterion. But the relevant claims, and the criteria for judging their rightness, and the valuable features and capacities can certainly be derived from a 'rational conception of human beings.' The latter will admittedly involve theoretical reflections concerning subjectivity, behaviour, normative logical principles, and so on as well as considerations concerning the biological nature of human beings and the irreversible historical development of a specific conception of right and justice. This approach to grounding unconditional moral commands is cast in less starkly monolithic terms than the Kantian approach, but it is certainly not impossible in principle.

3. The idea that properly moral action must always be undertaken 'out of duty' is also convincing only in a weaker sense than that intended by Kant. It is convincing in the sense that a rightly identified rule or ground for action should certainly be able to determine our actions even against the prompting of our actual inclinations. Actions that are 'contrary to better insight' cannot be right, any more than can rules of conduct that are exclusively directed towards the satisfaction of our own needs, inclinations, desires, or interests. But it does not appear convincing to claim that true moral 'worth' can only be ascribed to actions undertaken *because* of the fact that the maxims in question can be framed as a universal law. Not merely in relation to cases of heroic altruism – the apparent moral value of which causes Kant considerable difficulties in the *Metaphysics*

of Morals[10] – but also in relation to quite 'normal' cases of action, it is not at all obvious why someone who has done the right thing primarily on the basis of his inclinations cannot be said to have accomplished something morally 'valuable.' The fact that we should sometimes be rationally motivated to effective action independently of, or even contrary to, our particular inclinations does not necessarily imply that everything morally right or morally valuable depends exclusively on the primacy of purely rational motivation.

Even if we concede Kant's claim that the universal human capacity for 'rational motivation' is indeed the highest end of moral action, it does not yet follow of itself that every moral decision possesses value only if it is based on such a form of motivation. Nor does it follow from the demand that every principle of action be rationally 'acceptable' to all human beings that the choice or application of the relevant principle can only result from this criterion of acceptability. The idea that all the decisions and actions of rational beings must be motivated by the 'unmoved mover' of a purely rational will surely strikes us rather as a specific metaphysical position, to which there are in fact alternatives, or as a *fiat voluntas rationalis*, which can only be seen as a secularisation of a religious conception of morality.

Bibliography

Busch, W. (1979), *Die Enstehung der kritischen Rechtsphilosophie* Kants (Berlin).

Ilting, K-H (1972), 'Der naturalistische Fehlschluß bei Kant,' in M. Riedel, ed., *Rehabilitierung der praktischen Philosophie*, vol. 1, pp. 113–130 (Freiburg).

Krausser, P. (1968), 'Über eine unvermerkte Doppelrolle des kategorischen Imperativs in Kants *Grundlegung zur Metaphysik der Sitten*,' in Kant-Studien 59, pp. 318–130.

Oberer, H. (1973), 'Zur Frühgeschichte der Kantischen Rechtslehre,' in *Kant-Studien* 64, pp. 88–102.

---

[10] Again in the Introduction to the *Doctrine of Virtue*, Kant says that the maxim of 'promoting others' happiness at the sacrifice of one's own happiness, one's true needs, would conflict with itself if it were made a universal law' (6:393). Kant only avoids the implication that self-sacrificing acts must be treated as non-moral ones because, with regard to the duty of benevolence, he says that 'it is impossible to assign determinate limits to the extent of this sacrifice. How far it should extend depends, in large part, on what each person's true needs are in view of his sensibilities' (6:393). But we must ask whether Kant would properly regard an action in which we 'forget' our own needs in response to the distress of others as possessing any specifically moral value at all.

Ritter, Ch. (1971), *Der Rechtsgedanke Kants nach den frühen Quellen* (Frankfurt am Main).

Schmucker, J. (1961), *Die Ursprünge der Ethik Kants* (Meisenheim).

Strawson, P. F. (1976), 'Freedom and Resentment,' in *Freedom and Resentment and Other Essays* (New York).

4

The Transition from Common Rational Moral Knowledge to Philosophical Rational Moral Knowledge in the *Groundwork*

Dieter Schönecker

The *Groundwork of the Metaphysic of Morals* is the first work in which Kant speaks explicitly of conceptual 'transitions' from one sphere or domain to another. But Kant never made clear precisely how these transitions are to be understood or what their systematic function within the overall structure of the *Groundwork* ultimately is. No one disputes the fact that Kant always emphasised the central importance of systematic methodological considerations for philosophical reflection. In the Preface to the *Groundwork* itself, he refers explicitly to 'the method employed in this text' (Gr:392, 17) and to the 'path' he has pursued in relation to the entire project of a metaphysics of morals (Gr:392, 22).[1] Whereas the *Groundwork* as a *whole* proceeds analytically, the metaphysics of morals he intends to publish 'someday' in the future will be constructed synthetically (Gr:391, 16). Kant says, it is true, that the internal structure of the *Groundwork* 'turns out *consequently*' as it actually does (Gr:392, 22, my italics), articulated clearly in its three well-known sections. But it is not immediately obvious why a specific

[1] Kant's works are cited in accordance with the Academy Edition with respect to pagination and, where necessary, line numbers. The *Groundwork* is abbreviated as Gr, the line number corresponds to the opening word of the relevant citation in the German original, and roman numerals refer to the three relevant sections of the work. For the *Groundwork* (Gr), the *Critique of Pure Reason* (CPR), the *Critique of Practical Reason* (CPrR), the *Metaphysics of Morals* (MM) and the *Prolegomena* (Prol.), I have used the Meiner edition (Hamburg), and for the lectures on *Anthropology from a Pragmatic Point of View*, the Jäsche *Logic*, and the Mrongovius materials on *Moral Philosophy* (Moral M II), I have referred to the Academy edition.

transition [*Übergang*] is involved in each of these sections. And nor, as we have pointed out, does Kant really explicate the character of these transitions any further.

In all the literature surrounding the *Groundwork*, we find that very little attention has been paid to this problem.[2] Quite apart from the fact that almost all commentators make the mistake of treating the third section of the *Groundwork* as synthetically constructed, hardly anyone has provided a thorough examination of the 'transition problem' itself. And when this has been attempted, it has been pursued only in relation to the contrasting distinction between the analytic and synthetic methods. This distinction in Kant is of course notoriously unclear and controversial. It is thus symptomatic that some interpreters can regard their understanding of the synthetic method as entirely compatible with the content of the third section, although Kant himself describes the latter as analytic in character. Now it is possible to show that the third section also proceeds in analytic fashion without specific reference to the contrasting substantive distinction between the analytical and synthetic methods. And the same holds for the concept of a 'transition.' At least as far as the first section of the *Groundwork* is concerned, we can grasp the significance of the transition where it occurs, and clarify why Kant chooses to adopt this methodological procedure, with sufficient clarity without having to consider Kant's initial methodological observations in the Preface.[3] In the following discussion, I shall limit myself to this first

---

[2] See footnote 18. I should like to thank Dr. H. M. Baumgartner and Dr. H. Oberer for a number of valuable comments and suggestions from which the text has benefited. I should also like to express my gratitude to H. Dinker and B. Kraft for a stimulating exchange of views concerning this, and indeed many other, aspects of Kantian philosophy.

[3] I would like to point out here that we should distinguish between *presenting* an issue in an analytical or synthetic manner and *arguing* a case in an analytic or synthetic manner. In this sense, for example, we should distinguish between the question concerning Kant's mode of presentation in the first *Critique* and the question of whether he there argues his case analytically insofar as he proceeds logically and consistently from the 'fact' (*Prol*:274) of synthetic a priori propositions (in mathematics and pure natural science) and merely investigates how such propositions are possible – a procedure that evidently exposes him to the charge of circular reasoning (see Hösle 1990, p. 161). In the Jäsche *Logic,* Kant discusses the analytical and the synthetic method in the 'doctrine of method' that is principally concerned with the 'the clarity, the thoroughness and the systematic order' (§97) of the materials of knowledge. The 'analytic or synthetic method' (§117) reappears when he is enumerating and comparing various methods (§§115–120), such as the scientific method versus the popular method or the systematic method versus the fragmentary method. These methods concern not the logical status of the development or foundation of concepts and knowledge claims, but rather the manner in which actual acquired knowledge is presented. That is why Kant identifies the analytical method as

transition from 'common rational moral knowledge' to what Kant calls 'philosophical rational moral knowledge.' The second transition is much more difficult to elucidate effectively because that would require the kind of close interpretation of the entire project of the metaphysics of morals that cannot properly be developed here. In addition, as the secondary literature on the subject shows, there is already considerable controversy concerning the structure of the second section itself. And the famous – indeed infamous – difficulties surrounding the third section need not be mentioned in this context.

I shall briefly recall the underlying point and purpose of the *Groundwork* and the overall structure of the text (I). Then I shall specifically discuss the transition involved in the first section (II), analyse the way in which it is connected with Kant's critique of popular moral philosophy (III), and briefly summarise my final conclusions (IV).

I

In the Preface to the *Groundwork*, Kant explicitly unfolds his ambitious project of a metaphysics of morals as a pure *a priori* philosophy. It should already noted, however, that in the *Groundwork*, Kant deploys the concept of a 'metaphysics of morals' in various and not always immediately clear ways.[4]

---

more suitable 'for the purposes of popularity' and the synthetic method as more appropriate 'for the purposes of a scientific and systematic elaboration of our knowledge' (§117). One should therefore expect the *entire* text of the *Groundwork* to proceed *synthetically* insofar as Kant says explicitly that it would be 'quite absurd' for such an investigation 'to want to comply with popularity' (Gr:409, 25–26). On the other hand, Kant's discussion of analytic and synthetic method in his *Logic* also clearly supports the claim that the entire *Groundwork* proceeds *analytically* insofar as that discussion corresponds precisely to Kant's remarks in the Preface. In the *Logic* lectures, Kant says that the analytical method 'commences with the grounded and the conditioned and advances towards principles,' whereas the synthetic method 'moves on the other hand from the principles to the consequences or from the simple to the composed' (§117). This clearly implies that Kant's remark in the Preface about proceeding 'in turn synthetically from the examination of the principle and its sources back to common cognition' (Gr:392, 19) should not be interpreted to mean, as almost all commentators read it, that the 'examination of this principle' already belongs to the synthetic part of the enquiry. The examination in question belongs to the analytical part of the enquiry (*Groundwork* III), and it is only after this examination that one can advance from 'the principles to the consequences.' It is already obvious that the question we are addressing here is a complex one.

4 For this, see Bittner (1989), p. 14f.

Firstly, the expression 'metaphysics of morals' is a generic concept for designating the pure part of ethics. In this sense, Kant also describes the metaphysics of morals as 'pure moral philosophy' (Gr:389, 8) or as 'pure philosophy of morals (metaphysics)' (Gr:410, 31).[5] The task is to place this metaphysics of morals 'before' (Gr:388, 36) popular moral philosophy and practical anthropology (see Gr:409, 23;410, 18) precisely because all moral philosophy properly 'rests entirely upon its own pure part' (Gr:389, 26). In this sense, therefore, Kant distinguishes the pure philosophy of morals from the 'applied' philosophy of morals (Gr:410, 30). There is no doubt that Kant's principal ethical works, at least according to his own self-understanding, all form part of this 'metaphysics of morals.'

Secondly, Kant speaks of a metaphysics of morals that he intends 'someday' to provide (Gr:391, 16)[6] and for which he is presenting the *Groundwork* 'in advance' (Gr:391, 17). Despite all the difficulties involved, we can say that the originally projected work was eventually realised as the *Metaphysics of Morals* that Kant later elaborated in terms of the *Doctrine of Right* and the *Doctrine of Virtue*. The subsequent metaphysics of morals must therefore itself be distinguished from the *Groundwork of the Metaphysics of Morals*. Because a 'groundwork' for a metaphysics of morals, as pure moral philosophy, cannot itself be empirical, and because the empirical part of morals is also expressly designated in contrast with it as practical anthropology, the *Groundwork* as such is already 'pure moral philosophy.' Now a pure moral philosophy is nothing other than a metaphysics of morals. Thus the *Groundwork* is also itself a metaphysics of morals. We may conclude, therefore, that the metaphysics of morals is the generic concept that includes within itself both the 'actual' metaphysics of morals as well as the 'groundwork' for the latter.

Thirdly, Kant also recognises a metaphysics of morals as a particular part of the *Groundwork*, and one that, with some considerable difficulty, must be located and identified somewhere within the second section of the work.[7] And that would be at a point of transition to a metaphysics of morals that belongs within the *Groundwork* itself.

---

[5] See also Gr:390, 10 and 412, 6.

[6] See Gr:421, 32 (for the 'future' metaphysics of morals).

[7] It is true that Kant explicitly says that he '*now*' intends (Gr:427, 17, my emphasis) to 'step forth,…namely into the metaphysics of morals' (Gr:426, 28). But since this step essentially consists in a (renewed) analysis of the practical faculty of reason (Gr:427, 19ff.), the precise relationship between this and the earlier analysis of the same issue

In general terms, we must describe the metaphysic of morals (mm$_1$) as a pure moral philosophy. Like any system of ethics, its task is to determine which acts are morally demanded, forbidden, or permitted; in addition, it should be able to explain how and why moral rules and prescriptions can be binding upon us at all. But Kant says explicitly that he is pursuing a *pure* moral philosophy – that is, an ethics that is constructed in a *a priori* manner. The terms 'pure' or 'a *priori*' here simply signify, first, that the concepts employed, the moral imperative that is proposed, and the binding validity that is claimed in such an ethical theory are all non-empirical in source and character. Any philosopher who wishes to defend a metaphysics of ethics in this sense is therefore barred from making any appeal to the nature of human beings. For if it is the case that moral laws must possess universality and necessity with regard to their range and their intrinsically binding character, and if it is also true that empirical states of affairs or justifications based upon experience can neither possess or guarantee such universality, it follows that only an *a priori* ethics is capable of grounding the universality and necessity of moral laws upon the principle of reason. And since reason is a universal and identically appearing feature of all rational beings, the moral law must be applied to man as a rational being, even if it is true that he remains a sensuous being as well. The ethics that must accomplish this task is the metaphysics of morals (mm$_1$). Kant describes the task, method, and function of this metaphysics of morals in paragraphs 6–10 of the Preface (Gr:388, 15–391, 15): it must identify 'ethical laws' (Gr:389, 16) and the 'ground of obligation' (ibid.) solely '*a priori* in concepts of pure reason' (Gr:389, 18); it should prescribe its laws a priori to man 'as a rational being' (Gr:389, 29); it should identify 'the moral law in its purity and genuine character' (Gr:390, 8); and it should 'investigate the idea and the principles of a possible *pure* will' (Gr:390, 34). Indeed all of this 'is indispensably necessary, not merely because of a motive to speculation – for investigating the source of the practical basic principles that lie *a priori* in our reason – but also because morals themselves remain subject to all sorts of corruption as long as we are without that clue and supreme norm by which to appraise them correctly' (Gr:389, 36).

(Gr:412, 26ff.) remains unclear. In order to avoid possible misunderstanding, I shall distinguish, where necessary, between the metaphysics of morals as an overall concept and project (mm$_1$), Kant's 'future' metaphysics of morals (mm$_2$), and metaphysics of morals as part of Section II of the *Groundwork* (mm$_3$).

After describing the task of the *Groundwork* in these terms, Kant then adds that he also intends to provide a relevant metaphysics of morals 'some day' in the future. If this future metaphysics were simply identical with the metaphysics of morals as just described, it would be almost impossible to understand what the *Groundwork* itself was intended to accomplish. But what is it precisely intended to accomplish? Kant writes: 'The present groundwork is, however, nothing more than the search for and establishment of *the supreme principle of morality*, which constitutes by itself a business that in its purpose is complete and to be kept apart from every other moral investigation' (Gr:392, 3) The *Groundwork* therefore accomplishes a part of the task already identified as belonging to a metaphysics of morals (mm$_1$). First, it identifies and analyses ('seeks out') the concept of the moral law and the concepts directly connected with it ('the good will', 'duty'). Second, it answers (in 'continuation') the question as to 'how such a synthetic practical proposition is possible *a priori* and why it is necessary' (Gr:444, 35) – that is, it answers the question concerning the binding character of the Categorical Imperative. The analysis and demonstration of the moral law must precede 'every other moral investigation,' and the latter refers here to none other than the 'metaphysics of morals' that Kant himself intends 'some day' to provide (mm$_2$). The Preface already makes it quite clear what the task of this subsequent metaphysics will be: the 'application of the same principle [i.e. of the Categorical Imperative] to the entire system' (Gr:329, 8). If we also consider Kant's later reference to a 'future *Metaphysics of Morals*' (Gr:421, 32), the task of which would include the 'division of duties' (Gr:421, 31), it is easier to understand what such application implies: the *systematic* derivation of legal and moral duties for human beings from the Categorical Imperative and the organised exposition of these duties. It is generally recognised that this is effectively accomplished by the 'doctrine of right' and the 'doctrine of virtue' as presented in the later *Metaphysics of Morals*.

So what precisely does the present *Groundwork* accomplish? The Preface already clearly teaches us just how inappropriate it would be to regard the *Groundwork* as merely an exploratory or preliminary work, to treat it simply as a 'practice exercise' of some kind. The proper analysis and demonstration of the Categorical Imperative itself is the 'principal question' of the metaphysics of morals as a whole, and forms the basis on which we proceed to the systematic derivation and exposition of duties. The *Groundwork* is a metaphysics of morals insofar as it proceeds in an a priori fashion and conceptually unfolds the highest principle of morality. It is a 'critical' inquiry insofar as it draws upon the *Critique of Practical*

Reason in deducing the validity of the Categorical Imperative. And insofar as it constitutes a 'metaphysics of morals' and a 'critique,' it is also
an 'ethics,' although it does not yet contain an entire body of systematic
ethics.[8] Any attempt to draw a strict distinction here between metaphysics
of morals, ethics, and critique can only lead us astray – and this precisely
because the *metaphysics* of morals (mm$_1$) is indeed an *'ethics'* (Gr:387,
16), the fundamental part of which is provided by the *Groundwork*,
which in turn contains the essential *critical* element.

II

Whatever Kant himself understood by his talk of 'transitions', even the
most cursory attention to the relevant texts shows that these transitions
are certainly to be found. The concept of 'transition' here does not mean
that we simply move from term A towards term B without necessarily reaching the latter, in the sense that one might pass over from one
river bank to the other one, and where the transit consists essentially in
the crossing itself. The kind of transition we are talking about involves
reaching the other side, where the process of passage itself is not necessarily relevant to the matter. Thus Kant's first transition actually brings
us to the 'principle' (Gr:403, 35) of 'moral cognition on the part of common human reason' (Gr:403, 34), and thus to rational philosophical
knowledge. As we shall see, the second section of the *Groundwork* will
once again emphatically confirm that such rational philosophical knowledge is not an object of striving, but something that is actually attained
(Gr:412, 15–22). With regard to the metaphysics of morals (mm$_3$), it is
also true that such knowledge is actually attained. For if the 'resolution'
(Gr:444, 36) of the question as to how the Categorical Imperative is a
possible and necessary synthetic proposition 'no longer lies within the
limits of the metaphysics of morals' (ibid), then the preceding discussion
itself must lie precisely within those limits.[9] And since, as the heading of
Groundwork II clearly shows, the transition in question is only accomplished in this second section, the metaphysics of morals itself must be
located in this same section. In addition, the heading of *Groundwork*
III indicates that we are presented here with the transition *from* the

---

[8] In Section II (Gr:424, 12–14), Kant claims after all that 'all duties,' with respect to the
'kind of obligation' involved, have been 'set out completely.'
[9] See Bittner (1989), p. 15.

metaphysics of morals *to* the critique of practical reason itself. The former must therefore already have been attained at this point. And the critique of practical reason is also actually accomplished and not merely anticipated in a preliminary fashion. For Kant says that he here wishes to 'preface' the synthetic use of pure practical reason with a 'critique of this rational faculty itself' and indicate its 'main features' (Gr:445, 13 and 15). This is the proper 'business' (Gr:440, 27) of *Groundwork* III. Furthermore, the appropriate heading to the last section of the *Groundwork* is formulated in the Preface not simply as a 'transition' (Gr:446, 2) but as the 'final step' (Gr:392, 27).[10]

A formal examination of the relationship between the relevant transitions also confirms these findings. No one disputes the fact that the third section of the *Groundwork* does indeed substantively begin from the point where the second section ends. *Groundwork* II contains the transition to the metaphysics of morals, whereas *Groundwork* III contains the transition, the 'final step,' from this same metaphysics of morals to the critique of pure practical reason. The precise relationship between *Groundwork* I and II, on the other hand, is much more difficult to determine precisely. On analogy with the relationship between Sections II and III, it would be tempting to imagine that Section II begins essentially where Section I leaves off. On this supposition, the first transition would be that from common moral rational knowledge to philosophical moral rational knowledge, and the second transition would be that from the latter philosophical knowledge to the metaphysics of morals. And this would logically imply that we must ultimately identify philosophical ethical rational knowledge with popular ethical thought or popular moral philosophy. For the heading to *Groundwork* II speaks not of a 'transition from *philosophical moral rational knowledge* to the metaphysics of morals,' but of a 'transition from *popular moral thought* [or according to the formulation in the Preface from *popular moral philosophy*] to the metaphysics of morals.' On this reading, the *Groundwork* would simply present us with *four* forms of moral rational knowledge: common moral rational knowledge, philosophical rational knowledge (popular ethical thought or popular moral philosophy), metaphysics of morals, critique of pure practical reason. Thus Bittner (1989, p. 29) interprets the transitions as follows: 'The moral philosophy of the first section formulates the principle for common moral rational knowledge; this popular philosophy is grasped

---

[10] Similarly, Kant claims that we must 'advance by natural steps' towards the metaphysics of morals (Gr:412, 22) and 'take a step into the field of *practical philosophy*' (Gr:405, 23).

and developed afresh in the metaphysics of morals of the second section; the principle identified in this metaphysics of morals is itself grounded in the critique of practical reason which is sketched in part three.'[11]

This description of the first and third section of the *Groundwork* is absolutely correct. But it is very problematic to identify the moral philosophy of Section I (that is, philosophical moral rational knowledge) with the popular philosophy of Section II (for in speaking of 'this popular philosophy,' Bittner is clearly referring to what Kant calls 'popular moral philosophy,' or 'ethical thought'[12]). It is quite true, at least in a certain sense, that the findings of philosophical moral knowledge in *Groundwork* I are grasped afresh in terms of the metaphysics of morals in *Groundwork* II; and it is true that the concept of duty and the concept of the Categorical Imperative are clarified specifically in relation to the first analysis of the faculty of practical reason.[13] But that certainly does not mean that the philosophy from which Kant distances himself in Section II in order to attain a properly metaphysical perspective is identical with the philosophy to which he made transition in Section I. It is actually untrue to say that popular philosophy is 'grasped and developed afresh' in Section II – on the contrary, it is very sharply criticised – and it is only philosophical moral rational knowledge that is effectively developed here. One can show that there are actually five rather than four forms (or aspects) of moral rational knowledge in the *Groundwork*: (a) common moral rational knowledge, (b) philosophical moral rational knowledge, (c) popular ethical thought, (d) metaphysics of morals (mm_3), and (e) critique of pure practical reason. We have concluded that the relevant transitions are those between a and b, between c and d, and between d and e. With regard to the first transition in particular, it can and must be shown precisely how and where it finds its proper place within the first section of the *Groundwork*. In addition, we shall also show that close relationships also obtain between a and c and between b and d.

It is not difficult, therefore, to demonstrate that Bittner's interpretation is actually mistaken. It suffices in this respect to pay careful attention to

---

[11] See also Vorländer's 'Introduction' to the *Groundwork* (1965, p. XVIII), where he claims that the first section of the work leads from 'common moral rational knowledge to philosophical rational knowledge, and the second section *then* leads on to the metaphysics of morals' (my emphasis).

[12] See Gr:412, 17, where Kant even describes this as 'popular philosophy.'

[13] The metaphysics of morals (mm_3) showed simply through 'explicating *the generally received* concept of morality that an autonomy of the will is unavoidably connected with the same, or rather lies at its basis' (Gr:445, 2, my emphasis).

Kant's own words. The following quotation alone clearly shows that philosophical moral rational knowledge must be strictly distinguished from popular moral philosophy, and thus it reveals the untenability of the relevant interpretations by Bittner and Brandt (we shall return to the latter in what follows). Kant says explicitly: 'However, in order to advance by natural steps in this study [i.e. in the metaphysics of morals, D. S.][14] *not merely* from common moral appraisal [...] to a philosophical one, *as has already been done*, but *rather* from a popular philosophy which goes no further than it can by groping about with the help of examples to metaphysics' (Gr:412, 15 – my italics). If I am not mistaken, the significance of this passage, and the specific relevance of the formulations we have highlighted, has hitherto been entirely ignored in the secondary literature concerning the character of Kant's first transition. There can be no doubt, it appears to me, that Kant is here drawing an explicit distinction, and as clearly as one could wish, between 'philosophical appraisal' (referring unambiguously to *philosophical* moral rational knowledge[15] as distinct from *common* moral rational knowledge) and popular moral philosophy. Whereas *Groundwork* I advances from common moral rational knowledge to philosophical rational knowledge ('as has already been done'), *Groundwork* II itself advances ('rather') from popular moral philosophy to metaphysics. But this clearly implies that a transition has already occurred in the first section (that is, from common moral rational knowledge to philosophical moral rational knowledge). It also clearly shows that we cannot legitimately identify philosophical moral rational knowledge with popular moral rational knowledge.

Quite apart from the passage we have cited, which surely speaks for itself, it would also be entirely inappropriate to identify philosophical and popular rational knowledge precisely because the latter is explicitly described as merely 'groping about with the help of examples' (Gr:412, 17). And Kant repeatedly rejects such an approach: 'One could not give worse advice to morality than attempting to derive it from examples' (Gr:408, 28). On the contrary, Kant stresses that the 'concept of duty'

---

[14] Since 'this study' clearly refers back to the metaphysics of morals (mm₁) that has just been mentioned, the philosophical rational knowledge of the first section is therefore already itself part of the metaphysics in question.
[15] This is clear from the fact that Kant is adverting to what has 'already been done'. This can only refer to the first section, which, as the relevant heading implies, does indeed move from 'common moral appraisal' (that is, common moral rational knowledge) to philosophical moral rational knowledge. Philosophical 'appraisal' therefore refers precisely to this philosophical moral rational knowledge.

he is employing, – that is, the concept that he has drawn from common rational knowledge in the first section by means of philosophical conceptual *clarification* (Gr:397, 3) and *development* (Gr:397, 6) – has emphatically not been 'treated as a concept of experience' (Gr:406, 7). In the first section, philosophical rational knowledge already leads to an initial analysis of the concept of duty[16] and even to an initial formulation of the Categorical Imperative; it can only be regarded as absurd, therefore, to place such knowledge on exactly the same level as popular moral philosophy. Even a cursory examination of the text clearly reveals that Kant's transitions are not from a to b, from b to c, and from c to d, but rather from a to b, from c to d, and from d to e. And that means precisely that the *Groundwork* does indeed distinguish five rather than four different kinds (aspects) of moral rational knowledge.

The heading to the first section should already show beyond any doubt that we are presented here with a (first) transition to a philosophical form of moral rational knowledge, quite independently of the question concerning the specifically philosophical character of this rational knowledge. For the heading, which refers to this transition, *is* precisely the heading to the first section, and one may justifiably wonder what significance could possibly attach to the heading itself, as indicating the *content* of the first section, if the transition thus indicated could not actually be found within *Groundwork* I at all. How, then, despite this extremely obvious argument, can a well-informed interpreter such as Brandt (1988, p. 174) assume as something quite self-evident that the transition to philosophical rational knowledge does *not* indeed transpire in *Groundwork* I, or if so only in passing at the end of the section (so that what we have made a transition to does not itself appear within this first section)? The answer is easy to find: it is only in the very last paragraph of *Groundwork* I that Kant says that our common human reason 'is impelled on practical grounds to go out of its sphere and take a step into the field of *practical philosophy*' (Gr:405, 22). It is this passage that obviously provides the argumentative basis for Brandt's claim. And at first glance this certainly seems convincing enough. For Kant says here that common human reason must now move out of *its* sphere and into the field of practical philosophy, a field that thus has

---

[16] Indeed Kant explicitly emphasises that he is drawing on the philosophical clarification already accomplished in Section I: 'We have seen *in the first section* that in the case of an action from duty we must look not to interest in the object but merely to that in the action itself and its principle in reason (law)' (Gr:414, 13, footnote, my emphasis).

yet to be entered. If this remark were located at the very beginning of *Groundwork* I, we would not have a problem. One could simply regard the passage between pages 397 and 403 as the 'field of practical philosophy' that common human reason is to enter. But the remark in question comes right at the end of Section I. It therefore follows, as Brandt obviously concludes, that the philosophy that is to offer us 'help' (Gr:405, 32) only becomes the explicit object of consideration in *Groundwork* II. And that is also true. It is only because Brandt identifies *this* philosophy with philosophical moral rational knowledge that he is unable to discover any transition *to* philosophical rational knowledge within *Groundwork* I itself. In Brandt's analysis, the transition all but vanishes in being simply reduced to passing remarks of Kant's as he moves from one section to another. Yet Brandt's interpretation of the first transition is quite untenable. It is not true that 'the two final paragraphs address the transition announced in the title.' That actually takes place much earlier in the text, as we shall shortly see. And, most importantly, it is not true that the transition takes us '*from* the first *to* the second section' (my emphasis). In the first place, this would imply that absolutely no transition is effected within *Groundwork* I itself, which cannot possibly be right, as we have seen, and would contradict the whole point of the heading to the first section. And, the heading to the second section, or the very separation between the first two sections, would then no longer make any sense at all. In the second place, this would also mean simply identifying philosophical rational knowledge and popular moral philosophy, something that Brandt himself is most reluctant to do. Paradoxically enough, he interprets the transition in question as one to a philosophy that he describes as 'initially [...] *false*' (my emphasis) – namely, to popular moral philosophy.[17] In short, if Brandt's reading were correct, then *Groundwork* I and II would forfeit both their own individual character and their reciprocal connection, and even indeed their systematic significance in general. In this case, the only transition that Kant has managed successfully to accomplish would be that from common moral rational knowledge to the metaphysics of morals.[18]

[17] Brandt thus explains the formulation and content of the second heading by saying that 'common human reason [...] in seeking assistance falls first into the den of the empiricists' (Brandt, p. 175), and is only then saved from its predicament by the protective arms of metaphysics in the shape of a *philosophia practica universalis*.
[18] See also Gr:406, 5–8. As I indicated at the beginning, the commentaries shed precious little light here. Although Paton certainly addresses the question of analytic and

What then does Kant's first transition effectively achieve? Or, to put the question in another way: what does *Groundwork* I actually demonstrate, and why does Kant begin from a consideration of common moral knowledge in the first place? Kant makes his well-known claim that a good will is the only thing that can properly be regarded as unconditionally good right at the beginning of the *Groundwork*. The proper object of judgement in relation to morally relevant acts is neither the concrete consequence of an act, nor the (ultimate) intention behind an act, nor again the capacity to realise a desired end as an act. What we judge here is solely the good and firm intention that motivates an act. The intention (the will) itself is good if the maxim it embodies is universalisable

synthetic method, he does not discuss the 'transition problem.' Although he is broadly right to say that Kant tries to formulate the moral principle of common human reason as 'clearly as possible before he actually goes on to justify it' (Paton 1962, p.11), this completely ignores the distinction between *Groundwork* I and II. Wolff rather artificially constructs three different audiences that Kant is allegedly addressing in the three respective sections of the text (Wolff 1973, pp. 24–28). But he is right to observe that Section I essentially presents Kant's 'analysis of ordinary moral consciousness' (p. 33). Wolff calls this a '*real rational reconstruction*' (p. 55) of everyday moral consciousness, which presupposes that the latter *also in fact* acts in accordance with the principles articulated in the systematic reconstruction of its moral judgements. But he does not address the central problem and related issues in any detail. Kaulbach does address the transition question, but his own analysis is insufficiently precise and involves a number of errors: (1) He claims that the first section concerns 'the transition from common moral rational knowledge to the metaphysics of morals' (Kaulbach 1988, p. 15). In a certain sense, that is quite right, but Kaulbach fails to distinguish between different concepts of metaphysics here, and therefore interprets the second section too as a transition to the metaphysics of morals. He speaks imprecisely of 'thought' (p. 16) with reference to the first section and of the 'metaphysician' (ibid.) with reference to the second section; (2) the claim that the transitions in Section I and Section II both move 'in each case from a historically real form of moral thought to *their* a priori sources' (p. 16, my emphasis) is mistaken, at least with respect to the second transition. The second section does not lead us to 'the a priori origin' of popular moral philosophy – for what could that possibly mean? – but simply and roundly criticises the latter. Kaulbach later effectively recognises this himself when he says that the second transition is meant to show that we 'must move from a false philosophy of praxis based upon empirical sources to pursue the path of an a priori science of a metaphysics of morals' (p. 38); (3) the assertion that 'metaphysics' (what kind of metaphysics is meant here remains unclear) already provides, with the first two transitions, 'a justification of the validity claim of the "ought" that arises from the moral law in a kind [sic.] of transcendental deduction' utterly contradicts Kant's own remarks in this connection at the end of Section II. For the deduction is only presented in the third section. Freudiger regards Bittner's and Brandt's analyses of the transitions as 'acceptable interpretations' (Freudiger 1993, p. 63), which, as we have already shown, is clearly not the case. Freudiger himself pays no attention to the problem in question and claims that the metaphor of 'transition' offers 'hardly any' assistance (ibid.) in interpreting Kant's method in the *Groundwork*.

and if the motive for the act that follows from this maxim is grounded solely in respect for the moral law. Although Kant concedes that there is certainly 'something strange' (Gr:394, 34) about this idea of an intrinsically good will, he nonetheless claims it meets with 'the agreement even of common reason' (ibid), and indeed that it 'already dwells in our natural sound understanding' (Gr:397, 2).[19] In his lectures on ethics in the winter semester of 1784/5 – and it was in April 1785 that Kant received his first copies of the *Groundwork* – he strongly emphasises the same thought: '*Everyone* knows that nothing in the world is good without qualification except the good will' (*Moral M* II, p. 607, my emphasis).[20] The function of philosophical moral rational knowledge is simply (initially) that of *clarifying* (Gr:397, 3) the idea of the good will. But to clarify this idea does not merely mean reconstructing the concept of an intrinsically good will as the criterion that is effectively applied in our actual '*common* moral judgement' (Gr:412, 15, my emphasis).[21] It also means 'developing' (Gr:397, 6) this concept, in an emphatic sense of 'development', in relation to the concept of duty. For although the concept of duty 'contains' (Gr:397, 8) the concept of the good will, it does so 'only under certain subjective limitations and hindrances' (Gr:397, 7). Deriving his conclusion on two prior propositions, Kant furnishes the first fundamental definition of the concept of duty as follows: '*Duty is the necessity of an action out of respect for the law*' (Gr:400, 18). The law in question is the Categorical Imperative. With regard to the latter, Kant also claims that our everyday understanding 'always has

---

[19] 'Even children of moderate age feel' the specific character of an act performed from duty, according to Kant (Gr:411, 37).

[20] At the crucial point of his argument in the Preface (Gr:389, 5–23), Kant makes an analogous observation: '*Everyone* must grant that a law, if it is to hold morally, that is, as a ground of obligation, must carry with it absolute necessity' (Gr:389, 11, my emphasis). But the ground of obligation lies 'a priori simply in concepts of pure reason' (Gr:389, 18). It is therefore 'clear of itself from the common idea of duty and of moral laws' (Gr:389, 10) that there must indeed be a pure moral philosophy. The argument presented in the first two paragraphs of *Groundwork* I develops a negative strategy in demonstrating that the good will alone is good without qualification, and is also capable of being the highest good insofar as other possible candidates, as derived from traditional conceptions of virtue and the consequences of human action, can decisively be excluded. Kant's argument is based, amongst other things, on the premise that the ground of morality must lie in reason. Common human reason knows this, too, and also acknowledges the concept of the good will because it is the only relevant concept compatible with that premise.

[21] See the 'practical faculty of appraising' action.

this principle before its eyes' (Gr:402, 15; cf. 403, 36). It is not merely the concept of the good will, but also the concept of duty – in which the former is contained, and the moral principle that is connected in turn with the concept of duty – that is already fundamentally familiar to our everyday understanding: 'Thus, then, we have arrived, within the moral cognition of common human reason, at its principle, which it admittedly does not think so abstractly in universal form but which it actually has always before its eyes and uses as the norm for its appraisals' (Gr:403, 34).[22] What has 'already been accomplished' (Gr:412, 17) in G I, therefore, is the transition from an everyday form of ethics[23] to the first level of philosophical ethics.

But where precisely does this transition occur? There is one particular passage that more or less compels our attention here (Gr:397, 1–10). Readers of this part of the text carefully will clearly recognise that a certain switch of direction – namely, a transition – takes place here. In this passage, Kant passes from the concept of the good will, as it is already familiar to everyday ethics, to the concept of duty, which contains this concept of the will, and is even in a position to 'let it shine forth all the more clearly' (Gr:397, 10) precisely under certain limitations. Kant develops the concept of the good will in terms of the concept of duty, and thereby arrives at a first formulation of the Categorical Imperative, which is precisely the moral principle that corresponds to the moral consciousness of our everyday understanding. What this consciousness lacks, however, is simply a clear and abstract presentation of the case, and it is this lack alone that

---

[22] In his lectures on *Anthropology from a Pragmatic Point of View* (7:139), Kant distinguishes human beings in accordance with their disposition to 'common sense' [*Gemeinsinn*] (or sometimes: 'sound human understanding') or to 'systematic knowledge' [*Wissenschaft*]: 'The former are adept in applying rules in particular cases (*in concreto*), the latter in grasping rules as such and prior to actual application (*in abstracto*).' This corresponds closely to Kant's remark in the *Groundwork* that moral 'concepts and the principles belonging to them insofar as they are fixed a priori' should be 'set forth in their generality (*in abstracto*) if this knowledge is to be distinguished from common knowledge and called philosophical' (Gr:409, 12).

[23] Kaulbach (1988, p. 14) describes such ethics as an 'unconscious metaphysics'. Cf. MM: 216, where Kant says that every human being possesses within himself a certain metaphysics, 'although as a rule only obscurely.' See also MM: 206, where he claims that every human being of sound understanding is a kind of metaphysician 'without knowing it.' Kant makes an analogous claim in the context of theoretical philosophy: 'We are in possession of certain modes of a priori knowledge, and even the common understanding is never without them' (the heading of Section II of the Introduction to the *Critique of Pure Reason*).

distinguishes it from a philosophical moral consciousness.²⁴ Thus there is no real obscurity attaching to the concept of a 'transition,' at least as far as *Groundwork* I is concerned. It simply signifies the following: The analysis here builds upon something in the positive sense of taking over an already acquired insight (a conviction, a principle, a concept) and simply presenting the latter in a more universal and abstract form. The point in the text where this transition occurs can be located precisely.²⁵ The transition itself is not an independent part or element of the theory.

²⁴ A further difference consists in the fact that 'the philosopher may investigate' that upon which our sense of 'immediate respect' ultimately 'rests' (Gr:403, 26–27). This is what Kant undertakes in the third section of the *Groundwork*.

²⁵ Although this also raises certain problems. In paragraphs 4–7 of the first section of the *Groundwork*, Kant develops a teleological argument to 'test' the '*idea*' (Gr:394, 32, my emphasis) of a good will from the 'point of view' (Gr:395, 2) of the purposiveness of nature. Kant's procedure in Section I of the *Groundwork* is analytical, and he is essentially engaged here in conceptual analysis. It is only with the third section of the *Groundwork* that we can demonstrate that morality, and therefore also the good will, is indeed a reality rather than simply a '*chimerical* idea' (Gr:445, 6, my emphasis). Yet Kant already wishes to dispel the 'suspicion' (Gr:394, 35) that it is simply a 'a high-blown fantasy that forms the covert basis' of the conceptual idea (not of the assumed reality) of the good will (Gr:394, 36). That would indeed be the case if practical reason, because of the teleological constitution of human nature itself, were incapable in principle of being the moral 'governor' of the will (Gr:395, 1). To this extent, as we have already claimed, Kant's teleological argument does belong in the context of those observations on the concept of the good will that effectively prepare for the concept of duty itself, observations that are only really concluded with this argument (Gr:397, 1ff.). But in the light of this teleological argument, how are we to interpret the transition from common moral rational knowledge to properly philosophical moral rational knowledge? Are the observations on the concept of the good will in fact only concluded with the teleological argument, so that the transition to philosophical rational knowledge is accomplished immediately afterwards (Gr:397, 1–10), or does the teleological argument itself already belong to that philosophical rational knowledge? It is impossible to provide an unambiguous answer to this question.

Our analysis of the eighth paragraph of the first section (Gr:397, 1–10), within its systematic context, has shown that this clearly marks a significant turning-point in the text. For the concept of the good will is to be developed precisely through investigating the concept of duty that already implies and contains the former. Kant thus makes a transition from the concept of the good will to the concept of duty, and since it is the teleological argument that is still supposed to test the idea (the concept) of the *good will* (albeit from a specific 'point of view'), his procedure here would seem to be quite coherent. On the other hand, the concept of the good will appears as something so 'strange,' at least in some respects, to common human reason itself that Kant appeals to further considerations based on a philosophical argument that could already be regarded as part of philosophical rational knowledge. It is probably impossible to shed complete light on this problem either. Nonetheless, so it seems to me, the transitional character of this passage (Gr:397, 1–10) is so obvious that we should maintain our thesis that this is indeed the point at which Kant actually makes the transition in question. And since the

But why does Kant begin by building upon our common moral rational knowledge in the first place? In the Preface to the *Critique of Practical* Reason,Kant writes: 'A reviewer who wanted to say something in censure of this work [i.e. the *Groundwork*] hit the mark better than he himself may have intended when he said that no new principle of morality is set forth in it but only a new formula. But who would even want to introduce a new principle of morality and, as it were, invent it? Just as if, before him, the world had been ignorant of what duty is or in thoroughgoing error concerning the latter?' (CPrR: 8).[26] This passage is not actually as helpful for answering our question as it might first appear. The fact, if it is indeed a fact, that the principle of morality does not have to be invented because it has already long since been discovered and is already universally recognised, albeit in vaguer form, is not itself a sufficient ground for Kant's choice of 'method'

concept of duty possesses such momentous significance for the whole of Kant's moral philosophy, we can say that it is essentially this concept that qualitatively distinguishes moral rational knowledge proper from common moral rational knowledge. There is further evidence to support this contention.

As we shall see, the popular moral philosophers regard the concept of duty, which itself already contains the concept of the will, as a 'mere phantom of the human imagination overstepping itself through self-conceit' (Gr:407, 17). This sort of objection rests, amongst other things, on the assumption that man is 'too weak' (Gr:406, 21) to act from duty on account of the 'frailty and impurity of human nature' (Gr:406, 19). Popular moral philosophy typically argues that man 'uses reason [...] only to look after the interests of the inclinations' (Gr:406, 23). Reason thus cannot possibly fulfil the genuine task of 'serving' the moral self-legislation of mankind (Gr:406, 22). But this is precisely the task that Kant already identifies in the first section of the *Groundwork* as the 'true calling' [*wahre Bestimmung*] of reason (Gr:396, 20). We should have '*falsely* grasped the purpose of nature in assigning reason to our will as its governor' (Gr:394, 37, my emphasis) if we held that reason, as popular moral philosophy suggests, can only serve the interests of our inclinations. It is precisely '*not* to happiness,' Kant tells us, that 'reason is properly destined' (Gr:396, 11, my emphasis). The suspicion of fantasy would only be justified if reason only governed the will insofar as it determines the latter in relation to the interests of human inclinations. It is this suspicion that Kant wishes to contest. But where precisely would such a suspicion arise in the first place? In the context of the first transition, it would clearly arise from common human reason itself 'despite all its agreement' (Gr:394, 34) with the idea of the good will. This accords entirely with the role that common reason plays in the transition to the metaphysics of morals, as we shall indicate in more detail later. It is precisely within *cultivated* common practical reason that the natural dialectic unfolds. And it is perhaps no accident that human beings who characteristically harbour a certain hatred of reason are precisely those who also possess what Kant calls a 'cultivated reason' (Gr:395, 28).

[26] This, too, once again, clearly reveals that common human reason already possesses the concept of duty, as well as that of the intrinsically good will.

(Gr:392, 17) – namely, that of beginning from this supposed knowledge. Kant indirectly compares his own achievement in *Groundwork* I with the work of Socrates.[27] For he has, in the first instance, simply made our common human reason 'attentive to its own principle' (Gr:404, 4) and 'without in the least teaching it anything new' (Gr:404, 3). But that alone does not explain *why* he has done so. Why does Kant not simply begin directly with an abstract ethical enquiry into the various concepts he believes to be central and significant? There is only one plausible answer here: as a philosopher, he is not simply theoretically interested in identifying and grounding the moral principle in a precise and perspicuous fashion, but also wishes to see it *penetrate* our actual moral consciousness in a firm and reliable way.

As we have already noted, this essentially practical interest is one of the reasons why Kant undertakes to construct a metaphysics of morals in the first place. In accordance with the general doctrine of method required by practical reason, it makes perfectly good sense to accomplish this task by connecting it directly with the moral consciousness that is already present, rather than by pursuing it solely in the rarefied heights of pure philosophy. The fact that one *can* indeed make such a connection is of course grounded in the matter at hand itself. To make this connection precisely in relation to method and exposition pursued by pure philosophy has the strong pedagogical advantage of provisionally treating the moral principle in its own definite character as something that is not essentially alien to us. It allows us to expound it, on the contrary, as something that is very familiar to us and that only needs to be formulated precisely and subsequently defended against the kind of philosophical claims expressly based upon dialectical reasoning: 'A principle of morality must equally be comprehensible to the simplest understanding, because every human being must possess that principle' (Moral M II, p. 628). There is no contradiction in ascribing, on the one hand, an awareness of the moral principle to our everyday understanding, while recognising, on the other, that there is

---

[27] See Kant's remarks on method in the *Doctrine of Virtue* where he describes 'the dialogical (Socratic) method' as one that 'presupposes' that the learner's knowledge concerning the content of duty and morality is 'already present naturally in the pupil's reason and needs only to be developed from it' (MM:411). Through Socratic dialogue, the pupil 'comes to know his own principles of reason' (Jäsche *Logic*:150). This too is a further indication that the transition in question is already accomplished in the first section. The philosopher of the *Groundwork* effectively assists common moral rational knowledge to come to know its 'own principles of reason.'

a certain *natural dialectic* in this understanding that threatens at least to weaken the absolute firmness of that principle. It is because of this dialectic that we must develop a more precise definition and justification of the principle in question, and refute the claims of popular moral philosophy in the process.

III

Why does common human reason need any assistance from practical philosophy here, if, as Kant himself has already just claimed, it does not really require 'any science or philosophy' (Gr:404, 5) in general? Essentially our reason knows what is right and wrong, and knows what the relevant moral principle is. Nonetheless, it finds itself drawn into a *'natural dialectic'* here (Gr:405, 13). Moral laws should be acknowledged and followed without regard to, and sometimes even in opposition to, our own individual inclinations, needs, and *'pathological'* interests (Gr:413, 33). But it is precisely the sensuous nature of human beings that offers a 'powerful resistance' (Gr:405, 5) to the unconditional claim that duty makes on our behaviour. The human being stands at the juncture, as it were, of two determining forces, and this corresponds precisely to the way in which Kant conceives our nature. The human being is at once a sensuous and a rational being, at once determined and potentially determinable by reason and by sensibility. It is precisely from this multiple nature[28] that the *natural* dialectic[29] emerges: 'i.e. a propensity to rationalise against those strict laws of duty' (Gr:405, 13). The dialectic consists – and this is important in relation to the role of popular moral philosophy – *not* in the fact that human beings are affected by inclinations the pursuit of which would lead them to contradict the claims of duty, *nor* in the fact that human beings do actually behave immorally. It consists rather in the fact that human beings *rationalise* against the

---

[28] See Gr:424, 25–33.
[29] There is no contradiction between assuming the existence of some such natural dialectic and the fact that practical reason, as Kant remarks in the Preface (Gr:391, 20–24), is not 'wholly dialectical' as it is in its 'theoretical but pure use.' This is generally recognised as one of the three reasons why Kant initially restricts himself to writing a *Groundwork of the Metaphysics of Morals* rather than directly elaborating a *Critique of Practical Reason*. If towards the end of the first section (Gr:405, 30–35) Kant draws a parallel between a certain 'natural dialectic' and the intrinsic dialectic of theoretical reason, this merely points to a certain similarity rather than a structural affinity between the two.

moral laws. In the final analysis, it is quite true that this natural dialectic *'arises'* [*entspringt*] (Gr:405, 13, my emphasis) from the polarised force field of reason and sensibility. But it *'unfolds'* [*entspinnt*] (Gr:405, 30, my emphasis) internally 'within practical common *reason'* itself (ibid., my emphasis). It is reason itself that becomes entangled in this dialectic and threatens to forfeit the real knowledge that it already actually possesses, and that expressly philosophical moral knowledge is simply called upon to explicate further. This dialectical propensity tends 'to cast doubt upon the validity [...] upon the purity and strictness' of moral laws (Gr:405, 14). And it does so not (only) in the practical sense that it simply lets our inclinations run free and uncontrolled, but it also leads us to render such laws *'more accommodating* to our desires and inclinations' (Gr:405, 16, my emphasis). We thereby come to determine the laws themselves *through adaptation to human nature* and to 'corrupt' them in the process (Gr:405, 17). As soon as common human reason begins to *'cultivate* itself' (Gr:405, 31, my emphasis), it forfeits the very insight that Kant believes 'everyone' (Gr:389, 11) initially possesses, and indeed must possess if it is 'clearly evident of itself from the common idea of duty and of moral laws' (Gr:389, 10). And this insight, we remember, shows that the determination and binding validity of moral laws cannot properly be based on the nature of human beings. But this is precisely what happens, at least 'in terms of a motive' (Gr:389, 21), when cultivated common reason is 'seduced' (Gr:405, 1) into basing moral laws, in whatever manner, on human nature itself. For this can only generate maxims that are 'grounded in our needs and inclinations' (Gr:405, 26).

The only possible true source of moral laws, as Kant never tires of repeating, is reason itself as a property of rational beings in general. This is the argumentational context and basic reason for the fact that the 'assistance' that practical philosophy must supply consists in identifying the 'source' and 'correct determination' of the moral principle (Gr:405, 25). And that is precisely what the metaphysics of morals in its broadest sense is fundamentally called upon to accomplish.

Kant begins the second section by reminding us that 'we have so far drawn our concept of duty from the common use of our[30] practical

---

[30] The use of the possessive pronoun here ('our') also clarifies the relationship between the two forms of rational moral knowledge. For it is one and the same practical reason that is under consideration here. See also Gr:411, 9–11, where Kant says that the 'seat and origin' of all moral concepts lies in reason itself, and 'indeed in the most common human reason just as in reason that is speculative in the highest degree.'

reason[31]' (Gr:406, 5). But he immediately warns us not infer from this that the concept of duty has thereby been 'treated as an empirical concept' (Gr:406, 7). We have already pointed out briefly how Kant distinguishes between rational *a priori* ethics and merely empirical ethics. The metaphysics of morals is supposed to demonstrate the universality and necessity of moral laws by identifying *the reason that belongs to all rational beings* as the source of these laws. The very concept of moral laws implies that the latter are universally binding.[32] But they are only universally binding in turn if they are binding for all rational beings, and it is only when they are binding in this sense that they can also be said to possess the requisite necessity.[33] Universality and necessity must therefore not merely be identified and demonstrated *a priori*, but must also themselves be originally *a priori* in character. In this sense, moral concepts cannot in principle be treated as concepts of experience. In the first place, this is because experience can never demonstrate the universality and necessity of any laws. And in the second place, even if we could demonstrate the validity of certain practical rules for human beings, these rules would not necessarily be binding for all other rational beings insofar as we cannot legitimately infer anything about the nature of all rational beings solely on the basis of our own human nature. It thus follows, in the third place, that no anthropological knowledge can play any role in expounding a metaphysics of morals. And, in particular, the latter is not called upon to concern itself with the conditions under which human beings obey or ignore moral laws, or with the influence that inclinations may exercise upon the formulation and observance of moral maxims.[34]

---

[31] It is therefore precisely the achievement of the first section, and thus of philosophical moral rational knowledge, to 'draw' forth the concept of duty in this way. It is here that the transition to such knowledge is accomplished.

[32] It is a central Kantian claim that *conceptual* analysis demonstrates how necessity and universality properly belongs to the concept, and thus to the very meaning, of the moral 'ought': 'Morality cannot be constructed on the basis of empirical principles, for the latter yield only a conditioned rather than an absolute necessity. But morality *speaks*: You must do that, without condition or exception' (Moral M II, p. 599, my emphasis). For 'the Ought *signifies* the thought that a possible free act of my own would necessarily transpire if reason possessed complete power over our will' (ibid. 605, my emphasis).

[33] See Gr:442, 7: '...the universality with which these [i.e. moral laws] are to hold for all rational beings without distinction, the unconditional practical necessity which is *thereby* imposed upon them ...' (my emphasis).

[34] For this see MM: 404f.

Kant refers explicitly to the concept of universality, in the extensive sense just outlined, in order to argue 'that no experience could give occasion to infer even the possibility of such apodictic [i.e. moral] laws' (Gr:408, 18). The whole of the fourth paragraph of Section II (Gr:408, 12– 27) is concerned with this argument. Interestingly enough, Kant begins by speaking of a 'further' point, thus implying a *second* argument for his claim that experience can never properly supply the ground of ethics, or as he puts it at the very beginning of Part 2, that the concepts of ethics are not concepts of experience. To express it more precisely, Kant's claim that experience cannot furnish the proper ground for moral philosophy has two sides to it. One relates to the *extensive sense* in which moral laws are binding (Gr:408, 18), which is the essential concern of Kant's second argument (2); the other relates to the significance of particular examples, which is the essential concern of Kant's *first* argument (1) consisting of two parts (1a and 1b) – that is, effectively, of two arguments in turn. The first part (1a) is presented in Paragraphs 1–3 (Gr:406– 408, 11), while the second part (1b), rather clumsily expressed, is presented in connection with the second argument – namely in the fifth paragraph (Gr:408, 28–409, 8). This part, like the second argument, also is directed against the empirical prejudice with regard to grounding ethics, but is focussed specifically in a rather different manner. It attempts to show that the concepts of ethics cannot be 'drawn from experience' (Gr:407, 22) insofar as they cannot be 'borrowed from examples' (Gr:408, 29). In this regard, Kant offers two arguments that can only be briefly discussed here in relation to our immediate purpose: (1a) experience can never indubitably show that an act has been done entirely for the sake of duty because the presence of overt or covert incentives for the act in question can never be excluded. In this sense, therefore, the concept of duty cannot itself be derived from experience[35]; (1b) in order to recognise an act as an example of proper moral action, we must already possess a concept of what proper moral action is. Therefore, concepts of ethics cannot be acquired from the consideration of examples.[36]

---

[35] In the second section of the *Groundwork*, Kant says: 'It cannot be made out *by means of any example*, and so empirically, whether there is any such [moral] imperative at all' (Gr:419, 16).

[36] This argument (1b) is naturally different from argument (1b), but both are directed against the claim that one can derive moral concepts from examples in a quasi-inductive manner ('and so empirically,' Gr:419, 17). That may be the reason why Kant introduces argument (1b) after argument (2).

Argument 2 – the claim that moral laws are binding in an 'extensive sense' (Gr:408, 14) and thus cannot be derived from our specifically human experience – is much more important and is directed explicitly against a whole series of ancient and contemporary forms of moral philosophy. I shall therefore quote the relevant passage in detail: 'For, by what right could we bring into unlimited respect, as a universal precept for every rational nature, what is perhaps valid only under the contingent conditions of humanity? And how should laws of the determination of *our* will be taken as laws of the determination of the will of rational beings as such, and for ours only as rational beings, if they were merely empirical and did not have their origin completely a priori in pure but practical reason?' (Gr:408, 19). And Kant's lectures on ethics from the winter semester of 1784/5 reveal, even more clearly than the *Groundwork* itself, that he intends a critical and intensive engagement with the moral philosophy 'of recent times' (Moral M II, p. 620). As far as attempts to ground the 'principle of morality' are concerned, Kant distinguishes between empirical and rational principles according to the way in which they furnish external or internal grounds in each case. Thus, those who would reduce morality to culturally dependent factors such as education or habituation (like Mandeville or Montaigne) base their arguments upon external empirical grounds. The 'Epicureans' (Moral M II, p. 621) introduce happiness as the inner empirical ground of morality, whereas the 'English' thinkers (ibid.), as Kant calls them, appeal to some kind of moral sense (Kant names Hume, Hutcheson, and Shaftesbury in this connection). Wolff and Baumgarten, on the other hand, argue on the basis of inner rational principles. Finally, Kant also mentions the theological principle that appeals to the perfection of the divine will, and describes it as a rational external principle. But the 'principle of *one's own happiness*' represents the 'most objectionable' of all in Kant's eyes, and it is precisely to this principle that our common reason reduces the ultimate principle of morality whenever it is led astray by popular moral philosophy and entangled in the natural dialectic of reason itself.

Argument 1 is also directed against certain 'philosophers' who can be found 'at all times' in history (Gr:406, 14). In the first instance, Kant shares their view that it may be impossible to discover a single example of action undertaken purely for the sake of duty. But he draws a quite different conclusion from this fact, or perhaps we should rather say that it simply holds no interest for him. The philosophers in question infer from the impossibility of finding an incontestable example of such a thing that there have never actually been any actions performed for the sake of duty. And not only that, but they also hold such actions to be incompatible with human nature, which is exclusively governed by the interest of satisfying our desires and inclinations and which employs reason solely to pursue such purposes. The only form of practical reason these philosophers are prepared to ascribe to human beings is the rationality that belongs to hypothetical imperatives. Kant not only concedes to his opponents that it is 'absolutely impossible by means of experience to make out with complete certainty a single case' (Gr:407, 1) in which someone has acted solely out of duty, he even goes so far as to entertain strong doubts, from a pragmatic perspective, about the reality of purely moral dispositions. However, and this is the essential point, he insists that 'what is at issue here is not whether this or that happened,' but whether 'reason by itself and independently of all experience commands what ought to happen', and that therefore 'actions [performed from duty] .... are still inflexibly commanded by reason' precisely because 'this duty, as duty in general, lies, prior to all experience, in the idea of a reason determining the will by means of a priori grounds' (Gr:408, 1). Assuming that the concept of duty has been correctly identified in formal terms, the argument (1a and 1b) has therefore demonstrated that such a concept of duty can be neither derived from nor confirmed through experience. The other philosophers, whom Kant does not name, regard human beings as 'too weak' (Gr:406, 21) to act out of duty alone, but they 'did not, on this account, call into doubt the *correctness* of the concept of morality' (Gr:406, 17, my emphasis). What they called into doubt was rather the '*practicability*' (Gr:408, 5, my emphasis) of purely moral actions, a doubt that is, and must be, based upon 'experience' (ibid.) precisely because for these philosophers '*everything* is based upon experience' (ibid., my emphasis). But is it really possible, as Kant suggests, to doubt the practicability of our 'previous concept of duty' without actually challenging its correctness? Strictly speaking, the answer must be no. For if this 'duty, as duty in general, lies prior to all *experience*' within reason itself (Gr:408, 9, my emphasis) – if this *a priori* character already belongs to the *concept* of duty itself – then the empirical philosophers can hardly leave this concept in itself unaffected, and thus its very correctness as a concept. Speaking less strictly, however, we can distinguish between doubt concerning the *practicability* of *actions* performed from duty and doubt concerning the *correctness* of the *concept* of duty. In that case, the sceptics would simply be expressing their fundamental doubts about the moral strength of human beings, whereas Kant would simply be contesting the relevance of such considerations for the issue in question. The only thing that properly counts is the idea of morality as the necessity of performing an action out of respect for the moral law. Whether human beings are *practically* in a position to do so, *irrespective of their freedom* and thus of their *intrinsic* possibility for action, plays no role as far as the identification and definition of the concept of duty is concerned. And it is simply the purity of this concept that is at issue here.

It is this purity that attaches to the moral law, and thereby the purity of philosophy itself, that is therefore corrupted in principle by 'popular moral philosophy' (Gr:409, 17). The fundamental failing of the latter consists in its constant appeal to experience, and particularly to our 'knowledge of human nature (which we can only draw upon from experience)' (Gr:410, 9). We have already discussed the implications of this claim and the Kantian objections to it. What is interesting here is Kant's criticisms of the 'allegedly' popular character (Gr:409, 36) of this 'popular moral thought.' For it is this that so clearly reveals the connection with the natural dialectic of common reason, and thus also the connection between the various forms of moral rational knowledge (a, b, c, d) and their internal relationships ('transitions'). Kant tells us that 'true [...] *philosophical* [...] *popularity*' (Gr:409, 27) consists first in furnishing ethics with a solid foundation and then in making such ethics accessible to a broader public. As Kant reveals in the Preface, he believes the metaphysics of morals is 'capable of a great degree of popularity and suitability for the common understanding' (Gr:391, 35). That is precisely what distinguishes it from the relevant grounding part that must come first on account of its 'subtleties' (Gr:391, 37).

The popularity attaching to 'popular' moral philosophy, on the other hand, is unfortunate for two reasons: firstly, such an ethical theory does not represent a pure moral philosophy *a priori*; and secondly, it is also a matter of 'the greatest *practical* importance' (Gr:411, 18, my emphasis), even a 'desideratum of utmost importance' (Gr:410, 24), to determine moral laws as laws of the will *a priori*. Only then do they acquire 'genuine influence' (Gr:411, 15) because in this form they exercise an effect as a moral force that is greater than that which any 'extraneous [i.e. empirical] incentive' (Gr:411, 35) is capable of exercising. Kant sees the *practical* danger arising from any impure or 'mixed doctrine of morals' insofar as the latter, oriented as it is to human nature, lessens the binding force of moral laws. Such a doctrine, convinced as it is of the weakness of human nature, thus accommodates itself to such weakness and hence actual human inclinations as well. It thereby weakens the strictly binding character of moral laws and connects them with essentially empirical incentives. Such a doctrine is 'put together from incentives of feeling and inclination and also out of rational concepts' (Gr:411, 3) and merely reveals a spectacle of '*half-rationalised* principles' (Gr:409, 31, my emphasis). But is this not the very same mistake that is committed by our *cultivated* common reason? Is it not the latter that also casts doubt upon the purity and rigour of moral laws, which also renders moral laws 'more suitable to our desires and inclinations'? And is it not striking that the natural dialectic in which our common reason became entangled is defined precisely as a propensity to 'rationalise' against the strict laws of duty (Gr:405, 14), a propensity from which indeed 'half-rationalised principles' themselves arise? Nor can we fail to recognise a parallel with Kant's later elaboration of the metaphysics of morals. There, too, Kant emphasises the *a priori* character of the moral law. There, too, as in the *Groundwork*, he warns continually against the dangers of an empirically grounded ethics. He specifies such empirical ethics as a 'doctrine of happiness' (MM: 215), which cannot possibly be based on *a priori* principles: 'All apparently *a priori* reasonings [*vernünfteln* – my emphasis] here comes down to nothing but experience raised by induction to universality, a universality … so tenuous that everyone must be allowed countless exceptions in order to adapt his choice of a way of life to his particular inclinations and his susceptibility to satisfaction' (MM: 215–16.).

   Everything is suddenly clarified here if we simply remember the concept employed in the *Groundwork* to capture the 'powerful counterweight' of the inclinations and their satisfaction, from which the natural dialectic of reason arises: namely 'happiness' (Gr:405, 8). Moral laws 'command for everyone, without taking account of his inclinations' (MM: 216). But cultivated human reason does take account of precisely these human inclinations and of our striving for happiness. And that is why, on our argument here, such reason is (essentially) no different from that popular moral philosophy that also, amongst other things, appeals to 'happiness' (Gr:410, 6) as the basis and ultimate goal of its ethical precepts.[37]

---

[37] As we have seen, 'happiness' is not the only principle to which popular philosophy appeals. Other relevant principles include 'perfection,' 'moral feeling,' 'fear of God,'

The 'heteronomy of the will' (Gr:441, 1) is the characteristic feature of both popular moral philosophy and of the natural dialectic of reason. And this is particularly true with regard to the motive of happiness. Just as there is a fundamental congruence between sound human reason and philosophical human reason, on the one hand, so too there is a fundamental congruence between reason turned dialectical and popular moral philosophy, on the other.[38] But this congruence *only* obtains when our common reason 'cultivates itself' (Gr:405, 31). Is it therefore a question of merely theoretical speculation to ask whether it is not popular moral philosophy, amongst other things, that 'seduces' (Gr:405,1) our common human

and so on. (See Gr:410, 3–7). Kant interprets all such *'attempts'* to ground morality (Gr:410, 3, my emphasis) as characteristic of 'popular moral thought.' They all belong together by virtue of their intrinsically 'empirical' character. The formulation, the alleged rigour, and the theoretical grounding of such principles are always based on experience, and for Kant, in this connection, that means on our knowledge of human nature. But this knowledge fails to yield both the requisite universality of moral laws, since it excludes consideration of rational beings in general, and the requisite necessity of moral laws, since experience is always afflicted by an element of contingency. We should certainly not underestimate the rhetorical character of Kant's observations in this connection. If at first he had ardently embraced and fulsomely praised *that* practical reason we all possess in common – namely, our 'sound reason' or 'natural sound understanding' (Gr:405, 22;397,2) – we now find him fiercely attacking this 'disgusting hodgepodge of patchwork observations and half-rationalised principles in which shallow pates revel because it is something useful for everyday chit-chat' (Gr:409, 30). Clearly recognising that various different principles of morality can present themselves once we have 'conceded the basic concept of heteronomy' (Gr:441, 26), Kant does not merely refuse to distinguish (as later at Gr:441, 29–444, 34) between an empirical and a rational form of heteronomous moral principles, nor merely refuse to differentiate the various forms of popular moral philosophy. He simply presents the reader with a 'marvellous mixture' (Gr:410, 8) in which the principles of perfection, of happiness, of fear of God, of moral feeling, have been thrown together in one and the same popular moral philosophy – precisely because they are all based on experience. See Gr:410, 8–18, where Kant, after referring to this 'mixture,' immediately asks whether the moral law can be found 'at all with reference to the knowledge of human nature.' Later on, it is true, he does distinguish between the domains of anthropology, theology, and so forth (see Gr:410, 19–22). In fact, all moral philosophies founded on heteronomy ultimately refer back to the 'natural constitution of the subject' (Gr:444, 17), irrespective of whether their principles are *'empirical* or *rational'* (Gr:441, 33). To that extent we can say that the 'knowledge of human nature' does indeed form the general basis of all popular moral philosophy.

[38] Our common human reason, which in one sense, as Kant indirectly suggests, can no longer be 'distinguished' (Gr:390,14) from popular moral philosophy, is therefore dialectically contaminated. The former and the latter both comprehend morality in a 'mixed' form (Gr:390, 15), and that is precisely why popular moral thought 'does not even deserve the name of philosophy' (Gr:390, 13).

reason, and that 'cultivates' it?[39] Such philosophy is popular not insofar
as it is shallow, but it is 'commonly understandable' precisely *because* it
'renounces any well-grounded insight' (Gr:409, 29). It is actually popular,
Kant seems to believe, in the sense that it enjoys considerable support 'in
our times' (Gr:409, 15).[40] Popular moral philosophy corresponds to 'the
taste of the public' (Gr:388, 25) and 'finds favour' there (Gr:410, 3): 'For if
votes were to be collected as to which is to be preferred – pure rational cognition separated from anything empirical, hence metaphysics of morals,
or popular practical philosophy – one can guess at once on which side the
preponderance would fall' (Gr:409, 15). It is because Kant is pursuing the
cause of enlightenment rather than any purely theoretical interest that he
offers some 'assistance' in this situation – the assistance of the metaphysics
of morals.

IV

We can now summarise the conclusions of the preceding analysis. In the
Groundwork, Kant distinguishes five forms of rational moral knowledge.
He begins with the transition from our common moral rational knowledge
(a) to philosophical moral rational knowledge (b). His second transition,
however, takes popular ethical thought (c), and not this philosophical
rational knowledge, as its point of departure. He makes a transition from
popular ethical thought to the metaphysics of morals, or mm_3 (d). And
from the latter, he makes a final transition to the critique of pure practical
reason (e). Thus, whereas the third transition takes as its point of departure the position that results from the second transition, the relationship
between the first two transitions is different in kind: in the first section
of the *Groundwork*, Kant makes the transition from a to b, whereas in
the second section he makes the transition not from b to d but from c to
d. The first transition possesses an essentially affirmative function: Kant

---

[39] See Kaulbach (1988, p. 14), who claims that our common human reason tends to be
'oppressed' and misled by 'sophistical reasoning.'
[40] See also Hegel's remark on Kant in his *Lectures on the History of Philosophy*: 'In the
domain of practical philosophy the so-called theory of happiness generally prevailed at
that time, and morality was grounded upon impulses; the concept of man, the way in
which man was supposed to realise this concept, is grasped here in terms of happiness, in
terms of the desire to satisfy these impulses' (G. W. F. Hegel, *Werke*, vol. 20, Frankfurt,
p. 334). Kaulbach (1988, p. 38) specifically identifies Mendelssohn, Garve, Feder, Engel,
and Nicolai as 'popular philosophers' in the relevant sense.

shows that our common understanding of ethics corresponds precisely to what can in fact be formulated in terms of an *a priori* ethics. The second transition, on the other hand, accomplishes a kind of negative demarcation: it takes as its point of departure from popular moral philosophy, which is characterised by the fundamental error of attempting to ground ethics on happiness and experience in general, an error that is consciously identified as such and expressly avoided by the metaphysics of morals. Common moral rational knowledge thus already possesses the fundamental concepts belonging to a genuine ethical philosophy (the good will, duty, the Categorical Imperative). Philosophical moral rational knowledge expressly clarifies and develops these fundamental concepts in a positive relation to this our common ethical thinking, and the metaphysics of morals subsequently provides a final and definitive analysis that specifies and differentiates these concepts in a critical relation to popular moral philosophy. The critique of pure practical reason shows that these concepts can rightly claim objective reality. Thus, although common moral rational knowledge already possesses moral insight, as 'cultivated reason,' it finds itself entangled in a natural dialectic that is characterised by the same fundamental error that also afflicts popular moral philosophy. This error reveals the necessity of providing a precise conceptual analysis of the central issue in a metaphysics of morals. In a certain respect it is this moral philosophy itself that 'seduces' common moral rational knowledge and thus reveals why the latter requires 'assistance' from a metaphysics of morals in the first place.

Bibliography

Bittner, R. (1989): 'Das Unternehmen einer Grundlegung zur Metaphysik der Sitten', in Höffe, O., (ed.): Grundlegung zur Metaphysik der Sitten. Ein kooperativer Kommentar, Frankfurt, pp. 13–30.

Brandt, R. (1988): 'Der Zirkel im dritten Abschnitte von Kants Grundlegung zur Metaphysik der Sitten,' in Oberer, H., and Seel, G. (eds.): Kant. Analysen – Probleme – Kritik, Würzburg, pp. 169–191.

Freudiger, J. (1993): Kants Begründung der praktischen Philosophie. Systematische Stellung, Methode und Argumentationsstruktur der 'Grundlegung zur Metaphysik der Sitten,' Bern/Stuttgart/Vienna.

Hösle, V. (1990): Die Krise der Gegenwart und die Verantwortung der Philosophie, Munich.

Kaulbach, F. (1988): Immanuel Kants 'Grundlegung zur Metaphysik der Sitten.' Interpretation und Kommentar, Darmstadt.

Paton, H. J. (1962): Der kategorische Imperativ. Eine Untersuchung über Kants Moralphilosophie, Berlin.

Vorländer, K. (1965): 'Einleitung' zu Kants 'Grundlegung zur Metaphysik der Sitten,' Hamburg (reprint of third edition).

Wolff, R. P. (1973): The Autonomy of Reason. A Commentary on Kant's Groundwork of the Metaphysics of Morals, New York.

5

Reason Practical in Its Own Right

Gerold Prauss

All of the relevant German dictionaries we have previously consulted for philosophical purposes have failed us in one important respect.[1] None of them so much as mentions the fact, let alone furnishes the requisite examples for the fact, that the German word *eigen* can be employed in both a reflexive pronominal sense as well as in a possessive adjectival sense. This is ignored even with regard to compound expressions such as *Eigenliebe* (self-love) or *Eigenlob* (self-praise), where the relevant part of the compound provides the dominant element rather than the subsidiary element of meaning. For 'self-love' is not the love that one finds in oneself, in contrast to the love that another feels, but the love one feels *for oneself* rather than for someone else, and 'self-praise' likewise is something one bestows *upon oneself* rather than upon another. The possessive sense as distinct from the reflexive sense of the word – the sense that the love I feel towards myself can only be my love, that the praise I bestow on myself can only be my praise – is so self-evident, I believe, that is not explicitly expressed in such cases at all.

Yet it is precisely in the reflexive sense that Kant himself specifically employs the word *eigen*, although the possessive sense that is necessarily

---

[1] *Grammatisches-kritisches Wörterbuch der hochdeutschen Mundart* (J. Chr. Adelung), Leipzig 1793; *Handwörterbuch der deutschen Sprache* (J. Chr. Aug. Heyse and K. W. L. Heyse), Magdeburg 1833; *Deutsches Wörterbuch* (J. and W. Grimm), Leipzig 1862; *Deutsches Wörterbuch* (M. Heyne), Leipzig 1890; *Deutsches Wörterbuch* (M. Heyne), Leipzig 1905; *Trübners deutsches Wörtebuch* (ed. A. Götze), Berlin 1940; *Etymologisches Wörterbuch der deutschen Sprache* (F. Kluge), Berlin 1957; *Deutsches Wörterbuch* (H. Paul, W. Betz), Tübingen 1966.

connected with and harboured within the word also occasionally appears too. And this reflexive use seems to be rather frequent in the *Groundwork* in particular, although this may not indeed immediately catch our attention. I will therefore supply a number of relevant references to specific remarks that seem quite unambiguous to me,[2] and that any close analytical commentary on the *Groundwork* must certainly examine with care. For it appears to me that the reflexive character of these remarks, something to which no explicit attention has apparently been paid before, first opens up authentic access to a quite systematically decisive line of thought that Kant pursues in the third section of the *Groundwork*. In addition to noting the textual references already supplied, one can clearly see that the following references from pages 448–450 alone (cf. 448, 14, 20f.; 449, 10f.; 450, 23) can only be read and interpreted reflexively: one's 'own consciousness' (448, 14) must be glossed as 'self-consciousness,' one's 'own legislation' (449, 10f.) as 'self-legislation,' and, above all, one's 'own will' (448, 20) as 'will directed to itself' or as 'willing itself.'

From the overall context in which these remarks are made, we can also clearly see the real reason that prompts Kant to adopt a doubly problematic position with regard to the reality of freedom. He writes (1) that 'we can escape here from the burden that weighs upon theory' (Gr:448, 34f) because (2) 'every being that cannot act otherwise than under the idea of freedom is just because of that really free in a practical respect – that is, all laws that are inseparably bound up with freedom hold for him just as if his will had also been validly pronounced free also in itself and in theoretical philosophy' (Gr:448, 4f.). But a merely imagined freedom cannot be treated in the same way as real freedom because then action itself would also simply be something imaginary, amounting in reality to nothing but a concatenation of empirical events. But then it is only by demonstrating the reality of freedom, and demonstrating it precisely through 'theory,' that is, philosophy – that one can demonstrate a validly binding law for all

[2] 4: 422: 24; 424: 22, 33; 431: 20, 22; 433: 7, 23; 436: 24; 438: 18; 440: 7, 17; 441: 4, 18. One cannot of course expect that this emphatically reflexive sense simply reveals itself immediately in all these cases without further ado. This is ruled out by the fact that the word *eigen* is indeed generally used in German in a possessive sense. The analysis of the relevant passages demands the appropriate effort and attention on the reader's part in engaging closely and directly with the text. Anyone who explicitly tries to read *eigen* here in a genuinely possessive sense (as signifying 'mine *but not hers*,' 'mine *but not his*,' and so on.), will discover that all these cases, with full support of the relevant context, actually resist this reading and emphatically demand the reflexive interpretation. Citations refer to the *Akademieausgabe*, whereas citations from the *Critique of Pure Reason* refer to the first (A) and second editions (B).

action that arises from freedom. It is only because Kant's actual attempt to provide such a 'deduction' proved unsuccessful that he appears, after the *Groundwork*, to have regarded the task as insoluble in principle.

The reason for this actual failure is clearly revealed by the remarks that, as we have insisted, can only properly be read in a reflexive sense. Kant was actually unable to develop an adequate theory of subjectivity as intrinsic self-relation, a theory that would elucidate such self-relation not simply in general but in the specific theoretical and practical sense of one's 'own consciousness' and one's 'own will,' and would pay due attention to the relevant common features and specific differences involved here. But this failure also led Kant to underestimate the initial far-reaching and significant contributions he himself had already successfully made to clarify these matters. For the reflexive sense of the remarks that form a kind of bridge between pages 446f. and 451 is also an indication that the third section of the *Groundwork* is concerned, from the very beginning, with nothing less than this theoretically and practically complex self-relation of subjectivity itself. It is this self-relation that appears, under various terms and descriptions, on page 451f.: as something 'active in its own right' (Gr:452, 3), whose 'pure activity' (Gr:451, 33), further described as 'pure self-activity' (Gr:452, 9f.) and 'pure spontaneity' (Gr:452, 18), remains thoroughly ambiguous in both theoretical and practical respects. For this 'pure activity' is also described both as 'understanding' (Gr:451, 6; 452, 10) and as 'reason' (Gr:452, 9), or the 'intelligence' (Gr:452, 23f.) that makes us what we are, through which we produce 'ideas' (Gr:452, 18) and 'representations' (Gr:448, 20f.; 452, 32) 'from within ourselves' (Gr:451, 11), and is then further described, as earlier in the text, as our 'own will' (Gr:448, 20f.;452, 32) and even as the power of 'free choice' [*Willkür*] (Gr:452, 32).

It is clear, terminologically speaking, that we should take the last-mentioned characterisation of practical self-relation in particular very seriously since the *Critique of Pure Reason* also describes the *a priori* 'synthesis' that underlies all a posteriori synthesis in Kant's view as a 'free synthesis' [*willkürliche Synthesis*] (4: A 221, B 269). And the context clearly indicates that the word *willkürlich* is here being used in a sense that would have to be translated in English as 'voluntary' rather than as 'arbitrary.' If 'theoretical' concepts such as the synthesis that belongs to the cognitive process of the understanding can be interpreted in terms of practical concepts such as 'will' and 'choice,' and if the practical character of the will as the principle of action can in turn be interpreted in terms of theoretical concepts such as 'intelligence' or 'reason,' this only serves to

confirm how difficult it actually is to decide whether the self-relation of
subjectivity in Kant should be understood as theoretical or practical in
character, or somehow as both, and what precisely this would mean in
each case.

Given the difficulties of decisively resolving this question, Kant's insistence that he cannot lay claim to a 'positive concept of freedom' (Gr:447, 17)
because it is impossible to demonstrate the latter 'as something real in
ourselves and in human nature' (Gr:448, 26f.) is particularly surprising
because the very 'deduction' of moral obligation appears to depend on
it, as we have already pointed out. For Kant is at least equally insistent in
making the well-known claim: 'If, therefore, freedom of the will is presupposed, morality together with its principle follows from it by mere
analysis of its concept' (Gr:447, 8ff.; see also CPrR: 5:31, 24ff.). If the
question concerning the theoretical or practical character of the self-relation of subjectivity has not yet been adequately resolved or decided, then
it also remains an open question as to whether Kant may properly be in
a position to make use of a positive concept of freedom as an already
demonstrated actuality after all. For he is no less insistent, at least after
completing the first *Critique*, that he has indeed 'deduced' the 'categories'
as 'pure concepts of the understanding,' and thereby that 'absolute spontaneity' of the 'understanding' that he has already described as 'autonomy'
(cf. 5:196, 24; 20:225, 21ff.;18:250, 13ff., Refl. 5608). And this absolute
spontaneity, which Kant also characterises as 'freedom' (cf. 4:290, 24f.;
16:386, 18f.; 18:182f., 176), must at least have something in common with
that spontaneity that would be required for the proposed 'deduction' of
moral obligation. For the spontaneity in question here cannot be understood as itself already possessing a morally obligating character.

What prevents us from appealing precisely to this absolute spontaneity
as a freedom that has already been demonstrated as far as the 'deduction'
of moral obligation is concerned? For the freedom involved here is no
more empirically knowable than that of moral obligation itself, though
Kant, remarkably enough, repeatedly points this out only with respect to
the latter (see, for example, CPrR: 5:48, 20ff.). But this certainly does not
prevent Kant from treating freedom as the legitimately 'deduced' foundation of the *Critique of Pure Reason*. And it is simply inconceivable
that Kant would refuse to embark upon the project of the first *Critique*
simply because subjectivity as absolute spontaneity could never itself be
discovered within experience.

It seems to me that there is only one plausible reason why Kant does not
take, or even consider, the step we have suggested. And it comes to light

if we attempt, in his place, to provide this answer to the aforementioned question, a question that Kant himself probably failed to pose explicitly only because he regarded the answer as self-evident: we cannot introduce the absolute spontaneity of the understanding, or the 'freedom' and 'autonomy' that also already underlies all cognitive activity, as the required presupposition for a 'deduction' of moral obligation simply because such spontaneity is merely 'theoretical' in character. But we only have to formulate this hypothetical answer in order to appreciate its inadequacy. For it would immediately turn the whole enterprise of providing a transcendental theory of knowledge and experience – in short, Kant's entire theoretical philosophy – into nothing but a vicious circle, and destroy it in principle from the very start.

Formulated very briefly for the purpose of clarification, the fundamental thesis of Kant's theoretical philosophy amounts to this: knowledge or experience – in short, theory – can be explained only by reference to spontaneity. But if this were interpreted to mean that theory can only be explained through theoretical spontaneity, that all the elements through which it is built up can only be explained in purely theoretical terms, then the thesis would already presuppose precisely what it was supposed to explain by recourse to spontaneity in the first place, and would be quite incapable of saying anything illuminating about theory and the theoretical domain in general. For the situation is further complicated, as far as Kant is concerned, because he clearly cannot appeal to the kind of traditional 'receptive' conception of theory that he has expressly repudiated through well-known arguments of his own. Kant's task, on the contrary, is to develop a spontaneous, and thus entirely novel, conception of theory on the basis of spontaneity itself, rather than simply presupposing a conception already implied by spontaneity.

For precisely this reason we cannot also exclude the thought that absolute spontaneity as self-activity, in the reflexive sense of one's 'own' will and consciousness that is indivisibly theoretical and practical at once, should itself be identified as reason that is practical in its own right. It is this latter concept that first allows, and also requires, us to develop and distinguish both theory and practice, the latter understood here in the narrower sense in which it is generally contrasted with the purely theoretical domain. It effectively provides a 'deduction' that can, and indeed must, ground the reality of moral obligation. Close consideration of the argumentative context to which these expressly self-reflexive references belong suggests the following methodological proposal: over against the second *Critique*, which appears to abandon the task of providing such a deduction, we should read the *Groundwork*, historically and systematically, as evidence that Kant regarded the solution of this problem as something still to be accomplished (even if the *Critique of Practical Reason* seems to imply the opposite).

This concept of the will as a reflexive self-relation is crucially important not only in order to grasp the deduction of the intrinsic relation of the will to moral obligation, but also if we are to understand what Kant can possibly mean by a morally 'good' will, irrespective of whether the relevant deduction has already been accomplished or not. In conclusion here, I will show that Kant inevitably risks misinterpretation when he attempts, at least in principle, to determine the sense of the term 'good' with reference to 'the good will' unless we already clearly grasp the following: the relevant meaning of 'good' here arises exclusively from the idea of the 'will' as reflexive self-relation, a conception that Kant presupposes here, but never fully explicates as such.

We can already see this from the very first sentence of the first section of the *Groundwork*: 'It is impossible to think of anything at all in the world, or indeed even beyond it, that could be considered good without limitation except a good **will**' (Gr:393). Unfortunately, a purely external circumstance has served to obscure what Kant is effectively presupposing right from the beginning. For the fact that *both* of the last words of this sentence appear in the original text in bold type, unlike the form in which I have cited it here, only conceals the fact that the proper emphasis, in accordance with the intrinsic sense of the passage, belongs exclusively to the word 'will', and cannot possibly refer to the word 'good.' Bold print serves in Kant, and not merely in the *Groundwork* but clearly throughout his other writings as well, only to indicate a sort of text-internal title that draws the reader's attention to the themes, key words, or technical terms that are subject to analysis in the relevant discussion. In other words, this device is indeed used to indicate general emphasis, but never to clarify the specific meaning of a sentence by assigning a distinct and particular emphasis upon individual terms or words.

If we therefore ignore the bold type, as the context here requires us to, we see not only that the true emphasis can only apply to the word 'will,' as opposed to the word 'good', but also precisely why this is the case. From the beginning, from the very first sentence of the text, Kant is not concerned with the meaning of the term 'good,' which the actual formulation of the sentence itself indicates is already being presupposed here, but exclusively with identifying that which can be regarded as good 'without limitation,' or as 'absolutely' (394, 32), 'unconditionally' (394, 1) and 'utterly' (394, 3) good. For what initially appears unintelligible, and surely stands in need of further clarification, is precisely the idea of something that is 'utterly,' 'absolutely,' and 'unconditionally' good. The meaning of 'good' itself, on the other hand, appears entirely self-evident because it always signifies something 'relatively' and 'conditionally' good, rather than 'absolutely' or 'unconditionally' good. Kant, and anyone else, can easily find abundant examples of things that are good in the former sense of the term. But in every such case, this means 'good' only in the sense of 'useful,' 'good *for something*,' and thus '*relatively* good' – that is, relatively to the end for which it serves as a means. In every such case, in accordance with the specific end in question, something can 'also be extremely evil and harmful' unless 'a good *will* is present' [my emphasis, GP], or if 'the will' that is to 'make use' of such things 'is not good' (393, 11–17).

Kant's remarks here, which can only mean 'if this will itself is bad or evil,' clearly reveal one thing: the entire argument is unintelligible from the start unless we grasp that it applies to the bad or evil will as much as it does to the good will. Kant is concerned here not with clarifying the meaning of the term 'good,' but solely with that of the expressions 'absolutely,' 'unconditionally,' and 'without limitation'. It is therefore irrelevant whether we prefer to elucidate this meaning with examples of something '*good* without limitation,' 'unconditionally *good*,' or 'absolutely *good*,' or of something '*evil* without limitation,' 'unconditionally *evil*' or 'absolutely *evil*,' or '*bad* without limitation,' 'unconditionally *bad*,' or 'absolutely *bad*.'

The proper understanding of Kant's opening sentence thus crucially depends upon our grasping that its meaning is not merely preserved, but is only fully revealed when the term 'good' is replaced here by the terms 'bad' or 'evil.' for it is equally true to say: 'It is impossible to think of anything at all in the world, or indeed even beyond it, that could be considered bad or evil without limitation except a bad or evil **will**.' And this implies nothing less than the following: if there is indeed anything that can meaningfully be qualified as 'good,' or as 'bad' or 'evil,' then it is only a good, or a bad or evil, *will* that can be considered good 'without limitation' or bad or evil 'without limitation.'

Only if we put it this way can we clearly appreciate the exclusive character of Kant's claim and the full burden of proof he is effectively assuming here: whatever there may be in the world, or even beyond it, it is not *conceptually* possible that is, – it is quite *impossible* because it is intrinsically *self-contradictory* – for anything, however good or bad or evil it may be, to be so 'absolutely,' 'unconditionally' or 'without limitation,' unless

we are precisely speaking here of a *will*. This is therefore implied by the
very concepts that Kant deploys in his analysis and derives from his fundamental distinction between beings possessed of 'will' and beings of any
other kind. What precisely is this concept of the will, and the contrasting
concept of beings without a will, that must already have been fairly clear
to Kant himself in order to make the kind of claims he does here?

Indeed Kant seems to be so clear about the relevant distinction in
his own mind that he not only fails to develop it any further, but even
manages to conceal its significance somewhat by the language that he
actually employs. Thus, without further elucidation, he marks the distinction by speaking of the 'worth' [*Wert*], indeed of the 'absolute' (394, 32),
'unconditioned' (391, 1) or 'inner' (396, 4) worth of the will, in comparison with which anything else can only ever possess an 'external' worth
of 'usefulness' (394, 26). Kant even compares the will to a 'jewel' that
possesses 'its full worth in itself' and would still 'shine by itself' without
any reference whatever to 'usefulness.' For usefulness would never represent more than a 'setting' that could 'neither add anything to nor take
anything from' (394, 25–28) the worth of the will itself.

This mode of expression, however, can easily encourage the impression
that Kant is attempting to distinguish quantitatively between higher and
lower levels of worth here – as if he were making the remarkable claim
that different kinds of things cannot possess the highest worth and that
only one kind of thing – the will – can properly possess it.

Every interpreter who has ever struggled in vain to identify the criterion that would justify Kant's evaluation, and permit him to distinguish
between a high, a higher, and the highest worth, has fallen under this mistaken impression to a greater or lesser degree. No one appears to have realised that this insoluble issue is an entirely self-created pseudo-problem.
Kant is not concerned with a quantitative question at all when he speaks of
measure or 'estimation' [*Schätzung*] (394, 2, 16, 33) in relation to worth.
He is elucidating, or at least beginning to elucidate, a purely qualitative
question concerning a distinction between fundamentally different kinds
of things in this world, 'or indeed even beyond it.' This is the distinction
between that which is a will, and always stands in relation to itself, and
that which is not a will, and always stands in relation to something else,
but never to itself.

In order to illustrate the latter case, and to provide contrasting
emphasis, Kant deliberately chooses examples that seem very close to the
former case and can therefore easily be confused with it. He thus refers to
the 'talents of mind' such as 'understanding,' 'wit,' and 'judgement,' and

especially to 'courage, resolution, and perseverance in one's plans' (393, 7ff.). And it is only subsequently that he then mentions things that might seem to be more remote from the will itself – namely, the 'gifts of fortune': 'Power, riches, honour, even health and that complete well-being and satisfaction with one's own condition called *happiness*' (393, 13).

But while all this may at first sight seem to be more closely or more remotely related to the will, it is in fact entirely qualitatively distinct rather than quantitatively distinct from the latter. It is fundamentally different from and so little identical with the will that it represents precisely the 'other' of the will at whose disposal it always simply stands. The will is free to 'make use' (393, 12) of those things that can only be described as good or bad in each case *according to the way in which* the will 'makes' this 'use' of them (393, 10–13). It is precisely through the 'use' that first makes these things into a 'means' to a certain 'end' that they are external to the will that makes use of them and to the end for which they are used, that they must in principle be defined in terms of heteronomy.

But by the same token – and this is the decisive point that Kant himself never adequately clarified – the will that makes such use of things cannot in principle be itself something that the will in turn simply makes use of. That would merely produce the absurdity of an infinite regress in the self-use of the will. For one can only really 'use' something other than oneself, something from which one originally distinguishes oneself and to which one therefore stands in a special relation. The will that makes use of things cannot in principle be anything but this 'using' itself. For what we call 'will' is precisely the source of all using of anything, something that can therefore only ever use something that is other than itself.

Will in this sense stands in principle over against everything else that is not will, stands exclusively in a relationship to itself. This is the autonomy, the absolutely free or spontaneous self-determination, from which all 'using' as 'acting' first arises. It is only because will constitutes such self-relation as autonomous self-determination that it can be a will that, *when good*, is so 'absolutely,' 'unconditionally,' and 'without limitation,' or that, *when bad or evil*, is also so 'absolutely,' 'unconditionally,' and 'without limitation.' For in fact, the will is absolute, unconditioned, without limitation, and so on, quite irrespective of whether, as original self-relation, it likewise stands in relation to something other than itself, something that it makes use of for the sake of something else. And it is only in relation to the latter that the will can also be described as good or bad in a 'relative,' 'conditional,' or 'limited' sense – that is, as beneficial or detrimental with respect to someone or something else.

Only when the structure of the will has been identified and clarified in principle can we meaningfully ask *on what ground* a will that is already in its own right 'absolute' or 'unconditioned' or 'without limitation' can itself further be described as *good* absolutely, *good* unconditionally, *good* without limitation, or as *bad or evil* absolutely, *bad or evil* unconditionally, *bad or evil* without limitation. For such a will, and that means for Kant a morally good or evil will, can be useful or detrimental with respect to something else, can indeed through one and the same act be useful for one thing and detrimental for another, without thereby losing or gaining in the slightest anything for its character as a moral will.

The thing that has to this day prevented not only Kant but also his interpreters from fully explicating this idea of the will is the difficulty we have already discussed: that of grasping and articulating a self-relation that is practical as well as theoretical. To this day, Kant himself and his interpreters have failed to broach this problem, and when it comes to the really decisive point, they have generally fallen back upon interpreting the will itself in naturalistic and empirical terms as 'drive' or 'inclination' and so on.

But the decisive point emphatically reveals itself precisely when Kant attempts systematically to deduce the will not merely as an autonomous self-relation in general but over and beyond this as one that autonomously subjects itself to moral obligation. For only an autonomy that is always already present can also limit itself as a specifically moral autonomy; only an acting that is always already productive in its own right can also command itself to 'act *in such a way* …'; only a will that is always already active can determine itself in terms of the ought itself. But all of this is possible only on the basis of a further and additional ground that must somehow reveal itself through this autonomous willing and acting. It cannot be derived from the latter in a purely analytical manner but only, in a sense that still requires further clarification, in a synthetic fashion. In precisely this sense, therefore, that constitutes the entire problem that has not been properly resolved to this day – any deduction of the necessity for assuming such a ground as the free self-imposition of moral obligation can only proceed synthetically.

The fact that Kant did not actually succeed in presenting such a deduction himself certainly does not prove that the task is impossible in principle, and that our sense of moral obligation must therefore remain nothing but a 'fact of reason,' nothing but what Kant paradoxically enough describes as an 'a priori fact' (CPrR:5:31). There are those who still defend and exploit this position today, even though they could or should know better, precisely in order to claim that autonomy of itself – that is, analytically – already signifies moral autonomy, that willing of itself – that is, analytically – is already subject to moral obligation. Just because Kant himself failed to accomplish his task completely, these defenders simply transform moral philosophy as a rational enterprise into a dogmatic moral ideology that is as remote from Kant's intentions as it is possible to imagine. Even for the most refined Christian thinker, this inevitably converts autonomy back into heteronomy of one kind or another, and simply produces in an impoverished form of Christianity at best. For what is more authentically Christian than the thought that the subject can only be good or evil in a properly absolute sense insofar as it does not merely autonomously heed, or autonomously infringe, the demands of moral obligation, but rather in advance of both possibilities has already autonomously *imposed* moral obligation upon himself as something *to be* heeded? But if such imposition is not simply to imply a circular argument (an autonomous relation to morality on the basis of an autonomous relation to morality) that is ultimately vacuous, it cannot arise from an autonomy that is itself already moral, but only from an original autonomy that is itself still morally neutral. It can only arise from a reason that is indeed already practical in its own right, though precisely one that is thereby not yet or already moral.[3]

---

[3] For the fundamental importance of the concept of 'reason that is practical in its own right,' and its significance for the entire structure of Kant's philosophy, see G. Prauss, *Kant über Freiheit als Autonomie*, Frankfurt 1983.

6

Kant's Justification of the Role of Maxims in Ethics

Michael Albrecht

Kant's moral theory has been generally characterised in a variety of ways: as a formalist ethics, as an ethics of duty, as a deontological ethics, and so forth. But it is also an important feature of Kant's theory that it represents what we can call an 'ethic of maxims.' Otfried Höffe, one of the most thorough contemporary interpreters of Kant's thought, introduced this expression precisely to emphasise the central role played by the concept of a maxim in Kant's ethics.[1] For, after all, the Categorical Imperative does not command: Act in this (or that way), nor does it instruct us: Act in accordance with this (or that) intention. What it actually prescribes is: 'Act according to a maxim which can at the same time serve as a universal law.' This is the formulation that Kant provides in the *Metaphysics of Morals* (*Doctrine of Right*: 6:225). But in all the other passages, in all of his other works, where he attempts to define the Categorical Imperative, Kant always relates the latter explicitly to the role and significance of maxims.[2] It is precisely maxims, and maxims alone, as Höffe says, that form the authentic 'object' of the Categorical Imperative.

---

[1] Otfried Höffe, *Immanuel Kant* (Albany 1994), pp. 145ff.
[2] Oswald Schwemmer has identified nine such explicit formulations in Kant's work. See O. Schwemmer, *Philosophie der Praxis. Versuch zur Grundlegung einer Lehre vom moralischen Argumentieren in Verbindung mit einer Interpretation der praktischen Philosophie Kants* (Frankfurt am Main 1971), p. 133; Schwemmer, 'Vernunft und Moral. Versuch einer kritischen Rekonstruktion des kategorischen Imperativs bei Kant,' in *Kant. Zur Deutung seiner Theorie von Erkennen und Handeln*, ed. G. Prauss (Cologne 1973), pp. 255–273; p. 257.

The following considerations do not attempt, as part of a general historical interpretation of Kant, to elucidate his ethical thought as a whole, nor to decide the best way of characterising his ethics as a whole, but simply to clarify the question of an 'ethic of maxims' itself. In other words, I shall work to elucidate Kant's theory precisely insofar as it is an ethic of maxims, although there is of course no question that this formulation certainly captures a fundamental dimension of Kant's ethical thought as a whole. This will involve (1) clarifying Kant's concept of a maxim as such, (2) enquiring after the source of the concept in question, (3) liberating the interpretation of his 'ethic of maxims' from the numerous misunderstandings to which it has been subject in the Kant literature, (4) attempting to answer a specific question already raised in research on Kant but never satisfactorily resolved, and finally (5) raising a question that has never even been posed by Kant research – the question of an authentic *grounding* for an ethic of maxims. I shall not directly address the question of whether Kant is right concerning the kind of justification he offers.[3]

But why does this important and indeed frequently discussed problem of Kant scholarship still require this degree of further clarification? The reason, I believe, lies in the fact that the secondary literature has hitherto almost exclusively limited itself to examining the texts that constitute Kant's two principal works in the field of ethics, the *Groundwork of the Metaphysics of Morals* and the *Critique of Practical Reason*. But why has such scant attention been paid to Kant's other relevant texts in this connection? Surely this is because in his other texts, such as the *Observations on the Feeling of Beautiful and the Sublime* or the various lectures on 'Anthropology,' Kant speaks almost exclusively of 'principles' [*Grundsätze*] rather than of 'maxims.' It would appear that commentators were always wary of identifying the terminology of principles and maxims in Kant's work.[4] It is precisely here that we must seek the methodological

[3] Otfried Höffe, 'Kants kategorischer Imperativ als Kriterium des Sittlichen,' in *Zeitschrift für philosophische Forschung* 31 (1977), pp. 354–384; p. 356; reprinted in O. Höffe, *Ethik und Politik. Grundmodelle und -probleme der praktischen Philosophie* (Frankfurt am Main 1979), pp. 84–119; p. 86.
[4] The entry 'Grundsätze, praktische' in Eisler's *Kant-Lexicon* makes absolutely no reference to 'maxims,' and the entry 'Maxime' no reference to 'Grundsätze.' It hardly needs pointing out that Kant also employs the term 'Prinzip' as an equivalent for 'Grundsatz' (and thus also for 'Maxime') – see *Groundwork*: 4:422). The fact that Chapter 1 of the *Critique of Practical Reason* treats 'Grundsätze' as the broader and higher concept in relation to 'Maxime' and 'Gesetz' is no real cause for serious confusion since Kant never uses the word 'Grundsatz' when he is talking exclusively about 'the moral law' itself.

key for developing a better understanding of Kant's 'ethic of maxims.'
Kant did in fact use the terms 'maxim' and 'principle' as synonyms. For
the borrowed term *Maxime* was rightly recognised as French in origin,
the vernacular German equivalent of which was simply *Grundsatz*, or
'principle.'

This brings us directly to our first question: what precisely is a maxim?
In §1 of the *Critique of Practical Reason* (5:19), Kant defines maxims
as *subjective practical principles*. What does Kant understand by this?
'Practical' signifies that such principles determine a course of action, or
refraining from one – that is, are action-guiding determinations of the
will. They are thus rules 'in accordance with which the subject *acts*'
(*Groundwork of the Metaphysics of Morals*: 4:421 note), or more precisely 'wills to act' (*Doctrine of Right*: 6:225).⁵ Second, maxims represent
practical *principles*. On the one hand, this implies a certain intentional
persistence in the application of maxims, and on the other, a certain
importance with regard to the acting subject. Maxims are valid over time
and concern the continually ongoing series of particular cases to which
they must be applied. Acting in accordance with maxims over time thus
presupposes strength of will (*Doctrine of Virtue*: 6:394). As fundamental
principles [*Grundsätze*] they are also universal in character (A35/5: 19).
This does not imply a logical hierarchy, but simply underlines the fact that
the principles are important to the subject that entertains these maxims.

It should also be pointed out that Kant treats 'Regel' (rule) as a general term as well.
There are certainly passages where it is difficult to determine whether these words for
'principle' ('Grundsatz' or 'Prinzip') are being used as an equivalent for 'maxim' or are
being employed as the higher and more general concept. See the pioneering essay on this
issue by Rüdiger Bittner, 'Maximen,' in *Akten des 4. Internationalen Kant-Kongresses,
Mainz, 6–10 April 1974. Teil II.2: Sektionen*, ed. G. Funke (Berlin/New York 1974), pp.
485–498; p. 491.
⁵ Kant is already defining a maxim as a 'subjective principle of willing' in the *Groundwork*
(4:400, note). Kant's later formulation in the *Doctrine of Right* (6:225) captures precisely
the same thought and sounds as if it were intended to clarify a passage in the *Groundwork*
(4:421 note) that might easily be misinterpreted to imply that all actions proceed in
accordance with maxims. Kant is actually there referring to the distinction between the
objective 'ought' and its actualisation in and through the maxims of the subject. See also
Marcus Willaschek, *Praktische Vernunft. Handlungstheorie und Moralbegründung bei
Kant* (Stuttgart/Weimar 1992), p. 67. The formulation of the Categorical Imperative that
we have cited earlier (from the *Doctrine of Right*: 4:421) also reads as if it were intended
as a corrected and clarified version of the difficult formulation presented earlier in the
Groundwork (4:421). On the other hand, the difficulty involved in that formulation ('act
only in accordance with that maxim through which you can at the same time will that it
become a universal law') is also effectively reproduced in one of Kant's later formulations
from 1796 ('according to which you can at the same time will,' and so on) in the essay
Zum ewigen Frieden in der Philosophie (8:420).

If something is so specific to the individual subject as to be ethically irrelevant, it will not generally be made into a maxim in the first place, if the subject is to avoid falling victim to a certain 'micrology,' as Kant puts it. Whether 'I eat fish or meat, if both are agreeable to me' is ethically indifferent (*adiophoron*) (*Doctrine of Virtue*: 6:09). In his book on Kant's ethics, Harald Köhl says: 'We don't make maxims for ourselves with regard to anything and everything.' And he is quite right. But he is wrong to think that he is thereby contradicting Kant's view of the matter.[6]

Third, the fact that maxims are *subjective* must be understood in several senses. This simply means that maxims are not 'objective' – that is, they are not objective principles, or practical laws, that are binding for the will of every rational being (5:19). Kant calls these laws 'imperatives' and identifies the Categorical Imperative as the 'Fundamental Law' that underlies them all (5:30). Maxims are only ethically justified if they can satisfy the Categorical Imperative – are capable of being universalised – that is, can themselves be turned into laws. On the other hand, the maxims reveal themselves precisely thereby as those rules of action through which we are actually capable of pursuing what *should* happen. The unconditional *validity* of the moral law in no way implies that a given individual necessarily obeys it. The moral law finds its own application only through the maxims in accordance with which the subject wills to act.[7] The ethical demand is thereby extended to the maxims themselves: one *ought* to make maxims for oneself.

As subjective principles, our maxims, as distinct from the objectivity that consists in the mere form of universalisability, also possess a certain

---

[6] Harald Köhl, *Kants Gesinnungsethik* (Berlin/New York 1990), p. 60. Köhl even combines this with the claim that one can act according to maxims that one has not expressly chosen for oneself. Instead of examining the directly relevant concept of habituation in this connection, he feels entitled to raise the simple objection: 'The idea that we always act in accordance with maxims that we have consciously *chosen* for ourselves is empirically mistaken' (ibid.).

[7] *Groundwork*: 4:420f. note. See *Critique of Pure Reason*: B 830: 'Laws which are imperatives, that is, are objective *laws of freedom*, and which tell *what ought to happen*, although perhaps it never does happen ...'; B 840: 'Practical laws, insofar as they become at the same time subjective grounds of actions, that is, become subjective principles, are called *maxims*. [....] the *observance* of its laws' [i.e. those of morality] 'is effected [...] in accordance with maxims.' Mellin emphasises this point strongly: 'All practical laws, that is, laws in according with which something ought to happen ... must become such maxims ... if they are really to be acted upon. ... The practical law 'do not steal' may always remain what it is, but it is only acted upon once someone also ... makes it into a determining, that is, subjective principle, of willing and acting.' G. S. A. Mellin, *Encylopädisches Wörterbuch der kritischen Philosophie*, vol. 4, Section 1 (Jena/Leipzig 1801; reprinted Aaalen 1971), p. 173f.

'material content,' an 'end' in terms of which the subject grounds and justifies its maxims.[8] Marcus Willaschek is mistaken, therefore, when he writes that 'maxims precisely do not concern a specific concrete purpose, but the way in which we act.'[9] The preservation of health, or the love of truth, for example, may be purposes that are difficult to accomplish, but they are not questions of mere form, for they are ends of willing that one can make into maxims for oneself. Whether one actually does so depends upon the kind of person one is. Human beings are very different from one another and can therefore make different maxims for themselves, as Kant says, 'in accordance with the conditions of the subject' in question.[10] This does not mean that there can only ever be purely individual maxims in each case. Different individuals can certainly accept one and the same maxim. This is because maxims, as Kant says in the same place, are themselves determined by the *reason* present in the subject. Since every human being has access to reason, it is perfectly possible for one and the same maxim to be adopted by different people. On the other hand, it is quite possible for any individual to change significantly in the course of life. The fact that maxims are determined by reason does not of itself mean that one cannot change or abandon one's maxims. For rational reflection itself can precisely lead us to do so and encourage us to adopt other maxims for oneself.

This serves to highlight a further feature of the way in which maxims are intrinsically related to the individual subject: a maxim represents an obligation of the specific subject in relation to itself. The maxim does not express what one in general should do, but rather what a particular individual actually wills to do. Maxims are 'self-chosen,'[11] and this is a specific achievement of the subject insofar as it thereby binds itself in its actions to 'rules which it lays upon itself,' as Kant puts it.[12] Maxims therefore are not rules that may somehow appear binding in general, but simply those rules that an individual human being obliges himself to follow. The aspect of achievement involved here is effectively captured by Kant's observation that very few people actually have maxims in this sense.[13]

[8] *Groundwork*: 4:436; *Doctrine of Virtue*: 6:394f.
[9] Willaschek, *Praktische Vernunft*, p. 75.
[10] *Groundwork*: 4:421 note.
[11] 15/2:521 (Refl. 1179).
[12] *Groundwork*: 4:438.
[13] It is 'a rare thing' for individuals to act in accordance with principles (*Anthropology*: 7:292).

This is a view that Kant consistently continued to maintain throughout all the other changes and internal developments of his moral philosophy.

The last important aspect of Kant's concept of maxims lies in their acknowledged plurality. Whereas there is only one fundamental principle of morality, the Categorical Imperative itself, several different maxims are operative for any given individual who regulates his own action and conduct in a principled fashion. From an anthropological perspective, Kant is interested in the idea of 'character' as an inner coherence of our various maxims.[14] Of course, we have long since ceased to entertain the kind of high expectations with regard to character that are implied by Kant's conception of the importance of maxims. What we tend to understand by the term 'character' today corresponds rather to what Kant called the 'natural disposition' of human beings.[15] The plurality of maxims possesses systematic significance for Kant not merely because it reveals the need to establish an inner coherence amongst the various maxims of the individual subject, but also because it explains how different maxims of greater or lesser degrees of universality can nonetheless all be subsumed under the concept of a maxim.

For example, if someone proceeds to act in accordance with the maxim of living as independently as possible, then from this more general maxim he can derive a series of other maxims, such as that of not incurring debts, for example.[16] Or if someone has adopted the maxim of always treating his own body in such a way that he may continue uninterruptedly to engage in intellectual and scholarly labour for as long as possible,[17] then he can also adopt the maxim of not smoking his pipe more than once a day, for example.[18] Even if the more general maxims effectively concern one's conduct of life as a whole, whereas the other derived maxims translate these fundamental and far-reaching proposals into the actual labour of everyday life, this latter process also essentially involves subjective-practical principles – namely, maxims. For they, too, like the more overarching principles, are articulated in the light of the individual's rational reflection on the specific ends that are important for the conduct of one's life.

---

[14] *Anthropology*: 7:295;15/2:521 (Refl. 1179).

[15] *Anthropology*: 7:285.

[16] *Immanuel Kant. Sein Leben in Darstellungen von Zeitgenossen. Die Biographien* von Ludwig Ernst Borowski, Reinhold Bernard Jachmann, und Ehregott Andreas Christian Wasianski (Darmstadt 1968; reprint of the 1912 Berlin edition of Felix Gross, cited henceforth as *Biographien*), p. 64 (Borowski).

[17] Ibid., p. 52 (Borowski).

[18] Ibid., p. 150 (Jachmann).

They represent a persisting obligation over time which the subject lays upon himself precisely to decide relevant courses of action in accordance with these self-imposed rules of behaviour.

The examples we have offered here are not derived from Kant's texts. We have chosen alternative ones precisely because Kant's own illustrations, which the critical reception has continued exclusively to rely on to this day, are all negative examples of maxims that fail to comply with the Categorical Imperative – that is, of unethical maxims – and this has been a source of some confusion and uncertainty in interpreting Kant's intentions.[19] One can naturally discover a wealth of appropriate positive examples in the earlier biographies of Kant. The individual who desires to live as independently as possible is, of course, Kant himself, and in this connection his biographers all treat 'maxims' and 'principles' as synonymous terms. The examples in question can naturally claim moral validity only to the extent that they properly correspond to Kant's concept of a maxim. But since they do so correspond, they also serve to provide a vivid source of material for Kant's moral thought that has not effectively been exploited by the secondary literature in the past. There are other relevant examples we can draw from the Kant biographies that also fulfill the conditions of his concept of a maxim: Kant's principle of not offering money directly to beggars, but of giving financial support for the municipal administration of poor relief, for example.[20] Or a final example: the young Kant already dressed in accordance with the maxim of observing current fashion in order not to appear conspicuous.[21]

We can also shed further light on the question here, as so often, by carefully considering the historical sources of Kant's concept of maxims, and this is the second point I therefore wish to pursue. The concept in question probably derives from Jean-Jacques Rousseau. He was, of course, Kant's favourite author, and Kant had read all his books. There are three (and perhaps more) elements to Rousseau's notion of a maxim. In the first place, a maxim represents a concisely formulated rule for the conduct of life, an abbreviated expression of a general philosophical insight, for example: 'We

---

[19] Critical discussion generally concentrates entirely on Kant's examples in the *Groundwork* (4:421ff., 429 f.) and the *Critique of Practical Reason* (5:19, 27). Christian Schnoor has also examined other texts and has identified ten examples in total. C. Schnoor, *Kants Kategorischer Imperativ als Kriterium der Richtigkeit des Handels* (Tübingen 1989), p. 124, 129, 152f., 157, 159, 161, 178–180, 182; the only directly positive example Kant provides for making a maxim into a law is to be found in the *Doctrine of Virtue*, 6:393.

[20] *Biographien*, p. 66 (Borowski), p. 289 (Wasianski).

[21] Ibid., p. 56 (Borowski), p. 166 (Jachmann).

KANT'S JUSTIFICATION OF ROLE OF MAXIMS

lament those sufferings in others from which we do not feel entirely safe ourselves.[22] More recent German translators render Rousseau's term *maxime* as *Grundregel* or 'basic rule.' In the second place, a maxim for Rousseau articulates a general *practical* rule, as in the following example, also drawn from *Émile*: 'One should permit children to develop all the powers with which nature has endowed them.'[23] The German translator speaks here of a *Leitsatz* or 'governing principle.' In 1761, a year before *Émile*, Rousseau had published his *Nouvelle Héloise*, in which where he also lays particular emphasis on a third aspect of the idea of a maxim that the German translation renders as *Grundsatz* or 'basic principle.' For example, Rousseau writes: 'I maintain the basic principle that there should be no secrets between friends' ['J'ai pour maxime de ne point interposer de secrets entre les amis'].[24] The idea of a maxim here functions, as in Kant, as a general rule of conduct deliberately adopted by the acting subject. In other words a maxim is a fundamental practical subjective principle. Three components of the concept of a maxim can be clearly distinguished in Rousseau's use of the term: (1) Maxims are not merely a matter of formulating what we believe is morally right since they also express rules for governing one's own conduct ['aussi des regles de votre conduite']?[25]; (2) Although such maxims are certainly not unchangeable, they are relatively firm over time: an honest man would be properly ashamed to change his fundamental principles 'from one day to the next'[26]; (3) The ultimate human criterion to which we appeal in deciding which maxims to adopt is nothing other than 'reason' itself. It is a matter of fundamental principles, which, as Rousseau subsequently says, man's 'reason dictates to him' ['sa raison lui dictoit'], a formulation that Kant, as we pointed out earlier, more or less repeats verbatim.[27]

Kant employs the concept of a 'maxim' or 'fundamental principle' in a very similar fashion to one of the senses, as clearly distinct from the other two, in which the word *maxime* appears in Rousseau's writings. Kant first used the concept in this way in his *Observations on the Beautiful and the Sublime* of 1764. Rousseau's concept of maxim here appears

[22] J. J. Rousseau, *Émile*, p. 507. Rousseau is cited here according to the *Oeuvres complètes*, Bibliothèque de la Pléiade, vols. 4 (*Émile*) and 2 (*La Nouvelle Héloise*).

[23] *Émile*, p. 290.

[24] *La nouvelle Héloise*, p. 511. See *Biographien*, p. 58 (Borowski!).

[25] Ibid., p. 666.

[26] Ibid., p. 182.

[27] *Groundwork*: 4:421 note: '...which reason determines'; 4:426: '...which reason dictates.'

as *Grundsatz* or 'fundamental principle.' In 1764, Kant lays particular emphasis upon the fact that so few human beings act explicitly in accordance with fundamental principles (2:227) even though genuine virtue depends upon the latter (2:217f.). Kant is trying to show why we cannot simply rely on 'kind-hearted impulses' in the moral context (2:221). For virtue presupposes both conscious decision and constancy, or a certain 'resoluteness' [*Standhaftigkeit*] that can only be secured by recourse to 'fundamental principles' (2:221). On the other hand, Kant in 1764 also evaluates the function of maxims in an ambivalent manner: he thinks it is perfectly in order that so few human beings explicitly regulate their conduct in accordance with such principles, given certain qualifications and limitations of gender (2:232) and natural temperament (2:222). For fundamental principles, as expressions of rational reflection, are always potentially subject to human error – and erroneous principles create correspondingly greater harm precisely because their universality and the persistence with which they are entertained (2:227). This too is reminiscent of Rousseau, who believed that bad principles are far more damaging than uncontrolled passions.[28] As we shall see, Kant will later correct his own earlier evaluation of the matter in this respect. But Kant will nonetheless essentially retain his own *concept* of a maxim, or what he still defines in 1764 as a 'fundamental principle,' in spite of any other changes he would subsequently introduce in his ethical theory. And the concept is here already clearly distinguished from the concept of maxim as employed in the Wolffian tradition.[29]

From the beginning, Kant's concept of a maxim or a fundamental principle involves (a) a conscious decision that (b) is taken and applied by only a few individuals. For Wolffian philosophy, on the other hand, the concept implies that (a) *all* individuals always act in accordance with certain maxims that (b) they do not consciously formulate for themselves. The Wolffian philosopher Alexander Gottlieb Baumgarten defines maxims

28 *La nouvelle Héloise*, p. 98 note. Kant's relatively early lectures on ethics (that is, delivered for the first time between 1777 and 1780) clearly expresses his ambivalence in this regard : '... it is worse to perform evil from maxims than from inclination. But one must perform what is good from maxims' (27/1:368, lines 31–33 = 27/2.2:1502, lines 8–10.) Kant used Baumgarten's *Ethica* as his compendium for these lectures. His remarks relate directly to §246 in Baumgarten's text (see note 30).
29 Leaving aside the question of whether Kant was directly acquainted with Wolff, and if so which works in particular he had consulted, we are referring here to the Wolffian tradition of philosophy with which Kant was certainly very familiar through a variety of relevant sources.

as rules of conduct 'to which one becomes accustomed.'[30] It therefore represents a specific moral task for us to 'uncover,' as Wolff says – that is,to make conscious to ourselves precisely those maxims through which we are accustomed to 'direct' our 'course of action.'[31] From a historical perspective, therefore, Baumgarten must be excluded, contra Rüdiger Bubner,[32] as an 'immediate source' for Kant's approach insofar as Baumgarten himself explicitly endorsed this rather modern-sounding and specifically unreflective habituation to action-orienting maxims. From a more substantive perspective, this brings us directly to the third point mentioned earlier – namely the significant misunderstandings of Kant's 'ethic of maxims' on the part of his interpreters.

For it is repeatedly claimed that Kant believes that all individuals always act in accordance with maxims.[33] It is quite true, of course, that his actual claim to the contrary is simply an anthropological presumption on Kant's part. But this thesis alone already serves to distinguish quite clearly between Kant's position and that of the Wolffians, and it also helps to illuminate the specific achievement represented by Kant's concept of a maxim. It is also widely claimed that maxims for Kant are based on habits.[34] Once again, Kant's conception is thereby identified with a Wolffian notion of maxims that he was careful to differentiate unambiguously from his own. There is of course no textual confirmation in Kant's writings for such misinterpretations. In order to suggest

[30] Alexander Gottlieb Baumgarten, *Ethica philosophica* ([1]1740), §246. The remark did not appear in the second edition of 1751 (27/2.1: 800), but only in the modifications to the third edition of 1763 (p. 937). The changes and modifications of the third edition probably derive from Baumgarten himself. It is not known precisely which edition Kant used as a textual basis for his lectures (see note 28), and his actual copy of the compendium has unfortunately not been preserved. But Kant would not have needed to rely on this single passage for a knowledge of the Wolffian conception of unconsciously followed maxims.

[31] Christian Wolff, *Vernünfftige Gedancken von der Menschen Thun und Lassen* ([1]1720; Frankfurt und Leipzig [4]1733; reprinted and edited by H. W. Arndt, in C. Wolff, *Gesammelte Werke*, Abt. 1, vol. 4. Hildesheim/New York 1976), p. 117 (§190). This is repeated in almost exactly the same words in Zedler's *Universal-Lexicon*, vol. 19 (1739) under the entry for 'maxim.' The thought is further explicated as follows: 'In general every man possesses certain maxims or universal rules in accordance with which he directs his actions... At the same time it is true that the man himself cannot be clearly said to know these maxims even though he acts in accordance with them' (column 2254).

[32] Rüdiger Bubner, *Handlung, Sprache und Vernunft. Grundbegriffe praktischer Philosophie* (Frankfurt am Main 1976), p. 200.

[33] See Stephan Körner, *Kant* (Harmondsworth 1955), p. 133f., or Köhl, *Kants Gesinnungsethik*, p. 60.

[34] See, for example, O. Schwemmer, *Philosophie der Praxis*, p. 137.

the contrary, one must first invert the very sense of Kant's actual words, as Bubner has effectively done. In the *Metaphysics of Morals*, Kant says that 'ethical maxims...cannot be grounded in terms of habit' and that 'the subject would forfeit its *freedom* in the adoption of its maxim' if 'the realisation of ethical maxims were to become a matter of habit' (*Doctrine of Virtue*: 6:09). Bubner refers directly to this passage and summarises its significance in the claim that 'maxims...depend upon habit....'[35] In this connection, Kant's own distinction between acting from habit and acting according to maxims is particularly suitable for bringing out the character of maxims as he understands them: if someone lives his life in accordance with maxims, he helps to ensure a certain uniformity in decisions of the will that itself depends upon a free and conscious self-imposed obligation of the subject. On the other hand, while it is clear that everyone has his own habitual dispositions, this is precisely what cannot be claimed with reference to maxims. That is why Kant is convinced we cannot possibly say that everyone in fact acts in accordance with maxims. Kant's explicit view that action according to ethical maxims should not be made into a mere matter of habit directly contradicts the Wolffian position, which strove precisely for the habitualisation of virtue and explicitly sought out appropriate ways in which this might be accomplished.[36] For Kant, on the

---

[35] Bubner, *Handlung, Sprache, Vernunft*, p. 187. Bubner can only identify 'the doctrine of prudence' and 'the theory of maxims' (ibid., note 57) on the basis of a misquotation from Kant (*On Perpetual Peace*: 8:370). The second passage that Bubner cites in support of his claims about 'habit' derives from Kant's *Lectures on Pedagogy* (9:480). Placed in context, it runs as follows: 'Moral culture must be based upon maxims rather than on discipline.... One must try and ensure that the child habituates itself [*sich gewöhne*] (!)...to acting in accordance with maxims. Through discipline we are left with nothing but a habit [*bleibt nur eine Angewohnheit*] (!)...The child should learn to act in accordance with maxims whose rightness the child itself recognises.' If we disregard the slight linguistic clumsiness of the formulation, Kant's remarks here are perfectly consistent with the following passage: 'The greater the number of habits [*Angewohnheiten*] a man possesses, the less he can be considered to be free and independent.... One must therefore take care that the child does not [simply] habituate itself [*sich gewöhne*] to anything. One cannot allow the child to develop a habit.' Although the passages already cited (and that cited in note 37) relate solely to *ethical* maxims, Kant is also thinking, as we shall see, of maxims as such since he interprets the latter essentially in deontological terms (see *Critique of Pure Reason*: B 840).

[36] See, for example, Moses Mendelssohn, *Gesammelte Schriften. Jubiläumsausgabe*, vol. 2 (Berlin 1931; reprinted Stuttgart-Bad Cannstatt 1972). It is 'habit' that ensures that 'the moral man' is 'no longer conscious of himself in reliably acting out rules.' Kant's emphatic distinction between maxims and habits would lead to difficulties if we imagined that the reliable observance of ethical maxims is something that is easily produced (as something that might thus appear simply a matter of habit). But as far as the reliable observance of maxims is concerned, we should think here rather of Goethe's remark

other hand, moral action must depend upon freedom, whereas habit is itself an expression of unfreedom.[37]

A different misunderstanding, one of a more terminological character, is found in the work of Otfried Höffe. In his otherwise exemplary book on Kant, Höffe suggests that the universality of maxims consists in 'the way in which we lead our lives as a whole' – for example, as considerate or inconsiderate, as forgiving or vengeful, and so forth.[38] But it is immediately clear that these are quite inappropriate examples of what Kant means. Human behaviour can certainly manifest inconsiderateness and revenge – but it is difficult to imagine either as cases of consciously adopted maxims. What Höffe unconditionally wishes to insist upon is the distinction between maxims and practical rules. For Kant says that maxims contain within themselves a plurality of further practical rules (5:19). What is at issue here, as a matter of some importance for contemporary theory of action, is the relationship between two types of rules: relatively permanent maxims, on the one hand, and their rules of application, which naturally vary in accordance with specific situations, on the other. This distinction has produced some acute difficulties for interpreters of Kant's thought.[39]

('He only wins both life and freedom who must daily conquer them anew' – *Faust* II, Act V) rather than of the Aristotelian definition of virtue in terms of *hexis* or habitual conduct (*Nicomachean Ethics* II, 5) and the related traditional attempt to distinguish between a 'firmly established characteristic' and an 'easily changeable tendency' [*dispositio*]. See Joseph Gredt, *Die aristotelisch-thomistische Philosophie*, vol. 2 (Freiburg im Breisgau 1935), p. 304. For the concept of 'habitus' invoked in this connection is still clearly too close to what Kant means by 'Gewohnheit.' This difficulty also reappears in O. Höffe's article on 'virtue' (*Lexicon der Ethik*, eds. O. Höffe et al., Munich ²1980, p. 252). Virtue is interpreted here as a 'way of life' [*Lebenshaltung*], an 'accustomed' manner of acting that nonetheless, as Kant rightly sees, cannot simply rest on 'habit.' Höffe thus attempts to combine Kant and Aristotle by interpreting a virtuous 'way of life' precisely through the concept of 'disposition,' though it is understood here not as a changeable tendency but as an effective attitude that finds expression as 'character.'

[37] See *Doctrine of Virtue*: 6:407: 'for if it is a habit [*Angewohnheit*]...it is not one that proceeds from freedom, and therefore not a moral aptitude'; *Anthropology*: 7:147: '... Virtue is *moral strength* in fulfilling one's duty, something that can never become a habit, but ought always to arise entirely anew and originally from one's mode of thinking in general [*Denkungsart*].' Kant is here radicalising, under Rousseau's influence, the traditional criticism of habitual action that had already been expressed, for example, by Wolff (see *Thun und Lassen*, p. 69, §§116–118): if the individual fails to 'reflect upon whether his conduct is good or evil,' this 'sleep of conscience arises from habit [*Gewohnheit*].' That is why 'we must not permit our conduct to become any matter of habit before we possess a true and certain conscience [*ein richtiges und gewisses Gewissen*].'

[38] Höffe, *Kant*, p. 149.

[39] There are (at least) three areas of difficulty here that have led to various attempts at clarification: (1) by distinguishing between a 'rule' and a 'maxim' and identifying the former

But in order to safeguard this distinction, we certainly do not need to locate the maxims on such an exalted plane as Höffe attempts to do. The decision not to incur debts, for example, is a maxim that can simply be derived from a higher maxim – namely that of living an independent life. And yet we can also imagine that the derived maxim can also contain various further individual rules and precepts corresponding to specific requirements and opportunities. Could one not perhaps even say with Lewis White Beck that the rules in question are nothing but the particular applications of maxims in individual cases?[40] This would provide a convenient solution to the problem of defining the distinction in question.

In case this solution should appear to be all too convenient, we should also ask ourselves whether it is an indispensable feature of the concept of a maxim that the latter must contain further rules within itself. Can there be no maxims that do not themselves require any further rules?[41] It would be too simple to claim that we should then precisely be dealing with a rule rather than a maxim. Let us take our earlier example of smoking a pipe only once a day: is that simply a rule subordinated to the maxim of maintaining one's capacity for work? No, for it represents a maxim,

with a mere intention (Höffe, *Kants kategorischer Imperativ*, p. 362; *Ethik und Politik*, p. 93); (2) by interpreting the universality of maxims in terms of their independence 'of particular individuals' (Schwemmer, *Vernunft und Moral*, p. 258). Ralf Ludwig also refers in a similar fashion to 'the supra-individual claim to actualisation' that properly belongs to maxims (R. Ludwig, *Kategorischer Imperativ und Metaphysik der Sitten. Die Frage nach der Einheitlichkeit von Kants Ethik*, Frankfurt am Main 1992, p. 52); and (3) by refusing to take maxims as concrete rules for conduct and locating them instead on a deliberately abstract level, in accordance with Bittner's dictum: 'The maxim does not of itself tell us what we should actually do' (R. Bittner, 'Maximen,' p. 490). Influenced by this view, Höffe claims that a maxim contains 'no precise description of a concrete act' (*Kants kategorischer Imperativ*, p. 363; *Ethik und Politik*, p. 95). Maxims here therefore become 'the ultimate, most universal determining grounds' (p. 359) or 'the ultimate determinations of the will' (p. 360). Höffe has actually attempted to refine his interpretation further, for in the version of this essay published in book form in *Ethik und Politik*, he refers to 'the ultimate universal determining grounds … in the relevant context of action' (p. 89) and 'universal determinations of the will' (p. 91). And Höffe's formulations, as cited in note 38, also reveal his concern with providing further clarification and specification. It seems to me that all the attempts enumerated here simply serve to complicate Kant's concept of maxims unnecessarily.

[40] Expressed more precisely: in the context of a practical syllogism, the maxim constitutes the major premise that expresses a universal rule (valid for a variety of specific cases) – for example: 'always avenge an injustice'; the 'rule' constitutes the minor premise that subsumes a particular case under the major premise – for example: 'this lie would avenge an injustice.' The 'conclusion' of the practical syllogism would then be the decision to lie on this particular occasion. See Lewis White Beck, *A Commentary on Kant's Critique of Practical Reason* (Chicago ¹1960, p. 81).

[41] See Willaschek, *Praktische Vernunft*, p. 66.

albeit a derived one, that is grounded in reason and must be brought into play on a daily basis in order to control one's desire to smoke. Whether or not we can imagine subordinating further particular rules to this maxim does nothing to change its status as a maxim. For a person who pays due attention to his health, it is indeed a matter of considerable importance to decide as to whether or how much he should smoke on a daily basis.

Trivial matters are not relevant to the formation of maxims. For the latter are essentially universal principles for determining the will. But this dimension of universality cannot essentially concern, as Höffe's problematic interpretation suggests, the distinction between good and evil behaviour itself.[42] For according to Kant, no human being deliberately chooses to do evil for the sake of evil.[43] The universality that belongs to maxims reveals itself in the first instance less in their relationship to further subordinate rules than in their relevance for the way in which human beings lead their lives in general. Maxims are intrinsically important to the subject who adopts and subordinates his actual conduct to them.

This does not imply that all maxims as such are already ethical maxims. No one is evil for the sake of being evil, but there are certainly unethical maxims. This is the almost unanimous view amongst Kant's commentators.[44] But the commentators, to come to our fourth point, have failed to clarify the question of when and how the subject tests its maxims with regard to their ethical or unethical status that is, when and how the Categorical Imperative is applied to our maxims. In this connection, Bubner claims that we must have recourse to 'given maxims.'[45] And Höffe also says: 'In relation to the rich variety of our subjective principles (maxims) the moral maxims are specifically separated out from the non-moral ones.'[46] That would imply that maxims that are already given are only tested subsequently. But that is difficult to render intelligible: how should reason itself, which has led human beings in the first place to adopt this or that maxim and continually to determine their will in accordance with it,

---

[42] 'Maxims correspond rather to what the tradition had described as virtue or vice' (Höffe, *Kants kategorischer Imperativ*, p. 369; *Ethik und Politik*, p. 91).

[43] See *Anthropology*: 7:293f.: '... but man never recognises the evil within him as good, and there is therefore really no such thing as evil performed out of principles, but only evil that is occasioned by them.' See *Religion within the Boundaries of Mere Reason*: 6:36: 'The human being (even the worst) does not repudiate the moral law, whatever his maxims, in rebellious attitude (by revoking obedience to it).'

[44] See, however, the entry for 'Character' in the *Historisches Wörterbuch der Philosophie* (vol. 1, column 988) where it is assumed that all maxims are essentially ethical maxims.

[45] Ibid., the entry for 'Maxim' (vol. 5, column 943).

[46] Höffe, *Kant*, p. 151.

now once again, without special occasion, prompt them to test the maxim a second time? For the very advantage that accrues to a maxim – namely, its firmly rooted character – tends to resist the possibility of changing or abandoning the maxim in question. It is certainly true that we can change our maxims, but do we do so unless there is an accompanying change in our experience or rational reflection?

Kant himself is partly responsible for the difficulty here insofar as in the *Critique of Practical Reason* (5:27f.) he offered an example that seems to represent just such a subsequent testing of a maxim (the misappropriation of a bank deposit by someone whose maxim commands the further accumulation of property by all reliable means). Prompted by a given case, the agent examines his maxim and discovers that it is unethical because it cannot function as a universal law. With this and other similar examples, Kant is trying to show how we can properly test the universalisability of maxims that is demanded by the Categorical Imperative. Because the universalisation of unethical maxims cannot be conceived and/or willed without contradiction, unethical maxims cannot survive application of the test, although this is quite possible for other maxims that are diametrically opposed to one another. This is what Kant's examples are precisely intended to demonstrate.[47] The example of the deposit should not be over-interpreted, say in terms of a psychology of criminal behaviour. For then it would simply discourage people harbouring unethical maxims from risking the subsequent application of the Categorical Imperative to them.[48] It would therefore be inappropriate to interpret Kant's point here as concerned with the temporal relationship between the formation of maxims and the application of the Categorical Imperative. In this connection, we should note Kant's remarks a few pages later, which unambiguously resolve the problem involved here: 'as soon as we project maxims of the will for ourselves' we thereby become 'immediately conscious' of the moral law' (5:29). A maxim is tested when it is formulated, rather than subsequently when it comes to be applied. And this is precisely what Kant also has in mind in relation to his other examples in the *Groundwork* (4:421ff.) and the *Critique of Practical Reason* (5:19).

Johannes Schwartländer puts the matter thus: the unconditional demand of reason 'does not subsequently address the will, once it has formed its

---

[47] We can here ignore the fact that Kant thereby envisages the distinction between perfect and imperfect duties, and that between one's duties towards oneself and one's duties towards others (*Groundwork*: 4:421).

[48] See also Willaschek, *Praktische Vernunft*, p. 70.

subjective principles, but rather has always already and simultaneously addressed it.' The unconditional demand of reason 'thus concerns the very formation of maxims.'[49] Why is this the case? Because maxims are themselves an achievement of human reason. Individuals form maxims for themselves in relation to their individual courses of action. But they form these maxims through rational reflection, and reason itself, as something common to all human beings, is never merely a matter of the individual. Thus reason itself inevitably poses the question as to whether the intended subjective principle can also become an objective principle that is, a law that is binding upon every human being in the same circumstances.[50] In this sense, the formation of maxims, precisely because it transpires through reason, already refers us to the moral law itself.

To infer from this relationship between the formation of maxims and the form of lawfulness that there can only ever be moral maxims would be a misunderstanding. A will that was 'incapable of forming any maxim' that 'could at the same time represent an objective law' would be a 'holy will.' But the human will is not holy in this sense (CPrR: 5: 32). Maxims therefore are not *eo ipso* moral. But they are formed through rational reflection, and this relates them immediately to the intrinsic moral demand of reason itself.[51] But we human beings can fail to comply with this demand[52]; we can egotistically close ourselves off from others for example,[53] or we can 'throw dust into our own eyes,' as Kant puts it.[54] He

---

[49] Johannes Schwartländer, *Der Mensch ist Person. Kants Lehre vom Menschen* (Stuttgart 1968), p. 152. It would seem that Kant's thought underwent some significant development with respect to this question, although it is impossible to pursue this in any detail here. For in a 'Reflection' dating from the 1770s, we can still find Kant saying: 'First develop a character as such, and then a good character' 15/2: 514; Refl. 1162).

[50] It is certainly possible to criticise this qualification, but it seems required if we are to maintain the inner connection between the individual subject and his maxims in relation to the Categorical Imperative itself.

[51] That is why there cannot properly be any maxims that are neither moral nor immoral – that is, any morally neutral maxims. Apart from the two alternatives of being able or being unable to universalise one's maxim, there seems to be no third possibility, 'no intermediate position' as Kant says (*Religion*: 6:23 note). The question concerning acts that are neither commanded nor forbidden, but are permitted (*Doctrine of Right*: 6:223), is a question of right rather than one of morality. The Categorical Imperative does not distinguish between commanded, forbidden, and permitted maxims.

[52] This is because reason does not possess 'complete control' over the human faculty of desire. If it did, the subjective and the objective principle of volition (the maxim and the law) would be identical from the first (*Groundwork*: 4:400, note; see also *Critique of Practical Reason*: 5:32).

[53] *Groundwork*: 4:422 provides us with an example of a maxim 'based on self-love.'

[54] *Religion*: 6:38.

is solely concerned here, we should note, with the formation of maxims, and this never transpires without recourse to reason.[55] But human reason can be deaf to the unconditional claim it harbours within itself. Reason can place itself entirely in the service of inclinations of one kind or another, whether out of error or stupidity (*Groundwork*: 4:421, note).[56] Nonetheless, human beings ought to form maxims for themselves. But why precisely should they do so? Are not unethical maxims, which certainly exist as Rousseau reminds us, far worse than unethical acts? Kant later effectively revoked his original sympathy with this view of Rousseau, and if we ask precisely why he did so, then we also find ourselves asking after the ultimate foundation of his ethic of maxims, which brings us to our fifth and final point.[57]

In his *Anthropology*, Kant provides an example that he had already noted at the end of the 1780s and one that is particularly helpful in clarifying this final question. Kant writes: 'Even someone of bad character (like Sulla), if he also provokes revulsion through the brutality of his firmly rooted maxims, is nonetheless an object of admiration [*Bewunderung*].'[58] Kant does not mean to imply that bad maxims are better than none at all. 'Admiration' here is not an expression of moral approval but, as Kant sees the matter, there is still something worthy of admiration in this connection. In spite of his repellent conduct, Sulla is rightly admired because his acts were based on firmly rooted maxims.[59] Unfortunately it has proved impossible to determine which maxims Kant was specifically referring to

---

[55] Reason 'determines' our maxims, but does so 'in accordance with the conditions of the subject' (*Groundwork*: 4:422). Thus it is that our 'maxims arise' ... 'with the cooperation of reason' from 'desires and inclinations' (4:427).

[56] See *Anthropology*: 7:292: our 'principles' are sometimes 'false and defective'; *Groundwork*: 4:425: 'what is derived from certain feelings and propensities ... can indeed yield a maxim for us but not a law.'

[57] 15/2:869, lines 23–25 (Refl. 1518). This 'Reflection' is dated 1780–1789 and is found in a notebook Kant used for his frequently repeated lectures on anthropology. But since this text is clearly more carefully elaborated than the corresponding passages in the anthropology lectures that probably date from the first half of the 1780s, it would seem to be earlier, and may well derive from the end of the previous decade. It is now impossible to verify Adickes' claim (p. 867 note) that Christian Friedrich Puttlich's transcripts of Kant's lectures on anthropology (1784/5) relate to this particular series of lectures.

[58] *Anthropology*: 7:293. 'Sulla' is the Latinised form of the Greek name 'Sylla.'

[59] See *Anthropology*: 7:293: 'For although these principles may also sometimes be false and defective, nonetheless the formal aspect of willing as such to act in accordance with firm principles possesses ... something valuable and admirable in itself'. Cf. also *Pädagogik*: 9: 488: 'In the case of a bad man the character is very bad, ... although it is pleasing to see someone carrying out his intentions and standing firm.'

in this connection.[60] In Kant's eyes, Sulla had certainly not yet become the kind of shining figure of Roman history he later came to represent for Theodor Mommsen, for example.[61] For Sulla was still regarded as the cruel 'master in the art of criminality,' which he already appeared to be in the eyes of his contemporaries and of immediate posterity.[62] The maxims in question must therefore have involved the various measures and proscriptions by means of which Sulla systematically and mercilessly eliminated his political opponents once he had himself gained power. Such behaviour is repulsive, but it nonetheless evokes a kind of admiration in us insofar as these acts also clearly reveal the firmly rooted maxims underlying them. But why are firm maxims still worthy of admiration?

It is simply because maxims, whether good or evil, are not merely given to human beings directly by nature, in the way our immediate natural dispositions are given. Maxims are thus an expression of the freedom with which human beings actively give themselves, or at least *should* give, a 'character.' Not every human being forms maxims for himself, but every individual *ought* in fact to realise the capacity for freedom that is present in every human being. But how do human beings actualise their freedom? In Kant's view, they do so by binding themselves to self-chosen maxims. This is how human beings make their action independent of inner and outer nature and thus directly determine such action themselves.[63] Freedom is independence from the compulsion of inclinations, an independence grounded in the autonomy through which we 'give ourselves' the law.[64] It is quite true that maxims, considered by themselves, do not yet amount to the complete autonomy that is only attained when human

---

[60] The maxims in question here are certainly not the admirable ones involved 'when he resigned' (that is, when he willingly renounced power). See *DohnaWundlacken*, p.327.

[61] Theodor Mommsen, *Römische Geschichte* (Munich 2001), Book 4, Ch. 10.

[62] Lucanus, *De bello civili* I, 136. See especially Cicero, *De finibus* III, 75. The many reproaches traditionally cast upon Sulla (which never make mention of principles or any such thing) even included that of 'quaffing blood' – see Francois Hinard, 'La naissance du Mythe de Sylla,' in *Revue des Études latines* 62 (1984), pp. 81–97.

[63] *Anthropology*: 7:292: 'It is not a question here of what nature makes of man, but of what the latter makes out of himself,' and 7:294. See also 7:292: 'But to possess a character as such signifies that property of the will through which the subject binds himself to specific practical principles which he has prescribed unalterably for himself through his own reason.' See also 15/2:840, line 6f. (Refl. 1513): 'Maxims do not arise from nature: they must be thought out.'

[64] *Groundwork*: 4:446f.; *Critique of Practical Reason*: 5:33; *Doctrine of Virtue*: 6:408. See also 15/2, 842 (Refl. 1513): 'Moral freedom is independence from the compulsion of one's own inclinations, namely the capacity to act in accordance with maxims.' See p. 756, lines 22–24 (Refl. 1494).

beings actualise their freedom as a certain necessity precisely by subjecting themselves to the moral law. And insofar as human beings form subjective principles for themselves, they become aware that the latter must specifically be measured by the criterion of potential objectivity – that is, by the moral law itself. But the free and independent decision to form and adopt particular and determinate maxims, even considered on its own,[65] is already so significant in Kant's eyes that he can celebrate such a decision in positively hymnic terms in his *Anthropology*. There he speaks of an explosion, of a revolution, of a new epoch in the life of an individual (7:294). For human beings who give themselves maxims are effectively creating themselves, so to speak, insofar as they directly apply the human capacity for freedom to themselves through a free decision of their own. It is appropriate therefore that Kant speaks in this connection of 'a kind of rebirth' (ibid.).

We should note, however, that this does not simply hold for specifically ethical maxims. For Sulla, too, acted in accordance with maxims. In Kant's lectures on 'Anthropology' dating from the early 1780s, as Norbert Hinske has convincingly demonstrated,[66] and thus more or less contemporaneously with the *Groundwork*, Kant even went so far as to claim that a determinately formed character possesses a certain 'inner moral worth even if it is an evil character,' as opposed to human beings who 'fail to act in accordance with maxims at all.'[67] Kant has exaggerated here, and he never repeated his case in such words later. But it is quite clearly his considered view, both here and later, that without maxims, despite the danger of electing unethical ones, there can be no morality at all. And this position essentially resolves the ambiguities that attended his earlier writings. What still remains is Kant's conviction that it is a rare

---

[65] That is, without regard to the examination of maxims through the Categorical Imperative, something that itself, from the perspective of time, actually transpires simultaneously. The words from Kant's *Anthropology* that are cited in the following discussion – namely, 'revolution' and 'rebirth' – are *not* intended here (unlike *Religion*: 6:47) to refer to the *transformation* in one's maxims that can lead to a *virtuous* character, to the morally good human being. There are also other important ethical aspects as discussed in these pages (6:47) that differ significantly from what Kant generally says elsewhere concerning maxims, virtue, incentives, character, and so on. Willaschek, *Praktische Vernunft*, p. 128ff., also soon finds himself in serious difficulties when he tries to interpret the concept of 'character' (6:47) in the context of Kant's remarks in other works.

[66] Norbert Hinske, *Kant als Herausforderung an die Gegenwart* (Freiburg/Munich 1980), p. 40f.

[67] Immanuel Kant, *Menschenkunde oder philosophische Anthropologie*, ed. Fr.[iedrich] Ch. [ristian] Starke [= Johann Adam Bergk] (Quedlinburg und Leipzig ²1883; reprinted Hildesheim 1976), p. 346. See also 15/2:542, line 3f. (Refl. 1232).

thing for human beings to live by self-chosen maxims.[68] But distinct from the earlier writings, it is now quite clear that to form maxims for oneself is itself a moral demand, an 'ought,' that is binding upon every human being.[69]

Up to this point, we can properly speak of an anthropological grounding of an ethic of maxims: human beings ought to live in accordance with maxims in order to fulfil their vocation as beings intrinsically capable of freedom. But maxims are not *eo ipso* moral in character. Nonetheless, morality itself rests upon maxims, principles without which it cannot be actualised at all. Morality realises itself, in the individual case, when the Categorical Imperative is applied to maxims. Our final question, therefore, one that has never even been explicitly posed in the secondary literature and indeed was not specifically thematised by Kant himself, concerns why the Categorical Imperative relates directly to maxims, rather than to anything else, to acts or intentions for example. Why does living morally essentially mean living in accordance with ethical *maxims*? Clarifying this question reveals two aspects to the concept of a maxim: in the first place, a maxim represents a decision of the will concerning how one is to act; it is not the act itself. Or to express the matter in a more modern idiom: a maxim belongs to the motivational level of behaviour, and for Kant it is motive that essentially determines the moral quality of an act. The maxim expresses a disposition [*Gesinnung*][70] that human beings can freely give themselves and for which they are responsible. That is why the mere correspondence between an *act* and the moral law only yields legality for Kant. It is only the correspondence between the *maxim* of an act and the moral law that yields ethics or morality proper. For a legal act may be immoral – if the motive is immoral.[71]

---

[68] Kant is thinking not of gender or temperament here, but of the process of aging: *Anthropology*: 7:294, *Dohna-Wundlacken*, p. 331.

[69] See *Anthropology*: 7:295: '…thus to be a man with principles…must be something possible for the commonest human reason'; *Dohna-Wundlacken*, p. 324: 'A freely acting being must act in a way that is always based on maxims,' and p. 325: 'Man must always and everywhere…act on the basis of maxims.'

[70] For this concept, see *Groundwork*: 4:435: 'in dispositions, that is, in maxims of the will'; *Critique of Practical Reason*: 5:159: 'as disposition, in accordance with its maxim' [the maxim of the act]; *Religion*: 6:23 note: 'disposition (the inner principle of maxims)'; see also Kant's letter to Herz of April 1778: 'good dispositions that are built upon principles' (10: 230, lines 18–20).

[71] *Doctrine of Right*: 6:225. See *Groundwork*: 4:399: 'action from duty has its moral worth…in the maxim in accordance with which it is decided upon' (see *Pädagogik*: 9:475.); *Critique of Practical Reason*: 5:159: 'whether the action was also done (subjectively) *for the sake of the moral law*, so that it has not only moral correctness as a deed

In the second place, a maxim represents a decision to act in a uniform and consistent manner. A maxim must reveal a certain steadfastness that is, must exclude the possibility of deciding to neglect the maxim whenever a particular occasion or inclination might prompt such a thing. It merely betrays the sad state of current research on Kant when Ralf Ludwig in 1992 could describe the view that 'maxims permit exceptions' as a 'solid result of the discussion surrounding the status of maxims.'[72] For the very opposite is the case. It is quite true that the subject can alter or relinquish its maxims. But the maxims themselves always demand to be consistently followed over time.[73] The proposal not to incur debts but yet to make exceptions for particular occasions would not be worth the effort of trying to adopt as a maxim. It would not constitute a maxim in the first place. Someone who had adopted the unqualified maxim, yet nonetheless fell into debt, would not be acting in accordance with the relevant maxim and would thereby contradict the claim that not incurring debts is indeed a fundamental principle – that is, precisely a maxim – governing his behaviour. The Categorical Imperative relates directly to maxims precisely because the latter do not permit of exceptions, precisely because we can thereby rely upon individuals to act over time in accordance with the maxims they have given themselves.[74] For in this case, the individual is not simply oriented to purely singular and contingent examples of moral acts, but rather towards the exercise of virtue as such. But only the individual who repeatedly acts in a reliably moral fashion is properly virtuous – that is, is essentially supported and assisted by a steadfast commitment to maxims (*Doctrine of Virtue*: 6:394), over against the inconstant and vacillating character of our feelings and inclinations.[75]

And it is only the 'immutability' of maxims (CPrR: 5:33), as long as they are indeed ethical maxims, that also points to that *perfection* [*Vervollkommnung*] that is the ultimate end of virtue itself. If we were

but also moral worth as a disposition by its maxim.' See also Kant's preliminary notes for his 'Prize Essay' on *The Progress of Metaphysics*: 'The good will ... is not a phenomenon because it is oriented towards maxims and not towards acts that transpire within the world' (20:336, lines 18–20).

[72] R. Ludwig, *Kategorischer Imperativ*, p. 51f.

[73] Rüdiger Bubner has clearly recognised this: 'One may occasionally contradict one's maxims, but maxims possess validity only insofar as we actively conduct ourselves in accordance with them' (*Handlung, Sprache, Vernunft*, p. 191).

[74] Immanuel Kant, *Anweisung zur Menschen- und Weltkenntnis*, ed. Fr.[iedrich] Chr. [istian] Starke [= Johann Adam Bergk]. (Quedlinburg und Leipzig ²1883), p. 59. See 15/2:756, line 26f. (Refl. 1494).

[75] See *Critique of Practical Reason*: 5:118; *Anthropology*: 7:294.

speaking here of 'holiness' rather than 'virtue,' then we should certainly never be able to adopt maxims – that is, subjective principles that could represent something other than objective laws. The fact that human beings can never be 'holy' in this sense therefore also implies that our human capacity for morality that is, for virtue – can never be accomplished perfectly. Virtue always represents striving towards perfection, and never an attainment of perfection itself. But if virtue is to evince 'constant progress,' as Kant puts it (CPrR: 5:33), then virtue must avail itself of maxims. This 'progressus,' in Kant's eyes, is not accomplished through human beings' adopting ever more virtuous maxims, but through holding fast to the virtuous maxims they have already formed, through doing precisely what the concept of a maxim demands, despite the difficulties this imposes – namely, through showing strength of will in the pursuit and realisation of those maxims.[76] If human beings can be sure of earnestly trying to do so – and there is no absolute certainty here – then they can be said to possess virtue (CPrR: 5:33). Consideration of the concept of virtue thus also reveals just how crucial a proper understanding of the role of maxims is for the appropriate interpretation of Kant's ethical thought as a whole. Not all maxims are ethical maxims. Nonetheless, without maxims there can be no ethical conduct in human life precisely because morality is only effectively realised in and through the practical adoption of ethical maxims.

---

[76] Virtue is 'moral disposition in *conflict*' (*Critique of Practical Reason*: 5:84). Because of the influence of the 'inclinations,' virtue 'can never settle down in peace and quiet with its maxims adopted once and for all' since 'if it is not rising, it is unavoidably sinking. For moral maxims, unlike technical ones, cannot be based on habit' (*Doctrine of Virtue*: 6:409).

III

CRITIQUE OF
PRACTICAL REASON

7

The Form of the Maxim as the Determining Ground of the Will (*The Critique of Practical Reason*: §§4–6, 27–30)

Otfried Höffe

1. Overview

In the 'Analytic of Pure Practical Reason,' Book I of the second *Critique*, Kant undertakes to show that 'pure reason can be practical – that is, can of itself, independently of anything empirical, determine the will' (5:42, 4). In the context of this demonstration, Sections 4–6 are primarily concerned with the second, third, and fourth steps in an ultimately seven-part argument (with the concepts of pure form, universal legislation, and transcendental freedom, respectively). Since these sections briefly repeat the first step (the exclusion of 'material principles') and effectively anticipate the fifth, sixth, and seventh steps of the overall argument (the 'fundamental law,' the 'fact of reason,' and the concept of 'autonomy,' respectively), they constitute the essential core of the 'Analytic' that introduces the second *Critique*.

According to the initial definition that opens Section I (5:19), the argument must establish the existence not merely of subjective principles ('maxims') but also of objective practical principles ('practical laws') that can properly be recognised as 'holding for the will of every rational being' (ibid.). For only then, as Kant points out in the 'Remark' that follows, can pure reason be said to 'contain within itself a practical ground, that is, one sufficient to determine the will' (ibid.). In the first step of the ensuing argument (§§2–3), Kant comes to a twofold negative conclusion: (a) no maxims originating from an empirical will – namely, one determined by any preceding desire – can properly furnish practical laws (§2: theorem I); and (b): the governing principle of an empirical will – namely, self-love or the pursuit of one's own happiness – must therefore be excluded from consideration (§3: theorem III).

Whereas Kant's theorems I, II, and IV are presented in the expected and traditional form ('A is B'), theorem III is different: §4 begins hypothetically ('if ..., then') and the following two sections (§§5–6) are introduced in a similar fashion ('Supposing that ...'). One can of course formulate theorem III in a more traditional and emphatic manner: 'A rational being can only think of his maxims as principles which contain the determining ground of the will merely by virtue of their form.' But that would simply forfeit part of the point at issue: that Kant is here arguing for a certain possibility rather than already asserting something as a reality.

The hypothetical formulation reveals a specific argumentative strategy that is characteristic of the very project of a critique of practical reason, and particularly of the 'analytic' it involves, and one that is clearly evident right from the beginning of Kant's 'Remark' in §1 ('If it is assumed ..., then. ...'; 5:19). In contrast to a system of practical reason, or a metaphysics of morals, a critique cannot simply assume the reality of pure practical reason as something already given, but must first proceed to establish it. With this end in mind, Kant initially presupposes the reality of pure practical reason as given ('If. ....'), and then considers the relevant arguments that could successfully justify that presupposition through a series of methodical steps. Once the first two theorems have effectively excluded inappropriate principles, the third theorem (§4) returns to the originally formulated task of identifying maxims that are 'practical laws' (§1; 5:19), or more emphatically – 'practical universal laws' (5:27), and to the conclusion, already presented in the *first* step of the argument, that we must concern ourselves here solely with the form, as distinct from the matter, in such laws (5:27). Both §5 and §6, finally, presuppose the validity of the partial conclusions established in the preceding sections.

At the beginning of §4, Kant points out that in the first instance he is only undertaking a limited task. Whereas the principal original task demanded that maxims be 'cognized' as objectively binding upon us (5:19), he is here content simply to 'think of' them as such (5: 27). Kant turns to the further question, which is ultimately essential for genuine knowledge, of whether what is merely thought is also actual, only later in his discussion of the 'fact of reason.'

The *second* step in Kant's demonstration consists in an argument *e contrario*. Kant infers the uniquely appropriate governing principle directly from consideration of the inadequate and inappropriate alternative. Repeating the first step of his argument, regarding the inappropriateness of appealing to any material principles (ibid.), Kant concludes that it is the form and the form alone, the pure form, of our maxims, that furnishes the appropriate determining ground for the pure will.

In the *third* step of the demonstration, intimately connected as it is with the second, this pure form acquires a certain content of its own: that of universal legislation (§4, theorem III; 5:27). Here, as elsewhere, the qualifying term 'universal' possesses a purely explicating significance rather than a specifying significance. In accordance with Kant's strict terminological usage, 'law' and 'legislation' in the practical sphere are conceived as immediately 'binding upon the will of every rational being' (5:19). And the fact that a practical law can 'qualify for universal legislation' is simply an 'identical proposition' for Kant (5:27) – that is, one involving an analytical relation already contained in the concept of a thing (see *Critique of Pure Reason* B 10).

Presupposing that the possibility of universal legislation is the only relevant consideration, Kant clarifies and develops the ensuing and intrinsically twofold task or 'problem' in two further steps. The discussion of the first 'problem' (§5) contains the *fourth* step in the overall argument: Kant here elaborates the concept of a will that is determined solely by the form of law itself – namely, the concept of a 'free will.' Presupposing this concept, Kant proceeds in his discussion of the second 'problem' (§6) to identify the law that properly corresponds to such a will. As the second step of the demonstration has already revealed, the determining ground of the free will lies in the legislating form contained in the maxim, a form that corresponds, in accordance with the third step, to a universal legislation.

In his 'Remark' on §4, Kant takes a further *subordinate step*. He takes the pure form of legislation, universality itself, as the proper measure and criterion for the moral character of our possible maxims, and applies the test of universalisability to his famous example of the bank deposit. He thereby anticipates the *fifth* step in his demonstration, the identification of the moral law in the shape of the categorical imperative.

The *fourth* step of the demonstration effectively consists of four parts. Firstly, (a) the free will is defined negatively as 'altogether independent of the natural law of appearances, namely the law of causality' (5:29). Secondly, (b) this negative definition of the free will is evaluated positively insofar as it reveals freedom in the 'strictest – that is, in the transcendental – sense' (5:29). Thirdly, (c) by recourse to the third step of the argument the will now acquires a positive content as 'a will for which the mere lawgiving form of a maxim alone can serve as a law' (5:29). Kant's positive concept of freedom already makes its appearance here, and anticipates the essential theme of the third and fourth theorems, as well as his *seventh* step – namely, that concerning the autonomy of the will. In the fourth part of this fourth step, (d) Kant reverses the presentation of the argument: the legislating form of the maxim is 'the only thing that can constitute a determining ground of the will' (§6; 5:29).

Finally, in the 'Remark' to §6, Kant anticipates the *sixth* step of his demonstration, that concerned with 'the fact of reason' as developed in the two remarks to §7.

In the 'Preface,' Kant had explicitly drawn attention to the relevant conclusion of the first *Critique* that would prove so decisive for the argument of the second: that the concept of transcendental freedom can be presented 'only problematically, as something that is not impossible to think' (5:3). The second *Critique* is intended to resolve this still outstanding problem by establishing the 'objective reality' of transcendental freedom (ibid.). This would be tantamount to furnishing the speculative '*keystone* of the whole structure of a system of pure reason, even of speculative reason' (ibid.). Since Kant already accomplishes this purpose in essentials, albeit not yet with all the requisite clarity and detail, in §§4–6, these sections can properly be regarded not merely as the argumentative core of the 'analytic,' but as the truly decisive part of the second *Critique* as a whole. The most important steps of the argument can be summarised as follows:

(1) Kant derives the mere form of a maxim by excluding all material content from the will and its particular maxims. (§4, first paragraph)

(2) He explicates the mere form of a maxim as a universal law-giving. (§4, second paragraph)

(3) 'The most common understanding can distinguish without instruction what form in a maxim makes it fit for a giving of universal law and what does not' (5:27). Kant elucidates this claim with reference to the example of having in his hands a deposit 'the owner of which has died without leaving any record of it' (5:27). (§4, first paragraph of the 'Remark')

(4) Through his example of the deposit, Kant also alludes to the 'desire for happiness' and all associated empirical determining grounds that are intrinsically unfit for any universal legislation, whether internal or external in character (5:28). (§4, second paragraph of the 'Remark')

(5) We can represent the mere form of law to ourselves only through the faculty of reason. Since this form is no possible object of the senses, it

cannot belong to the order of appearances and the law of causality that governs them. This demonstrates, once again *e contrario*, that a will that is determined solely by its law-giving form is a free will in the strictest transcendental sense of the term. (§5)

(6) But a will that is independent of all material, and thereby material conditions, must be capable of being determined in some way, and the law-giving form itself is the only other remaining source of determination. (§6)

(7) It is quite true that freedom and an unconditioned practical law 'reciprocally imply each other' (5:29). But since we can never become immediately conscious of our freedom, nor infer its reality on the basis of experience, 'our *cognition* of the unconditionally practical' must begin from the moral law itself. Kant shows that we can become immediately conscious of the latter by appeal to an example of extreme conflict between duty and inclination, between the moral demand for honesty and the pragmatic desire to preserve one's life, and contrasts this conflict with the pragmatic considerations involved in choosing between a short-lasting 'highly pleasurable' inclination and a more long-term interest in the quality of one's life. (§6, 'Remark')

2.   §4: Mere Form and the Deposit Example

In order to clarify the structure of his argument *e contrario*, Kant repeats, in the first part of theorem III, the decisive negative conclusion already established in the first two theorems: namely, that any material content must be excluded as a possible determining ground for the pure will. One can certainly ask whether Kant has not performed the relevant exclusion a little too hastily since his argument is here concerned only with sensuous material, rather than with any 'material' even of a non-sensuous or super-sensuous character. But the answer to this problem is provided by the further conceptual development of Kant's argument. In the context of practical philosophy, Kant understands the term 'material' to signify any object, sensuous or super-sensuous, whose reality can be desired. The decisive point is that some desire is always presupposed with regard to material principles of whatever kind: namely, the pleasure promised by the actual existence of what is desired. (In accordance with the ambiguity attaching to the concepts of 'bonum' and 'malum,' the relevant object of desire or aversion essentially concerns well-being or its opposite, rather than good or evil; cf. 5:57ff.) The pleasure one takes in the possible future reality of an object, the anticipation of pleasure, is just as much an empirical question as the pleasure we actually experience in the existence of the object of desire. That is why Kant rightly says that 'it is impossible to see a priori which representation will be accompanied with *pleasure* and which with *displeasure*' (5:58). To banish all reference to material content is therefore not to deny the will any possible object or determinacy. But it is to exclude the pleasure taken in the existence of an object as the decisive determining ground of the will. Since the question of pleasure is beside the point here, the distinction between 'more refined delights,' like those associated with 'cultivating one's spiritual talents' (§3; 5:24), and those of a more sensuous character, is entirely irrelevant as far as a critique of practical reason is concerned.

Aristotle, of course, regarded the intellectual and philosophical life, the *bios theôrêtikos*, as the highest form of life that can be enjoyed by human beings (*Nicomachean Ethics* X, 6–7). Kant would not deny that such a life can provide the highest and most sustained kind of human activity, or indeed that it can procure the highest kind of human pleasure. Nonetheless, so his argument implies, one cannot claim *a priori* that this particular human being *A* at this moment of his life *t* must desire to pursue this kind of theoretical pleasure that belongs uniquely to the spiritual life.

Our spiritual or intellectual delights, indeed all of our more refined delights, necessarily involve a certain pleasure, and thus also certain empirical distinctions both between different individual subjects and between different phases in the life of the same individual subject. Whenever, therefore, material content provides the determining ground, as Kant summarises the point in §4, the 'rule of the will' is subject to an 'empirical condition' – namely, 'the relation of the determining representation to the feeling of pleasure or displeasure' and 'therefore not a practical law' (5:27).

Tacitly presupposing an exclusive disjunction (for it is a question of either matter or form, and there can be no third term), the second part of the theorem identifies 'form' as the only possible alternative once 'matter' has been excluded. The concept of form that Kant employs here is not adequately captured by Korsgaard's claim, with reference to the *Groundwork*, that it essentially concerns the relationship between the act to be performed and the purpose to be realised. As an example, Korsgaard discusses the maxim 'I shall beat Alex in order to relieve my anger' and the relationship between the propositions – namely, 'I shall beat Alex' and 'I wish to relieve my anger' (Korsgaard 1996, p. 75f). But from a Kantian perspective, Korsgaard has not here provided a maxim at all, nor even one of the rules that are contained within a maxim in Kant's sense. On analogy with Kant's examples in the second *Critique*, such as those 'to let no insult pass unavenged' (5:19) or 'to increase my wealth by every safe means' (5:27), or even those in the *Groundwork*, the relevant maxim would be framed rather as follows: 'I wish to relieve my anger by every safe means.' The (morally problematic) rule contained within the maxim would run like this: 'If it appears to be a safe way of relieving my anger, then I shall go and beat someone.' In this case, I would perform a violent act, which, according to Kant, directly contradicts the principle of justice (cf. 5:61). In Kant's perspective, this rule, and the maxim behind it, both imply a material determining ground for the will – namely, the desire to relieve one's anger by any relevant means.

But 'form' as Kant understands it does not simply coincide with the 'ought' either. For a pure rational being, one that is not confronted by the demands of an ought at all, can also act in accordance with mere form. Indeed such a being, a 'holy' being in the 'ontological' sense, even always acts in accordance with mere form. As Kant explains in the *Groundwork* (4:431, 436) and the second *Critique* (5:27), what is at issue here is the pure form of law: universal legislation itself.

This interpretation is confirmed by Kant's remarks in his *Lectures on Logic*. In the Introduction, specifically the section 'On Cognition in General,' Kant defines matter as the 'object' and form as 'the *way* in which we know the object' (9:33). If we apply this to the central issue of the second *Critique* – namely, the will and its appropriate determining ground – then 'matter' signifies the object of the will and 'form' signifies the specific way, detached from all expectation of pleasure, in which we will (rather than know) the object. The relevant alternatives are therefore: the pure form of willing, or the form of the maxim – that is, universal lawfulness, on the one hand – or the impure form – that is, a lack of universal lawfulness – on the other. Once again, the additional predicate 'universal' here (5:27) is intended in an explicating sense rather than a qualifying sense. Kant is not contrasting a universal with a more limited form of legislation, but simply emphasising the decisive feature of law-giving itself – its universality. It is only by virtue of this feature that mere form can exercise the criterial force that it does in Kant's 'Remark.'

Kant tests 'what form in a maxim makes it fit for a giving of universal law and what does not' (5:27) by considering the maxim 'to increase my wealth by every safe means' (ibid.). What is at issue is not the agent's intention of increasing his wealth, but simply the agent's attitude, here described by Kant as 'avarice,' in being prepared to use all means he really considers safe in order to procure his ends. Kant's test of universalisability is concerned with the immoral attitude involved, which is precisely revealed as such through the moral inadequacy of certain means. Contrary to widely received opinion in this respect, Kant is not concerned with any specific means or rules in regard to human conduct. How someone might actually increase his wealth is a technical question in Kant's view, one that is properly addressed by considering the best available means with respect to a given intention. Whether increasing my wealth actually contributes to my happiness is a purely pragmatic question, but it becomes a moral one, as we already realise on reading the very first section of the text, once the 'determination of the will' is at issue (5:19). As far as the cultivation of our faculties is concerned, the relevant question is whether we always employ them in a sincere and honourable way, or occasionally use them in order to deceive others, and whether we employ them indifferently without regard for the needs of others or in a benevolent and helpful manner.

The same is true of the *Groundwork*, once again right from the beginning, including even the Preface insofar as the latter speaks of the will 'without any empirical motives' (as distinct from 'determining grounds') or of the 'pure will' (4:390). Kant is making the same point when he claims in the striking opening sentence of the first section that it is 'impossible to think of anything at all in the world, or even beyond it, that could be considered good without restriction except a *good will*' (4:393). In addition, Kant is essentially concerned, both in the *Groundwork* and in the second *Critique*, with a 'universal' determination of the will that vouchsafes the relevant propositions the status of principles in the strict sense, ones that contain within themselves 'several practical rules' (5:19). If a rule is already something universal, and a maxim possesses universality at a second level, Kant can regard a (practical) law as possessed of a still higher universality, that universality at a third level that is 'cognized as objective – that is, as holding for the will of every rational being' (ibid.). This universality is binding upon finite and pure rational beings alike, and amongst finite rational beings upon human beings and non-human beings alike insofar as they are possessed of reason and sensibility. It is only with regard to such principles that the inclinations of a human being can express something like character: 'in the present case my avarice' (5:27).

Kant tests the universalisability of avarice indirectly – namely, in relation to a rule that is not universalisable even though it falls under the relevant principle (see 'a case for my maxim'; ibid.). Kant uses the famous example of the deposit, which has become a familiar one in philosophy since the discussion in Plato's *Republic* (I 333b–d). A few years later,

Hegel managed to convince himself (in the essay on *Natural Law* of 1803, esp. pp. 462; Knox translation, pp. 77f., and in the *Phenomenology* of 1807, in the section on 'Reason as Tester of Laws,' pp. 322f.; Miller translation, pp. 256–262) that he had effectively refuted Kant's appeal to this example and with it the basis of Kant's moral philosophy as a whole. And subsequent generations of Hegelian thinkers have continued to share the same opinion without ever subjecting it to careful scrutiny through close examination of Kant's actual text (for further discussion of Hegel's critique of Kant, see Allison 1990, 184ff. and Ameriks 2000, chapter 7).

The first task is to clarify the relevant concept of the 'deposit.' Since the days of Roman law, a deposit has signified a moveable good handed over to another for safekeeping free of any charge. The legal act involved is the 'pactum depositi,' the contract of custody, and is to be distinguished from that which is given into custody, the deposit itself. The legal manual that formed the basis for Kant's lectures on 'natural law' (Achenwall/Pütter 1750/1995, §379: 124f.) defines the 'pactum depositi' as a contract 'through which a moveable good belonging to another is handed over for safekeeping free of charge' ('quo custodia rei alienae mobilis gratis suscipitur'). Although the term 'deposit' is occasionally understood to mean not (merely) the good in question, but (also) the underlying contract, Kant's own formulation is unambiguous. A deposit 'in my hands,' as he puts it, is the thing itself rather than the contract (5:27).

The next point to observe is that Kant is not concerned with just any deposit, but solely with one that could serve as 'a safe means' for increasing my wealth if and when 'the owner has died without leaving any written record of the same' (5:27). Kant thus specifically discusses the case of a deposit handed over for safekeeping without any identifiable written proof of the event, and therefore in an act of trust, a deposit that cannot be reclaimed now that one of the initial parties is deceased.

Hegel rightly treats the deposit as a case of 'property,' but raises two objections to Kant's treatment of the example. Firstly, according to Hegel, the thought-experiment of universalisability simply produces a tautological result: 'If property exists, then property must exist.' And secondly, so Hegel claims, Kant has not even undertaken to 'show that something like property must exist' at all (Hegel, 1803, p. 463). Instead of attempting to do so, Kant has merely presupposed the legally established system of property rights as something already given. Let us begin by examining the second objection in specific relation to Kant's example of the deposit.

Even if it is true that something like a deposit, at least in some form or other, may actually exist in almost every developed human culture,

Kant does not presuppose such a thing as actually given in reality. All his argument requires is the conceivability of some such practice. It is even enough that we can imagine something, whether in actuality or merely in terms of a thought-experiment, that could serve as a safe means for increasing my wealth, but that might also contradict moral demands. Kant's argument merely presupposes that there are certain means for accumulating wealth that must be regarded differently from a moral perspective, some that are compatible with morality and some that are not, and that those that are indeed incompatible, like the deceitful means at issue, can be identified and excluded by means of the relevant thought-experiment.

But Kant therefore also disposes of Hegel's first objection. Kant does not conclude that 'if property exists, then property must exist.' What he does is to exclude certain forms of acquiring property as morally illegitimate ones. In the strict sense, Kant is not concerned with the institution of contract, nor even with that of property itself. He is simply concerned with the non-universalisable character of a certain means, of the safe and easy act of deception. But even the latter is simply the mediating instance here. For what Kant is ultimately contesting is the view that our 'desire for happiness' (5:28) is ever suitable for grounding a universal practical law. Kant demonstrates this unsuitability, something that even 'the most common understanding can grasp without instruction' (5:27; see also 87, 153 and 155), by reference to an example of 'avarice' (5:27), one of the 'cold' passions 'acquired in the course of culture' as opposed to one of the 'inflamed' and 'innate' passions that are 'natural' to us (Kant's *Anthropology*: 7:267f.).

According to Kant a 'passion' is an 'inclination that hinders reason from comparing it, in respect of a certain choice, with the sum of all inclinations' (*Anthropology* §80: 7:265). Such passions, these 'cancers for pure practical reason,' thus produce an acute 'foolishness' insofar as we here take one aspect of the relevant end as if it were the whole and simultaneously close ourselves off from other possible inclinations. For both reasons, we effectively forfeit the happiness that could ensue from regarding the totality of our inclinations. In the example of the denied deposit, however, Kant does not actually criticise avarice along pragmatic lines, as an expression of foolishness. On the contrary, he focuses directly upon the carefully meditated act of denying a deposit if there is no evidence to show that it was ever made. Nor does Kant actually repudiate avarice as such, for while it is indeed an 'entirely mean-spirited' passion, it is one that is 'not always morally reprehensible' (7:274). Kant only criticises avarice insofar as it makes use of immoral means – namely, of a carefully calculated act of deception.

Kant's example of the denied deposit shows the unsuitability of the relevant maxim of avarice as far as the possibility of universal legislation is concerned. Likewise, *e contrario*, it shows the suitability of universalisability as the appropriate criterion for practical moral laws. For, so Kant argues, the law that one could deny any deposit for which no record exists would simply 'annihilate itself' (5:27). This self-annihilating character corresponds to the stricter criterion presented in the *Groundwork*, concerning the maxims that cannot consistently be conceived without contradicting our unremitting or 'perfect' duties and those that cannot consistently be willed without contradicting our meritorious or 'imperfect' duties (4:424). Kant thus discusses the case of a perfect duty towards others – namely, a duty of right.

Because Kant also says that universalising the relevant case of deception would mean that 'there would be no deposits at all' (5:27), one might be tempted to interpret his argument in 'consequentialist,' social-pragmatic, or ultimately empirical terms. Thus, the act of handing over the deposit, the contract of custody, counts as a socially binding rule or form of interaction, an institution that is defined by advantages and obligations, that creates certain expectations, that establishes a coherent relationship between one's own acts and those of other people, and thus facilitates a regulated life in common. The denial of the deposit would therefore undermine the reliability and credibility of the institution in general, and if everyone acted in like manner, there would soon no longer be anyone to make such a deposit in the first place. On this interpretation, universalising the relevant maxim would simply destroy the institution in question, and with it a certain possibility of rational social life.

Such reflections are correct enough but they are beside the point as far as Kant's argument or the precise question at issue is concerned. Considered in purely consequentialist terms, the source of such a general disappearance of social trust is neither here nor there. It is irrelevant whether it arises from specific lack of honesty or from the fact that people have sometimes proved unable, despite the best of intentions, and perhaps because of unanticipated difficulties, to return the deposit entrusted to them, and so on. Kant is only interested in the moral perspective in general, in the underlying determination of the will itself, in the relevant maxim (5:19) or inclination (5:27; see *Groundwork*: 4:402; 'But it is quite different to be truthful out of duty than out of a concern for the unfortunate consequences').

The fact that there would 'exist no deposits at all' (5:27) if one adopted the maxim in question, according to Kant, itself speaks against the right to deny the deposit in one's hands. This 'non-existence' must be understood in terms of the aforementioned 'self-annihilating' character of the universalised maxim (5:32; cf. 28). As something that has been handed over for safekeeping, the deposit is not a gift, but the legal property of another that can be reclaimed by the owner or the owner's heirs. If the deposit is denied, it forfeits its own essentially defining character as something belonging to 'another,' and its 'essence' as property is destroyed or, as Kant puts it, 'annihilated.'

Generally speaking, the properly moral moment, morality itself, reveals itself for Kant not in our acts, but rather – and this is the principal argument against the consequentialist interpretation – in the determining grounds of those acts. And similarly, in the example of the deposit, Kant is not concerned with the question of whether the individual in question actually returns it or not. For it is quite possible that the deposit entrusted to me is destroyed by fire or is stolen from me by someone else. Kant is simply concerned with the potential decision to 'deny' the deposit (5:27), with a case of mendacity and deceit, and thus with avarice as the underlying motive of the will.

In the consequentialist interpretation, the result of universalising the maxim, as Kant identifies it – namely, its 'self-annihilating' or 'self-destroying' character – does not figure at all (5:28). For a world where nobody is willing any longer to entrust deposits to anyone because of their disappointed expectations in the past, where everyone prefers to hide their valuables in the mattress or bury them in the garden, may well be unattractive, but it is certainly not inconceivable. We can only identify the logical contradiction – rather than, as Korsgaard assumes (1996, p. 92), the practical contradiction – that is involved here when we turn our attention from the (desirable or undesirable) consequences and concentrate exclusively upon the maxim itself. What, then, does it mean to 'increase my wealth by every safe means'? (5:27).

Since a contract of custody implies a duty to return what has been entrusted, refusal to do so signifies retention of the property of another without recognising it as another's property. The case of a deposit knowingly and deliberately retained for oneself results from the 'intrinsically self-contradictory' maxim to recognise something as the property of another and simultaneously to deny its status precisely as another's property. (Contrary to the view of Willaschek, 1992, p. 333, no great act of judgement is required to decide which of the two maxims – whether to deny the deposit or not – is properly to be described as the moral).

Rejecting the principle of happiness as the decisive criterion in respect of morality is so important to Kant that after presenting his principal criticisms of such a view in 'theorem II,' he returns to the issue once again in 'theorem III.' Here Kant objects to those 'intelligent men' (5:28) who have proposed the maxim corresponding to our desire for happiness as a universal practical law. Is he thinking here (as in §3; 5:24) of figures such as Epicurus, expressly mentioned a little later amongst the list of those who have identified practical material determining grounds for the will? In §3, Kant was primarily concerned with elucidating the idea of reason as determining the will immediately and 'not by means of any intervening feeling of pleasure or displeasure' (5:25), with the contrast between the mediate and immediate determination of the will in general. Here in §4 he is discussing the contrast between 'harmony' and its 'extreme opposite' – 'the most terrible conflict' (5:28). The principle of (one's own) happiness, turned into a law, leads directly to the kind of terrible conflict that recalls Hobbes' war of all against all: 'For then the will of all has not one and the same object but each has his own (his own welfare)' (ibid.). And it can only be a contingent matter if pursuit of one's own welfare actually proves to be compatible with the intentions and desires of others. But such an occasional and contingent harmony contradicts the task of articulating a strictly universal structure of moral legislation.

The concept of universalisation is generally interpreted simply in social terms, in relation to all possible individuals, expressed by Kant negatively for cases of maxims that cannot be willed or even conceived as binding on all persons. But the second paragraph of the 'Remark' in §4 modifies this interpretation by indicating that empirical determining grounds are 'no more fit for inner legislation' than they are for universal external legislation (ibid.). That is because 'within each subject now the influence of one inclination preponderates and now that of another' (ibid.). And this reveals, once again *e contrario*, alongside the more familiar case of 'inter-personal universalisation' or 'general concord' (ibid.) a further 'intra-personal' form of universalisation. This latter would thus furnish the criterion for those equally legitimate moral norms that are hardly ever mentioned, let alone properly acknowledged, in contemporary moral philosophy, which is focussed exclusively on the social domain – what Kant calls 'duties towards oneself.'

3.   §5: A Free Will

In 'Problem I,' Kant attempts to elucidate the idea of a will that determines itself solely through the mere law-giving form of universality itself.

Kant's decisive preliminary argument here claims that the 'mere form of a law can be represented only by reason' (5:28). The further course of the argument follows directly from this: that this form is 'not an object of the senses,' that it 'consequently does not belong amongst appearances,' that it is 'distinct from all determining grounds of events in nature in accordance with the law of causality' (ibid.). But such independence from all natural causality is freedom, and indeed freedom 'in the strictest pluse – that is, in the transcendental sense' (5:29).

Kant does not further elucidate the concept of transcendental freedom here since he presupposes the relevant discussion already provided in the *Critique of Pure Reason* (see the 'Preface' to the second *Critique*; 5:3). In the first *Critique*, in the decisive analysis of the third antinomy (freedom versus determination), transcendental freedom signifies that peculiar 'causality through which something takes place, the cause of which is not itself determined, in accordance with necessary laws, by another cause antecedent to it' (B 474). Whereas freedom generally is taken to imply a certain spontaneity, transcendental freedom consists in 'an *absolute spontaneity* of the cause, whereby a series of appearances, which proceeds in accordance with laws of nature, begins *of itself*' (ibid.; see B 831). In terms of its conceptual status, transcendental freedom is an 'idea' (B 476). That Kant essentially retains this conception of transcendental freedom in the second *Critique* is perfectly clear from a couple of relevant passages. In the Preface to the second *Critique*, Kant already emphasises that transcendental freedom is to be taken 'in that absolute sense in which speculative reason required it, in its employment of the concept of causality, in order to rescue itself from the antinomy' (5:3). And in the 'critical elucidation of the analytic of pure practical reason,' Kant tells us that transcendental freedom must be conceived as 'independence from everything empirical and so from nature generally' (5:97). But absolute spontaneity consists precisely in just such independence.

Kant does not specifically analyse, as a foil for the concept of transcendental freedom, the kind of comparative and pragmatic freedom he had himself evoked in the first example in the 'Remark' following 'Problem II,' where he compares 'love of life' in general to the possible consequences of 'lustful inclinations' and accords clear priority to the former (5:30ff.). But even there he does not actually speak of comparative freedom, and thereby loses an opportunity to emphasise the exceptional significance of transcendental freedom by way of contrast. (Kant himself only speaks of the 'comparative concept of freedom' where the determining natural ground, as with a projectile in free motion, can be described as internal to the acting object: cf. 5:96.)

Transcendental freedom represents the strictest concept of freedom because, if we clearly analyse the matter for ourselves, we can see that all other concepts of freedom still permit some degree or moment of material determination. In the case of such comparative freedom, such as the 'psychological freedom' involved in a 'merely internal chain of representations in the soul' (ibid.), we are always only more or less free, but never absolutely free. On the other hand, freedom in its transcendental shape is not susceptible to further intensification. As an 'absolute spontaneity' of causality, such freedom signifies an original and absolute 'beginning,' and is properly described as 'transcendental' precisely because it concerns the conditions of possibility for initiating a series of appearances in and of itself.

As Kant reminds us in the Preface to the second *Critique*, the concept of transcendental freedom is presented 'only problematically' in the first *Critique* (5:3). At first sight, §5 of the second *Critique* merely seems to come to the same conclusion, albeit now in relation to practical reason as capable of determining the will rather than to the cognitive function of speculative reason. For the problem that is to clarified by recourse to transcendental freedom, as we have seen, is initially presented hypothetically: 'Assuming that ... .' And in fact, Kant addresses the question of the objective reality of this freedom only in the 'Remark' to the next section (§6). Nonetheless, he does make considerable advance upon the conclusions already provided by the first *Critique*. For 'problematic judgements' are not the same as 'hypothetical judgements.' According to the theory of judgement presented in the first *Critique* (§9), a problematic judgement belongs under the heading of 'modality'. The modality of judgements 'contributes nothing to the content of the judgement' but 'simply concerns the value of the copula in relation to thought in general.' Problematic judgements are those in which affirmation or negation is taken as merely *possible* (optional)' (B 100). In this sense, the solution to the third antinomy simply implies that it is 'not impossible to think' the idea of transcendental freedom. 'Hypothetical' assertions, on the other hand, concern the *relation* between judgements: the 'if ... then' or 'ground ... consequence' relation. What is new here, as compared with the first *Critique*, is that the initial proposition identifies the rational domain in which alone transcendental freedom can attain objective reality. This domain is, as we know from §1, is that of the will. But it is also a new claim, as we know from §4, that, in the case of the will, objective reality, or the second category of modality, arises solely from the fact that 'the mere law-giving form of a maxim alone can serve as a law' (5:29).

Kant has therefore already come to a certain decisive conclusion in the course of the analysis: the transition from problematical modality ('possibly') to assertoric modality ('actually'), from the claim that it is 'not impossible to think' something to the claim that something is 'objectively real,' is only successfully accomplished with respect to transcendental freedom if 'the mere law-giving form of a maxim alone' not only 'can serve' as a law, but actually does so serve. What is new, therefore, is that we now know how this transition, how this bridge from one modality to the other, is to be established. But this observation must also be qualified: we may have come to possess significant knowledge in this respect, but it is still far from complete. For Kant does not continue the relevant analysis in detail here. He will later speak of the 'fundamental law of pure practical reason' (§7). But we still need to know whether, or that, this transition can convincingly be demonstrated: is there actually such a bridge? The positive answer to this question lies in the givenness of the fundamental law, in the 'fact of reason' or the 'fact of pure reason' (5:31).

In view of the familiar distinction between the 'positive' and 'negative' conceptions of freedom, the will initially appears to be free in a merely negative sense: 'as altogether independent of the natural law of appearances, ... the law of causality' (5:29). But since 'the merely law-giving form of a maxim alone' serves as a law for the will, the latter can also be described as free in a positive sense. Without explicitly introducing the concept of autonomy, Kant already effectively anticipates this theme in §5: the will considered for itself is not a relationship to objects at all, but represents the self-relation of pure reason itself, and as such is free in a positive sense. (In the *Metaphysics of Morals*, Kant will modify this formulation by introducing the distinction between 'will' [*Wille*] and 'choice' [*Willkür*], claiming that the will cannot be called either free or unfree and that only choice can properly be described as free. See 6:226.)

4. §6: Freedom and the Moral Law

Kant's discussion in 'Problem I' is both completed and in a sense reversed in the discussion in 'Problem II.' If the former is concerned with the free will as fitted for assuming law-giving form, the latter is concerned with the law as fitted for determining the free will, with the law that 'alone is competent to determine it necessarily' (5:29). Kant's answer to the relevant problem runs as follows: 'The law-giving form, insofar as this is contained in the maxim, is therefore the only thing that can constitute a determining ground of the will' [or more precisely and emphatically: a sufficient determining ground of the will] (ibid.). In principle, this answer was already presented earlier in the text insofar as it corresponds directly to the concluding observations in §5. In that context, however, Kant was discussing the will, whereas here in §6 he is concerned with the law-giving form.

The 'Remark' emphasises the strictly complementary character of the two discussions. In that respect, it is best read as more than simply an elucidation of 'Problem II.' The remark bears equally upon both 'Problems' and draws upon both discussions for the resulting conclusion: 'Freedom and unconditional practical law thus reciprocally imply each other' (ibid.).

This qualification of practical law as 'unconditional' (also repeated a few lines later) did not appear in the two preceding sections (§§4–5), or indeed anywhere else earlier in the text. Again the qualification here is clearly intended in an explicating sense rather than in a specifying sense, as in the earlier example of 'universal' practical laws (5:27) and the later example of 'pure' practical laws (5:30). For Kant's original demand, at the very beginning of the work, that practical laws must 'hold for the will of every rational being' (§1; 5:19) cannot be fulfilled by any 'conditional' or 'impure' practical laws. For in the latter case, empirical determining grounds would inevitably come into play and thereby contradict the concept of a practical law in its universally binding character for all rational beings. On the other hand, this twofold explication of practical laws as 'pure' and 'unconditioned' is not redundant insofar as it introduces a new dimension to the formulation provided at the beginning of the text. For we only know that practical laws are unconditionally binding once we have properly grasped the concept of transcendental freedom (§5) as an absolute spontaneity that is subject to no conditions whatsoever. And the 'pure' character of practical laws is derived from insight into the concept of 'mere law-giving form' that has already been developed in §4.

The 'Remark' raises the important and far-reaching question concerning that 'from which our *cognition* of the unconditionally practical *begins*, whether it be from freedom or the practical law' (5:29). Kant has already suggested the answer to this question in the Preface with his distinction between the 'ratio essendi' and the ratio 'cognoscendi' (5:4): cognition cannot begin from freedom since we possess no immediate awareness of the latter and cannot possibly infer its reality from experience. But we can become immediately aware of the moral law by 'attending to the necessity with which reason prescribes pure practical laws to us and to the exclusion of all empirical conditions to which reason directs us' (5:30).

Kant connects our immediate consciousness of the moral law with a certain condition that he introduces parenthetically. However, this is not strictly a 'conditioning condition,' as in the relation of ground and consequent, but rather what we might call a condition of application ('as soon as'). And here Kant effectively anticipates a central theme of section §7 – namely, the fact of (pure) reason, when he tells us that the immediate consciousness in question is given 'as soon as we draw up maxims of the will for ourselves' (5:29). This awareness therefore requires an effort, and represents an achievement. It runs counter to the thoughtless absorption in everyday life and involves deciding to adopt rules, even subjective principles – that is, maxims – for the conduct of life. Remarkably enough, Kant does not define such maxims in any further detail; they could be any maxims whatsoever, rather than necessarily moral ones. This would be to impute universality or law-like character to every maxim, and the crucial distinction between mere maxims in general and maxims fitted to become laws, already established in §1, would disappear. But in the case of an immoral maxim, such as the principle of 'increasing my wealth by every safe means,' familiar from the example of the appropriated deposit (5:27), one could hardly become immediately conscious of the moral law. Just as Kant speaks a few lines later of universal practical laws, we may well ask ourselves whether here too he is not already thinking specifically of moral principles rather than of any principles whatsoever: in deciding to adopt moral principles, and indeed only then, does one become immediately aware of the moral law. Nonetheless, the principal thesis behind the 'Remark' stands independently in its own right: one cannot become conscious of freedom in an immediate manner, but solely through the moral law or morality itself.

In spite of having separated the moral law so emphatically from any possible sensuous conditions, Kant does make an appeal to 'experience' towards the end of the 'Remark' (5:30). But experience is not being invoked here in order to ground morality or freedom, something that would simply conflate the distinction between the 'is' and the 'ought' and would certainly involve a radical inconsistency in the overall argument. The reference to experience is supposed to confirm the order in which the two concepts properly stand to one another – namely, that it is 'morality which first discloses to us the concept of freedom' (ibid.). For the purposes of his demonstration here, Kant conducts the argument on two levels. Although he does not use the expression, Kant refers first to the kind of 'pragmatic' freedom that is intrinsically oriented to one's own welfare, before proceeding to identify that authentically moral – that is transcendental – freedom that excludes any such orientation.

Kant begins by discussing another passion, this time the 'natural (innate)' and 'inflamed' passion of lustful desire (see Kant's *Anthropology*: 7:267f, where it is described as 'sexual inclination'). Instead of simply assuming the supposedly irresistible power of such desires, Kant suggests we consider the case of someone who knew that, after 'gratifying his lust,' he would instantly be hanged on the gallows standing outside. If we ask ourselves whether such a man 'would not then restrain his inclinations,' Kant is rightly convinced that 'one need not conjecture very long for the reply' (5:30). Here he is alluding to what we have called 'pragmatic freedom', the freedom to limit or restrain a currently predominant inclination in favour of the higher-level inclination of the love of life in general. But there is a freedom over and beyond such considerations. For anyone who was similarly 'threatened with immediate execution' unless 'he give false testimony against an honourable man,' Kant says, would have to admit 'without hesitation' that it would at least be 'possible' for him to refuse such a thing (ibid.).

The discussion of 'truthfulness in opposition to lying' (5:61) usually plays a particular role in Kant's work. One only has to consider the prohibition on false promises in the *Groundwork* (4:402; 422; 429), the remark in the essay on *Perpetual Peace* that 'honesty is better than all politics' (8:370), or the repudiation of the 'supposed right to lie from philanthropic motives' (8:423–30). From the possibility of refusing to give false witness, Kant rightly concludes that someone 'therefore judges that he can do something because he is aware that he ought to do it, and recognises within himself that freedom which, but for the moral law, would have remained unknown to him' (5:30; see 155 and 158). The first part of Kant's formulation anticipates the central doctrine of the 'fact of reason' ('Man can do something because he is aware that he ought to do it'), while the second part, indeed the whole remark, essentially confirms 'the moral law as the *ratio cognoscendi* of (transcendental) freedom.'

Bibliography

Achenwall, G./Pütter, J. S. 1750/1995: *Elementa Iuris Naturae / Anfangsgründe des Naturrechts*, Latin/German edition, edited. and translated by J. Schröder, Frankfurt am Main.

Allison, H. E. 1990: *Kant's Theory of Freedom*, Cambridge.

Ameriks, K. 2000: *Kant and the Fate of Autonomy*, Cambridge.

Hegel, G. W. F. 1803: *Über die wissenschaftlichen Behandlungsarten des Naturrechts, seine Stelle in der praktischen Philosophie und sein Verhältnis zu den positiven Rechtswissenschaften*, in: *Werke in zwanzig Bänden*, vol. 2,

Frankfurt am Main 1970, 434–530. English translation: *Natural Law. The Scientific Ways of Treating Natural Law, Its Place in Moral Philosophy, and Its Relation to the Positive Sciences of Law*, translated by T. M. Knox (Philadelphia 1975).

Hegel, G.W.F. 1807: *Phänomenologie des Geistes*, in *Werke in zwanzig Bänden*, vol. 3. English translation: *Hegel's Phenomenology of Spirit*, translated by A. V. Miller (Oxford 1977).

Korsgaard, C. 1996: *Creating the Kingdom of Ends*, Cambridge.

Willaschek, M. 1992: *Praktische Vernunft. Handlungstheorie und Moralbegründung bei Kant*, Stuttgart.

8

'On the Concept of an Object of Pure Practical Reason' (Chapter 2 of the Analytic of Practical Reason)

Annemarie Pieper

In the second chapter of the second *Critique*, Kant explicitly addresses three questions: (1) What is the object of practical reason? (5:57–65) (2) What are the categories through which practical reason determines this object? (5:65–67) (3) How does the faculty of practical judgement mediate between action and the moral law? (5:67–68) As a response to these questions, Kant develops a theory of ethical judgement for assessing the unconditionally binding character of the claim to validity that is raised by any moral judgement. He attempts to determine both whether this claim can be justified and how it can be rendered practically effective.

1. The Object of Practical Reason

Kant defines the object of practical reason, as distinct from the cognitive object of theoretical reason, as an envisaged consequence of an act of freedom. Such an object is not something already given, like a natural object, but something which must first be brought into existence through a specific kind of act. The constituting conditions for such a thing lie within the faculty that initiates the production of ethically relevant objects – namely, the will itself.

The will does not automatically heed the prescriptions of practical reason, but can also be determined by non-rational factors (by feelings of pleasure and displeasure, or by objects that are agreeable or useful) to which it may accord priority over such prescriptions. It is imperative, therefore, to distinguish between an object that owes its existence to freedom and an object that is actualised in the course of satisfying a natural need. In order to separate these two kinds of objects clearly from one another, Kant suggests that we should conceptualise the objects generated by the principle of freedom through the categories of good and evil, and conceptualise the objects actualised in pursuit of the principle of happiness through the categories of well-being and distress. This distinction has the advantage of permitting us to separate the analysis of morality entirely from empirically motivating factors that invariably possess a simply factual rather than normative character.

Kant is attempting therefore to understand good and evil exclusively as 'modes' or 'categories' of freedom rather than as empirical predicates of any kind. But since the human will is always subject to two principles – namely, the principle of happiness and the principle of freedom – the faculty of desire finds itself confronted by two different kinds of demand: an imperative to select the best appropriate means for the realisation of a particular end from which we may expect an increase in our happiness (well-being), and an imperative to perform our duty for its own sake, regardless of any feelings of pleasure or displeasure that may be involved. Since the human will is not a 'holy will,' one invariably already committed to morality, it naturally tends, because of its immediate involvement with bodily needs, to accord priority to such needs. The will evaluates 'objects' as good (or evil) either because they represent good (or bad) ends for satisfying certain given needs and desires, or good (or bad) means for realising such ends. But understood in this sense, 'good' and 'evil' would simply amount to empirical concepts devoid of any moral significance. They would merely prescribe our acts in a hypothetical rather than categorical manner, and the striving for happiness would be the only relevant ground for human conduct.

Hence, according to Kant, if the concepts of good and evil are to possess properly moral and thus normative significance, they must be reconstructed as 'consequences of the *a priori* determination of the will' (5:65). From the empirical perspective, the concepts of good and evil provide our point of departure for the determination of the will: good or evil is simply what makes me happy or unhappy (or what is useful or detrimental) and thus motivates me to actions directed toward my own well-being. From the moral perspective, on the other hand, it is autonomous reason that furnishes the proper point of departure for reconstructing the concepts of value. Unlike the principle of happiness, which has an effect upon the will in accordance with natural necessity as *causa efficiens*, autonomous reason exercises a 'causality from freedom' as *causa finalis* by presenting the will with a normative law (the moral law) as '*the supreme condition of all good*' (5:62).[1] Good and evil, as 'objects' of practical reason, are then nothing but an 'effect' or 'consequence' of the freedom that in turn understands itself as the 'cause' of this normative causality. Kant designates the product of this activity either as the moral law or as the good, depending on whether the act of practical self-determination is analysed in terms of its formal unconditional character (the ought) or in terms of its qualitative content (morality).

Kant thus identifies an empirical act as one that begins from a feeling of pleasure or displeasure, and that directs the will to those ends that would satisfy our desire for happiness. A moral act, by contrast, originates in practical reason, whose normative causality commands the will to examine all of its desires in the light of the moral law and evaluate their possible consequences in moral terms. In the final analysis, the categories of good and evil are applied exclusively to 'objects', which are subject to such moral evaluation.

'Thus good and evil is, strictly speaking, referred to actions, not to the person's state of feeling, and if anything is to be good or evil absolutely (and in every respect and without any further condition), or is to be held to be such, it would be only the way of acting, the maxim of the will, and consequently the acting person himself as a good or evil human being, that could be so called, but not a thing' (5:60).

In claiming that the principle of freedom itself, rather than the concepts of good and evil, constitutes the *a priori* source of morality, as the condition of the moral law (*ratio essendi*), Kant is essentially repudiating all hedonistic, utilitarian, and metaphysical ethical theories. For such theories always attempt to ground morality in some ontological principle and thereby all commit what G. E. Moore called the 'naturalistic fallacy'. Assuming that the human striving for happiness is something ethical in its own right, hedonistic and utilitarian theories effectively identify happiness with the good and thereby elevate an actual fact into a normative principle: what all human beings actually do becomes what is right,

---

[1] In the *Nachlass*, Kant expands on this as follows: 'We explain free acts in accordance with the laws of human nature, but we do not thereby recognise these acts as determined by the latter; otherwise we would never regard them as contingent and claim that they could and should have transpired differently. In free acts reason is involved not merely as a cognitive, but also as an effective and moving *principium*. How reason ... can assume the place of a natural cause is something we cannot understand' (*Nachlass*: 5612; *Materialien*, p. 41).

and thereby good. It is quite true that attempts to provide a metaphysical foundation for ethics, such as that developed by Plato in the *Republic* through recourse to the idea of the good, would certainly avoid the charge of vainly trying to derive 'the ought' from empirical existence. But since the idea of the good is still interpreted here in relation to being itself, albeit some kind of supra-empirical being in the sense of eternal presence, the origin of 'the ought' is illegitimately located in an ontological principle. Quite apart from the logical impropriety of ascribing normative force to the factical or intelligible domain in its own right, any attempt to ground morality on some actually existing epitome of the good (such as happiness, the idea of the good, or the will of God) essentially violates the principle of freedom for Kant. And that can only result in heteronomy: man would no longer determine himself through practical reason, would no longer determine how he ought to will in accordance with a law of his own, but would allow himself to be determined externally instead (through nature, through some metaphysical construct, or through some non-human being over and beyond himself).

If normative validity is legitimately to be ascribed to the concepts of good and evil, then ethics must appeal to an irreducible *a priori*, a principle of obligation that can define good and evil in properly moral terms. Kant therefore reconstructs the logical genesis of moral action in terms of the following conceptual sequence: freedom – the moral law – good and evil – formation of the will – action. 'This is where we must explain the paradox of method in a critique of practical reason, *namely, that the concepts of good and evil must not be determined in advance of the moral law*' (5:62). The proper object of pure practical reason is therefore the will insofar as the moral law commands it not simply to strive unreflectively for happiness, but to examine its maxims from the perspective of what is morally good and evil, and thereby determine whether such maxims correspond to the law of freedom or not, and thus whether they are normatively justified or not.

2. Good and Evil as Categories of Freedom

Kant analyses the will-determining capacity of practical reason from a twofold perspective. On the one hand, he employs the concept of causality to describe the intrinsic relationship between reason and the will, interpreted as an essentially normative relationship rather than an ontological relationship.[2] On the other hand, he focuses upon the categorial status of the concept of causality itself and investigates the functional role of a causality of pure reason as far as moral-practical judgements are concerned.

When Kant speaks of a 'causality from freedom' in the context of the moral determination of the will, the qualification 'from freedom' emphasises that we are not talking about the causality of nature, where a cause exercises an effect in a mechanical fashion, and acts therefore as the consequence of an external stimulus rather than spontaneously from freedom. Nonetheless, Kant continues to employ the concept of 'causality' in relation to practical reason precisely because he wishes to emphasise that the freedom in question here cannot be identified with arbitrariness. For practical reason too generates laws of its own that possess universal validity and determine a relevant object. On the other hand, the difference between this process and the way in which theoretical reason (of the understanding) determines its object is so fundamental that the two concepts of causality involved must be distinguished unambiguously from one another.[3] It is decisive for the causality of freedom that practical reason (the cause) determines the will (the effect) not through any law of nature, which would simply eliminate freedom altogether, but solely through its own normative force or compulsion.[4] This 'force' proceeds from the law (the moral law) that practical reason expresses as a strictly categorical claim: always and everywhere consciously and deliberately to affirm freedom for the sake of freedom. This 'law of freedom' (5:65) results from an act of reason itself. Practical reason does not act in a lawless manner, and the 'first' act through which it initially produces itself as practical reason consists precisely in the production of the law of freedom. If practical reason occurred somewhere outside or above the human

---

[2] 'Moral laws in themselves possess no *vim obligatoriam*, but contain nothing but the norm [*Norm*]' (Kant: *Nachlass*: 7097; *Materialien*, p. 96).

[3] See Beck 1974: 'Freedom is a kind of causality in which the cause of the act is not one of two phenomenal events. We cannot comprehend this kind of causality. We can only comprehend relations of cause and effect when both terms of the connection are events in the same spatio-temporal series' (p. 139). One should merely add that this incomprehensibility is twofold in character: it is *theoretically* impossible to grasp an effect as the consequence of a non-phenomenal cause, and it is *practically* incomprehensible how a non-phenomenal cause can exercise a phenomenal effect.

[4] 'One must compel oneself to perform well-considered and morally good acts. Hence *imperativi*. The cause is as sensuous as the spontaneity belonging to it, and the original movement derives from this. The more one is capable of compelling oneself, even with a pragmatic compulsion, the freer one is' (Kant, *Nachlass*: 6998; *Materialien*, p. 107).

domain, it would require no law and would already coincide immediately with the moral will. Freedom would not then be something demanded of us, and the will would already affirm its freedom *ab ovo*. For we human beings, on the other hand, reason and will are not immediately identical because the body also makes its claims and thereby determines the will empirically in terms of the causality of nature. To that extent, practical reason finds itself compelled to address the body, against the empirical will, and to exercise coercion in the shape of the 'ought.' But in a sense, practical reason simultaneously cancels this normative force or compulsion insofar as it grasps it explicitly as an expression of original freedom. The will is subject to the ought because what it ought to do brings it to freedom in the first place. It thereby reveals itself precisely as a good will that wills what it ought to do.

If we examine the conceptual structure of moral judgements, we can see that the synthesis involved here is accomplished precisely through categories of freedom. In this context, too, Kant refers back to the specific conditions of knowledge already explored in the first *Critique* in order to distinguish precisely between the respective functions of the understanding as distinct from those of practical reason. A theoretical judgement organises empirical material (the sensuous data furnished through intuition) through the categories of the understanding in order to render it capable of truth, whereas a moral judgement normatively determines the empirical will (inclinations, interests, impulses, desires) in order to qualify it as good or evil through the categories of freedom. But Kant emphasises that a moral judgement is not a cognitive judgement, even though it formally exhibits a comparable structure to the latter. For a moral judgement is not concerned with determining the being of any existing entity (a natural object), but solely with evaluating the maxim of the will with respect to its normative validity. In this connection, the empirical genesis of the maxims in question is irrelevant – for they are all personal rules formed through the individual pursuit of particular ends on the basis of the natural desire for happiness. The moral judgement concerns the ethical status of our maxims, and practical reason alone determines the genesis of this status. Practical reason offers the '*form of a pure will*' (5:66) that represents the unconditioned 'ought' of the postulate of freedom and provides the appropriate perspective for the moral evaluation of the empirical will.

This 'pure will,' constructed by analogy with transcendental apperception as the pure consciousness of theoretical reason, involves an 'I will' that must be able to accompany all my practical deliberations and that is

oriented *a priori* to the morally good.⁵ Just as the truth-grounding function of the 'I think,' in accordance with Kant's logical theory, finds expression in the twelve forms of judgement, so too the 'I will' of pure practical
reason unfolds its morally grounding force in terms of twelve practical
categories. Kant claims that these categories 'in relation to the supreme
principle of freedom become cognitions immediately and do not have
to wait for intuitions in order to receive meaning; and this happens for
the noteworthy reason that they themselves produce the reality of that to
which they refer (the disposition of the will), which is not the business of
theoretical concepts' (5:66). The characteristic feature of these practical
categories is therefore that they require no 'application' to the empirical sphere because what is actually willed in fact cannot determine our
knowledge of what ought to be willed. It is quite true that it is the empirical will that finds itself addressed by the moral law. But unlike a case
of sensuous perception, which guarantees that an instance of theoretical
knowledge is not only necessarily and universally valid but also objectively substantive, the empirical will itself plays no role in determining
the objective validity of moral-practical judgements. For the empirical
will stands under the conditions of nature, and is therefore incapable of
deciding upon the binding character of such judgements or of qualifying
what ought to be done in terms of good or evil. That something is 'actually' obligatory is determined solely through the categories of freedom,
which in turn compel the empirical will to subject itself to the form of
the pure will and thereby to abstract from all wishes and desires it in fact
possesses. Not what I actually will, but what I actually ought to will,
essentially decides the moral character of the relevant judgement and the
act that results from it.

The '*table of the categories of freedom with respect to the concepts of
the good and the evil*' (5:66) comprehensively presents the *a priori* principles generated by practical reason as a moral demand addressed directly
to the empirical will. These normative principles are not synthetic *a priori*
judgements such as those of pure theoretical reason. The judgements of
pure theoretical reason are constitutive for our knowledge of nature only
because they result from the *a priori* application of the categories of the
understanding to time as the pure form of intuition required for all given
sensuous content. The categories of practical reason, on the other hand,
need no such application in the first place, and can therefore be formulated

⁵ 'Freedom is the apperception of oneself as an intellectual being, something that is active'
(Kant, *Nachlass*: 6860; *Materialien*, p. 40).

directly through autonomous practical reason as postulates of freedom, and thus expressed immediately as moral principles.[6]

Within each of the four groups of categories, Kant specifies the types of judgement in accordance with the sensuous and natural aspect they derive from the interest-governed nature of the empirical will. But both the 'sensuously conditioned' and the 'sensuously-unconditioned' principles are formulated *a priori* – that is, from the perspective of the rational concepts of good and evil as the two fundamental modifications of freedom. Whatever derives from freedom possesses the formal structure of the ought and the substantive character of the good. As practical categories of *quantity*, Kant identifies maxims, prescriptions, and laws, which can be articulated as individual, collective, and universal principles. Let us assume that man is a rational being whose will is indeed initially formed, whether individually or collectively, in relation to empirical conditions (with specific interests and inclinations), but that this will can always be evaluated from the perspective of good and evil. We may then formulate the quantitative categories of freedom as normative principles in this way: (1) Of your subjective maxims, let only those that are directed to the good as the sum total of freedom be binding rules upon your action. (2) Of the norms and values that are recognised as inter-subjectively binding in your community, let only those that are directed to the good as the sum total of freedom be binding rules upon your action: (3) Let your will be determined at all times by the moral law as the principle of freedom binding on all rational beings in relation to what you ought to do.

Kant identifies practical categories of *quality* as the rules that determine whether we perform, omit, or exempt ourselves from certain actions. These categories categorically demand: (1) Always hold to principles that are consistent with the moral law. (2) Reject those principles that cannot pass the test of the categorical imperative. (3) Only override principles whose moral character is otherwise self-evident when there are good – that is, morally justifiable – grounds for doing so.

---

[6] Beck regards the section on the categories of freedom as the most difficult and obscure portion of the second *Critique*. He claims that the 'sparseness and lack of clarity' (op. cit., p. 125) of the conceptual construction here force the commentator to provide little more than suggestions and conjectures about Kant's intentions. It is quite true that Kant's remarks in this connection are extraordinarily sparse and are certainly not as immediately intelligible as he supposes. But I have the distinct impression that Beck's interpretation (op. cit., pp. 142–151), which differs significantly from that presented here, pays insufficient attention to the fact that the categories of freedom are reconstructed here specifically 'with respect to the concepts of the good and the evil' – that is, from the perspective of morality, and must therefore be read as moral postulates or imperatives.

The principles that Kant summarises as practical categories of *relation* are those concerned with persons, with their state or condition, and with the reciprocal interaction of persons. Kant understands 'person' to mean the human and natural being who is nonetheless called upon to assume freedom, the being through whose reason the voice of morality sounds forth – as in the original sense of the Latin *'personare.'* Insofar as the categories of relation express *a priori* relations in general (substance-accident, cause-effect, reciprocity), so the practical relational principles demand the formation of a human character that is always prepared to give priority to moral rather than merely natural considerations: (1) Always act as a free being that only contingently possesses bodily needs as well. (2) Subject the formation of your will to the causality of freedom manifested in the moral law. (3) In forming your own will, respect the freedom of other persons who are likewise morally obligated to consider your freedom.

The practical categories of *modality*, according to Kant, concern what is permissible, what is dutifully required, and what is a matter of perfect duty – and the opposites of these. It is a question of the morally possible, the morally actual, and the morally necessary. These practical categories yield the following normative principles: (1) Hold always to the moral law, which enables us to distinguish between morally permissible and impermissible acts in our practical judgements. (2) Give priority to the duties prescribed by the moral law over the satisfaction of needs and the pursuit of happiness. (3) Act always out of duty (in terms of morality) rather than merely in conformity to duty (in terms of legality).

The twelve categories of freedom are not cognitive categories, because they are not concerned with grounding our theoretical knowledge of empirical objects at all. The categories of freedom must rather be read as instructions for action that direct the will to form its practical judgements in the light of the *a priori* reconstruction of the moral forms of judgement, and never to regard empirical desires as legitimate unless they are first evaluated in the light of the category of freedom. The normative principles that are implicit in the categories of freedom reveal themselves in the last analysis as modifications of the good as determined by the moral law, as specified by Kant in accordance with the logical table of judgements. From a quantitative perspective, the good presents itself as the morally legitimated determining ground of an individual, collective, and universal human subject. From the qualitative perspective, the realisation of the good as an unconditional ought is commanded in terms of universally binding rules of action. From the relational perspective, the good appears as the complex of relations within which the subject constitutes itself as an autonomous person in association with other autonomous persons. From the modal perspective, the good reveals itself lastly as the possible, actual, or necessary execution of a duty. In all cases of *a priori* moral self-determination of a human being through practical reason, the good functions essentially as the representative of freedom itself.

3. The Practical Faculty of Judgement

Insofar as practical reason is capable of determining the will immediately in relation to what ought to be willed, no specific practical faculty for making judgements is required. There is nothing to be 'applied' here because the categories of freedom are 'pure' – that is, are normatively binding independently of all empirical interests. A practical faculty of judging is not required because practical reason does not need to go out beyond the moral law, which it has itself constructed as the representative instance of freedom, in order to demonstrate the 'objective' validity of the law in question. Since the substantive moral character of the good, as object of the ought, is also generated through reason itself, the faculty of judging shows itself to be redundant as a mediating factor, something that is most certainly not the case where cognitive judgements are concerned. The categories of the understanding cannot generate their objective validity from simply within themselves, and can confirm that claim to validity only in relation to a material content that is supplied to it from another faculty altogether – that of sensuous intuition. The particular data of sensibility and the universal forms of the understanding stand over against one another in an unmediated manner, and without the faculty of judgement there could be no objective knowledge at all. The theoretical faculty of judgement must illuminate our intrinsically 'blind' intuitions through its schematising activity by moving constantly between the particular and the universal and thereby fill our intrinsically 'empty' categorial concepts with material content. It is only after once the faculty of judgement has successfully accomplished this by 'subsuming' the particular under the universal or by 'applying' the universal to the particular, after rendering each conformable to the other through the activity of the imagination, that we can speak of true – that is, substantive (objective) and valid (categorially grounded) – knowledge.

   If Kant is nonetheless forced to develop a procedure of typification that is analogous to the schematism of the theoretical faculty of judgement, and thus to install a specific practical faculty of judgement even though here there are no moral 'particulars' that need to be subsumed under a moral universal, he does so because the human will is also determined by external and non-rational factors. Since the latter are defined by their given ontological character rather than their deontological character, they immediately raise the problem of properly clarifying the difference between the 'is' and the 'ought' in particular cases. And neither the understanding nor practical reason as such are best-suited to resolve this difficulty. Practical judgement is called for when we must relate a particular (a natural expression of the will) that has not yet been morally evaluated to the moral universal (the moral law as representative of the twelve modifications of freedom) and moralise the particular in question by making it subsumable under the moral law in the first place. As Kant writes: 'The concepts of good and evil first determine an object for the will. They themselves, however, stand under a practical rule of reason which, if it is pure reason, determines the will *a priori* with respect to its object. Now, whether an action possible for us in sensibility is or is not a case that stands under the rule requires practical judgement, by which what is expressed in the rule universally (*in abstracto*) is applied to an action *in concreto*' (5:67).

The problem that creates the need for such practical judgement lies in the fact that two entirely distinct systems of rules initially stand over against each other without mediation, and must therefore first be rendered conformable to one another. [7] But how can an unconditionally obligating demand (the postulate of freedom) be applied to circumstances and events belonging to the world of appearances, to things over which the moral law can have no power insofar as they are all subject to the necessity character of laws of nature? The causality of freedom and the causality of nature govern different domains of objects – the good on the one hand,

---

[7] Otfried Höffe identifies a frequently overlooked affinity between the Kantian and Aristotelian theories of judgement in the domain of ethics. He is concerned above all to counter the objection that Kant simply devalues human individuality and banishes the dimension of experience from ethics altogether. Höffe certainly concedes that Kant's approach disempowers experience, but stresses that it does so only in relation to moral self-determination. For we can only strictly speak of autonomy if the will is capable of determining its actual willing independently of experience (through practical reason alone). 'Judgement grounded upon experience is disempowered in favour of a form of judgement independent of experience, namely 'the judgement of pure practical reason', [...] because only the latter can properly decide upon the genuinely moral moment in question' (Höffe 1990, p. 545). But in Kant's view, the faculty of judgement that does depend upon experience (like Aristotle's concept of *prohairesis*) still makes an indispensable contribution to the appropriate evaluation of a situation in the light of a practical rule (and thus to the concrete exercise of judgement in particular cases).

and nature on the other – neither of which can in principle be reduced to
the other. No 'is' can be derived from an 'ought' and no 'ought' can be
derived from an 'is.' How then can practical judgement exercise the mediating function in 'moralising' the particular or empirically 'materialising'
the universal without committing the 'naturalistic fallacy'?

In the *Critique of the Power of Judgement*, Kant distinguishes two
specific types of judgement: determining and reflective. Theoretical
judgement belongs to the former type. For it subsumes a given particular under an equally given universal by developing a schema that, being
at once sensuous and cognitive in character, can mediate between the
understanding and the faculty of intuition. All cognitive judgements rely
on schemata that generate the relevant synthesis. These schemata permit
the categorial articulation of sensuous data and thus facilitate the process of subsumption. The faculty of reflecting judgement, on the other
hand, which Kant introduces in the context of aesthetic and teleological
judgements, is involved when only the particular is given (namely, objects
experienced as 'beautiful' or 'sublime,' or natural products that appear
to be self-generating and self-sustaining) and the universal required for
subsumption is not. The universal provided by the understanding and the
universal as defined by practical reason are both incapable of legitimating judgements concerning organisms and objects of art. Here the faculty
of judgement can only render the particular susceptible to judgements
through 'reflecting' rather than schematising activity. In·so doing, the
faculty of judgement makes use of a principle of its own in order to frame
an aesthetic or teleological universal: the principle of purposiveness.

To which of these two types of faculty of judgement would the kind of
practical judgement discussed here seem to belong? It is quite clear that it
cannot simply be assigned immediately to either of them. If it is to determine content, it would have to subsume given particulars (the factual-
empirical determinations of the will) under a given universal (the moral
law). But that is precisely the problem since the moral law is not a universal in the ontological order of things and is therefore inapplicable to
the objects of nature as such. In order to exercise its reflective function,
the practical faculty of judgement, based on the principle of purposiveness, would have to discover an appropriate universal for the given particular. But it cannot accomplish this either because it already possesses
the universal – namely, the moral – law, which it no longer needs to seek
out and identify. The dilemma with which the faculty of practical judgement is confronted is clear. If practical judgement attempts to schematise
content, it fails because the particular belongs to the ontological order

and the universal belongs to the deontological order. And that means that nothing in nature as such conforms to the latter, and no schema can be developed where the sensuous component is lacking. But if practical judgement attempts to exercise its reflecting function, it also fails because the universal is already given. But the universal in question can neither be applied nor be replaced by any other universal construed on the basis of the principle of purposiveness. For the aesthetic and the teleological forms of judgement can, in principle, only make regulative rather than constitutive use of their relevant principles, and this falls far short of what is required for practical judgement.

In order to resolve this difficulty, Kant proposes a special procedure peculiar to practical judgement. Although this procedure is different from and independent of the processes of schematism or reflection as such, it nonetheless remains oriented to the determining and reflecting method of the faculty of judgement in general – namely, the method of typification. Now Kant also describes typification as a kind of schematism. And this is legitimate to the extent that typification projects or sketches a certain model that enables us to relate two heterogeneous components meaning-fully with one another insofar as it expressly brings them both together in a shared context. But since the moral law and its modifications, the categories of freedom, are in principle not possible sensuous objects, Kant seeks to identify the kind of schema that can function as the 'type' for the moral law. The only possible candidate to serve such a role for the moral law is the law of causality, which represents the lawfulness of nature in general. The causality of nature furnishes an appropriate schema for the causality of freedom because it precisely fulfils the two conditions that are required if the moral law is to be applied successfully to the empirical determinations of the will: (1) as the principle for any actual knowledge of nature, it establishes a connection with the empirical realm; (2) as law, it guarantees a necessary relation between cause and effect:

'Physical causality, or the condition under which it takes place, belongs among the concepts of nature, whose schema transcendental imagina-tion sketches. Here, however, we have to do not with the schema of a case in accordance with laws but with the schema of a law itself (if the word schema is appropriate here) [...]. To a natural law, as a law to which objects of sensible intuition as such are subject, there must correspond a schema, that is, a universal procedure of the imagination (by which it presents *a priori* to the senses the pure concept of the understanding which the law determines). But no intuition can be put under the law of freedom (as that of a causality not sensibly conditioned) – and hence under the concept of the unconditioned good as well – and hence no schema on behalf of its application *in concreto*. Thus the moral law has no cognitive faculty other than the understanding (not the imagination) by means of which it can be applied to objects of nature, and what the understanding can put under an idea of reason is not a *schema* of sensibility but a law – such a law, however, as can be presented *in concreto* in objects of the senses and hence a law of nature, though only as to its form. This law is what the understanding can put under an idea of freedom on behalf of judgement, and we can, accordingly, call it the *type* of the moral law.' (5:68–69).

This crucial passage clearly reveals Kant's determination not to end up by erasing the distinction between the 'is' and the 'ought,' the two realms he had been so careful to separate from one another in order to establish the proper independence of the validity of moral claims in relation to everything empirical. If he now elevates the law of causality as the 'type' of the moral law, and presents it as the underlying schema for the moral evaluation of the empirical processes of the formation of the will, he does so essentially because the understanding and practical reason alike can legitimately be compared as intrinsically legislative authorities in their own right. Just as the understanding generates the law of the causality of nature, so too practical reason generates the law of causality of freedom. And it is precisely this generation of the form of lawfulness that enables us to see how we can harmonise empirical and moral willing, factual and normative validity, without simply eliminating the distinction between morality and nature. Kant emphasises 'the *form of lawfulness* in general' (5:70) as the common element of the two kinds of causality, without thereby claiming that one kind may ultimately be reduced to the other, since he also insists upon the radical difference between moral and empirical determination of the will. He thus avoids the naturalistic fallacy that arises when an essentially empirical significance and ontological status is inappropriately ascribed to the causality of freedom.

Typification, as Kant emphasises in different ways, is a process of schematising without reference to the imagination. *Theoretical* judgement is dependent upon the image-producing capacities of the imagination, since the schema here would otherwise lack the necessary sensuous and aesthetic components and would be incapable of serving as a model for the synthesis of material content and categorial form. *Practical* judgement, on the other hand, in order to prevent an ontological interpretation of its own normative synthetic judgements, must exclude the function of the imagination that is necessarily required for the constitution of objects of knowledge. If practical judgement employs the understanding as a schema for moral claims, a relation to the sensuous world is still retained here insofar as the cognitive faculty of the understanding is fundamentally related to the senses without the 'material deliverances' of which its own concepts would remain emptily abstract. At the same time, however, the *theoretical* relation to the sensuous world is ignored when practical judgement draws upon the pure law of the understanding as the type of the moral law in its quasi-schematising process of mediating between normative moral claims and the empirical will. For practical judgement is concerned solely with the validity of the law of causality to which the understanding that has constructed it lays claim, and not with the realm to which this law is applied – namely, the determined natural order. But practical reason also lays claim to the very same validity in relation to its own law of the causality of freedom, and it likewise disregards the realm to which the moral law is applied – namely, that of all empirical willing determined by the desire for happiness. In this way, the concrete content and circumstances that fall under the jurisdiction of the law in any particular case are disregarded in principle: the ontological and the normative realm (will and morality) are separated from one another, but they are nonetheless capable of being related to one another through the laws that govern them.

The way in which practical judgement employs the law of causality as the type of the moral law while simultaneously distancing itself from the schematising procedures of the theoretical faculty of judgement effectively brings it into a certain proximity with the reflecting faculty of judgement, and in particular of teleological judgement. [8] This proximity derives from

---

[8] The practical faculty of judgement *qua* reflecting judgement can certainly also be interpreted as an expression of aesthetic judgement, especially if we bear in mind the significance of the *sensus communis* for the exercise of judgement in particular cases and the role of the imagination in furnishing sensible images that can represent the ideal. Urs Thurnherr has thus attempted to locate 'the very heart of Kant's moral philosophy in his aesthetic thought' (Thurnherr 2001, p. 82) and emphasised the distinction between projecting and acknowledging maxims. 'Whereas the process of determining or projecting maxims presents itself as a task for our common understanding as a practical-aesthetic faculty of judgement, the process of assuming, of actively *acknowledging*, maxims constitutes the proper object of the will as practical reason' (ibid., p. 90; cf. also Thurnherr 1994). Peter Müller, on the other hand, interprets practical judgement in teleological terms and speaks of a 'moral teleology' in this connection. Since reason is 'autotelic' with respect to its practical function, Müller follows the approach of Nicolai Hartmann and describes the teleology in question as 'the categorial form of human freedom' (Müller 1983, p. 434). It seems to me that we can recognise both an aesthetic and a teleological aspect to the practical faculty of judgement as a form of reflecting judgement, depending on which of its relevant tasks we are seeking to clarify. When we formulate the categorical imperative in analogy with a law of nature, we will appeal to the teleological

the shared regulative function that the moral law exercises with respect to the will and the principle of purposiveness exercises with respect to nature. In the *Critique of the Power of Judgement*, Kant employs the critical concept of the 'as if' in order to show that although our judgements here possess no constitutive significance (with regard to grounding our knowledge of objects), they can nonetheless claim an equal validity with cognitive judgements as far as the self-referential judgements of the reflecting faculty of judgement are concerned. We are indeed permitted to understand specific phenomena of nature in purposive terms – that is, as if nature itself acted according to purposes. Although this assumption is only permissible subjectively (in relation to the faculty of judgement itself) and not objectively (in relation to nature), this hypothesis has shown its real value with regard to natural organic processes that cannot be explained in a purely causal-mechanical fashion. Where, therefore, the category of causality fails us, the teleological power of judgement appeals to the principle of purposiveness to formulate the appropriate connections of cause and effect. Thus ants and bees form states ('as if' they had developed concepts of an expressly social community that would then function as the cause of the division of labour they actively pursue); the river leaves certain deposits ('as if' it intended that a certain kind of tree should take root there); beavers build houses for themselves ('as if' they were architects).

This critical perspective of the 'as if' also underlies the particular judgements of the practical faculty of judgement insofar as the latter hypothetically presupposes, in applying the moral law to the empirical will, that practical reason can indeed determine the will, just as the understanding determines nature through the category of causality. This approach represents a kind of thought-experiment one must perform in order to decide upon the moral status of a given maxim: Represent to yourself that the proposed rule of action should acquire the status of a law of nature that would ineluctably determine the human will. Would you then, on this supposition, still be able to will what it is that you *de facto* will? Kant believes that just such 'a rule of judgement under the laws of pure practical reason' (5:69) plays a very considerable role in our everyday conduct and

perspective in order to elucidate the comparison between the causality of nature and the causality of freedom with respect to the form of lawfulness in general. But we could also refer to 'sublimity' ('the starry heavens above' and 'the moral law within') in this connection. And we can appeal to the aesthetic of reflecting practical judgement when we consider not so much the compelling character of both forms of causality, but rather their effect upon our sensuous-feeling nature.

behaviour. As Kant says: 'Ask yourself whether, if the action you propose were to take place by a law of the nature of which you were yourself a part, you could indeed regard it as possible through your will. Everyone does, in fact, appraise actions as morally good or evil by this rule' (5:69). One can of course always will to act in such a way that it will procure advantage for oneself, and welcome mendacity and deception as advantageous strategies to pursue in this connection. But one cannot rationally will this if one were to suppose that all human beings were forced by their very nature to act in pursuit of their own advantage. Kant had already expressed this thought in the formula of the categorical imperative as presented in the *Groundwork*: to assess the morality of an act by determining whether its maxim could still be willed if it were to be regarded as a universal law of nature (4:421; 437).

The practical faculty of judgement therefore evaluates the action-grounding rules of the empirical will with respect to their moral status by reflecting upon whether its maxims could determine the will as if they were laws of nature. Kant finds this procedure entirely convincing because 'even the commonest understanding' (5:70) already orients itself by this approach and thus affords the support of general experience in this regard. It is legitimate to employ the law of nature as the type of the law of freedom as long as one does not conflate the type with the law. That is always what happens whenever the typification is also extended beyond the form of lawfulness to the realm of application itself, and the perspective of 'as if' is thereby transformed into the perspective of 'thus it is' (thus committing the naturalistic fallacy).[9] As the type of the moral law, the causality of nature is not conceived here as a law that grounds any knowledge of objects. It rather merely serves for the practical faculty of judgement as a model through which it may represent a normative determination of the

---

[9] See Konrad Cramer 1996: 'In the good we conceptualise the single *value* which provides the norm for all material value. ..... It is not for every being that understands the good that the latter can present itself as something that *ought* to be pursued. It cannot so present itself for a holy will, although the latter, as Kant says, must always remain the ultimate paradigm by reference to which we should orient the determination of our own will. Even the holy will must be conscious that what it effortlessly performs is indeed the good, i.e. what properly claims unconditional esteem. A holy will does not perform what is good unconsciously, but it *performs* what is good *because* it is good. We, on the other hand, *ought* to perform what is good because it is good. ... Once we understand this, we also immediately understand the prescriptive force with which the moral law presents itself *for us*. It is because this normative moment, definitive for the good, is already immediately embedded in his explication of the propositional content of the moral law itself that Kant avoids committing the naturalistic fallacy from the very outset' (p. 324f).

will (the causality of freedom) in analogy with the compelling force of a
law of nature. This model enables us, in every particular situation relevant
to an action, to perform the required thought-experiment. And this identifies the obligatory character of an already accomplished or intended act
independently of its actual or possible results or of any personal interests
involved, and only considers the consequences that would ensue if the act
were executed under the conditions of a law of nature. A moral act would
not forfeit its status as a representative instance of freedom if it were represented as transpiring within a world where all agents act according to
the selfsame maxim. In such a world, a non-moral or an immoral act, on
the other hand, similarly represented, would imply the loss of freedom in
general, and thereby contradict its own claim to freedom.

Kant's chapter on the 'typic' clearly shows that he situates the practical
faculty of judgement in a space between determining and reflecting judgement. Practical judgement 'schematises' without recourse to the imagination and 'reflects' without recourse to the principle of purposiveness. And
it does so through recourse to a typification that helps practical judgement to determine the nature of the human will by reference to the moral
law. In this connection, practical judgement thereby clearly reveals that
the causality of nature and the causality of freedom, with respect to their
shared form of lawfulness, both possess the same compelling force, even
if this force articulates itself in terms of different kinds of claim to validity
depending upon the different realms in which it is applied: in terms of an
objective validity claim or a normative validity claim. Moreover, practical judgement reveals that the moral law can actually exercise an influence upon the formation of the will, and thereby effectively confirms 'the
golden rule' that already performs a significant practical role in orienting
our everyday understanding of morality. If the law of nature and the law
of morality both share this same compelling character, then the former
can legitimately be invoked as the type of the latter in order to reveal, by
projecting the thought of an entirely immoral world, what the true cost of
a world devoid of the moral law would be for individuals who conceive of
themselves as free and rational beings.

Kant concludes the chapter on the typic with an explicit critique of moral
empiricism and what he calls the 'mysticism of practical reason' (5:70f.).
The problem with systems of morality based on either of these approaches,
according to Kant, lies in the absolute emphasis ascribed either to the particular or to the universal. In both cases, there is effectively no room for
the kind of practical judgement that moves back and forth between the
will and 'the ought' through the typifying procedure we have described.

It is only in this way that practical judgement avoids both the mistake of trying to distil normatively binding principles from actual given desires (our pursuit of happiness) and the complementary mistake of ascribing the essentially factual validity of a law of nature to the moral law. Whereas the empiricist identifies happiness with the good, thereby cancelling the distinction between empirical fact and moral norm, the mystic transforms the type of the moral law into a schema that is employed to present the imaginary construct of an invisible divine realm, based on allegedly super-sensuous intuitions, or of a society of purely rational beings, as if they were something actual. Both the empiricist and the mystic illegitimately ontologise the normative dimension, the one by dogmatically enthroning the empirical world of the senses, the other by hypostasising the intelligible world of the super-sensuous. Kant regards the *'empiricism* of practical reason' as more dangerous because it 'destroys at its roots the morality of dispositions' and helps to 'degrade humanity' precisely by raising empirical interests to 'the dignity of a supreme practical principle' (5:71). The 'enthusiasm' associated with the *'mysticism* of practical reason' (5:70), by comparison, is much less dangerous because, for all its extravagant claims, it never questions 'the purity and sublimity of the moral law' (5:71) that it earnestly strives on the contrary to preserve.

Bibliography

Beck, L.W. 1960: *A Commentary on Kant's Critique of Practical Reason.* Chicago.

Cramer, K. 1996: 'Metaphysik und Erfahrung in Kants Grundlegung der Ethik,' in *Kant in der Diskussion der Moderne*, eds. G. Schönrich and Y. Kato. Frankfurt am Main, 280–325.

Höffe, O. 1990: 'Universalistische Ethik und Urteilskraft: ein aristotelischer Blick auf Kant,' in *Zeitschrift für philosophische Forschung* 44, 537–563.

Materialien zu Kants 'Kritik der praktischen Vernunft,' eds. R. Bittner and K. Cramer. Frankfurt am Main 1975.

Müller, P. 1983: *Transzendentale Kritik und moralische Teleologie. Eine Auseinandersetzung mit den zeitgenössischen Transformation der Transzendentalphilosophie im Hinblick auf Kant.* Würzburg.

Thurnherr, U. 1994: *Die Ästhetik der Existenz. Über den Begriff der Maxime und die Bildung von Maximen bei Kant.* Tübingen/Basel.

Thurnherr, U. 2001: 'Urteilskraft und Anerkennung in der Ethik Immanuel Kants,' in *Anerkennung. Eine philosophische Propädeutik*, eds. M. Hofmann-Riedinger and U. Thurnherr. Freiburg/Munich, 76–92.

9

The Dialectic of Pure Practical Reason in the *Second Critique* (CPrR:107–121)

Eckart Förster

1. Book II, Chapter 1: 'On a dialectic of pure practical reason in general'

The very first paragraph of Book II of the *Critique of Practical Reason* presents serious difficulties of interpretation for any reader who is already familiar with the first *Critique*. For the claim that pure reason 'always has its dialectic,' not only in its theoretical use but also in its practical use (CPrR:107, 6), directly contradicts the *Critique of Pure Reason* of 1781. The earlier text had defined dialectic explicitly as a 'logic of illusion' that created the mere 'semblance' of objective assertions (CPR A 61). It is quite true that Kant there understood the antinomies, just as he would in the second *Critique*, as a kind of fortunate confusion insofar as they compel human reason to reflect upon its own limits and to distinguish clearly between phenomena and noumena, between appearances and things in themselves. But at the same time this distinction was also intended to secure the fundamental possibility of genuine morality precisely because the moral law relates directly to freedom, and thus to the noumenal realm, rather than to the sensible world of appearances. And in the first *Critique*, Kant had expressly denied that practical reason also possessed a comparable dialectic. That is why he ascribed to practical reason what he calls a 'canon of pure reason' (CPR A 795ff.; see also A 12) that should contain the fundamental *a priori* principles for the correct employment of the cognitive faculty: 'If there be any correct employment of pure reason, in which case there must be a *canon* of its employment, the canon will deal not with the speculative but with the *practical employment of reason*' (CPR A 796f.). At the time, Kant still shared Rousseau's view that the true principles of morality must be transparently clear even to our ordinary human reason.

Kant revised his views on this question after reading the first review of the *Critique of Pure Reason*, which appeared in the *Göttingischen Anzeigen von gelehrten Sachen* in 1782. For Kant now realised that not only had the chapter on the 'Canon of Pure Reason' been quite misunderstood, but more importantly that there was actually no such clear unanimity concerning the principles of morality. That is why he felt compelled to compose the *Groundwork of the Metaphysics of Morals* in 1785, which represented precisely 'the search for and establishment of *the supreme principle of morality*' (*Groundwork*: 4:392, 3f.). Here for the first time, Kant speaks of a 'natural dialectic' afflicting our ordinary human reason, one that consists essentially of a propensity to 'rationalize' over the strict laws of duty, to apply occasional exceptions and restrictions to these laws, thus bending the latter to comply more easily with our wishes and inclinations (4:405, 12ff.). This simply robs such moral laws of their 'dignity', which consists precisely in their purity and strictness. But this is not enough to generate an antinomy as defined by the first *Critique*: i.e. 'a conflict within the laws ... of pure reason' (CPR A 407; see also *Metaphysik Dohna*: 28:620). For to speak of an antinomy in the strict sense, we require two mutually contradictory judgements or propositions whose validity can nonetheless be demonstrated in each case from principles of reason. Kant clearly saw that the revolutionary significance of his discovery of the antinomies lay in the fact that it compelled reason not simply to recognise possible errors in its mode of argumentation, but also to acknowledge a fundamental contradiction within its very laws.

In the *Critique of Practical Reason*, Kant therefore identifies the relevant dialectic as the consequence of reason's attempt to discover the absolute totality of conditions governing a given condition, and not, as he had in the *Groundwork*, as a conflict between the law of reason and the maxims based on wishes and inclinations. This naturally brings the argument into proximity with the problematic of the first *Critique*, where it is precisely theoretical reason's search for the unconditioned ground of all conditions (see CPR A 307f.) that inevitably entangles it in dialectic. In the context of moral philosophy, this totality, this unconditioned dimension, must be grasped as the ultimate object and goal of practical reason precisely because the unconditioned is already implied in the moral law as the determining ground of the will. But we still have to ask whether, and if so in what sense, this ultimate object also involves the kind of conflict between two equally necessary rational conditions that constitutes an antinomy as defined in the first *Critique*. In this connection, we should first look a little more closely at the concept of the unconditioned as the object of pure practical reason.

For Kant this object, which is also said to be 'the whole, the complete good' (CPrR:110, 35f.), implies both morality and the happiness that should accompany morality. Following the precedent of classical philosophy, Kant describes it as 'the highest good'. In the earlier stages of his development, Kant had already examined the various theories concerning the highest good amongst the Stoics, the Epicureans, the Cynics, and the Platonists (see Düsing 1971). And in this connection he was primarily preoccupied by the question concerning the conditions for the possible realisation of the highest good. Once Kant had clearly understood that only reason, rather than God, can properly be regarded as the origin of the moral law, then the question concerning human motives and incentives, the subjective grounds for performing moral actions, inevitably became a particularly acute and pressing issue. How can a morally appropriate act arise simply from our insight into the morally good? In his pre-Critical phase, Kant regarded the solution to this problem as the authentic philosopher's stone: 'We can form no concept for ourselves as to how the mere form [representation] of an act can possess the power of an incentive. Yet this must be so if morality is to transpire, and experience confirms this' (*Reflections*: 19:183). That is why Kant was particularly interested in those ancient theories of the highest good that regarded it essentially as the highest ideal of human existence, one that we could strive and make every effort to attain in the course of human life itself. This outlook is particularly clear in the case of the Stoics and the Epicureans. Expressed at its simplest, according to Kant, the Epicurean argues that the conscious adherence to maxims oriented towards happiness produces virtue, whereas the Stoics claim that the consciousness of virtue necessarily results in happiness (see CPrR:111). We shall examine Kant's criticisms of both these views in more detail in what follows. Here we shall simply point out that the problem concerning the possible realisation of moral actions can no longer be formulated in these terms once we accept that reason can be practical in and of itself and that the mere representation of the moral law is indeed sufficient to determine the will to action. If the problem concerning the highest good once again becomes a burning issue for the second *Critique*, the true significance of this concept must be grasped and analysed in a new and different context.

According to Kant, the dialectic of pure practical reason is revealed as soon as we attempt to provide a close and careful definition of the concept of the highest good. In order to assess Kant's arguments properly here, we should first remind ourselves of the particular 'error of the ancients' to which Kant refers in the second chapter of the 'Analytic' of pure practical reason. According to Kant, the Greek thinkers made the mistake of identifying the concept of the morally good with the concept of the highest good, and therefore with 'an object which they intended *afterwards* to make the determining ground of the will in the moral law' (CPrR:64, 28–30; my italics). But Kant has already shown that no object external to the moral law, of whatever kind, can ever be the determining ground of the pure will. Only the moral law itself can play this role. This law is therefore a formal law that abstracts from all objects. But it only abstracts from all objects as far as the determining ground of the pure will is concerned. For naturally we can no more conceive of a willing without objects (in the broadest sense) than we can conceive of a law without an object domain for it to govern. If we consider the issue from the perspective of potential action, on the other hand, then it makes no sense to abstract from the objects or purposes of the will. In any complete analysis of moral consciousness, the determination of the will and the objects of action must always constitute a unity. That is why Kant can also write that 'the moral law alone must be viewed as the ground for making the highest good and its realisation or promotion its object' (CPrR:109, 23–25).

This merely restates the conclusion that can already legitimately be drawn from the 'Analytic' of pure practical reason. But in the final section of the chapter under discussion here, Kant also formulates his conclusion in a way that appears to go beyond what has already been argued and that has consequently led to significant disagreements amongst his commentators. If the moral law as the highest condition of virtue is 'already included' (CPrR:109, 35f.), along with the concept of happiness, in the concept of the highest good, then the highest good is precisely 'not merely *object*: the concept of it and the representation of its existence as possible by our practical reason are at the same time the *determining ground* of the pure will' (CPrR:109, 35f.). But this seems to contradict Kant's simultaneous claim that the highest good is 'not to be taken as the *determining ground*' of pure practical reason (CPrR:109, 23). And Kant now further insists that human reason must at least be able to conceive of the possibility of successfully realising its own actions. If the highest good as the ultimate purpose of the will were itself impossible, the moral law – which is meant to be a component of the highest good, and demands its realisation – would itself be false precisely because it was unrealisable: 'If, therefore, the highest good is impossible in accordance with practical rules, then the moral law, which commands us to promote it, must be fantastic and directed to empty imaginary ends, and must therefore in itself be false' (CPrR:114, 6–9).

Kant's formulations in this regard have attracted criticism from many commentators. For to elevate the highest good into the determining ground of the will in this way would seem to involve a repudiation of the principle of autonomy itself (see the overview of the relevant literature in Albrecht 1978, pp. 152–66). Thus, Lewis White Beck, in his commentary on the second *Critique*, claims: 'But we must not allow ourselves to be deceived, as I believe Kant was, into thinking its possibility is directly necessary to morality or that we have a moral duty to promote it, distinct from our duty as determined by the form and not by the content or object of the moral law' (Beck 1960, p. 245).

The interpretation of these difficult passages from the second *Critique* clearly depends on (1) the precise sense in which the highest good (in Kant's sense) can be described as 'not merely object,' and (2) the precise way in which the impossibility of realising the highest good can be said to imply the falsity of the moral law.

1. Although the argument of the 'Analytic' defines the moral law as purely formal in character, even there Kant already points out that it is not a question of simply formulating a prohibitive concept of this law. On the contrary, the moral law should furnish the sensible world with 'the form of a world of the understanding' whose 'counterpart should exist in the sensible world' (in accordance with the relation between *'natura archetypa'* and *'natura ectypa'*). Thus the idea of the moral law prescribes a nature 'in which pure reason, if it were accompanied with suitable physical power, would produce the highest good' (CPrR:43, 11f.). The highest good is therefore not some object external to the will itself, not something that might 'afterwards' act, or indeed fail to act, as the determining ground of the will. The highest good is itself the realisation of the moral law within our world. The law, considered as the condition of one of its component parts – namely, virtue – is therefore already 'included' in the concept of the highest good rather in the way in which the ground plan is contained in the idea of a completed building (with the important distinction that the law, unlike the ground plan, also demands its 'counterpart'

in the sensible world). It is only in this sense that the representation of the highest good can also be morally determining with regard to the will.

The moral law must be realised (as far as this is possible) by human beings – that is, by finite rational beings who determine their action through positing ends and purposes for themselves. In the final analysis, all individual ends must be subsumed under the moral law. This gives rise to moral ends that cohere with the ends of all other rational beings. A practical law such as the moral law is characterised precisely by the fact that it 'makes everything harmonious' (CPrR:28, 9) and offers all rational beings a common purpose or 'one and the same object' (CPrR28: 13). That is why Kant also speaks of practical laws as laws belonging to a 'kingdom of ends', which he understands as a totality of all ends and purposes – whether moral or purely individual – in systematic connection with one another (*Groundwork*: 4:433). In this sense, the promotion of the highest good as a kingdom of ends is itself therefore an end that is prescribed for us through the moral law.

2. The realisation of one's own happiness belongs amongst the ends that any finite rational being inevitably pursues on the basis of its own finite nature. The securing of one's own happiness is certainly not a duty because, as Kant emphasises in the *Metaphysics of Morals*, we cannot meaningfully turn what everyone does by nature anyway into a moral duty (cf. MM 6:386). It is also the case that the realisation of one's own happiness cannot be made into a pure moral end, cannot be the same shared object of striving, because the particular conditions of one's own happiness are different for each individual and essentially depend upon empirical circumstances. Happiness is indeed the end of 'every rational but finite being and therefore an unavoidable determining ground of its faculty of desire' (CPrR:25, 12–14). But it is not a determining ground of the *pure* will. That can only be provided by a practical law that 'must contain *the very same determining ground* of the will in all cases and for all rational beings' (CPrR:25, 23f.). To this extent, therefore, the representation of one's own happiness in the concept of the highest good is not determining for the moral will. But we can certainly draw the following conclusion: if a kingdom of ends ought to be possible, and the highest good ought to be capable of realisation in the world, then the moral and the natural ends of those rational beings who ought to promote this realisation must be systematically connectable with one another, at least in principle. If nature itself, within which alone I can realise my ends and of which I am myself a part, were such as to systematically exclude a happiness proportionate to virtue, this would be tantamount to a contradiction

within reason (that is, an antinomy). For it is indeed always 'only one and the same reason' (CPrR:121, 4f) that both prescribes the moral law to us and bears a 'commission from the side of sensibility which cannot be refused' (CPrR:61, 26f.). Or, as Kant expressly puts it: 'For, to need happiness, to be also worthy of it, and yet not to participate in it cannot be consistent with the perfect volition of a rational being that would at the same time have all power, even if we think of such a being only for the sake of an experiment' (CPrR:110, 27–31).

2.   Book II, Chapter 2: 'On the dialectic of pure reason in determining the concept of the highest good'

In distinguishing between the 'supreme' and the 'complete' as the two relevant components in the concept of the highest good, Kant explicitly returns to the distinction we have been attempting to clarify. Virtue is the *supreme* condition of the highest good because virtue itself is unconditioned, – that is, not subject to any other condition. But the *complete* good also involves the realisation of the 'object of the faculty of desire in rational finite beings' (CPrR:110, 23) – that is, of a happiness that is not itself unconditionally good, but that always presupposes virtue as the condition of its goodness. But for the highest good, we must be able to think both of virtue and a happiness corresponding to it as systematically united. The question is, precisely how this is possible?

It is here that the deeper significance of Kant's discussion of the Epicurean and Stoic positions is properly revealed. For both these schools, although in directly opposite ways, had posited the unity of virtue and happiness in the highest good by assuming a fundamental identity between these two underlying principles: the Epicureans identified happiness and virtue, and the Stoics defined virtue as the consciousness of one's own virtue. They both proceeded on the assumption therefore that 'wholly identical acts' lay at the basis of both virtue and happiness. But Kant, in his pre-Critical reflections on this question, had already pointed out that it was Christian morality that first clearly revealed the fundamental distinction between the concepts of virtue and happiness. The Christian perspective was the first one to present the moral law with a strictness and purity that no human behaviour could ever fully equal, to emphasise that a happiness properly correspondent to this law can never be attained in this world because of our human 'lack of holiness' (*Reflections*: 19:120). 'The teacher of the *evangelium* rightly assumed that the two *principia* of our behaviour, virtue and happiness, were separate and independent of one another [*verschieden und ursprünglich*]. He showed that the connection [*Verknüpfung*] between them does not lie in nature (as known in this world). He told us that we may nonetheless take comfort in believing in this connection. But he placed the condition for it very high, and in accordance with the holiest law' (*Reflections*: 19:238, cf. 174f.). The Stoics and the Epicureans had therefore struggled in vain to construe an 'identity' beneath 'essential and irreconcilable differences in principles' (CPrR:111, 33ff.). In the 'Analytic' of the *Critique of Practical Reason*, Kant himself, without historical references, finally presented the concept of a practical law in its purity, in clear distinction from any principles of self-love. In this way, he was able to clarify on purely conceptual grounds the fundamental difference between maxims of virtue and maxims concerning one's own happiness (CPrR:25f.; see Willaschek 1995).

3. 'The antinomy of practical reason'

Right up to, and indeed including, the *Critique of Pure Reason* in 1781, Kant had assumed that we ourselves *could* be the creators of such a highest good. For the cause and ground of true universal happiness is nothing other than a 'freedom partly motivated and partly restricted by moral laws' (CPR A 809). Happiness would therefore necessarily result from the reciprocal exercise of virtue. The mistake committed by the Stoics was simply the assumption that consciousness of one's *own* virtue can already intrinsically ensure happiness. In Kant's view, we would only be able to enjoy this happiness if we could also presuppose that 'everyone does what he should do,' and that is precisely what but for Kant we cannot do. According to the first *Critique*, therefore, the realisation of happiness, for which as virtuous agents we must nevertheless be able to hope, must also be transferred to the life beyond this one and thus ascribed to the mediation of God (CPR A 811; 813). Thus Kant in 1781 does not yet presuppose the influence of God on the physical world.

For reasons that cannot be explored further here (see Förster 1998), Kant abandoned this position soon after the publication of the first *Critique*. In the *Critique of Practical Reason*, Kant interprets happiness exclusively in empirical terms as 'the harmony *of nature* with [one's] whole end' (CPrR:124, 23f.; my emphasis). Since we exercise no thorough or permanent influence upon nature, and since nature itself 'does not depend on the moral dispositions of the will' (CPrR:113, 31ff.), we can no longer regard ourselves, even in principle, as the reciprocally acting causes of our own happiness. It is only therefore now that we are indeed faced by an *antinomy* of pure practical reason.

4. 'The critical resolution of the antinomy of practical reason'

To say that matters are 'just the same' (CPrR:114, 27) with regard to both the antinomy of pure practical reason and that of pure speculative reason seems, at least at first sight, to be highly misleading. In the final analysis, it was the antinomies of theoretical reason that drove Kant to develop the critical philosophy in the first place, as he explained in a letter to Christian Garve (*Briefwechsel*: 12:225). Transcendental idealism appeared to be the only way of resolving the problem of the antinomies. And Kant's treatment of the antinomies could also therefore be taken as an indirect demonstration of the truth of such an idealism (see CPR A 507f.; *Prolegomena*: 4:292). There is nothing corresponding to all of this in relation to the antinomy of practical reason. For the latter indeed already presupposes the idealistic framework of the critical philosophy itself. But there are also significant differences between the two discussions from a formal point of view. The thesis and antithesis presented by the practical antinomy are not two opposed and mutually contradictory judgements, like their theoretical counterparts in the antinomy of speculative reason. Nor is it the case in the practical antinomy that each of the opposed propositions 'finds conditions of its necessity in the very nature of reason' (CPR A 421). As Kant himself notes, the first of the two opposed propositions, which claims that the striving for happiness produces the ground for a virtuous disposition, is '*absolutely false*' (CPrR:114, 29). And the second proposition, which claims that the disposition to virtue necessarily produces happiness, is only equally false if I base it upon experience. Hence all that is needed to resolve this 'antinomy' for Kant is to show that it is 'not impossible' for a virtuous disposition to possess a proportional and corresponding 'happiness as an effect in the sensible world' (CPrR:115, 2 ff.).

The claim that this is 'not impossible' affords a certain, albeit rather weak, connection with the third antinomy in the *Critique of Pure Reason*, and it is this that allows Kant to draw a parallel between the two discussions. In the first *Critique*, of course, neither of the two contradictory judgements could be described as absolutely false; indeed, either of them could possibly be true. The 'antithesis' in the third antinomy is actually true insofar as it is restricted to the sensible world. For then it formulates a principle that is constitutive for all empirical knowledge – namely, the principle that in this domain, everything transpires in accordance with the laws of the causality of nature. The 'thesis,' on the other hand, which claims that we must also assume a further causality of freedom for the full explanation of phenomena in the world, could be true if we were compelled to assume, in addition to the appearing world, a super-sensible world that related to the phenomenal world as ground to consequence. And it is indeed precisely that that is supposed to be the result of the entire dialectic here. The antinomy of theoretical reason is resolved insofar as the causality of nature is related exclusively to the realm of appearances, and freedom is related exclusively to the realm of things in themselves. But theoretical reason cannot transcend this fundamental distinction: it can obtain no insight into the actuality or the possibility of a causality of freedom. Theoretical reason must simply acknowledge that nature and freedom 'do not conflict,' and that the latter is therefore 'not impossible' (CPR A 558).

We can see how Kant feels entitled to pursue a comparable strategy in the *Critique of Practical Reason* as well if we reformulate the antinomy in such a way that it also presents us with two contradictory propositions, both of which can be justified by appeal to rational principles (on this, see Beck 1960: 248):

Thesis: the highest good is possible.

Antithesis: the highest good is not possible.

Demonstration of the thesis: the moral law requires the realisation of the highest good.

Demonstration of the antithesis: the connection between virtue and happiness is neither analytical nor synthetic a priori, nor synthetic a posteriori – that is, empirically given.

Resolution of the antinomy: the antithesis is true of the sensible world where the laws of nature have exclusive sovereignty. The thesis may be true of the intelligible world because the synthetic connection of virtue (as ground) to happiness (as consequent) is not absolutely impossible.

The distinction between the sensible and the intelligible worlds, which theoretical reason itself is compelled to acknowledge, is therefore sufficient to resolve the practical antinomy as well. For this shows that it is not impossible for a causality other than that of nature to produce the required connection between my virtue and 'happiness as an effect in the sensible world' (CPrR:115, 5f.), even if theoretical reason cannot obtain any insight into such a connection. We have come to see that this connection is in principle not impossible. And in addition, one can now add: not only must theoretical reason draw this distinction between two worlds as a consequence of its own acknowledged antinomies, but it must also conceive of itself as a noumenon belonging to an intelligible world. For theoretical reason must necessarily presuppose that its own judgements are not causally determined by natural objects if it is to avoid falling into a performative contradiction (see *Groundwork*: 4:448). And practical reason, for its part, recognises the moral law as an intelligible determining ground of human freedom. And that is how Kant can regard the practical antinomy of the second *Critique* as resolved: for 'it is not impossible that the morality of disposition should have a connection, and indeed a necessary connection, as cause with happiness as effect in the sensible world, if not immediately yet mediately (by means of an intelligible author of nature), a connection which, in a nature that is merely an object of the senses, can never occur except contingently and cannot suffice for the highest good' (CPrR:115, 2–8).

The alleged antinomy therefore does not represent a genuine internal conflict within the laws of practical reason, but merely an apparent conflict between the legislative powers of theoretical and practical reason. It is thus so easy to resolve precisely because the required distinction between the sensible and intelligible worlds has already been established by theoretical reason, and is one that practical reason must itself presuppose. This 'antinomy' is therefore not nearly as serious as Kant seems to suggest. Whether his resolution of the antinomy serves effectively to remove every trace of dialectic from the concept of the highest good is of course another question. In this connection, we might point out that in his later writings, beginning with *Religion within the Limits of Reason Alone*, but also and especially in the *Opus Postumum*, Kant subjects the concept of the highest good and his associated doctrine of postulates to still further fundamental revision (on this, see Chapter 10 by Friedo Ricken in the present volume, and Förster 1998).

The remaining paragraphs of the section entitled 'Critical resolution of the antinomy of practical reason' actually contribute nothing further to the understanding of the resolution in question. They merely try to shed some further light on the mistaken attempt of both earlier and later thinkers to explain the possibility of the highest good without appealing to the concept of an intelligible world. Their mistake, according to Kant, lay in wrongly assuming that our consciousness of the feeling of satisfaction or self-contentment, which *results* from moral action and can be sensibly experienced, is itself capable of *determining* the will morally. But Kant has already shown in detail in the 'Analytic' that it is only the representation of the moral law itself, rather than any feeling that precedes and underlies reason, that is capable of determining the will in terms of morality.

It is also in this sense that we must read Kant's remark that the mistake lies in believing that we can ever discover any proportionate correspondence between virtue and happiness 'in *this life* already (in the sensible world)' (CPrR:115, 23f.). If that really meant that the highest good is only possible in a world beyond, as Kant himself still claimed in the *Critique of Pure Reason* (A 811), then the promotion of the highest good 'in this world' as demanded by the moral law would only relate to virtue. And the resolution of the practical antinomy would not then require the possibility of an 'intelligible author of nature' who could bring about 'happiness as effect in the sensible world' (CPrR:115, 4ff.) in due accordance with our moral conduct.

5. 'On the primacy of pure practical reason'

In 1781, in the *Critique of Pure Reason*, Kant made the following claim: 'The legislation of human reason (philosophy) has two objects, nature and freedom, and therefore contains not only the law of nature, but also the moral law, presenting them at first in two distinct systems, but ultimately in one single philosophical system' (CPR 840). But even in 1788, in the *Critique of Practical Reason*, Kant was still unable to provide such a single, internally unified, philosophical system (something he only managed to do, at least partially, in the *Opus Postumum*). Here in the second *Critique*, he could only express the hope that he might 'some day' succeed in deriving the unity of practical and theoretical reason on the basis of a single principle (CPrR:91, 2ff.). But in addition to their legislative character, each of the two faculties of reason are also interesting in their own right. In 1781, Kant framed this in terms of the questions 'what can I know?' and 'what should I do?' and in 1788, in terms of the striving to elucidate the highest *a priori* principles of our knowledge of objects, or of the determination of the will in relation to an ultimate and complete end (see CPR A 805 and CPrR:5:120). Once the legislative capacities of both theoretical and practical reason had been completely exhibited in the respective 'Analytics' of the two critiques, it was impossible to avoid addressing the question concerning the possible unity of these two fundamental interests of reason. For on the one hand, 'it is still only one and the same reason' (CPrR:121, 4f.) that judges in accordance with *a priori* principles, whether in the theoretical or the practical context. And on the other hand, reason in the theoretical context found itself compelled to restrict knowledge to the realm of possible experience, while in the practical context, it found itself equally and necessarily referred to concepts belonging to the super-sensible world.

Nonetheless, as Kant takes pains to show in this final section of the relevant chapter, there is no fundamental conflict within the interests of reason. On the contrary, the theoretical interest of reason must be 'subordinated' to the practical interest of reason, which thereby acquires its primacy. And there are a number of rational considerations that indicate why this should be the case.

If the enterprise of practical reason could only regard and assume as given what has been established by theoretical reason, then the latter would clearly enjoy primacy. But if certain theoretical judgements are inevitably and simultaneously bound up with the practical interest of reason, judgements that theoretical reason can neither confirm nor deny, then we must ascribe primacy to practical reason. Now, through the moral law, we are actually conscious that reason itself can be practically determining. This law requires the promotion of the highest good in the world. But such a good is only possible, so Kant will attempt to demonstrate in the chapter that follows, on the assumption of the existence of God and the immortality of the soul. If this demonstration is successful, then the propositions asserting that 'God exists' and 'the soul is immortal' are two theoretical, albeit unverifiable, propositions that nonetheless belong to an unconditionally valid practical law. This is because, as Kant has explicitly argued, the impossibility of the highest good would imply the falsehood of the moral law itself. That is why he describes both of these theoretical propositions as postulates of pure practical reason. In addition, we must acknowledge a third postulate – that of human freedom – which expresses the necessary condition of the moral law itself. All three postulates would then represent theoretical propositions validated or demanded by practical reason. But what has theoretical reason to say in this connection?

One the one hand, it is theoretical reason's own interest in precisely these ideas – namely, the freedom of the will, the immortality of the soul, the existence of God – that constantly tempts it to transcend the limits of possible experience: 'It [sc. theoretical reason] follows the path of mere speculation, in order to approach them, but they fly before it' (CPR A 796; cf. A 798). That is why reason is compelled to submit itself to a critique of its own cognitive powers – that is, to an investigation and determination of its limits. This leads reason to recognise that it is unable through its own resources alone to decide between the thesis and antithesis of the dynamical antinomies: with respect to the intelligible world it can only adopt an agnostic position and therefore entertain the possibility of such a world while claiming no theoretical insight into it.

On the other hand, on the basis of its own law-like character, reason strives constantly to bring the sensuous data of experience into ever more comprehensive unities and establish the greatest possible systematic unity in the totality of its knowledge. But it cannot accomplish this without employing ideas of the super-sensible world at least as regulative principles. And the transcendental deduction of these ideas must therefore be regarded as 'the completion of the critical enterprise' (CPR A670). For, as Kant puts it, the 'speculative interest of reason makes it necessary to regard all order in the world *as if* it had originated in the purpose of a supreme reason' (CPR A 686; my emphasis).

Theoretical reason cannot therefore be indifferent to what practical reason, which is after all 'still one and the same reason,' succeeds in demonstrating in the context of its own domain. On the contrary, theoretical reason finds itself compelled 'to compare and connect' the propositions that are inseparable from practical reason 'with everything that lies within its power as speculative reason' (CPrR:121, 12f.). But this implies a recognition of the primacy of the practical interest of reason over the theoretical interest of reason in the very connection between both. And this recognition also presupposes that reason can only be practical through representing the moral law to itself. If the determination of the will could only be effected 'pathologically' on the basis of a preceding feeling – that is, of a sensuous principle belonging to the theoretical domain – theoretical reason could only reject its subordination to practical reason as an illegitimate 'demand' (CPrR:120, 34f.). The inevitable result of this rejection would be a 'conflict of reason with itself' (CPrR:121, 22f.). But it is precisely the purpose of Sections 6 through 9 of Chapter 2 of the second *Critique* to show in more detail that no such internal conflict actually exists.

Bibliography

Albrecht, M. 1978: *Kants Antinomie der praktischen Vernunft*, Hildesheim.

Beck, L. W. 1960: *A Commentary on Kant's Critique of Practical Reason*, Chicago.

Düsing, K. 1971: 'Das Problem des höchsten Gutes in Kants praktischer Philosophie,' in *Kant-Studien* 62, 1, pp. 5–42.

Förster, E. 1998: 'Die Wandlungen in Kants Gotteslehre,' in *Zeitschrift für philosophische Forschung* 52, pp. 341–362.

Henrich, D. 1992: 'The Moral Image of the World,' in Henrich, *Aesthetic Judgement and the Moral Image of the World*, Stanford, pp. 3–28.

Willaschek, M. 1995: 'Was sind praktische Gesetze?', in *Proceedings of the Eighth International Kant Congress*, Memphis 1995, edited by H. Robinson, Vol. II, Part 2, Milwaukee, pp. 533–540.

10

The Postulates of Pure Practical Reason
(CPrR:122–148)

Friedo Ricken

The 'unavoidable problems set by pure reason itself,' Kant tells us in the Introduction to the second edition of the *Critique of Pure Reason*, 'are *God, freedom,* and *immortality*' (B 7). Notwithstanding the '*loss* of its fancied possessions which speculative reason must suffer, general human interests remain in the same privileged position as hitherto, and the advantages which the world has hitherto derived from the teachings of pure reason are in no way diminished. The loss affects only the *monopoly of the schools,* in no respects the *interests of humanity*' (B xxxif). The dogmatic proofs that the schools had traditionally provided for the immortality of the soul, the freedom of the will, and the existence of God had never succeeded in reaching the public mind or exercising any influence upon its convictions on account of 'the unfitness of the common human understanding for such subtle speculation' (B xxxii). And the 'purely speculative interest of reason' in these three themes remains 'very slight indeed,' as Kant goes out of his way to emphasise in the section of the text he calls 'The transcendental doctrine of method.' 'If, then, these three cardinal propositions are not in any way necessary for *knowledge*, and are yet strongly recommended by our reason, their importance, properly regarded, must concern only the *practical*' (A 798–800/B 826–8).

But whereas the critique of speculative reason fails to exercise any influence upon our common human understanding of God, freedom, and immortality, it nonetheless confers great authority on these issues insofar as it brings the Schools to recognise that they themselves 'can lay no claim to higher and fuller insight into a matter of universal human concern than that which is equally within the reach of the great mass of people (ever to be held by us in the highest esteem)' (B xxxiii). In matters that concern all human beings without distinction 'nature is not guilty of any partial distribution of her gifts', and with respect to 'the essential ends of human nature,' the highest philosophy itself must bow to 'the guidance which nature has bestowed upon even the most ordinary understanding' (A 831/B 859). The truths of God, freedom, and immortality are not therefore ones of which the Schools can claim to be 'the sole authors and possessors [...], reserving the key to themselves, and communicating to the public their use only.' On the contrary, the Schools should limit themselves in this regard 'solely to the cultivation [*Kultur*] of universally comprehensible, and, for moral purposes, sufficient forms of proof' (B xxxiii).

These remarks clearly reveal the essential task and starting point for Kant's doctrine of the postulates: it is concerned with the 'cultivation' – that is, the clarification and development – of universal human insights. That is why Kant can say, in the second *Critique*, that 'the kind of cognition' it involves in a sense already 'approaches popularity' (CPrR:10, 24f.). In the third *Critique*, Kant expresses the essential insight that must be cultivated as follows: 'As soon as human beings begin to reflect on right and wrong, at a time when they still indifferently overlooked the purposiveness of nature, [...] the judgement must necessarily have occurred to them that it could not in the end make no difference if a person has conducted himself honestly or falsely, fairly or violently' (CPJ:458, 9–14).

1.   The postulates and pure practical faith

As a first step, it will be useful to sketch the general line of argument that has led Kant to introduce the doctrine of the postulates. The starting point, or *ratio cognoscendi* (CPrR:4, 33), for the doctrine is our own consciousness of that fundamental law of pure practical reason 'by which reason determines the will immediately' (CPrR:132, 10f.). This determination of the will is entirely independent of any theoretical presuppositions. Since the moral law is apodictically certain in its own right, it requires 'no further support by theoretical opinions as to the inner character of things, the secret aim of the order of the world, or a ruler presiding over it, in order to bind us most perfectly to actions unconditionally conformed to the law' (CPrR:142, 27ff.). The rational will that is to be determined by the moral law must assume that observance of the moral law is possible. The will stands under the unconditional demand of the moral law and thus 'requires these necessary conditions [sc. the postulates] for observance of its precept.' When Kant immediately adds that 'the postulates are [...] *presuppositions* having a necessarily practical reference' (CPrR:132, 12–14), he is identifying a twofold necessity here: the unconditional obligation imposed by the moral law and the necessary conditions for its observance. In the first *Critique*, Kant expressed the same line of thought as follows: 'Now since there are practical laws which are absolutely necessary, that is, moral laws, it must follow that if these necessarily presuppose the existence of any being as the condition of the possibility of their *obligatory* power, this existence must be *postulated*' (A 633f./B 661f.). To 'postulate' here means to 'require.' What is necessarily required, according to the second *Critique*, is the possibility of the highest good: 'If, therefore, the highest good is impossible in accordance with practical rules, then the moral law, which commands us to promote it [...] must in itself be false' (CPrR:114, 6–9).

We must distinguish between the determination of the will through the moral law and the necessary object of a will that is determined through this law. Freedom is 'the condition of the moral law,' but the 'ideas of *God* and *immortality* are not conditions of the moral law but only conditions of the necessary object of a will determined by this law' (CPrR:4, 9–12) – that is, conditions of the highest good. The postulates of the immortality of the soul and the existence of God therefore stand or fall with Kant's doctrine of the highest good. They have no force whatsoever unless Kant can show that 'the promotion of the highest good [...] is an a priori necessary object of our will and inseparably bound up with the moral law' (CPrR:114, 2–4). For the moment, I will leave this question to one side, although I will return to it later in discussing the postulate of the existence of God. For now, I will presuppose that the moral law indeed requires us to promote the highest good, and will analyse the conclusions that Kant draws from this claim.

The will can only respond to the unconditioned demand to promote the highest good on the assumption that reason holds the highest good to be possible. But the claim that the highest good is possible is itself a theoretical proposition and thus an object of theoretical reason. The claim presupposes three further propositions: that the theoretical concepts of freedom, immortality, the soul and God are pure rational concepts with no corresponding intuitions; that they can therefore contribute nothing to the 'cognition *of these objects*' (CPrR:135, 9); but that they do indeed '*have objects*' (CPrR:135, 7f.). Practical reason thus compels us to assume the theoretical or 'objective reality' [*objektive Realität*] (CPrR:135, 6f.)

of freedom, immortality, and God precisely because 'practical reason
unavoidably requires the existence of them for the possibility of its object,
the highest good, which is absolutely necessary practically, and theoretical reason is thereby justified in assuming them' (CPrR:134, 24–27).
A few lines earlier, Kant had spoken of the 'possibility of those objects of
pure speculative reason' (CPrR:134, 19), rather than of their 'existence'
[Existenz]. And in Religion within the Limits of Reason Alone, Kant
argues that 'the minimum of cognition (it is possible that there is a God)'
must already be 'subjectively sufficient' for any duty that can be laid upon
anyone (6: 154, 16–18). And Kant is speaking here of real possibility as
distinct from the purely logical possibility that belongs to any non self-
contradictory proposition (see CPR B xxvi, note).

The Critique of Pure Reason defines an 'Idea' as 'the indispensable
condition of all practical employment of reason' (A 328/B 385). The second Critique develops and explains this conception in further detail: the
postulates 'give objective reality [objektive Realität] to the ideas of speculative reason in general [...] and justify its holding concepts even the possibility of which it could not otherwise presume to affirm' (CPrR:132,
13–18). But what does the concept of 'objective reality' mean here? We
can only heed the demand of pure practical reason to promote the highest
good if we assume that the highest good is indeed possible. The assumption that the highest good is possible, and similarly the assumptions of the
existence of God, freedom, and immortality, are therefore necessary conditions of our own efforts to realise the highest good, and thereby causal
factors that exercise an influence within the phenomenal world. The ideas
of speculative reason become ' immanent and constitutive inasmuch as
they are grounds of the possibility of making real the necessary object of
pure practical reason (the highest good)' (CPrR:135, 27–29).

Kant understands 'a postulate of pure practical reason' as 'a theoretical proposition, though not one demonstrable as such, insofar as it is
attached inseparably to an a priori unconditionally valid practical law'
(CPrR:122, 22–25; see also 11, 28–41). So far we have been concerned
exclusively with the propositional component of Kant's claim here. We
have seen that it involves certain existential assertions: the postulates
assume 'that there are such objects [sc. freedom, immortality, God]
(CPrR:135, 21). Let us now consider the act of entertaining these postulates or holding them to be true. Here Kant distinguishes 'three degrees:
opining [Meinen], believing [Glauben], and knowing [Wissen]. Opining
is such holding [Fürwahrhalten] of a judgement as is consciously insufficient, not only objectively, but also subjectively. If our holding of the

judgement be only subjectively sufficient, and is at the same time taken as being objectively insufficient, we have what is termed *believing*. Lastly, when the holding of a thing to be true is sufficient both subjectively and objectively, it is *knowing*' (CPR A 822/B 850). Holding the postulates to be true therefore is a '*belief* and, indeed, a pure *rational belief* since pure reason alone (in its theoretical as well as in its practical use) is the source from which it springs' (CPrR:126, 10–13).

Kant further clarifies the concept of pure rational belief by drawing a distinction between postulates and hypotheses. Postulates and hypotheses alike arise from a need on the part of pure reason. Pure speculative reason feels a need to explain the order and purposiveness of nature and therefore assumes some kind of God as the ultimate cause of both. Reason here infers a necessary but not sufficient condition for what it is to be explained. Explaining the purposiveness of nature by reference to a God may well be the best available hypothesis, but we cannot know that it is the only possible explanation. Such a hypothesis therefore 'cannot be brought further than the degree of being the most reasonable opinion for us human beings' (CPrR:142, 17f.). The physico-theological demonstration of the existence of God is therefore insufficient to ground belief in this regard. Speculative reason holds a certain hypothesis to be true because of reason's need to find an explanation for the phenomena.

Holding a postulate to be true cannot be a question of knowing, because a postulate can never be theoretically demonstrated. It is therefore a question of an objectively insufficient 'holding.' But how does this become a subjectively sufficient holding – that is, believing? Why does pure reason feel a need for holding the postulates to be true? It feels this need, in accordance with Kant's definition of the problem, because a relevant postulate is 'attached inseparably to an a priori unconditionally valid *practical* law' (CPrR:122, 24f.). The subjective ground for holding the postulate results from the duty to make the highest good 'the object of my will so as to promote it with all my powers' (CPrR:142, 20f.). I can only comply with this duty if I presuppose the possibility of the highest good. That I make the highest good my end and purpose thus presupposes that I hold the postulates to be true. The subjective ground of holding this to be so is therefore my obedience to the moral law that commands the promotion of the highest good. The need for holding the postulates to be true arises from the will to heed the moral law in the first place. Pure rational belief is subjectively sufficient because 'the subjective effect of this law, namely the *disposition* conformed with it and also made necessary by it to promote the practically possible highest good' (CPrR:143, 4–6; cf. 11, 37–39; 125, 25–32), presupposes this rational belief that the latter is possible.

   Holding the postulates to be true is therefore something that is only subjectively sufficient for those who have made the highest good their end. In the second *Critique*, this conclusion is merely suggested. It is 'the upright man' who says 'I *will* that there be a God,' and so on (CPrR:143, 24f.). And Kant tells us further that pure practical rational belief 'has itself arisen from the moral disposition' (CPrR:146, 10). On the other hand, the first *Critique* is quite explicit that 'this rational belief is based upon the assumption of moral dispositions. If we leave these aside, and take an individual who is completely indifferent with regard to moral laws, the question propounded by reason then becomes merely a problem for speculation, and can, indeed, be supported by strong grounds of analogy, but not by such as must compel the most stubborn scepticism to give way.' But no human being is entirely free of interest in such matters. For one who lacks the appropriate moral sentiments or dispositions, still 'enough remains to make him *fear* the existence of a God and a future life.' For this only requires that we can never apodictically demonstrate the impossibility of the existence of either (CPR A 829f./B 857f.).

2.   The existence of God

Kant's 'deduction' (CPrR:126, 14) of the postulates (CPrR:124, 21–125, 30) takes its point of departure from the concept of happiness. He defines the latter as 'the state of a rational being [...] in the whole of whose existence *everything goes according to his wish and will*' (CPrR :124, 21–23). Happiness in this sense therefore rests upon the harmonious correspondence between nature and the wish and will of human beings, and therefore also requires the harmonious correspondence between nature and the will that is determined by the moral law. But action in accordance with the moral law cannot of itself produce this correspondence. On the one hand, nature does not determine the moral law precisely because the latter commands through 'determining grounds that are entirely independent of nature and its harmony with our faculty of desire' (CPrR:124, 26–28). On the other, the moral law does not determine nature because the morally acting agent 'is not also the cause of the world and of nature itself' (CPrR:124, 26–28). Nonetheless, as far as the practical task of pure reason is concerned, 'such a connection is postulated as necessary: we *ought* to strive to promote the highest good (which must therefore be possible). Accordingly, the existence of a cause of all nature, distinct from nature, which contains the ground of this connection, namely of the exact correspondence of happiness with morality, is also *postulated*' (CPrR:125, 2–8). This cause is 'a being that is the cause of nature by *understanding* and *will* (hence its author), that is, *God*. Consequently, the postulate of the possibility of the *highest derived good* (the best world) is likewise the postulate of the reality of a *highest original good*, namely of the existence of God' (CPrR:125, 20–25).

The main difficulty in understanding Kant's argument here lies in his use of the terms 'world' and 'nature.' Are they being employed in the same or in a different sense? First of all, I shall clarify the concept of 'the best world' with which Kant here identifies the highest good.

The first *Critique* develops the concept of a world that 'would be in accordance with all moral laws.' Given the freedom of rational beings, such a world *could* exist, and in accordance with the moral law, *ought* to exist. This 'moral world [...] is thought merely as an intelligible world because we leave out of account all conditions (ends) and even all the special difficulties to which morality is exposed.' It is thus 'a mere idea, though at the same time a practical Idea, which really can have, as it also ought to have, an influence upon the sensible world,' and thus possesses an objective reality (CPR A 808/B 836). In this moral world, morality is necessarily connected with a corresponding and proportionate happiness inasmuch as 'freedom, partly inspired and partly restricted by moral laws, would itself be the cause of general happiness, since rational beings, under the guidance of such principles, would themselves be the authors both of their own enduring well-being and of that of others. But such a system of self-rewarding morality is only an idea, the carrying out of which rests on the condition that *everyone* does what he ought to do' (CPR A 809f./ B 837f.). But since this is not the case, the necessary connection between happiness and morality can 'only be hoped for if a *supreme reason*, which governs according to moral laws, is likewise posited as underlying nature as its cause' (CPR A 810/B 838).

The existence of God is not postulated here 'because there is not the least ground in the moral law for a necessary connection between morality and proportionate happiness' (CPrR:124, 30–32), but because not everyone actually does what in accordance with the moral law he ought to do. But how can Kant justifiably conclude from this to the existence of God as the 'cause of nature'? How should God, as the cause of nature, make good the defect that results from the fact that not everyone acts in accordance with the moral law? If God were understood as the cause of nature, this would

indeed eliminate the defect in the world of nature and permit happiness
to be realised in the realm of nature. But a few lines later, Kant expressly
denies this idea: the sensible world certainly does not present this practically necessary connection between the two elements of the highest good.
That is why we must assume a world in which they are indeed so connected 'as a future world' (CPR A 811/B 839). The inconsistency can only
be resolved if we adopt a twofold concept of nature here. Firstly, there is
nature, which is 'merely an object of the senses' (CPrR:115, 6f.). But Kant
cannot be, secondly, referring to this concept of nature when he says that
happiness depends upon the 'harmony of nature' (CPrR:124, 23) with
the moral self-determination of the human will. For in relation to nature
merely as an object of the senses, this harmony 'can never occur except
contingently' (CPrR:115, 7). He can, therefore, only be referring to nature
in a noumenal world.

In the *Groundwork*, it is the 'kingdom of ends,' expressly defined there
as the *'mundus intelligibilis'* (4:438, 17), that corresponds to the concept
of the 'best world.' The kingdom of ends is the systematic connection of
'rational beings as ends in themselves and of the ends of his own that
each may set himself' (4:433, 22f.). Kant identifies two conditions in this
regard: the categorical imperative would have to be universally observed,
and the 'kingdom of nature and its purposive arrangement' would have
to 'harmonise' with the will that is determined by the moral law (4:438,
35–37). The universal observance of the categorical imperative here is
only a necessary but not a sufficient condition for allowing all members of
the kingdom attain an end of happiness that also includes all of their own
particular ends. Nature pays no heed to whether a human being is worthy
of happiness, and, as Kant's discussion of Spinoza in the third *Critique*
indicates, the righteous are also thereby 'subject to all the evils of poverty,
illness and untimely death, just like all the other animals on earth, and
will always remain thus until one wide grave engulfs them all together'
(CPJ:452, 25–28).

The moral law obligates human beings to make 'the natural end which
all men have' (*Gr*:430, 19) – namely, their own happiness, into a reciprocal end with regard to one another. 'For, the ends of a subject who is an
end in itself, must as far as possible be also *my* ends' (*Gr*:430, 24–27).
This law remains binding upon us as rational beings, although we cannot thereby expect that the two necessary conditions for attaining the
prescribed end – namely, its universal observance and the corresponding harmony of nature – will ever be fulfilled in this world (*Gr*: 438,
32–439, 3). But if there is a duty to promote a happiness corresponding to

moral worthiness, then pure reason not only possesses 'the warrant, but also the necessity, as a need connected with duty, to presuppose the possibility of this highest good' (CPrR:125, 26–28). In precisely what way, though, is this necessity intrinsically connected with duty?

The first *Critique* alludes to Leibniz's distinction between the kingdom of grace – that is the kingdom of ends that is governed by the highest original good – and the kingdom of nature, in which rational beings 'can expect no other consequences from their actions than such as follow in accordance with the course of nature in our world of sense.' And Kant concludes that to 'view ourselves as in the world of grace [...] is a practically necessary idea of reason' (CPR A 812/B 840). The assumption of the best noumenal world (rather than of incentives: cf. A 807/B 835) is therefore a necessary *presupposition* for the determination of the will by the moral law. Kant develops this line of thought in further detail in the Preface to the first edition of *Religion within the Limits of Reason Alone*.

There Kant tells us that morality requires 'no material determining ground [...], that is, no end' (*Religion*:3, 17f.). The laws of morality are binding simply through their mere form of universal lawfulness. But this does not exclude the possibility that they possess a 'necessary reference' to an end – 'namely, not as the ground but as necessary consequences' of maxims framed in accordance with the Categorical Imperative. 'For in the absence of all reference to an end no determination of the will can take place in human beings at all' (*Religion*:4, 13–17). The action resulting from the determination of the free power of choice [*Willkür*] by the moral law exercises a certain effect. This is not an end for the sake of which the free power of choice is determined, but a consequence that arises from this determination of the will. This free power of choice requires more than an indication concerning *how* it shall act, for it must also necessarily ask *where* its action leads in accordance with its choice. For 'it cannot possibly be indifferent to reason how to answer the question, *what is then the result of this right conduct of ours*, nor to what we are to direct our doings or nondoings, even granted this is not something fully in our control, at least as something with which they are to harmonize' (*Religion*:5, 2–7). It is a natural need 'to think for all our doings and nondoings taken as a whole some sort of ultimate end which reason can justify' (*Religion*:5, 16f.). This ultimate end, the highest good, is the necessary and sufficient condition of every other end that we set for ourselves (*Religion*:6, 31f.). If the need to think an ultimate end for ourselves were not fulfilled, this would represent a 'hindrance to moral resolve' (*Religion*:5, 18).

Let us summarise this interpretation and ask how it coheres with the text of the deduction offered in the second *Critique*. The moral law demands the 'production of the highest good in the world' (CPrR:122, 4) or the 'striving to produce and promote the highest good in the world' (CPrR:126, 1–3). It thus requires us, in the language of the *Metaphysics of Morals*, to make our own perfection and the happiness of others into our end (MM: 385, 30–386, 14). The end required here cannot be attained in the sensible world, where the connection between happiness and morality can only be a contingent one (CPrR:115, 5–8). A single 'wide grave' finally engulfs everyone 'all together (whether honest or dishonest, makes no difference here)' (CPJ: 452, 27f.). Hence duty can only command us to 'realise the highest good according to the utmost of our capacity' (CPrR:144, 34). The harmony of 'the kingdom of nature with the kingdom of morals' (CPrR:145, 32) that is required for the necessary connection of happiness and morality is only possible in a noumenal world. But the will can only determine itself to promote the highest good in the sensible world if it holds the highest good to be possible. The best world, which can only be thought as a noumenal world, is therefore a necessary practical idea.

On this interpretation, Kant's argument leads directly to God as the sovereign of the kingdom of ends (Gr:439, 13). But the deduction offered in the second *Critique* actually aims to demonstrate God as 'the cause (and hence the author) of nature' (CPrR:125, 21). As such, God is supposed to accomplish what rational beings in this world are not in a position to accomplish – namely, 'a necessary connection between morality and the proportionate happiness of a being belonging to the world as part of it and hence dependent upon it' (CPrR:124, 30–33). But what do the terms 'nature' and 'world' mean here? In what world is the connection between happiness and morality established? The reference to God as the author of nature might suggest that Kant is attempting much the same kind of thing as the proofs for the existence of God traditionally offered by theoretical philosophy. Kant would then be referring to nature and the world in the visible and sensuous sense of these terms. As the author of nature, God thus establishes the harmony between the kingdom of morals and the kingdom of nature within the sensible world. He would thereby have to intervene in the natural order of the sensible world in order to secure the connection between happiness and morality. But this assumption appears absurd since the righteous 'will always remain' subjected by 'nature' to the evils of sickness and death (CPJ:452, 24–27). According to this objection, Kant's argument demonstrates the existence of God as the sovereign of the kingdom of ends or the kingdom of grace, whereas what Kant actually claims is that his argument, like the traditional proofs of God, demonstrates the existence of God as the creator of the visible world.

Kant's deduction can only be defended against this objection if we recognise that he is using the terms 'world' and 'nature' in a twofold sense, although it is true that he does not make this fact entirely clear. The aim of his demonstration would then be to show that the 'kingdom of nature' and the 'kingdom of ends' must be 'thought of as united under one sovereign' (Gr:439, 12f.). This follows from the fact that the kingdom of nature has been created for the sake of the kingdom of ends. For the final end and purpose of God in creation is simply the highest good (CPrR:130, 29–32). The end and purpose of the sensible world lies in the noumenal world, where nature and morality are in harmony. The highest good, which we have a duty to realise in the sensible world as far as our powers permit, is only possible in the noumenal world. The critical resolution of the antinomy speaks of a nature 'that is *merely* an object of the senses' (CPrR:115, 6f., my emphasis). A super-sensible concept of nature is therefore clearly required for the proper resolution of the antinomy. The deduction implies 'the existence of a cause of *all* nature, distinct from nature' (CPrR:125, 5f., my emphasis). Kant's reference to 'all nature,' here distinguished from nature in the narrower sense, could be understood as embracing both sensible and noumenal nature. It is also possible that, in Kant's phrase about 'the supreme cause of nature, insofar as it must be presupposed for the highest good' (CPrR:125, 19f.), the subordinate clause introduced by 'insofar' refers not only to the 'supreme cause' but to 'nature' as well.

The concept of the highest good opens up a fresh perspective upon the moral law. For the highest good must be regarded as a divine command, though without thereby compromising the principle of moral autonomy. The moral law, through the concept of the highest good, leads directly 'to *religion*, that is, to the *recognition of all duties as divine commandments*' (CPrR:129, 18f.). The moral law prescribes an end for me that I cannot accomplish through my own powers. I must therefore assume a being that can accomplish what is unconditionally prescribed as a duty. For this being to realise the end prescribed by the moral law presupposes that the moral law prescribes what this highest will properly wills. The highest being would not realise the relevant end if it were not its own end, and if the command to realise this end were not the proper expression of its own will. It is the moral law that thus permits us to recognise the ultimate end and purpose of God in the creation of the world. It is the same end that the moral law prescribes to us and that can only be realised by the highest being. If we ask about 'God's *final end* in creating the world,' we can only name *'the highest good'* as such an end (CPrR:130, 29–32).

3. The immortality of the soul

A postulate requires that a necessary condition for the fulfilment of a prescription of pure practical reason be itself fulfilled. What then is the prescription from which the postulate of immortality arises? Kant actually gives no precise answer to this question. According to the Preface of the second *Critique*, it seems to derive, like the postulate of the existence of God, from the demand for the realisation of the highest good: 'The ideas of *God* and *immortality* are [...] only conditions of the necessary object' of a will that is determined by the moral law (CPrR:4, 10–12). This is also Kant's starting point for the deduction of this postulate: 'The production of the highest good in the world is the necessary object of a will determinable by the moral law. But in such a will the *complete conformity* of dispositions with the moral law is the supreme condition of the highest good. This conformity must therefore be just as possible as its object is, since it is contained in the same command to promote this object' (CPrR:122, 4–9). But when he comes to list the postulates later in the text, Kant says that the postulate of immortality 'flows from the practically necessary condition of a duration befitting the complete fulfilment of the moral law' (CPrR:132, 21–23; see also 124, 7–12). Here the deduction of the postulate does not presuppose the demand to realise the highest good. Immortality is immediately presented simply as the necessary condition for the complete fulfilment of the moral law. And the demand to realise the highest good is a necessary and sufficient premise for the deduction of the postulate. But this does not exclude a mediate reference to the highest good: immortality is a necessary condition for the complete fulfilment of the moral law, and the latter in turn is a necessary condition of the highest good. But the complete fulfilment of the moral law would also be required even if the will possessed no necessary object. The postulate of immortality therefore merely presupposes the determination of the will through the moral law, and is independent of the doctrine of the highest good.

The introductory remarks from the deduction we have cited (CPrR:122, 4–9) attempt to derive the postulate of immortality from the demand to realise the highest good *in the world*. But what concept of the world is being employed here? The highest good ought to be realised in the sensible world. But this demand does not lead of itself to the postulate of immortality. For it is a duty that mortal human beings ought to fulfil to the best of their ability. The concept of the world here must therefore also include the noumenal world. The 'production of the highest good in the world' necessarily requires not only the realisation of the end pre-scribed by the moral law (see MM:385, 30–386, 14), but also the infinitely extending advance towards holiness.

The actual starting point for Kant's deduction here is the practically necessary demand for holiness, which can only be fulfilled through an unending process. For 'in accordance with principles of pure practical reason it is necessary to assume such a practical progress as the real object of our will' (CPrR:122, 14–16). This idea is also found, presented quite independently of the doctrine of the highest good, in the chapter concern-ing incentives of the will. Although the ideal of holiness is 'not attainable by any creature,' it nonetheless represents 'the archetype [...] which we should strive to approach and to resemble in an uninterrupted but endless progress' (CPrR:83, 25–27). 'This endless progress is, however, possible only on the presupposition of the *existence* and personality of the same rational being continuing *endlessly* (which is called the immortality of the soul)' (CPrR:122, 17–20).

Kant's argument presupposes a moral teleology. It proceeds on the assumption that the complete fulfilment of the moral law is the ultimate vocation of the human being. Kant speaks of 'the moral vocation of our nature' (CPrR:122, 26). It is through the fact of reason that we become consciously aware of this vocation. This moral vocation and the holiness of the moral law can only be united with one another by recourse to the postulate of immortality. Without this postulate we would be confronted by the following possibilities. In the first place, we would have to regard the moral law as incapable of fulfillment. We would thereby be renounc-ing our own moral vocation. And the moral law would simply become an unfulfillable and thus meaningless law. Or we should effectively have to deny the holiness of the moral law. We could, secondly, fulfill it only at the cost of making it into something '*lenient* (indulgent) and thus conformed to our convenience' (CPrR:122, 32f.). Or again we might fall victim to moral 'enthusiasm' in a vain hope of acquiring 'complete holiness of the will' (CPrR:122, 35). All of this would amount to nothing but arrogance, self-deception, and self-conceit. We would thereby transgress the limits established by pure practical reason (CPrR:85, 37) and forget that the only moral level upon which we human beings stand is marked not by holiness, but by '*virtue*, that is, moral disposition *in conflict*' (CPrR:84, 33f.), and by respect for the moral law. All of these alternative possibilities would only hinder our 'constant *effort*' (CPrR:123, 2f.) to observe the strict and inflexible but nonetheless true moral law.

This endless progress should not be conceived as a process in time. The uninterrupted and continuing existence of the human being is 'a magnitude (*duratio noumenon*) wholly incomparable with time' (*The End of All Things*, 8:327, 9f.) and of which we can only form a negative conception. Since beings in this state of super-sensible existence are not subject to temporal conditions, they cannot be an object of possible experience for us. This duration and state is therefore 'capable of no determination of its nature other than a moral one' (8:327, 30f.). The concept of infinite duration here is a purely negative one that simply tells that 'reason in its practical intent toward its final end can never have done enough on the path of constant alterations' (8:334, 10–12).

4.   Theoretical reason and pure practical rational belief

What Kant calls rational belief or faith [*Glaube*] depends upon theoretical philosophy insofar as the latter has to show that the existence of those objects posited by the postulates can indeed be *thought*. In order to be able to think an object, I require a relevant concept, and it must be possible to assert the objective validity of this concept without contradiction. In order to think the 'Ideas' of reason, I require concepts that are not derived from experience and whose application is not itself limited to experience. For they can also be applied to objects beyond all possible experience. These concepts are the categories. Practical rational belief thus presupposes the deduction of the categories in the *Critique of Pure Reason*, which shows that they 'are not of empirical origin but have their seat and source a priori in the pure understanding' and that they can indeed 'be referred to *objects in general* independently of intuition of these objects' (CPrR:141, 16–19). The dialectic of the first *Critique* has shown that the concepts of God, freedom, and immortality involve no internal contradiction and that their corresponding objects are therefore logically possible (CPR B xxvi–xxix). They are '(transcendent) *thoughts* in which there is nothing impossible' (CPrR:135, 3f.).

These concepts acquire objective reality through the law of pure practical reason, although they cannot be *known* precisely because there are no corresponding intuitions for these concepts. The postulates cannot therefore be synthetic *a priori* judgements of theoretical reason for the latter always presuppose intuition. The 'theoretical cognition of pure reason' receives a certain 'increment' through the postulates, albeit one that simply means these 'merely thinkable' concepts are now 'declared assertorically to be concepts to which real objects belong' (CPrR:134, 21–24). And this is an assertion that pure practical reason compels pure theoretical reason to make. This extension of theoretical reason is not therefore a matter of any theoretical extension of speculative knowledge. But theoretical reason can nonetheless make a negative, critically religious use of this 'increment' in order to counter the anthropomorphism that appeals to alleged experience and the fanaticism that calls upon supposedly supersensible intuitions (CPrR:135, 33–136, 4). Kant demonstrates these points explicitly in relation to the concept of God.

The supreme cause, as the deduction of the postulate of the existence of God indicates, must be the ground of the harmony between nature and the supreme determining ground of the will of rational beings – that is, must possess a 'causality in accordance with moral disposition.' This implies 'a being that is the cause of nature by *understanding* and *will*' (CPrR:125, 15–22). This concept of God is further qualified later in the text: the predicates through which we think God are 'understanding and will, considered moreover in the relation to each other in which they must be thought in the moral law, and hence only to the extent that a pure practical use is made of them' (CPrR:137, 7–9). Although the concepts of will and understanding are derived from our own nature, this involves no false anthropomorphism or extravagantly assumed knowledge of supersensible objects. For these concepts abstract from all other features of the human will and understanding to leave only 'what is required for the possibility of thinking of a moral law; thus there is indeed a cognition of God but only with practical reference' (CPrR:137, 18–20).

The concept of God properly belongs therefore to morality rather than to natural philosophy or metaphysics. Kant repeats the crucial steps of his earlier criticism of the ontological argument (CPR A 592–603/ B 620–631) and the physico-theological argument (A 620–630/B 648–658) for the existence of God (CPrR:138, 16–139, 37). Since every existential assertion is synthetic, the existence of God cannot be demonstrated from the mere concept of the most perfect being. And the attempt to infer the existence of God from the order and purposiveness of the world can only lead us to the concept of an author that is wise, good, and powerful, and so on. On this path of enquiry, the concept of God always remains 'a concept of the perfection of the first being not determined precisely enough to be held adequate to the concept of a deity' (CPrR:139, 34–36). It requires supplementation if it is properly to lead to the concept of a being that is all-powerful, all-knowing, and absolutely good in every respect. The only possible recourse for theoretical reason here would be the ontological argument that Kant has already refuted. But the physico-theological proof can be given a valid sense if it is further supplemented by the moral proof of the existence of God. The object of pure practical reason presupposes an author of the world who is characterised by the highest perfection. 'He must be *omniscient* in order to cognize my conduct even to my inmost disposition in all possible cases and throughout the future, omnipotent in order to bestow results appropriate to it, and so too *omnipresent, eternal*, and so forth' (CPrR:140, 4–7).

According to the *Critique of Pure Reason*, the physico-theological proof is 'the oldest, the clearest, and the most accordant with the common reason of mankind [...] It would therefore not only be uncomforting but utterly vain to attempt to diminish in any way the authority of this argument' (CPR A623f./B651f.). The third *Critique* explains the power of this argument for human reason in general by indicating how the physico-theological proof 'without noticing it mixes into its inference the moral ground of proof, which is present and so deeply moving for every human being.' It is only the moral ground of proof that produces that conviction in which 'everyone feels most deeply his vocation; the physico-teleological argument, however, has only the merit of guiding the mind on the path of ends in the contemplation of the world, and thereby to an *intelligent* author of the world' (CPJ:477, 29ff.).

Bibliography

Guyer, P. 1977: 'In praktischer Absicht: Kants Begriff der Postulate der reinen praktischen Vernunft,' in *Philosophisches Jahrbuch* 104, 1–18.

Silber, J. R. 1959: 'Kant's Conception of the Highest Good as Immanent and Transcendent,' in *The Philosophical Review* 68, 469–492.

Silber, J.R. 1969: 'Die metaphysische Bedeutung des höchsten Guts als Kanon der reinen Vernunft in Kants Philosophie,' in *Zeitschrift für philosophische Forschung* 23, 538–549.

Walsh, W. H. 1963: 'Kant's Moral Theology,' in *Proceedings of the British Academy* 49, 263–289.

Winter, A. 2000: 'Der Gotteserweis aus praktischer Vernunft,' in Winter, A., *Der andere Kant*, Hildesheim, 257–343.

Wood, A. 1970: *Kant's Moral Religion*, Ithaca, New York.

IV

LEGAL AND
POLITICAL PHILOSOPHY

11

On How to Acquire Something External, and Especially on the Right to Things (A Commentary on the *Metaphysics of Morals* §§10–17)

Kristian Kühl

The first part of the *Doctrine of Right* presents Kant's analysis of 'Private Right' in three chapters (§§1–40). The discussion of the 'General principle of external acquisition' in §10 introduces the second chapter on 'How to *acquire* something external' (6:258, my emphasis). The discussion in §10 supplements the previous discussion of 'How to *have* something external as one's own' (6:245–257, §§1–9, my emphasis), which had merely grounded the necessity of rightful possession in terms of the rightful postulate of practical reason, which asserts the possibility of distinguishing between 'what is externally mine or yours.' In §10, Kant is concerned with the actual realisation of this possibility.

The analysis in §10 treats of acquisition in general, and draws conclusions that also hold for the next three sections of the text: that on 'property right,' or one's right to things [*Sachenrecht*] (§§11–17), that on 'contract right,' or one's rights to persons [*Personenrecht*] (§§18–21), and that on 'rights to persons akin to rights to things' [*das auf dingliche Art persön-liche Recht*] (§§22–30). This becomes quite clear at the end of §10, where Kant outlines his 'Division of the *acquisition* [*Erwerbung*] of something external that is mine or yours' (6:259, my emphasis).

The specific title of §10 makes no particular reference to original acquisition, nor to the acquisition of external things, but speaks solely of the general principle of external acquisition. Hence paragraphs three and four do not properly belong in §10 insofar as they only relate to property right, which is first discussed in §11 (a point convincingly argued in Ludwig 1988, p. 65).

Kant begins §10 with definitions intended to apply to any external acquisition whatsoever:

(1) *Acquisition* of something occurs 'when I bring it about that it becomes *mine*' (6:258).

(2) Acquisition is *original* when it is '*not derived* from what is another's' (6:258, my emphasis).

Between these two definitions, Kant has also inserted another one: 'Something external is originally mine which is mine without any act that establishes a right to it' (6:258). But he should actually have formulated this definition in hypothetical form since he explicitly lays down at the beginning of the second paragraph that 'Nothing external is originally mine' (ibid.). But an original – non-derived – acquisition is supposed to be possible. And it is also possible, although Kant makes no reference to this in §10, that there is something originally mine – namely, *internally mine*, as the only innate right: the right to external freedom itself (6:237).

That 'Nothing external is originally mine' (6:258) clearly applies to the ownership of physical objects (that is, 'things' in the sense defined by §90 of the Civil Law Code) since they are by definition something distinct from me as subject and only become mine through acquisition (for example, through a unilateral act of choice or indirectly through contract). As far as intellectual or spiritual property is concerned, no external acquisition is involved. Intellectual achievements must simply be developed, although under specific conditions they too may be accorded certain legal protection. That Kant seems to have realised this himself is perhaps suggested by the second paragraph of §55: 'Anyone has an incontestable property in anything the substance of which he has himself made' (6:345).

But as far as external things are concerned, they must first be acquired. This remains the case even if we entertain the idea of an original 'community of what is mine and yours (*communio*)' (6:258). If we imagine an actual historically given 'primitive community (*communio primaeva*),' then individual property would only rightfully exist insofar as it was derived from this community itself.

The second paragraph of §10 fails to clarify the precise relationship between what initially appear to be two contradictory claims:

(1) The condition of community (*communio*) of what is mine and yours can never be thought to be original but must be acquired (by an act that establishes an external right).

(2) The possession of an external object can originally *only* be possession in common, or can be both original *and* in common.

Now Kant certainly qualifies the first claim: for it seems that we can, albeit 'problematically' (6:258), at least conceive of an *original* community (*communio mei et tui originaria*).' It is supposedly possible to think of such a community, though this too remains unclear, as based upon 'principles' rather than simply on history.

Instead of identifying these 'principles,' the third paragraph proceeds directly and immediately to discuss '*the* principle of external acquisition' (ibid.). Formulated without the accompanying parentheses, this principle can be presented as follows.

Three conditions must be satisfied for something to be mine:

(1) I must bring it under my power.

(2) I must have the capacity to make use of it as an object of my choice.

(3) I must will that it be mine.

Each of these conditions is specifically qualified in a way that subjects the process of external acquisition to the general principles defining a freely based doctrine of right:

(1) I must 'bring something under my power' in accordance with the universal law of right (and thus with the external freedom of others).

(2) I must 'use something as an object of my choice' in such a way as to realise the postulate of practical reason.

(3) I must be able to relate 'the will to possess something' to the 'idea of a possible united will.'

With regard to the acquisition of property right (as defined in §§11–17), the division that Kant presents at the end of §10 (6:259f.) involves three points:

– in terms of the matter (the object), we are concerned with the acquisition of a *corporeal thing.*

– in terms of the form (the kind of acquisition), we are concerned with *property right* as the right to a thing.

– in terms of the basis of the acquisition in right, we are concerned with *an act of unilateral choice*, although Kant points out that this is only 'an aspect of the way acquisition is carried out' (6:260).

In §11, Kant undertakes to answer the question: 'What is a right to a thing?' (ibid.). The term 'property right' refers to that part of private right involving 'laws having to do with things being mine or yours' (6:261). It thus delimits the domain concerning the right to things from other domains, such as tort law, concerning contractual rights, or family law, concerning personal relationships.

'Property right' is usually defined as a 'right to a thing (*ius reale, ius in re*)' (6:260) that belongs to a legitimate owner 'against every possessor' of a thing. Kant accepts this as a correct 'nominal definition' as far as it goes, but is nonetheless dissatisfied with it insofar as it fails to clarify the precise *relationship between persons and things*. Through his insistence that rights also necessarily involve duties, Kant emphatically rejects the view still commonly entertained in civil law that the owner's right relates directly to things. But it is only human beings, and not things, that can be bearers of rights (thus the stolen object now in the physical possession of the thief does not itself 'bindingly' refer back to the rightful owner of the thing).

Kant defines the property right of the owner of a thing not in terms of a *direct and immediate* relation to the thing, and of an indirect relation to its illegitimate possessor, but as an immediate right against such a possessor making use of the thing. The relation of right thus obtains between the owner and the possessor, and property grants a right over against the possessor with respect to the thing. The way in which property right regulates the relations between persons differs from other regulations governing such relations only in that the former *relates* essentially to the capacity for disposing over *things* (material objects). The correlative object of any relation of property right is therefore a human being rather than a 'rightless' thing. This is the basis for the possible limitation of an owner's right that may be required in relation to other persons, the right that §903 of the Civil Law Code defines as that 'of disposing of a thing in whatever way one pleases and excluding others from any possible intervention.'

The discussion in §11 can be supplemented by Kant's extended note at the end of §17. Thus the concept of 'property' [*Eigentum*] – and property is the most important right in this connection – already and correctly appears in the first paragraph concerning one's right to things (as proposed in Ludwig 1988, p. 68).

The free and all-inclusive disposal over the substance of a thing, which Kant connects directly with the concept of 'property (*dominium*)' (6:270), requires an objective restriction to material things. This directly excludes the possibility of treating the human being as an object of property.

The question of whether a human being can properly be 'the owner of himself' (6:270) makes no difference to the concept of property as a right to things. To decide whether a human being can 'dispose of himself as he pleases' (through suicide or self-mutilation for example), we must consider the 'right of humanity,' which involves a problematic responsibility on the part of every individual for 'the humanity of his person' (see §6 of the *Doctrine of Virtue*: 6:422f. For further discussion of this question in relation to the penal law, see Kühl 1991, p. 174 and Höffe 1979, p. 31).

And the question of whether anyone 'can be the owner ... of other human beings' (6:270) must be answered categorically in the negative. One cannot treat other human beings as one pleases by appeal to the principle of property. Kant's opposition to obsolete forms of slavery and serfdom is clearly evident here. One might also note the remark in the 'Division' of the subject in the Introduction: 'These would be human beings without personality (serfs, slaves)' (6:241). Whether this perspective also permits us to criticise modern forms of 'dominion over human beings' grounded in the economic ownership of means of production will depend upon our interpretation of Kant's general conception of the 'relation of dominion.' (See §30: The relation of 'servants' to the head of the household is certainly compared here with property right in terms of possession, but Kant clearly denies that the head of the household is thereby permitted to treat them as if he were an 'owner.' And there could never be a contract to this effect either, because no valid contract is possible where one party 'relinquishes his entire freedom and thus ceases to be a person' [6:283]. See also paragraph four in General Remark D at the end of §49 [6:330] and paragraph four of §55 [6:345].)

In the second paragraph of §11, Kant pursues the rather obscure observations in the second paragraph of §10 concerning the possibility of original collective possession, and thus addresses the problem of *grounding*, or more precisely *justifying*, the rightful acquisition of property. Kant proposes a *real definition* of property as: 'A right to the private use of a thing of which I am in ... possession in common with all others' (6:261).

This possession *in common* is supposed to be 'the only condition' (ibid.) of the possibility of *private* property! Without reference to common possession, we cannot explain how the right of an owner who is not 'in possession' of a thing is violated by another's illegitimate use of that same thing.

But in addition to the assumption of collective possession, we must also recognise a further condition if the owner is to impose upon all others an 'obligation' to refrain from making use of something that belongs to him. No unilateral demand on my part can possibly create the relevant obligation here. This demand only becomes a binding obligation on others 'through the united choice of all who possess in common' (ibid.).

This 'united choice of all' justifies restrictions on the external freedom of anyone and everyone. If this restriction is supposed to concern ownership of a thing, we must also assume 'possession in common ... with all others' (ibid.). The 'obligation' towards others with respect to things is created by the 'united choice' that possesses all things in common, that permits particular individuals to own and appropriate specific things under particular conditions. The private property that results thus proceeds from the consent of all those who possess in common (the 'social foundation' of private property). This can also justify a social restriction on private property and the withdrawal of certain things, such as land and the means of production, from private control (that is, returning them to collective possession through 'socialisation'; for example, see Kühl 1984, 307ff., for a detailed defence of this argument). The individual foundation of the doctrine of right means that the united will of all does not define collective possession as common property with respect to land, for example (see Kant's reference in §15 to Mongolia where 'all the land belongs to the people' [6:265]). If the external freedom of everyone is taken as the underlying principle, then anyone must be able to take possession of anything capable of being owned as long as this does not infringe the freedom of others. Private ownership thus enjoys priority as long as the private property of one can be rendered compatible, in accordance with a universal law of freedom, with the private property of others (this is the 'rational foundation' of private property; one could equally well speak of a 'freedom-based theoretical foundation' of property in this connection).

In §12 and §13, Kant discusses the initial and original acquisition of a specific thing or kind of thing – namely, that of land. The overemphasis upon the question of land with respect to other 'moveable' things that finds expression here serves to reveal the specific historical limitations of certain aspects of Kant's theory of property.

In §13, Kant relates the postulate of practical reason presented in §2 to the acquisition of land. On this principle, any land can be acquired in the original sense. It is 'the original community of land in general' (6:262) that furnishes the ground of the possibility of such acquisition. This is rather surprisingly 'demonstrated' by reference to the specific fact that 'the spherical surface of the earth unites all the places on its surface' (ibid.). For otherwise human beings would simply be dispersed along an infinite plane in such a way that they 'would not come into any community with one another' (ibid.). And Kant makes a similar point in his discussion of 'cosmopolitan right' in §62: 'Nature has enclosed them all [sc. all nations on the earth] together within determinate limits (by the spherical shape of the place they live in, a *globus terraqueus*)' (6:352). Can we say therefore that property and perhaps even right in general arises not merely from the necessity of maintaining external freedom, but also from the 'nature of things,' from the actually given conditions and circumstances of human beings as inhabitants of the earth? Is the earth the natural condition of right itself, the surface of the earth (as a sphere) the natural condition for the ownership of land? Or is this simply a symbolic way of vividly representing a concept of right and property that is essentially grounded in reason?

These questions must be left unanswered for the present (but for further consideration of different interpretations of the significance of the spherical character of the earth's surface for the theory of right and property in general, see Brocker 1987, pp. 107ff. and p. 193f.). And here one should also simply indicate the absence of any discussion of the exploration of extraterrestrial space, something that has now of course already begun.

The heading of §14 designates the rightful act of acquiring a corporeal thing as one of 'taking control (*occupatio*)' (6:263). It is the act of taking control that first leads to concrete private possession of a thing as property. Despite the aspect of power suggested by the expression of 'taking control' [*Bemächtigung*], the acquisition of property must be considered as a rightful act rather than as a violent act.

The unilateral character of 'taking control' here does not simply make it into an arbitrary empirical act, precisely because this unilateral character is universally acknowledged as such; it is 'the united and therefore solely law-giving will' (6:263) which permits the 'taking control' in the first place. But the latter does presuppose something that already follows from the universal law of right: the 'priority in time' that belongs to the first taking possession of something (ibid.). If this were ignored, then 'taking control' would violate the freedom of the one who first took possession of the thing in question.

The practical significance of this 'priority in time' is revealed in §15 (6:266), where Kant criticises the practice of colonisation. For prior acts of appropriation and taking control must also be respected even if they have been carried out by 'savages.' It is true that Kant does not explicitly discuss whether such respect must be forthcoming if such 'savages' refuse to enter into 'a civil constitution' with their 'visitors.'

The more detailed treatment of the three 'aspects' (*attendenda*) belonging to the original acquisition of things (6:258f.), which was 'excluded' from the discussion in §10, specifically clarifies and expands upon the concept of 'taking control' of a corporeal thing (which is precisely why this concept and its three aspects do not properly belong in the more general discussion of §10). The first aspect – that of 'apprehension' – indicates the physical taking possession of an object. In spite of its obviously empirical and conditioned character, such 'apprehension' is not a matter of arbitrary choice since it must respect the 'priority in time' already mentioned: it may only be extended to things that do not already belong to another.

The second aspect – that of 'giving a sign (*declaratio*)' – indicates the specification or marking of something as my own. This is what makes my property recognisable as such to others and thereby reveals to them the limits of their own exercise of freedom.

Both these aspects are unilateral acts and hence cannot on their own establish a rightful obligation on the part of others. It is only the third aspect – that of 'appropriation (*appropriatio*)' – that can establish such obligation. Although appropriation also represents a unilateral act of will from the perspective of the appropriating agent, it must also be conceived as the 'act of a general will (in idea) giving an external law through which everyone is bound to agree with my choice' (6:259). If all three aspects are taken into account, 'taking control' of a thing establishes property with due agreement of all others, who are simultaneously obliged to refrain from using the thing in question themselves.

The act of taking control, with its three aspects, thus rules out the idea that some empirical aspect, such as further developing or working upon the object, can serve to legitimate the acquisition of property (§15; for further discussion of the relationship of this material to Kant's *Vorarbeiten*, see Ludwig 1988, 71ff.). Such further development of an object is 'nothing more than an external sign of taking possession' (6:265). Neither the original 'apprehension' nor the 'demarcation' of an object, as empirical acts, can create or establish the right to property as a normative phenomenon. In addition, someone who further develops or works upon the object of another does not thereby recognise the priority of the owner's legitimately grounded right to the property. And, finally, property does not involve an immediate relation between a person and an object, but rather a relation between human beings with respect to an object, one that only becomes an acknowledged relation of right through the (necessary and explicitly conceptualised) agreement of all.

We should of course note that prevailing civil law allows someone who develops and works upon a thing to acquire property if through the development of some material or materials he produces a new 'moveable thing' (§950 of the Civil Legal Code). The previous owner thus forfeits his ownership but is entitled to financial compensation from the new owner (§951 of the Civil Legal Code). While this regulation thus acknowledges the 'actual development' of a thing, it should not be understood to imply the principle of the 'priority of labour over capital' (see Schapp 1989, §13 II).

There is some overlapping of subject matter in §15 and §17, which properly belongs at the end of the treatment of property right insofar as these sections – such as §8 and §9 on the possession of external things as one's own – principally concern the transition from provisional acquisition in the state of nature to conclusive acquisition within the context of a civil constitution. I should like to draw attention to a couple of points that seem to me to be particularly important and worthy of further discussion in this connection.

(1) In the civil condition, it is 'the a priori united will' that 'alone determines what is right, what is rightful, and what is laid down as right' (6:267). Does this imply that it is the task of the political legislator to organise an appropriate system of property rights? Or is the sole task of the state simply to secure the provisional system of property characteristic of the state of nature? Is the state merely supposed to guarantee the pre-political limits of property or should it positively strive to secure the conditions for realising rights to property or restore such conditions if they have disappeared? It seems clear that a welfare state system does not properly correspond to a freedom-based theory of property because it must constantly attempt to 'redistribute' the results of the actual exercise of freedom in this domain. On the other hand, Kant's theory of property seems to imply that the state has an obligation to promote a fairer distribution of opportunities with regard to freedom and property (for further discussion and detailed justification of this argument, see Kühl 1984, pp. 264ff.; in a similar vein, see the earlier contribution by Luf 1978, pp.124ff.; for further discussion of this kind of social extension of the theory of rights, ranging from the sympathetic to the highly critical, see Deggau 1983, pp. 248ff.; Kersting 1984, pp. 243ff., and 1986, p. 309; Ludwig 1987, p. 153; Baumann 1994, p. 147; Wildt 1997, p. 159). One could appropriately describe such a political order as a 'social state that serves the promotion of freedom' (Höffe 1981, p. 255).

(2) Does the universal obligation to enter into a civil state arise from the fact that freedom is threatened by 'a condition in which there is constant danger of conflict' where human beings share a common space (Höffe 1979a, p. 209)? Or is it provisional property that creates our duty to enter the state because the former requires positive regulation in terms of principles of right, because the 'potential conflict harboured by the state of nature' is specifically grounded in the 'manifold character of equally justified conceptions of right and interpretations of civil law which apply the

natural laws of what is mine and yours in each case in accordance with their own concepts of right' (Kersting 1991, p. 130)?

In conclusion, I should like to provide my own answer, at least in outline, to these two questions, taking them in the reverse order.

With regard to the second question: the architectonic of Kant's theory of right suggests that it is the merely provisional character of property in the state of nature that drives us forward to the idea of conclusive property within the context of a civil constitution – that is, within a political state. Kant's doctrine of right begins with the discussion of private right (6:245), and the latter begins with two chapters that deal respectively with what it means 'to have something external as my own' (6:245) and 'to acquire something external as my own' (6:258). Both chapters are centrally concerned with something external as a corporeal object that I can be said to have or to acquire – namely, a thing. The possibility of, and the justification of, property with regard to a thing thus serves to introduce the doctrine of right itself. But in his analysis of private right, Kant is not content simply with grounding the concept of property as a rational right in general. For that would not yet allow the concept of property with regard to a thing to appeal specifically to this right. If this right is to be completely secured, we require a political state with laws governing property and courts capable of deciding upon conflicts involving property. In other words, property itself demands that we leave the state of nature, and even justifies us in exercising the appropriate coercion upon other provisional owners of property. That is why Kant can say in the *Corollary* to §8 (in Chapter 1 of the *Doctrine of Right*): 'If it must be possible, in terms of rights, to have an external object as one's own, the subject must also be permitted to *constrain* [*nötigen*] everyone else with whom he comes into conflict about whether an external object is his or another's to enter along with him into a civil constitution' (6:256). Kant returns to this idea in §15 (in Chapter 2 of the *Doctrine of Right*), where he presents it as 'a principle of private right, in accordance with which each is justified in using that coercion which is necessary if people are to leave the state of nature and enter into the civil constitution, which can alone make any acquisition conclusive' (6:264). This idea is finally confirmed in the first section (on 'The right of the state') of Part Two of the *Metaphysics of Morals* (on 'Public right'), where at the end of the 'Remark' to §44, Kant writes: 'So if external objects were not even *provisionally* mine or yours in the state of nature, there would also be no duties of right with regard to them and therefore no command to leave the state of nature' (6:312–13). The specific connection between private right and public right is spelled out at the beginning of §42: 'From private right in the state of nature there proceeds the postulate of public right: when you cannot avoid living side by side with all others, you ought to leave the state of nature and proceed with them into a rightful condition, that is, a condition of distributive justice' (6:307).

Consistent and compelling as the overall argument may appear to be, its necessity derives 'merely' from the rather unequal and disproportionate structure of the *Doctrine of Right* itself. For it gives such prominence to the concept of property that the explication and justification of other rights (such as those concerned with human life, the body, personal freedom, the right to free movement, reputation, or sexuality) either receives only cursory treatment or is simply ignored altogether. If Kant had attempted to legitimise the kind of rights I have just mentioned by way of example, he would probably have come to positive conclusions with regard to most of these cases. His own conclusions regarding the sphere of personal freedom, for example, are clear from a prominent passage in the Introduction to the *Doctrine of Right* concerning the 'only innate right': 'Freedom (independence from being constrained by another's choice), insofar as it can coexist with the freedom of every other in accordance with a universal law, is the only original right belonging to every man by virtue of his humanity' (6:237).

But although it is certainly necessary to provide rational legitimation for the specific personal rights that Kant himself failed to examine in detail here, it is even more important to recognise, as Kant emphatically does, that a civil constitution, and thus a political state, is also indispensable if such rights are properly to be secured and perfectly realised. For in regard to such rights, human beings 'can never be secure against violence from one another' (6:312). Indeed force and violence are even more likely to be encountered in relation to rights in the more personal sphere of individual freedom than in those directly connected with property itself (one only need compare crimes against property that do not involve violence – such as theft, embezzlement, fraud and deception – with violent criminal offences involving physical compulsion, deprivation of liberty, or sexual assault). One can therefore also only be secure of one's rights in this respect if there is a political state to guarantee and define the limits of such rights and to ensure their actual protection through courts of law where necessary. And a situation where everyone simply does 'what seems right and good to himself' (6:312) can also arise where there is no direct conflict between owners of property or non-rightful possessors. This situation must therefore also be avoided in the sphere of human interaction where 'things' are not involved at all. It is thus not merely the right to property but every rationally legitimated individual right to freedom that demands the transition to, and the possible coercion to enter into, the political state.

I should also like to make a few comments with regard to the first of the two questions that were raised earlier. Although this claim has been widely contested, I have argued elsewhere that Kant's theory of right and property effectively implies 'a social state that serves the promotion of freedom' and furthers the just distribution of opportunities with regard to property and freedom (see Kühl 1984). Objections to this line of argument have generally been based upon an appeal to the text of Kant's *Doctrine of Right*. It is quite true that the text in question forbids the identification of external freedom conceived as independence from the coercive will of another (6:237) with a freedom conceived in terms of the equal distribution of opportunity in the economic sphere for example. And there is no explicit reference to any such thing in the *Doctrine of Right* itself. And there are likewise no references, or at least no explicit ones, in this part of the text to the broader social and political dimensions of a constitutional state that is oriented exclusively to the protection of freedom and property. Thus in §9 (Chapter 1), Kant claims that 'a civil constitution is just the rightful condition, by which what belongs to each is only secured, but not actually settled and determined' (6:256). It is true that Kant qualifies this view somewhat in §15 (Chapter 2) when he writes: 'The indeterminacy, with respect to quantity as well as quality, of the external object that can be acquired makes this problem (of the sole, original external acquisition) the hardest of all to solve' (6:266). But this does not imply that the state should play an active role in establishing equality of opportunity with regard to the acquisition of property or in imposing specific limits upon actual or potential appropriation.

In spite of these conclusive observations, however, there are passages in the text of the *Doctrine of Right* that suggest we should take the actual opportunities for acquiring property into account and consider the idea of limiting the actual power of private property. Thus in §46, Kant demands that positive laws 'must not be contrary to the natural laws of freedom and of the equality of everyone in the people corresponding to this freedom, namely that anyone can work his way up from this passive condition to an active one' (6:315). Since the 'active condition' in question is essentially connected with the issue of property, one could conclude from this demand that no one should be denied the opportunity of working to become a property owner in his own right. It is true that the text leaves it an open question as to whether we should be considering actual opportunities or merely rightful possibilities in this connection.

And the situation is similar with regard to the suggestion for limiting property. Kant's *Doctrine of Right* criticised attempts to fix the permissible amounts of property and possessions, as was common in the special commissions (the socalled *Fideikommisse*) of the time, because this would restrict individuals in the acquisition of property and their pursuit of economic independence (for further discussion, see Kühl 1984, 286f.). Kant actually ascribes an active role to the state as far as the abolition of privileges is concerned: 'From this it follows that within a state there can also be no corporation, estate or order which, as owner of land, can pass it on in accordance with certain statutes to succeeding generations for their exclusive use (in perpetuity). The state can repeal such statutes at any time, provided it compensates those who are left' (6:324). Again it is true that Kant does not, at least explicitly, draw the conclusion that might seem to be suggested here – that the state can eliminate not only special privileges with regard to rights, but might also intervene to challenge actual concentrations of power based upon accumulated property in the interests of extending the possibilities of further acquisition of property for all.

While these 'suggestions' in the *Doctrine of Right* may do something to open up Kant's work in the direction of the modern conception of the 'social state,' it is far more important in this regard to reflect upon and to extend the fundamental principle of his theory of right – namely, the universal law of right, which is also the law of the united will of all (see 6:267, 16–18). As the embodiment of the united will of all, the state must also legislate in accordance with the universal law of right in relation to questions of property (6:230). Whether indeed this universal law of right is concerned solely with the coexistence of the rightful freedoms of everyone, or whether it must also take into consideration the actual conditions for the realisation of freedom, is the final remaining question that has at least now been clearly formulated as such.

According to Kant, equality as 'a principle of universal human right,' with all its consequences for the domain of rights, is already implied 'in the principle of innate freedom,' since freedom and equality are 'not really distinct (as if they were members of the division of some higher concept of a right)' (6:238). If freedom and equality are to be treated neither as unconnected and independent principles, nor as mutually competing concepts, then equality cannot be understood in terms of actual equality of possessions. For this would generally exclude freedom of action with regard to things insofar as the latter always leads to changes in the distribution of property. The principle of equality must rather be related directly to that of freedom. It is specifically defined in terms of freedom for everyone insofar as this freedom can be exercised consistently with the like freedom of others in accordance with a universal law. This does not merely involve, on the negative side, the elimination of privileges that obstruct the realisation of freedom, but also implies, on the positive side, the creation of conditions for the actual realisation of freedom in the social, and particularly in the economic, sphere (even if Kant does not specifically emphasise 'questions concerning empirical success in realising freedom'). But this means that Kant's theory of right, and its underlying principle of freedom defined in terms of equality, is not simply restricted to the purely formal equality of right itself, but also demands the promotion of equality of opportunity. But in this respect, practical reason requires no recourse to a 'universally valid concept of happiness' because the principle of equality of opportunity allows everyone to realise his own conception of happiness, whatever that may be.

The lawfully defined freedom that initially grounds the possibility of acquiring property also provides the principle for limiting the acquisition of private property. Since private property is itself grounded in the principle of freedom, it cannot simply be left to itself or detached from the universal context of human freedom in general. The universal law of right indicates as much precisely by insisting on the compatibility of one individual's freedom with the same freedom of every other individual. This clearly establishes the principle of universality and reciprocity as the condition of all freedom, including the freedom that manifests itself in the acquisition of property and the accumulation of capital.

Bibliography

Baumann, P. 1994: 'Zwei Seiten der Kantschen Begründung von Eigentum und Staat,' in *Kant-Studien* 85, 147f.

Brocker, M. 1987: *Kants Besitzlehre. Zur Problematik einer transzendental-philosophischen Eigentumslehre*, Würzburg.

Deggau, H-G. 1983: *Die Aporien der Rechtslehre Kants*, Stuttgart.

Höffe, O. 1979: 'Recht und Moral: ein Kantischer Problemaufriß,' in *neue hefte für philosophie [sic]* 17, 1ff.

Höffe, O. 1979a: 'Zur vertragstheoretischen Begründung politischer Gerechtigkeit: Hobbes, Kant und Rawls im Vergleich,' in O. Höffe, *Ethik und Politik*, Frankfurt am Main, 195ff.

Höffe, O. 1981: 'Die Menschenrechte als Legitimation und kritischer Maßstab der Demokratie,' in J. Schwartländer (ed.), *Menschenrechte und Demokratie*, Kehl, 241ff.

Kersting, W. 1984: *Wohlgeordnete Freiheit. Immanuel Kants Rechts und Staatsphilosophie*, Berlin/New York.

Kersting, W. 1986: Review of Kühl, 1984, in *Zeitschrift für philosophische Forschung* 40, 309ff.

Kersting, W. 1991: 'Eigentum, Vertrag und Staat bei Kant und Locke,' in M. P. Thompson (ed.), *John Locke und/and Immanuel Kant*.

Kühl, K. 1984: *Eigentumsordnung als Freiheitsordnung. Zur Aktualität der Kantischen Rechts und Eigentumslehre*, Freiburg/Munich.

Kühl, K. 1991: 'Die Bedeutung der Kantischen Unterscheidungen von Legalität und Moralität sowie von Rechts- und Tugendpflichten für das Strafrecht – ein Problemaufriß,' in H. Jung et al. (eds.), *Recht und Moral*, Baden-Baden, 139ff.

Ludwig, B. 1987: Review of Kühl, 1984, in *ARSP* 73, 153ff.

Ludwig, B. 1988: *Kants Rechtslehre*, Hamburg.

Luf, G. 1978: *Freiheit und Gleichheit*, Vienna/New York.

Schapp, J. 1989: *Sachenrecht*, Munich.

Schmidt-Jortzig, E. 1998: 'Eigentum und Privatautonomie,' in *Recht – Eine Information des Bundesministeriums der Justiz*, 1ff.

Wildt, A. 1997: 'Zum Verhältnis von Recht und Moral bei Kant,' in *ARSP* 83, 159ff.

12

'The Civil Constitution in Every State Shall Be a Republican One'

Wolfgang Kersting

The six 'preliminary articles' that Kant introduces in the first section of his essay *Toward Perpetual Peace* formulate the negative conditions for securing peace between states. These principles have the status of laws that prohibit or permit certain courses of action universally – that is without exception. In contrast to the three 'definite articles' presented in the second section of the essay, they are based upon experience and thus make no claim to a completeness rigorously derived from a single principle. They envisage the sort of preventive measures that belong to the conventional repertoire of political action concerned with avoiding war and maintaining peace, and represent the indispensable, empirically identifiable conditions for a legally secured peace between states. These preliminary articles can procure a kind of preparatory peace that is simply an absence of war. But a mere absence of war cannot yet itself be regarded as a positive presence of peace. In order to advance from the absence of war to the presence of peace, we must also embark upon the path of right itself. It is only through recourse to principles of right that states and human beings can properly establish and achieve peace amongst themselves.

1. The state of war and the state of peace

If we translate the absence of war, as sketched in Kant's preliminary articles, into the contractual language of classical political philosophy, we immediately recognise that it is simply the state of nature, and thus a state of war after all. There is no real contradiction here since Kant has structural reasons for regarding the state of nature as itself a state of war. For in the state of nature, there are no non-violent legal procedures, independent of a contingent distribution of power, for regulating conflict and for securing and preserving social order. It is therefore a condition in which real or potential insecurity and latent aggression continue to prevail, a condition in which everyone must simply wait for the next 'outbreak of hostilities' (8:349). Kant interprets the fundamental political opposition between war and peace in philosophical terms as essentially a question of right. He thereby formulates a challenging and emphatic concept of peace that treats any political establishment of peace that is essentially based upon superior power and deterrent threat as a merely negative peace, and thus simply as a continuation of the state of war. And an absence of war merely based upon the current balance of power or constellation of superior forces, or even upon mutually agreed political conduct in accordance with the preliminary articles for perpetual peace, would still remain fragile, contingent, and structurally insecure in character. And although this is certainly preferable to an outbreak of violent conflict, it fails to provide the slightest grounds for any lasting non-violent coexistence amongst states.

Further measures and efforts are therefore required if the absence of war is to prove enduring, if those in a state of nature are ever to live in a condition of friendly coexistence, if the negative freedom characterised by the absence of war is ever to become a positive condition of peace. This condition of peace must therefore expressly be '*established*' (8:349). This involves the existence of specific legal structures, grounded upon rationally justifiable principles of right, which institutionally serve to shape the political constellations of power and government. Until this is accomplished, until neighbouring states have shown their mutual readiness to abjure war by entering jointly into a system of law-governed freedom permitting the legal and non-violent regulation of conflict, it is entirely rational for everyone to treat and regard any neighbour remaining in a state of nature as a real or potential enemy, to be 'permanently armed and ready for war' (*Reflections*: 19: 7646). This holds equally for particular individuals in a social state of nature and for political communities in an international state of nature. Under normal circumstances, under specific legal and political conditions, we would only treat someone as our enemy if he has infringed our rights in some way or other; here the enemy is only revealed as such through the violent infringement of right itself. In the state of nature, on the other hand, whether this prevails in the relations between individuals or in the relations between communities and states, the right of each is already infringed by everyone else insofar as this general state of lawlessness exists at all. Hence Kant can speak of a '*laesio per statum*,' an infringement of right that is structural in character and imposed by general conditions of existence (see *Reflections*: 19:7647; 23:211).

It follows directly from this interpretation of the state of nature that we necessarily possess the right to abandon this state. 'There should be no war; neither that between myself and yourself in the state of nature, nor between ourselves as states which although internally governed by law, nonetheless exist externally in a lawless condition (in relation to one another)' (MM: 6:354). Kant therefore claims that 'all men who can mutually affect one another must belong to some civil constitution' (8:349, note). Hobbes also teaches that we must abandon the state of nature, but his political philosophy only offers a single way out of the state of nature as far as individuals are concerned. And Hobbes can provide no institutional solution whatsoever for the renewed state of nature that results from the relations between states themselves. The Kantian way out of the state of nature leads us much further than this. And Kant's philosophy of law offers a peaceful solution, grounded in principles of right, for all the conditions that characterise the state of nature. It is not merely the state of nature prevailing between individuals that is to be replaced by an established order of right; the state of nature prevailing between political states must also be overcome through a legal constitution based upon principles of right. And even the state of nature that prevails between individuals and foreign states to which they do not belong is also to be replaced by appropriate legally sanctioned provisions and regulations (see 8:24).

This comparison with the political philosophy of Hobbes clearly indicates the audacity of Kant's own theory of rightfully secured peace. Whereas Kant wishes to achieve a condition of peace through overcoming the international state of nature by appeal to principles of law, Hobbes can only look for peace *within* the international state of nature as a way of simply preserving the absence of war for as long as possible. Hobbes's strategy for peace depends essentially upon rational mistrust. The essential idea is that war can be avoided as long as each party makes the cost of breaking the peace so high for everyone else that no one can reasonably hope to gain anything for himself by doing so. The fundamental thought here implies a balance of mutual deterrence that requires one state to ensure military parity with any rival state if this balance is to be maintained. But whenever one party threatens in time to become

more powerful, the other must attempt in turn to anticipate such developments by increasing its own military preparedness. The politics of deterrence itself thus inevitably produces a spiralling process of preparation
for armed conflict. Kant therefore attempts to ground the condition of
peace through an established legal order rather than through any balance
of mutual deterrence. For Kant, the aggressive dynamics of the state of
nature cannot ultimately be contained by prudential arrangements of this
kind, but must finally be brought to an end through recourse to a 'civil
constitution' (8:349). Individuals and states are categorically required by
reason itself to establish such a constitution properly framed in accordance with pure principles of right.

The three definitive articles for perpetual peace formulate the positive
conditions of legal right for any truly genuine and comprehensive peace.
At the same time, they also describe three different steps in the general
direction of legal right – concerned respectively with the right of citizens,
the right of nations, and the right of citizens of the world – that must all be
taken if the state of nature is definitively to be overcome. Kant claims that
this 'division is no arbitrary one but is necessary with reference to the idea
of perpetual peace' (8:349, note). Perpetual peace arises from a system of
right that can regulate all potential conflicts within the world of external
freedom. Now there is always the possibility that lawless violence can
arise between individuals, between states, and also between states and
individuals (who belong to foreign states or to no state at all). Any truly
comprehensive programme for avoiding conflict-generated violence must
therefore bring all areas of potential conflict under the aegis of right. A
programme for genuinely lasting and comprehensive peace must contain
and combine measures for establishing peace at the individual level of the
citizen of the state, at the international level of states in relation to one
another, and at the cosmopolitan level of the citizen of the world.

One might object that the question of internal constitutional right should
not play any role at all in a theory concerning peace between nations,
and that Kant himself has described his own rationally grounded peace
contract precisely as a philosophical project for an international order of
right. But Kant counters this objection with an argument that is central
to his explication of the first definitive article. This argument essentially
involves two theses. According to the first thesis, there is a close connection
between the political constitution of a particular state and its relationship
to other states, and this already essentially allows us to distinguish between
those constitutions that actively encourage war, those constitutions that
are not conducive to maintaining peace, and those intrinsically peaceful

constitutions that effectively hinder war. According to the second thesis, a republican constitution is one that directly favours peace and that, for internal structural reasons, already gives heed to rational demands concerning the principles of right. Reason itself therefore has immediate and twofold cause to endorse a republican constitution for the state. Firstly, because the latter is the only form of civil organisation that properly corresponds to the innate right to freedom that human beings possess as such. And secondly, because it promotes the establishment of an international order of legal right. The idea of a peaceful international order, derived from pure principles of right, thus has a further civil and constitutional premise. And it is an essential part of Kant's philosophical project for perpetual peace to explain and clarify this premise. That is why the first definitive article for perpetual peace among states contains a rational demand that is essentially motivated by considerations of civil and international law: 'The civil constitution of every state shall be republican' (8:349).

2.   The necessary elements of a republican constitution

According to Kant, a republican constitution is one that is 'established, first on principles of the *freedom* of the members of a society (as individuals), second on principles of the *dependence* of all upon a single common legislation (as subjects), and third on the law of their *equality* (*as citizens of a state*)' (8:349–50). Kant further characterises a republican constitution explicitly as 'the sole constitution that issues from the idea of the original contract on which all rightful legislation of a people must be based' (8:350). The underlying contractarian conception of social and political legitimacy in Kant's argument here clearly recalls that of Rousseau's *Social Contract*. Kant regarded Rousseau's notion of a 'confederation of citizens' as the authentic 'ideal of constitutional law,' and treated the idea of the social contract as a universally binding criterion of right for every existing social and political confederation (*Reflections*: 14: 6593). We can only replace the state of nature with an established order of right, in a manner compatible with the intrinsic human right to freedom itself, if all individuals are united under a general legislative will to the laws of which every individual is subject in precisely the same way. This contractarian union furnishes the model for all legitimate rule in accordance with rational principles of right. The internal normative structure of such a contractually constituted community already contains *in nuce* the normative structure of any republican constitution.

The organised legislative power, in duplicating the original contractarian union, exercises a proper and legitimate dominion because its laws are inevitably just in character. 'The legislative authority can belong only to the united will of the people. For since all right is to proceed from it, it cannot do anyone wrong by its law. Now when someone makes arrangements about another, it is always possible for him to do the other wrong; but he can never do wrong in what he decides upon with regard to himself (for *volenti non fit iniuria*). Therefore only the concurring and united will of all, insofar as each decides the same thing for all and for each, and so only the general united will of the people, can be legislative' (*The Metaphysics of Morals*, 6:313–14). We should note that such a conception of justice, based upon the unanimity and equal participation of all concerned, requires no specifically moral presuppositions and no special moral sense for justice. It does not prevent those who are to participate in this general expression of will from freely pursuing their own interests. Justice here consorts perfectly well with self-interest, but only on the condition that it pay equal regard to the self-interest of all concerned. Kant therefore defends an essentially procedural conception of justice that determines the justness of a law in accordance with the process through which it has been established. Laws are just laws when the process of establishing them reflects the process of contractual agreement itself, when they are the agreed result of a decision in which all those concerned have the same right to participate (see Mauss 1992).

The idea of a properly republican constitution, and the principles of legal freedom and equality directly connected with it, thus acquires a much clearer profile when interpreted in the context of this contractarian conception of the general will. In a state with a republican constitution, the freedom of human beings lies in the right to subject themselves solely to laws that can be accepted and acknowledged by everyone. Or as Kant expresses it: 'My external (rightful) *freedom* is ... the warrant to obey no other external laws than those to which I could have given my consent' (8:350, note). Since everyone possesses this right, the freedom of human beings in general must imply existence under laws that can be equally accepted and acknowledged by all.

The external rightful freedom of human beings cannot be determined independently of the concept of law. Kant makes it quite clear that the usual well-known definition of rightful freedom as 'the warrant to do whatever one wants provided one does no wrong to anyone' is essentially meaningless because it reveals itself on closer inspection as nothing but an 'empty tautology' (8:350, note). All laws imply a certain limitation of freedom, although of course they do not always limit freedom in a legitimate fashion. A non-tautological and rationally based determination of the external rightful freedom of human beings must therefore be connected directly with the concept of intrinsically just and legitimate laws. And since Kant's procedural conception identifies just laws precisely as laws that can command universal acceptance, this permits a definition of the private sphere of rightful freedom that is based a priori upon the equal legislative right of all. My external rightful freedom lies in my having to obey only those laws to which, in my shared legislative capacity with everyone else, I could have given my full assent. We should note how his definition links the innate human right to freedom directly to the sphere of constitutional right. We could almost say that Kant presents an Aristotelian position modified in accordance with *a priori* principles of reason. For the fundamental freedom that rightfully belongs to human beings can only adequately be explicated from the perspective of a republican constitutional order, and this freedom is already intrinsically interpreted here in terms of its potential concrete realisation in a system of law legislated through the general will.

The principle of equality is also intimately connected with the coordination of social action through universally acknowledged laws. For the idea of inequality with regard to rights is something to which 'the general will of a people in the original contract (which is yet the principle of all rights) would never agree' (8:350, note). Equality of rights implies the rejection of privilege and discrimination in general and requires the equal distribution of juridical power and unrestricted access to all legitimate legal measures. It is entirely incompatible with hereditary subjection, with particular rights and privileges for the nobility, and with all other ways of encouraging special rights and limiting legitimate ones. Equality of rights is guaranteed by transferring the principle of legislation to the united general will itself. It is quite obvious that the idea of the original contract, the concept of a united legislative will, and the typically republican constitutional principles of freedom and equality – all serve reciprocally to explicate one another. The autonomy of the citizen, already expressed in the legal concept of the *contractus originarius*, directly defines and determines the rightful freedom that belongs to the citizen as a human being – the freedom to subject oneself solely to laws that are capable of commanding universal assent – and thus establishes a condition of universal equality before the law. The 'principle of rightful dependence,' on the other hand, which Kant also mentions alongside the principles of freedom and equality, is not itself a characteristic feature of a republican constitution. Since 'this principle is already present in the concept of a state constitution as such' (8:350, note), it cannot contribute anything specific to the concept of a republican constitution.

A civil constitution can only properly be described as republican therefore if it corresponds to the principles of the essentially shared legislative capacities of all as possible citizens of the state, of the freedom of all as human beings, and of the equality of all as subjects – that is, of the equality of all before the law. And it is these characteristic properties of right that is also explain why a republican constitution is 'the sole constitution that can lead toward perpetual peace' (8:350).

3. The republican constitution as a constitution oriented towards peace

Kant's argument that a republican constitution favours and promotes peace, that this form of political constitution is structurally pacific in its very character, is a clear and simple one. 'When the consent of the citizens of a state is required in order to decide whether there shall be war or not (and it cannot be otherwise in this constitution), nothing is more natural than that they will be very hesitant to begin such a bad game, since they would have to decide to take upon themselves all the hardships of war …' (8:351). Again we should notice that Kant's argument does not attempt to justify itself by appealing to pacifist convictions, to a specific sense of justice, or to any other morally demanding principles. It is based entirely on rational reflection and considerations of self-interest. The same minimalist approach to motivational justification is expressed in Kant's famous dictum that the 'problem of establishing a state, no matter how hard it may sound, is soluble even for a nation of devils (if only they have understanding)' (8:366). A republican-minded 'nation of devils,' autonomously legislating its own laws and possessed of rational understanding, would never decide to initiate a war of aggression. Whenever human beings are capable, as autonomous citizens, of deliberating and deciding with one another concerning matters of common interest, they will wish to avoid initiating any war. They will reflect upon the costs that the prosecution of war would inevitably lay upon themselves, and they will immediately realise that it cannot be in their own interest to bear such burdens. One should remember of course that Kant's argument here concerns only wars of aggression rather than wars waged as a matter of self-defence. Since the riches and pleasures of an aristocratic prince remain essentially unaffected by war, it is an easy matter for such a ruler to act with capricious contempt for his fellow human beings and declare a war whenever and for whatever reason he deems appropriate. Citizens, on the other hand, who have no one else to shoulder the costs of war and will thus feel the full effects of the burdens of war themselves, have no conceivable interest in starting a war in the first place.

The republican constitution corresponds directly with the idea of political self-determination: it elevates the 'subject' to the level and status of 'citizen' and transforms political heteronomy into political autonomy. Whereas in a non-republican constitution the subjects essentially lack a voice, citizens who mutually recognise one another as free and equal autonomous members of the state can effectively express and articulate their own interests in a universally shared process of will-formation within a framework of guaranteed rights. And it cannot be in the interests of citizens to initiate and prosecute a war. This is why the republican constitution typically functions in the interests of peace. Hence we can also expect political communities with republican constitutions to encourage the idea of a perpetual peace amongst states.

This line of thought is of course too plausible to be entirely new. Erasmus, in his tract of 1517, *Querela pacis*, had already argued that any declaration of war should be conditional upon the consent of an entire people. And when Montesquieu examined the relationship between different political constitutions and the kinds of foreign policy they pursued, ascribing a belligerent character to monarchies and a peaceful one to republics, we can naturally interpret this as an anticipation of Kant's own reflections in this connection (see *De l'esprit des lois* IX, 2). But after witnessing the recent revolutionary events in France, many of Kant's contemporaries certainly doubted the claim that a republican constitution intrinsically promotes peace rather than war, and were even tempted to draw the opposite conclusion. Whereas the spectacle of the French Revolution led Kant to celebrate the potential beginning of a new age of freedom, the conservative critics of the revolution interpreted its totalitarian Jacobinism and its aggressive nationalism as the beginning of a new age of ideology. They heard the new revolutionary propaganda, they feared the resulting enthusiasm and the unfamiliar new political passions that took hold everywhere, and they certainly could not bring themselves to endorse Kant's civic rationalism or to regard human self-interest as a reliable basis and guarantee of reason and freedom.

From the Burkean perspective of Friedrich Gentz, it was obvious that the revolution had brought war rather than peace. In his critique of Kant's essay *Toward Perpetual Peace*, Gentz argued that the revolutionaries were attempting 'to unite all peoples of the earth in one great cosmopolitan federation' and were thus 'creating the cruellest world-wide war that has ever rent and shattered society' (Gentz 1800/1953:494). Hegel raises a similar objection to Kant's claims, albeit in rather more objective tone and with specific reference to politics in England. We cannot be so sanguine about the rational character of the people and must surely concede that 'whole nations are often more prone to enthusiasms and subject to passion than their rulers are. In England, the entire people has pressed for war on several occasions and has in a sense compelled the ministers to wage it' (*Philosophy of Right* §329, Addition). Whether or not Hegel's interpretation of the history in question is correct, it is certainly true that there have been, and are, such things as popular wars, that an enthusiasm for war can seize an entire people who are even prepared to be utterly destroyed through 'total' war. On the other hand, certain political developments in the domain of international relations since the Second World War have prompted others to reconsider Kant's thesis in this respect and to support it with an extensive body of material evidence (see Gilbert 1992).

In his essay *Toward Perpetual Peace*, Kant formulates his claim about the structural peace-enhancing tendencies of a republican constitution in a very simple and straightforward way. Once the principle that all citizens should be capable of deliberating and deciding in common upon such matters is accepted, no ruler could decide upon a war simply because no citizens would ever 'decide to take upon themselves all the hardships of war' (8:350). One can of course develop the thesis in much more detail. One could point out that in a community with a republican constitution, there is also an open culture of public opinion, that social learning processes have free room to develop, that a differentiated process of political will-formation is possible, and that where such deliberative and reflexive rationality is operative, it is very difficult to persuade citizens to undertake aggressive wars and military interventions.

But there was a good reason why Kant chose to formulate his argument so simply in the essay *Toward Perpetual Peace*. All the aforementioned rational advantages of the republican constitution could only properly be developed in the context of an actually existing republican polity with an unrestricted and uncensored public sphere. But Kant's argument concerning the republican constitution can also be treated as a thought-experiment that can be performed by those who currently wield power if they wished to exercise that power, as they are *a priori* obligated to do, in conditions where citizens actually deliberated and legislated for

themselves as well. That is why Kant expresses the argument in a form
that is susceptible to logical operationalisation, and thus recalls the universalising procedure and the appeal to non-contradiction in his moral
philosophy. One could speak of a criterion of universal and communal
legislation: a law is legitimate if it could have been universally so decided
upon, if those who are affected by it had also been involved in its legislation. The advantage of this operationalisation is obvious: the rational
manner of determining right characteristically developed within a republican constitution is rendered independent of any specifically democratic
form of government and social organisation, and can unfold its effective
potential in every actually existing form of political state. These reflections already begin to touch upon the theme of the third and most extensive section of Kant's discussion on the first definitive article. Here Kant
explores the chances and possibilities of actually realising republican
principles under adverse institutional conditions, and provides the appropriate conceptual means for a reform-oriented compromise solution to
the problem.

4.   The form of sovereignty and the form of government

The first definitive article for a contract securing peace in accordance
with philosophical principles of right falls into in three parts. The first
part enumerates the three principles of a republican constitution. The
second part presents the argument for the essentially peace-promoting
character of the republican constitution. The third part offers Kant's
extremely abbreviated and unclear theoretical outline for a republican
constitution in the context of an original reformulation of the basic distinctions that Aristotle already made in framing his own theory of the
political constitution. The central issue here turns on the distinction
between the form of sovereignty (*Herrschaftsform*, or *forma imperii*) and
the form of government (*Regierungsart*, or *forma regiminis*). Aristotle
had already distinguished the various forms of sovereignty 'according to
the different persons who have supreme power within a state' in terms
of '*autocracy, aristocracy* and *democracy*' (8:352). But we must also distinguish between 'despotic' and 'republican' forms of government – that
is, between a community governed according to pure principles of right
and a community that ignores such principles. Kant does not therefore
adopt Aristotle's constitutional schema, with its contrast between three
good constitutions that are compatible with proper government and three

deviant ones that are not. He makes no attempt to combine these quantitative and qualitative principles of classification, but presents them as independently defining and distinguishing features. Thus he can distinguish two diametrically opposed forms of government with respect to the rightful character or otherwise of the way in which they exercise their rule, and he can distinguish three forms of sovereignty that are indifferent from this perspective (see Bien 1972).

Kant has included this abbreviated theoretical outline of a possible republican constitution in the first definitive article of his essay because, as he indicates himself, he does not wish simply to identify a republican with a democratic constitution. Such an identification might seem quite plausible: the republican constitution is grounded in the idea of an original contract; freedom under universal laws refers back to the general legislative will; a democratic concept of sovereignty finds expression in such a will for sovereignty; the right to dominion – legislative authority – can only rightfully be ascribed to the united will of a people. How else should a subject become an autonomous citizen if not within the context of a democratically organised system of legislation? But if the republican constitution were simply identical with the democratic one, then the 'desired result' of perpetual peace that principally motivates the first definitive article could only be expected from actually existing democratic governments. And in view of the political circumstances of Kant's time, this would imply that the genuinely peaceful influences and effects of a republican constitution could only make themselves felt subsequent to a successful democratic revolution. On the purely conceptual internal level of the rational grounding of right, the form of political organisation coincides precisely with the rightful order of social life: a pure society of right is itself immediately identical with democracy. But once we turn to the question concerning the concrete realisation of right – the actual application of the rational principles of right and the effective power of reason within history – the two factors of political organisation and the order of right as such fall apart from one another. The unconditional validity of right as grounded in reason then assumes the form of an imperative that is addressed to all who exercise actual rule in the historical world and that commands the exercise of this power in accordance with the principles of rightful freedom and rightful equality. Once the dualism between form of sovereignty and form of government has been introduced and theoretically elucidated in this way, we can no longer simply identify the republican constitution with the democratic constitution: the democratic constitution leads to the democratic form of sovereignty and the republican constitution leads to the republican form of government.

The importance of the third part of Kant's discussion for the development of his general argument lies in providing the appropriate conceptual framework for mediating the normative level of pure principles of right with the empirical realities of politics and history. The legitimating paradigm for a politically self-organising society based on the idea of an original contract is thus an 'idea' of reason that transcends any possible immediate realisation. And Kant interprets this idea as the duty, binding on every empirical form of political authority, to exercise its power in accordance with republican principles. Thus it is the form of government, rather than the form of sovereignty, that here becomes the means of realising the concept of republicanism. But the possibility of republican rule is thereby rendered independent of the form of sovereignty. The peaceful effect that is to flow from the republican constitution in the international context is therefore also rendered independent of the particular form in which political authority is invested. The desired effect now depends instead on the precise manner in which the ruler or holder of political authority actually exercises that authority. The appropriate realisation of the demand expressed in the first definitive article would naturally require every state to be transformed into a republic – that is, into a democracy with some system of popular representation and an appropriate division of powers. But the project of perpetual peace does not have to wait for the realisation of this democratic internationalism. For it is also possible to fulfil the demand of the first definitive article in an indirect and roundabout fashion – namely through a republican style of exercising power that imitates the way in which a republic does so. Even in the historical absence of actual republics, therefore, the project of perpetual peace can still legitimately place its hopes on a republican approach to government on the part of states that are not themselves republics.

This clearly reveals the sharp divergence between Rousseau's own general position and Kant's reconstruction of Rousseau's concept of the social contract in the context of a philosophical theory of right based upon pure principles of reason. For Kant, the democratic plebiscitary origin of a law, something that is supposed to guarantee legislative justice, can be replaced by a methodical thought-experiment. And the 'sovereign,' conceptualised as an idea of reason in accordance with rational principles of right, can therefore also be represented by any empirical executant of power and authority. Rousseau's political philosophy, on the other hand, expressly requires us to identify the general will with civic sovereignty, to identify the *volonté générale* and the *volonté de tous*. For Rousseau, freedom is a material form of self-determination that can never in principle be delegated. This concept of freedom thus carries the political implication that all citizens must participate directly in the process of political decision making. In Rousseau's eyes, legitimacy can only be ascribed to a direct and plebiscitary exercise of democracy. The establishment of an essentially representative system of democratic government thus already violates the intrinsically unalienable character of self-determining freedom. For Rousseau, the assembly of the citizens, the ensemble of the empirical wills of all citizens, is the only medium in which the *volonté générale* can properly realise and manifest itself.

Kant's outline of 'a perfectly *rightful constitution* among human beings' (*The Metaphysics of Morals*: 6:371) envisages a free community as an uncoerced association of free and equal human beings oriented towards the determination and realisation of right. The contract to which such individuals subscribe constitutes the fundamental law of a rational political state, and functions in the historical context as the proper criterion for assessing the justice of actual positive laws. This contract expresses the sovereign will of rational right, and is therefore binding on every empirical legislator. The empirical legislator must be grasped as a representative of the general will and therefore cannot simply act *jure divino* or on the basis of his own *de facto* power. The empirical legislator can act solely as a representative of the legitimate legislative demands of an open system of justice that corresponds to the pure concept of the rightful state.

Kant's concept of republicanism cannot be reduced to some general maxim governing the appropriate exercise of power. For in addition to the specifically rights-oriented ethical component, it also possesses an emphatic institutional component. This latter aspect remains rather difficult to discern, however, since Kant's brief sketch here does not contain enough explicit discussion of the institutional conditions of political representation and the division of powers that are decisive for any republican conception of government. And in fact, Kant himself further obscures the distinction between the criteria of ethical and institutional republicanism when he entertains the possibility that autocrats may also exercise 'a kind of government in conformity with the spirit of a representative system' – that is, may exercise power and authority in such a way as if the legislative will were that of the united citizens of the state (8:352). In the final analysis, the three relevant criteria (anticipating the legislative decisions that would be taken by all those affected by any law, the division of powers, and a system of representation) are simply different expressions of the single fundamental principle of a constitution fashioned in accordance with rational principles of right – namely, that legislative authority properly lies in the united will of the people, and that every actual empirical ruler, with respect to law, cannot act simply on the basis of his own presumed power but must look upon himself explicitly as a representative of sovereign power exercised in accordance with rational principles of right. And Kant's extremely obscure criterion for the division of powers also broadly points in the same direction when he describes a despotic system that violates the principle of the division of powers as a 'high-handed management of the state by laws the regent himself has given, inasmuch as he handles the public will as his own will' (8:352).

In contrast with Rousseau, therefore, Kant refuses to treat any particular empirical system of government as the only legitimate one. In the context of Kant's philosophy, the question concerning the personal exercise of power is merely of subsidiary significance. Whether one individual rules, or some rule, or all rule is not itself important. What matters is the form of government in the sense of the way in which power is exercised. The form of government is 'either republican – that is, government in accordance with freedom and equality – or despotic, as a will that fails to bind itself to these conditions' (23:166). Neither republicanism nor despotism require a particular form of political state. Both kinds of government are compatible in principle with any particular form of sovereignty. It is possible for the spirit of the original contract to be rendered effective or to be despised in any form of political state. In the actual historical context of existing state power, exercised by specific forms of sovereignty generated under contingent conditions, the idea of a pure republican constitution, as the fundamental law for a pure society of right, comes to acquire the status of a system of rules for properly limiting the exercise of power and authority. Kant's rationally based constitutionalism is not primarily concerned with replacing historically established forms of government but with progressively transforming their inner character in accordance with republican principles. This republicanism thus articulates the idea of a republic as it appears in an alien form, and attempts to promote the incorporation of the spirit of the original contract into political systems that have already developed under fortuitous natural conditions of violence and are themselves essentially resistant to this spirit.

5.   Republicanism and republics

The process of realising a rational constitution involves a process of republicanising the spirit of political authority, and culminates in the fully republican exercise of such authority. States are initially created through violence rather than by any process of mutual agreement. Although rational consensus defines the rightful and legitimate origin of state power, violence clearly represents its actual historical origin. History shows that the political state based on right has arisen from and thus depends upon pre-existing systems of unchallengeable power. But the actual capacity to establish law is not sufficient to demonstrate the right to lay down rightful law in the first place. Considered in accordance with rational principles, proper legislative competence belongs solely to the united will of the people, and authority is only rightfully exercised when it restricts itself to the application of laws the community has legislated for itself. The fact that the political state based on right first arose from and depended upon the contingent historical basis of forms of rule established by force thus stands in direct contrast to the authentic dependence of political authority on the idea of the original contract. If the pure republican constitution ultimately underlies every form of political authority, then this authority is only legitimate when it is exercised in accordance with pure rational constitutional principles. This demand to promote the republican character of government thus inexorably recalls the problem of legitimacy that applies to all political authority. It rejects traditional attempts at justifying political power and reveals the essentially derived character of royal or princely authority. A monarch might appeal to Kantian philosophy to resist the threat of revolution, but he cannot claim any divine right in order to legitimate his power. He need not relinquish his position to some new empirical representative of a rightful rational sovereign, but he must acknowledge the latter as the only source of his own legitimacy. The ruler is consequently bound to accept and to observe 'the principles of a republican form of government for gradually limiting his political power through the voice of the people' (23:166). Hence the republican form of government also represents a programme for securing proper political legitimation.

In an essentially reformist spirit, Kant mediates the conflict between the purely rational conception of a republic and existing historical forms of political authority by appeal to a deliberate and ongoing realisation of a free and law-governed order of social life. Kant's rational sketch of a republic constituted in accordance with the laws of reason, of a non-coercive political state made up of rational beings, thus presents 'the eternal norm for any civil constitution whatsoever' over against the historical and contingent political state that has emerged from conflict and violence. The mediation between the two leads to 'the evolution of a constitution in accordance with natural right' (7:87). Kant conceived of this process as a kind of marriage between reason and authority, and the events of the French Revolution encouraged him in hoping that this evolution would continue to unfold in the future. Promoting the spirit of republican government introduces characteristic features of a free law-governed constitution into the empirical structures of political power and authority and helps to shape political institutions increasingly in accordance with the concept of right.

This reformist process of realising principles of right has its end in the establishment of a republic. Kant clearly distinguishes between the concept of republicanism and the concept of a republic, but he makes it unmistakably clear that the realisation of rational right can only be properly fulfilled in a republic and that an actual historical republic is the only appropriate empirical expression of a society organised in accordance with pure principles of right. A republican form of government – one exercised in a republican spirit – may well be able, as Kant repeatedly emphasises, to satisfy the people in general, but it remains a provisional arrangement with regard to principles of right. It is only when the 'evolution of a constitution in accordance with natural right' finally leads to a republic 'in the literal sense' (6:341), to a 'democratic constitution in a representative system' (23:166), that public right loses its provisional character and is properly acknowledged in its peremptory character, that an 'absolutely rightful condition of civil society' is established (6: 341).

The 'form of sovereignty' and the 'form of government' are mutually related concepts that can only be applied to the 'pre-republican' phase of history, to the period preceding the actual establishment of a republic proper. The traditional forms of the political state, along with the external distinction between sovereign and subject, will disappear once the republican 'form of government' finds objective realisation as a republic, once its characteristic principles are properly institutionalised and articulated within the context of an independent and self-contained constitution (for hitherto they have been effectively applied solely in the context of a morally oriented constitutionalism that is, in the last analysis solely through the will of monarch who has proved to be enlightened or at least prudent with regard to matters of right). It is only a republic that can transform a people of 'subjects' into one of political 'citizens.' It is only here that formerly personal authority and sovereignty is properly transformed into the objectively realised authority and sovereignty of the law.

It is only in a republic that freedom properly becomes 'peremptory,' as Kant puts it. This clearly reveals the intrinsic superiority of a republic from the perspective of rationally grounded right. For if freedom only becomes peremptory in a republic, then the relationship between a republican and pre-republican forms of sovereignty precisely mirrors that between the state of nature and the civil state. We can formulate this in another way: it is only in a republic, characterised as it is by the sovereignty of law independent of persons, that the shadow of the state of nature is finally dispelled: 'Any true republic is and can be only a *system representing* the people, in order to protect its rights in its name, by all the citizens united and acting through their delegates (deputies). But as soon as a person who is head of state (whether it be a king, nobility, or the whole of the population, the democratic union) also lets itself be represented, then the united people does not merely *represent* the sovereign: it *is* the sovereign itself. For in it (the people) is originally found the supreme authority from which all rights of individuals as mere subjects (and in any event as officials of the state) must be derived; and a republic, once established, no longer has to let the reins of government out of its hands ...' (6:341). Kant interprets the *telos* of historical progress from the perspective of right as a republic in which the '*law* itself rules and depends on no particular person' (ibid.), in which the constitutional state has been emancipated from all connection with traditional and personally based forms of power and authority and has thus effectively acquired its own autonomy and independence precisely because it 'forms and preserves itself in accordance with laws of freedom' (6:318). And this clearly articulates the fundamental difference between the pre-republican political state that is grounded in authority and the rational political state that is essentially grounded in freedom.

For human beings living under the conditions of finitude, a republic provides the best attainable form of social organisation for the realisation of right. As far as the social world is concerned, the republican form represents a stage of perfection analogous to that of morality as actualised reason. The moral human being is defined by the way in which reason autonomously governs the personality, the way in which the individual subjects all action and desire to the regime of reason itself. And a republican society is comparably defined by the way in which universally acceptable laws autonomously govern everyone equally, the way in which they express the general will and thereby regulate social life, the way in which they constitute principles for legitimate authority and coercion and thus bring the power of the executive into harmony with the intrinsic human right to freedom itself.

Bibliography

Bien, Günther 1972: 'Revolution, Bürgerbegriff und Freiheit. Über die neuzeitliche Transformation der alteuropäischen Verfassungstheorie in politische Geschichtsphilosophie,' in *Philosophisches Jahrbuch* 79, 1–18.

Gentz, Friedrich von 1800: 'Über den ewigen Frieden,' in Kurt von Raumer: *Ewiger Friede, Friedensrufe und Friedenspläne seit der Renaissance*, Freiburg 1953, 461–497.

Gilbert, Alan 1992: 'Must Global Politics Constrain Democracy? Realism, Regimes, and Democratic Internationalism,' in *Political Theory* 20, 8–37.

Kersting, Wolfgang 1993: *Wohlgeordnete Freiheit. Immanuel Kants Rechts- und Staatsphilosophie*, Frankfurt am Main.

Langer, Claudia 1996: *Reform nach Prinzipien: Untersuchung zur politischen Theorie Immanuel Kants*, Stuttgart.

Maus, Ingeborg 1992: *Zur Aufklärung der Demokratietheorie. Rechts- und demokratietheoretische Überlegungen im Anschluss an Kant*, Frankfurt am Main.

13

Commentary on Kant's Treatment of Constitutional Right (*Metaphysics of Morals* II: General Remark A; §§51–52, Conclusion, Appendix)

Bernd Ludwig

I

It is only in §51 (6:338) of the *Metaphysics of Morals* – that is, in the second half of the discussion of 'Constitutional Right' – that Kant introduces a distinction that is fundamental to his exposition of the theory of the state. For here Kant distinguishes between the 'pure idea of a head of state,' which is already implied in the concept of a commonwealth as such (*res publica latius dicta*) and enjoys 'objective practical reality,' and a 'physical person' who is 'to represent the supreme authority in the state and to make this idea effective on the people's will'. In the preceding sections, §§45–49, he has already introduced 'the state *in idea*,' the state 'as it ought to be in accordance with pure principles of right' and that essentially serves as a 'norm' (*norma*) (§45; 6:313) for every commonwealth. In the remaining sections (§§51–52),[1] Kant proceeds to discuss the various forms in which the political authority is expressed in and as a 'physical' head of state.

---

[1] The intrinsically transparent architectonic of Kant's theory of constitutional right was somewhat obscured by certain peculiarities of the printed text of 1797. The 'state in idea' is presented in §§45, 48, 46, and 49 (taken in this order); §47 leads via a theorem concerning 'the original contract' to §§51 and 52 which discuss the person of the head of state; and §50 falls outside the schema altogether. For a presentation of the text as Kant originally intended it, see Ludwig 1988, 75ff. Although the reconstructed text alone reflects the clear architectonic and the line of argument that underlies Kant's presentation of constitutional law, the twofold structure of the discussion following is also clear from the printed version of 1797.

But it is only in the succeeding year that Kant explicitly develops the conceptual distinction that underlies the architectonic framework of his earlier discussion. And this is the contrast between a *'respublica noumenon'* and a *'respublica phaenomenon,'* which Kant presents in *The Conflict of the Faculties*. After he has first criticised the British monarchy as a deceptive 'example' for a supposedly ideal model of political authority (7:90, 16), Kant goes on to discuss the general problem concerning the relationship between the idea of a constitution and its actual realisation: 'The idea of a constitution in conformity with the natural right of human beings [...] lies at the basis of all forms of the state, and that commonwealth which, thought in accordance with this idea through pure rational concepts, is called a platonic *ideal* (*respublica noumenon*) is no empty fantasy, but rather the eternal norm for any civil constitution in general and one which banishes war. A civil community organised in accordance with this idea is a presentation of the latter according to laws of freedom as given in experience (*respublica noumenon*)' (7:90). Even though the discussion is not yet couched in the authentic critical terminology of phenomena and noumena, Kant had indeed already articulated the same distinction with comparable conceptual precision in the 'Conclusion' containing 'further explanatory remarks' that he added to the second edition (1798) of the *Doctrine of Right*: '... what can be represented only by pure reason and must be counted among *ideas*, to which no object given in experience can be adequate – and a perfectly *rightful constitution* among human beings is of this sort – is the thing in itself. If then a people united by laws under an authority exists, it is given as an object of experience in conformity with the idea of the unity of a people *as such* under a powerful supreme will, though it is indeed given only in experience, that is, a rightful constitution in the general sense of the term exists' (6:371). In one of his preliminary notes for *The Conflict of the Faculties*, Kant had even applied this critical terminological distinction directly to his doctrine concerning the different forms of state in a way that provides a useful key to the overall structure of his theory of political right: '*Respublica noumenon* or *phaenomenon*. The latter assumes three forms, whereas the *respublica noumenon* takes only one and the same form' (RR: 19:609). Kant explicates the first of the two concepts mentioned in §51 – namely, the 'objective-practical' concept of a head of state in general, in the preceding sections in the context of a highly Rousseauean discussion of sovereignty and the division of powers (something that cannot further be developed here). But he explicates the second concept, that of a (physical) head of state – through an ideal-typical presentation of the three classical types of state (monarchy, aristocracy, and democracy) in the context of his ensuing theory of constitutional forms as presented in the *Metaphysics of Morals*. This two-level exposition of political right is clearly based, as a brief review of other Kantian remarks from the same period has already shown, on the critical distinction between 'appearances' and the 'thing in itself,' between *respublica phaenomenon* and *respublica noumenon*.

We should also recall Kant's claim in the 'Preface' to the *Metaphysics of Morals* that 'toward the end of the book' he had dealt with certain issues that are 'currently subject to so much discussion, and are still so important, that they can well justify postponing a decisive judgement for some time' (6:209). It seems reasonable to conclude that traces of this 'discussion' can be found particularly, if anywhere, in Kant's doctrine of the *respublica phaenomenon*. For we can hardly ascribe a comparably provisional character, arising from the conditions of the time, to the exposition of the 'idea' of the state that is supposed to provide, as we saw, an '*eternal* norm for every civil constitution.' And this conclusion is surely supported by the fact that Kant's thoughts on the different political forms of the state underwent considerable development even in the couple of years that separate the essay *Toward Perpetual Peace* and the *Doctrine of Right*. The considerable 'discussion' to which Kant alludes was, as we shall see, essentially the echo produced in Germany by the events of the French Revolution (and the corresponding 'counter-revolutionary' political response to those events in Britain). These connections may not always be particularly obvious to the reader of today, but examination of the preliminary notes and studies that have come down to us clearly reveals that Kant effectively developed some of his central ideas through a close and immediate engagement with the political issues and realities of the time. In the *Doctrine of Right*, this implicit relationship to contemporary discussions finds its systematic expression in the fact that the mediation between the rightful idea of the state and the political domain as a 'practised doctrine of right' (*Toward Perpetual Peace*: 8:370) constitutes a specific theme in its own right. For its part the principal discussion, which is contained in §51 and §52, is itself already anticipated – as is only to be expected in an analysis of *metaphysical* first principles – in the preceding treatment of Private Right. It will become clear, quite independently of any particular prompting through the actual 'discussions' of the moment, that this theme is an indispensable component of any philosophy of right that is not simply concerned with developing 'a platonic ideal of the state,' but also remains seriously engaged with the freedom of human beings in the here and now.

2

Here we can do little more than indicate the intimate systematic
connection between Kant's 'idea of the state' and the preceding sections
of the *Doctrine of Right*. This connection is evident, amongst other
things, from the way in which the division of powers in the state is already
anticipated through the architectonic of private right – that is, the doctrine of 'what is externally mine or yours in general' (6:245). For the three
chapters dealing with private right (the theory of possession, the theory
of acquisition, and the theory of acquisition dependent subjectively upon
the decision of a court of justice) correspond to the three propositions
in a 'practical syllogism' (6:313) and represent the legislative, executive,
and judiciary dimensions of the state. In short, the threefold articulation
required in the sphere of external private right (in relation to law, the principle of subsumption, and legal judgement) is reflected in the three distinct
powers or authorities of 'the state in idea.'

In expounding his theory of the political division of powers or authorities, Kant explicitly underlines the comparative and normative function
that intrinsically belongs to this concept of 'the state in idea' – namely,
'that condition in which the constitution conforms most fully to principles
of right', which is what 'the well-being of the state (*salus rei publicae* ...)'
properly consists in (6:318). The 'complete constitution of the state'
(6:316) that finds appropriate expression in this *ideal* consists in the coordination and subordination of the three authorities in accordance with
the practical syllogism: law, subsumptive rule, and legal judgement. And
this syllogism provides the basis for every specific legal judgement. This
clearly shows that for Kant the idea of the state is identical with the idea of
institutionalised right. The concept of an 'entirely pure political constitution' that Kant develops in this way is therefore nothing but 'the idea of a
republic' – as he explicitly says in his preliminary notes for the *Conflict of
the Faculties* (RR: 19:609). Kant summarises his argument in §51 of the
Doctrine of Right: 'The three authorities in the state, which arise from the
concept of a *commonwealth* as such (*res publica latius dicta*), are only the
three relations of the united will of the people, which is derived a priori
from reason. They are a pure idea of a head of state, which has objective
practical reality' (6:338). The architectonic structure of the *Metaphysics
of Morals*, to which we have already alluded, presents the theory of
authorities in the context of a theory of 'the state in idea,' the *respublica
noumenon*, while it presents the theory of the forms of state in the context of the *respublica phaenomenon*. This means that the three classical

forms of the state (monarchy, aristocracy, and democracy) are interpreted as relations of a *physical* 'superior' representing *all three* authorities with respect to 'the multitude of the people considered severally as subjects' (6:315).

In his discussion of the forms of the state, therefore, Kant proceeds on the (entirely realistic) assumption that legislative authority in particular is not based upon the empirical will of the people: the person who embodies 'the supreme authority in the state' thus 'makes this idea effective upon the people's will' insofar as he represents all three authorities 'which arise from the concept of a commonwealth as such' as a physical individual (6:338). In contrast to Rousseau, therefore, autocracy, aristocracy, and democracy are not for Kant forms of executive authority that are essentially subordinate to the sovereign will of the people, but are rather the specific organised forms of sovereignty itself. This is emphatically formulated in §51, where Kant points out that, as far as the theory of the forms of state is concerned, the monarch should more properly be described as an 'autocrat' (one who rules by himself, rather than one who governs himself). It is also evidently implied by Kant's explicit remark that in the autocratic form of state, 'only *one* person is the legislator' – for it is quite obvious here that Kant is no longer addressing the question concerning the political division of powers. The forms of the state as such, as Kant stresses, thus belong merely to 'the machinery of the constitution'. They are 'only the letter (*littera*) of the original legislation in the civil state,' which – as 'old empirical (statuary) forms which served merely to bring about the submission of the people' – may 'therefore remain as long as they are taken, by old and long-standing custom (and so only subjectively), to belong necessarily' to that machinery (6:340).

Kant had initially broached the question of the 'superior' or 'head of state' (as a 'physical person') and the 'subjects' (the people as a multitude) – as we saw this formulated in §51 – in an earlier section dedicated to the 'Transition from what is mine or yours in the state of nature to what is mine or yours in a rightful condition generally' (see §41; 6:306f.). In that connection, he pointed out that the 'union' of head of state and subject cannot properly be called 'society': for they are not 'co-ordinated' with one another as 'fellow members', but 'subordinated' to one another as 'commander' and 'subject.' In his earlier preparatory notes for the *Metaphysics of Morals*, Kant had made this point in almost identical terms: 'The head of state and the people, as the ruler, can never be one and the same person insofar as the latter merely obeys while the former merely commands (for while we can certainly think a connection or union between these two,

we cannot think here of a society *superior et subiectus*), and consequently
the people cannot rule in and through itself, but only through choosing
specific representatives from amongst itself' (*Vorarbeiten* 23: 161). In
the last line here, Kant introduces an idea that does not, astonishingly
enough, appear in the corresponding section of the *Doctrine of Right*:
that of *representation*. All forms of the state – simply because they necessarily involve a certain relationship between a head of state and the people
qua subject and are therefore forms of dominion – are representative in
essence. For the head of state, as representative of the will of the people,
represents the general will as distinct from the popular will. Kant thereby
counters the criticism that was mounted from conservative quarters
against the supposed Rousseauism of his essay *On the Common Saying*
of 1793 (see also *Toward Perpetual Peace*, 8:366). The non-representative
republic projected by Rousseau is a form of state that would be appropriate for angels or gods, and is therefore nothing more – but also nothing
less – than an *ideal* as far as human society is concerned.

A further significant consequence of Kant's decision to liberate the
concept of the *respublica phaenomenon* from the physical separation of
the three powers or authorities (which now simply belongs to the *respublica
noumenon*) clearly reveals itself in the concept of 'despotism.' In the conceptual context of the *Doctrine of Right*, despotism represents an explicit
perversion of the 'state in idea' insofar as it directly involves a usurpation
of legislative authority by executive authority (§49). Despotism cannot be
immediately linked with any specific external organisation of the body
politic (for qua *respublica phaenomenon* and *e definitione* not one of the
three forms of state is 'physically' characterised by a division of powers)
and we cannot expect therefore to establish any particular conceptual
relationship between despotism and any of the three forms of the state.
This means that the question of despotism can only be addressed in relation to the idea or 'eternal norm' of the state. A polity that, irrespective of
its external form as autocracy, aristocracy, or democracy, is governed in
such a way that the head of state treats the legislative will as his own private will stands closer to the 'ideal of despotism' than it does to the ideal
of a republic. Whereas the theory of the forms of the state relates solely to
the internal structure of the *respublica phaenomenon* – with a deliberate
systematic intention that, as we shall see, distinguishes Kant's position
here from that adopted in the essay *Toward Perpetual Peace* – the opposition between despotism and the concept of a republic belongs only to
the sphere of the *civitas noumenon*. But here the question concerning the
specific form of the state has no particular significance in its own right.

Measured against the ideal on the other hand, states as they actually appear can certainly be governed in a 'despotic' or a 'republican' manner. In this sense, Kant can stress, in the *Conflict of the Faculties*, that the republican constitution may be 'either in accordance with the *form of the state*, or in accordance simply with *the mode of government*, with respect to the unity of the head of state (the monarch) analogous to the laws which a people would give itself in accordance with universal principles of right' (7:88). Kant therefore already introduces the concept of the 'despotic' definitionally in the context of his discussion of the 'state in idea' (§49). And his theory of the forms of the state is only referring back to this when he contrasts despotism, and the way in which it effaces the distinction of the powers and authorities in the state, directly with the *ideal* of a pure republic in which such a distinction is expressly acknowledged.

3

If we now look back from this perspective to the essay *Toward Perpetual Peace*, we can clearly see that Kant in 1795 had not yet systematically separated the idea of the 'head of state' from the concept of the different 'forms' of the state. Since the theory of the forms of the state presented in the *Metaphysic of Morals* only assumes its proper character and significance in the light of this separation, it is worth pausing to discuss this point in a little more detail here. The two relevant distinctions (between the three forms of the state and between a despotism and a republic) that the *Doctrine of Right*, fully in the spirit of the critical philosophy, relates to the *phenomenon* and the *idea* of the state respectively, are both applied directly to the *form* of the state as such: as 'form of sovereignty (*forma imperii*)' and as 'form of government (*forma regiminis*)' (8:352). Whereas the first distinction thematises the person of the ruler according to the three forms of the state (as autocracy, aristocracy, or democracy), the second aims to differentiate between republicanism and despotism and thus to separate the power of ruler and government. Kant's argument here is principally designed to show that republicanism and democracy are not identical (*Toward Perpetual Peace*, 8:351) and that the latter is rather 'necessarily a despotism.' In light of our earlier discussion of constitutional law in Kant, this cannot fail to appear problematic: for by 1797, the conceptual distinction between despotism and republicanism on the one hand and that between the three forms of the state on the other finally lie on quite different and distinct levels of argument.

The essential idea behind Kant's argument in 1795 – and the contrast with the later conception of the *Doctrine of Right* – can nonetheless be clarified by looking at his preparatory studies for the essay *Toward Perpetual Peace* (see *Vorarbeiten* 23:165f.). There Kant distinguishes in a rather traditional manner between the 'substance' and the 'form' of the state (rather than between the 'idea' and the 'appearance' of the state). And he defines the substance of the state, as he also does in the actual essay *Toward Perpetual Peace*, in terms of the *forma imperii* ('one, or some, or all') and the form of the state in terms of the *forma regiminis*. This latter 'form of government' can be either despotic or republican in character. It is despotic in a 'mere democracy' (a democracy 'in itself' where the 'sovereign' simultaneously directs the 'government'), and it is republican in a 'democracy in a representative system,' as well as in the first two forms of the state where the 'heads of state' simultaneously 'represent' the people – if they have 'expressly assumed the principles of a republican mode of government for the gradual limitation of their power in the state through the consent of the people.' On the other hand, a king who represents the rights of the people is 'amongst all despots the best,' whereas aristocratically exercised power is 'somewhat worse,' and democratic despotism is 'the worst of all.'[2]

In these preliminary studies, republicanism is clearly characterised by two specific, and conceptually independent, features: on the one hand by the separation between legislative and executive authority, on the other by some kind of representation – that is, by the actual separation between the people and the head of state. Since, in the nature of the case, the people and the head of state are not identical in the forms of monarchy and aristocracy, the latter both necessarily fulfil the demand for representation.[3] They can therefore already be described in terms of 'republicanism' through the fact that they have expressly assumed a form of government that anticipates the concept of the division of power or authority. But it is obviously also the case that a 'democratic constitution in a representative system' can also be 'republican,' and of the three forms of the state, this is indeed for Kant the one that best realises a form of government that is 'appropriate' to rational concepts of right. But as far as democracy in its *non-representative* form is concerned, Kant says that

---

[2] An ideal is 'the representation of an individual being as adequate to an idea' (*Critique of the Power of Judgement*: 5:232). See also *Critique of Pure Reason* B 596.

[3] See Kant, *Vorarbeiten*: 23:166: 'The first two forms of the state as heads of state represent the people at the same time, while the third is not in itself [!] representative at all'. See also 23:160.

the people 'as the sovereign' is at the same time 'the kind of government which is despotism.'

As is well-known, this negative judgement of non-representative democracy can also be found in the published version of *Toward Perpetual Peace*: 'Any form of government which is not *representative* is, strictly speaking, *a meaningless form* [*eine Unform*], because the legislator cannot be in one and the same person also executor of its will (8:352). Kant makes this point in support of the charge of despotism that had been raised against 'democracy in the strict sense of the word' (ibid.). In this text, Kant clearly develops the idea of republicanism in conceptual opposition to that of democracy precisely by appealing to the concept of representation – that is, the institutional difference between the sovereign and the people.

The published version of Kant's essay did not take up the alternative concept of a 'democratic constitution in a representative system,' which he had himself already deployed in his preliminary studies. But the overall structure of Kant's argument even in the essay *Toward Perpetual Peace* really only becomes clear against the background of the complete fourfold schema presented in those studies: as representative forms of the state, democracy, aristocracy, and monarchy can all be interpreted in terms of republicanism (and indeed democracy pre-eminently so according to the preliminary studies). In contrast to the other two forms of the state, however, there is (also) a non-representative kind of democracy, and it is precisely this kind of democracy for Kant that necessarily 'grounds' a non-rightful exercise of executive power where 'all, who are nevertheless not all, decide' (*Toward Perpetual Peace*: 8:352). In the undifferentiated critique of democracy that is presented in this essay, Kant tacitly presupposes the concept of democracy taken in its non-representative sense, as it was understood in the Attic constitutions of ancient Greece as a direct kind of legislation and government (see RR: 19:595, 14ff.). And this suggests that Kant is conceptually (that is, 'necessarily') identifying democracy with an absence of representation – and therefore also simply identifying democracy with despotism. In the first instance, it is not entirely clear precisely why Kant should discuss democracy here solely in this sense of non-representative rule, and his assertion that democracy cannot be a 'kind of government in conformity with the *spirit* of a representative system' simply because 'there everyone wants to be ruler' hardly amounts to a convincing argument (*Toward Perpetual Peace*: 8:353).

If we critically assess the critique of democracy in Kant's essay in relation to the argument of the *Metaphysics of Morals*, the earlier conception clearly appears problematic. For if the forms of the state present different forms of constitution that makes the idea of the head of state 'effective upon the people's will,' then there is no systematic place for the (entirely conceivable) idea of a non-representative democracy *within* Kant's theory of the forms of the state. The fact that Kant actually does thematise democracy within the theory would seem to suggest a conceptual confusion that identifies a 'meaningless form' (*Toward Perpetual Peace*: 8:352), a perversion of the *ideal* of a pure republic, with a possible *realisation* of the state as a phenomenon. Yet this would clearly represent an unforgivable error in the context of the critical philosophy itself. And indeed in one of his 'Reflections', Kant refers explicitly to the despotic democracies of antiquity in this connection: 'There can be despotic governments, but there can be no despotic constitution on the part of the state' (RR: 19:595). Despotism as such cannot possibly represent an adequate ideal of the state precisely because it realises only *one* of the relevant powers or authorities involved. In this respect, we can see that the position that Kant develops in the preliminary studies is no better either. For insofar as that discussion locates non-representative democracy along with aristocracy and monarchy as possible forms of the state (and co-ordinates representative democracy as the third form of representative state in relation to both of the latter), it has already in principle violated the distinction between *respublica noumenon* and *respublica phaenomenon*.

But the systematic separation of Kant's theory of despotism from his theory of the forms of the state, which is effectively accomplished in the *Doctrine of Right* in 1797, is no mere architectonic detail. For it is also expressly reflected in the changed presentation of the different forms of the state, and this of course has political consequences of its own. If we overlook this, then the development of Kant's thought here inevitably appears simply confused. In the essay *Toward Perpetual Peace*, as we saw, Kant's demand for the most comprehensive possible form of representation led to a categorical rejection of democracy and an emphatic preference for monarchy (interpreted there in the closest possible affinity to republicanism): 'It can therefore be said that the smaller the number of persons exercising the power of a state (the number of rulers) and the greater their representation, so much the more does its constitution accord with the possibility of republicanism [...]. On this basis it is already harder in an aristocracy than in a monarchy to achieve this sole constitution that is perfectly rightful, but in a democracy it is impossible except by violent revolution' (*Toward Perpetual Peace*: 8:353; see *Vorarbeiten*: 23: 432).

Although Kant repeats this comparative ordering of the forms of the state in the work of 1797, he also emphasises that the discussion is guided by considerations of practical efficacy: 'It is easy to see that the autocratic form of the state is the *simplest*, namely the relation of one (the king) to the people, so that only one is legislator [...] It is true that, with regard to the *administration* of right within a state, the simplest form is also the best' (6:339). In the *Metaphysics of Morals*, Kant makes no attempt whatsoever to provide any internal-juridical principle of evaluation for his axiological presentation of the forms of the state (and thereby effectively returns to the view, traditional since Aristotle, that the question concerning the particular form of the state is of merely secondary importance). But now Kant also clearly indicates that it is possible to evaluate and compare the advantages and disadvantages of the three forms of the state as far as the anticipation of a republic is concerned. And from this overall perspective, Kant finds himself obliged to revise the summary judgement he had earlier expressed in the essay *Toward Perpetual Peace*. Continuing his line of argument, Kant now says 'With regard to *right* itself, however, this form of state [sc. autocracy] is the most dangerous for a people, in view of how conducive it is to despotism. It is indeed the most reasonable maxim to simplify the mechanism of unifying a nation by coercive laws, that is, when all the members of the nation are passive and obey *one* who is over them; but in that case none who are subjects are also *citizens of the state*' (ibid.). Kant's earlier evaluation of the forms of the state is effectively reversed here. Monarchy now appears as a form of state conducive to the despotism that was treated in Kant's earlier essay as a 'necessary' attribute of democracy. Kant's position with regard to political right in 1795 is vanquished here by the critical distinction first introduced in the *Metaphysics of Morals* in 1797.

Kant's view that the different forms of the state are equivalent from the specifically juridical point of view is also clearly revealed in his discussion concerning the legitimate alteration of civic constitutions. The sovereign – and in the context of the *respublica phaenomenon*, this means the head of state who represents the three authorities of the state as a physical person – can change the constitution if the latter 'cannot well be reconciled with the idea of the original contract' (6:340). Such a change in the constitution cannot simply rest with the 'discretion' of the head of state, although the restriction that restrains such change seems remarkably weak. In this connection, Kant refers explicitly to one, and significantly only one, restriction on the 'free choice' (ibid.) of the sovereign: it is the preference of the people which indicates what sort of constitution would appear 'more to its advantage.'[4] The king, the nobility, and the whole of the population as a 'democratic union' (6:341) are therefore all different potential representatives of the people. The *Doctrine of Right*, as we have seen, systematically and emphatically thematises the possibility of representation *prior* to the distinction between the different forms of the state, and no longer deploys the concept of representation, as it had been used in the essay *Toward Perpetual Peace*, in order to discredit democracy as a form of the state.

Kant's '*pure* republic' is – like Plato's ideal city – a norm, but it is not – in contrast to Rousseau – a specific exposition of the state (see *The Conflict of the Faculties*: 7:91, 6). Kant's republic is in fact non-representative in character since as 'the state in idea' it is simply self-rule of the people *sensu stricto*, and all laws in such a republic, according to §46 of the *Doctrine of Right*, are unanimously acknowledged (see RR: 19:609, 30). The republic as a phenomenon, on the other hand, or every appropriate realisation of the state, is always representative in character. The head of state and the subject are not identical in person. But it must harmonize 'in its effect' with the idea of a 'pure republic' that is entirely independent of the different forms of the state (6:340). 'In its effect' signifies administered as if by a personally separate executive governing in accordance with laws that could have sprung from the united will of the people (of an enlightened people). A '*true* republic' – a formula that now signifies the most perfect possible exposition of the 'idea of a republic' in an actually existing state[5] – is not merely representative in general, but is also a 'system representing *the people*, in order to protect its rights in its name, by all the citizens united and acting through their delegates (deputies)' (6:341). The 'political' distinction between democracy, aristocracy, and autocracy thus amounts in the final analysis to one concerning the way in which a specific group of relevantly qualified individuals is selected, like a parliament elected by citizens as distinct from a clique of aristocrats or

---

[4] It is quite possible that Kant is making a critical allusion to Sieyès in this connection: 'The nation is always at liberty to reform its own constitution. When the constitution is a matter of controversy, the nation cannot avoid attempting to frame a perfect constitution. (...) A body bound by constitutional rules can only decide in accordance with these rules. It cannot furnish a different constitution. (...) Even if the Estates General were convened, they would not be justified in deciding anything concerning the constitution. This right belongs to the nation alone, which – as we constantly repeat – is bound to no particular forms and conditions at all' (*Qu'est-ce que le tiers état*, p. 172).

[5] See also Kant's remarks on the idea of an 'example' and the concept of a 'true constitution' in *The Conflict of Faculties*: 7:90, 14f. (In this connection, see Unruh 1992, pp. 85ff.)

a dynastic monarchy. Only representative democracy, liberated from all historical particularity (6:100 and 369), furnishes an appropriate – that is, a 'true' exposition of the idea of a republic in an example drawn from experience. And as long as no such democracy exists, it remains 'the duty of monarchs, even though they rule *autocratically*, to govern *republicanly* (not democratically), that is, to treat the people in accordance with prin-ciple that conform to the spirit of the laws of freedom (such as a people of mature reason would prescribe for itself), even if the consent of the people has not literally been sought' (7:91). Kant repeatedly emphasises that his own concept of a democratic constitution has very little in common with Rousseau's concept of a state appropriate for 'a people of Gods', thereby indicating just how much he has learnt from Hobbes about a constitution for the people. For a multitude only becomes a people through the will of an individual or a collective body – that is, by means of representation. In the note to §52 of the *Metaphysics of Morals*, Kant consequently points out how 'the monarch's sovereignty wholly disappeared [...] and passed to the *people*' (!) once Louis XVI convened the Estates General (6:341; see RR: 19:595f.). But even if Kant treats the French Estates General as 'the people' here, any speculation concerning a possible, albeit covert, demand for direct democracy on Kant's part is entirely misplaced. The people, considered as a person with rights, is for Kant simply the body of repre-sentatives chosen by all citizens. Speculations about any covert theory of direct democracy here (as in Mauss 1992, pp. 18 and 199f.) effectively evaporate once we properly understand the architectonic of the *Doctrine of Right*. In the systematic context of his general argument, Kant treats the non-representative form of popular sovereignty merely as an 'idea.'

4

Kant's preference for representative democracy as the 'true' republican form of the state was already clear from the preliminary studies for the essay *Toward Perpetual Peace*, which we have already discussed. The long-established view that Kant essentially regards the monarchical form of the state as the best way of promoting republicanism in his sense thus effectively reflects the eccentric perspective that Kant defends in *Toward Perpetual Peace*. It is therefore worth enquiring into possible external reasons that may have motivated the 'exceptional' position of the essay in this respect.

It is not difficult to find a partial answer to this question. The common tendency to identify the French constitution under the Convention of 1793 with the institution of Athenian democracy (see Biester 1793) provides, as we saw, the immediate background to the discussion of the forms of the state in the essay of 1795. Kant here presents democracy as a 'meaningless' form of state where 'everyone wants to be ruler,' and that acknowledges no division of powers or authorities in the state – that is dispenses with laws and replaces them with decrees (Kant's remark about everyone deciding about a single individual seems to recall the ancient Greek practice of 'ostracism'). If Kant had not expressly distanced his view of the conditions in France, for all his sympathy for the disappearance of the *ancien régime*, from the Jacobin position, if he had not acknowledged the actual possibility of reform as far as the monarchical system in Germany was concerned, he might well have forfeited any genuine opportunity for influencing the contemporary political debate. For in that case, it is quite possible that the censuring authorities would never have permitted the publication of his essay in the first place – and given his earlier difficulties with Wöllner in 1774 (see *The Conflict of the Faculties*: 7:5ff), Kant certainly had ample reason to be cautious in this respect.

The response to the political disorder in France on 26 October 1795, shortly after the publication of the essay *Toward Perpetual Peace*, changed the character of the 'discussion' (as the 'Preface' to the *Metaphysics of Morals* put it) concerning the appropriate contemporary form of the state. As the executive authority, the 'Directory' of the 'French Republic,' as Kant now explicitly describes it, must consult 'the council that represents the entire people.' This would contrast with the British monarchy, which has resisted this political innovation and thus effectively revealed itself as a reactionary 'political machine' merely executes the absolute will of the monarch – and thereby marks a distinct historical regression (RR 19:606f.).

These remarks derive from the aforementioned fragment connected with the *The Conflict of the Faculties*. The fragment in question was composed, as the reference to the activities of the French 'Directory' indicates, after the publication of the essay *Toward Perpetual Peace*, but certainly before the definitive version of the second part of *The Conflict of the Faculties*. It is therefore very close in time to the composition of the *Doctrine of Right*. And in the latter text, we also encounter similar criticisms of the British political affairs (see 6:319, 19–320, 10, although the reference is not explicit), and it is clear that Kant's already cited remarks about how 'to simplify the mechanism of unifying a nation' (6:339) are simply the tip of the iceberg in a much larger question. Kant's emphatic sympathy for France, which could only be glimpsed between the lines in the text of 1797, finds clear expression a good two years later in *The Conflict of the Faculties*.

The *political* background to Kant's changed perspective with regard to monarchy and democracy in the writings composed after 1795 can also be specifically reconstructed. In Kant's eyes, the 'Directory' in France clearly represented a historical chance for 'democratic republicanisation' after the revolutionary turmoil that had divided the country in the immediately preceding period. But the particular stimulus to develop an adequate *theoretical* basis for a critical theory of the state came from a different quarter. In July 1796, Friedrich Schlegel had published his *Essay on the Concept of Republicanism, prompted by Kant's Essay on Perpetual Peace* in the journal *Deutschland* (see Herb/Ludwig 1994, pp. 468ff.). This contains pointers not only to the (new) idea of the head of state as a 'physical person' that combines the three authorities of the state in a single individual (§51; 6:338f.), but also to Kant's already cited remark that it is only the *respublica phaenomenon* that has three distinct political forms. For Schlegel explicitly emphasises that it would be 'quite senseless to divide the authentic (republican) state according to the specific form of government'.

5

In the historical reception of Kant's theory of constitutional law, one of the most intensely discussed topics has always been the question concerning the right to resistance or rebellion (see Unruh 1992, 194ff. for an overview of the debate). That Kant, as a philosophical protagonist of republicanism, or, in more contemporary terms, of constitutional democracy, should so stubbornly reject the idea that a people possesses a right to rebellion under certain circumstances seems initially quite surprising. In the first review of Kant's *Doctrine of Right* to appear, Friedrich Bouterwek already felt obliged to conclude his discussion by reproaching Kant for expecting his readers to accept 'the most paradoxical of all paradoxical propositions: the proposition that the mere *idea* of sovereignty should constrain me to obey as my lord whoever has set himself up as my lord, without my asking who has given him the right to command me' (6:371).

Now we must clearly distinguish at least three things in the present context: (1) a people's 'right to rebellion' against 'the legislative head of state' (6:320); (2) an individual 'right' on the part of a particular citizen to oppose specific commands of 'one who possesses authority'; (3) a right of the citizen to complain against political measures that violate the laws of equality. Such 'complaints (*gravamina*)' are permissible, as Kant sees fit to observe merely in passing (6:319; see *The Conflict of the*

Faculties: 7:89). As far as the second 'right' is concerned – that of *individual* opposition to an authorised command – Kant naturally also has something to say. For he specifically qualifies the traditional injunction 'Obey the authority who has power over you' (*Romans* 13) by adding in parenthesis, '(in whatever does not conflict with inner morality)' (6:371). This idea, of course, is hardly original, and Thomas Hobbes had already expressed similar reservations and qualifications 150 years before: 'In all things not contrary to the Morall law, (that is to say, to the Law of Nature) all Subjects are bound to obey that for divine law, which is declared to be so, by the Lawes of the Commonwealth' (*Leviathan*, chapter 26, paragraph 40). Kant certainly understands his formulation of this article as a definitive material restriction of the state's claim upon our obedience, for he explicitly emphasises elsewhere (in a 'Reflection' from the 1780s) that one may at least resist certain commands 'in those cases which could never enter into a proper *unionem civilem*, like forms of religious compulsion for example. Or the compulsion to perform unnatural offences like assassination etc. etc.' (RR: 19:594f.). And in *Religion within the Boundaries of Mere Reason* in 1793, Kant writes: 'The proposition, "We ought to obey God rather than men," means only that when human beings command something that is evil in itself (directly opposed to the moral law) we may not, and ought not, obey them' (6:99). This all follows directly from Kant's rational political 'theology,' which is also clearly formulated in the 'General Remark (A)' that we have been discussing: '... the saying "All authority is from God" [..] is not an assertion about the historical basis of the civil constitution; it instead sets forth an idea as a practical principle of reason: the principle that the presently existing legislative authority ought to be obeyed, whatever its origin' (6:319).

In attempting to answer the question of whether he should obey a specific authorised command, the citizen must always listen to the voice of the moral law itself (for the authorised command alone can never simply and automatically exculpate him), a law that Kant of course describes in the imagery of a 'divine commandment.' And here we simply encounter John Locke's famous insight that the only solution to this dilemma is an appeal to God himself. The question concerning who should judge here between the state and the individual citizen cannot of course be answered by referring to any power on earth at all. For the individual citizen alone can decide this only by reference to the court of conscience ('forum poli'; 6:235). And the individual alone is therefore answerable, as Locke puts it, on the last day before the highest judge of all men (see Locke, *Second Treatise on Government*, §20f.).

As far as the alleged right to resistance or rebellion on the part of *the people* against 'the legislative head of a state' is concerned, on the other hand, Kant responds with the same vigour, and the same arguments, as did Hobbes had in his time. For we cannot even derive any metaphorical sense from the question of who could stand as judge between a people and the head of state. For it is only through *representation* (or through *authority*, in Hobbes), only *through* the head of state as such, that a multitude first becomes a *people*, first becomes a bearer of a *united* political will (6:318, 23).

At this point, we should note that Kant also offers a further argument that is explained in the 'Appendix' to the *Doctrine of Right*. This argument clearly shows that Kant's repudiation of an alleged right to rebellion is more than a merely passing addition to the text that might subsequently be changed or revised. For in Kant's eyes it is only through submission to a universal legislative will that a rightful (that is, lawful) civil condition is possible in the first place. Every rightful resistance to this legislative will would presuppose a law of right that would itself refer back to a higher rightful legislation not subject to the original one. This leads inevitably either to the contradiction of a highest authority that is not the highest, as Kant says (6:320 and 372; RR 19:569, 33f.), or to an endless regress, as Hobbes had already said: '[To set] the Lawes above the Soveraign, setteth also a Judge above him, and a Power to punish him; which is to make a new Soveraign; and again for the same reason a third, to punish the second; and so continually without end, to the Confusion, and Dissolution of the Common-wealth' (*Leviathan*, chapter XXIX, 9). Hobbes's argument certainly differs from Kant's in its detail, but comes to the same conclusion. In the final analysis, this question concerns more than a specific issue of constitutional theory, but arises directly from the concept of right that underlies both arguments here. The distinction between *meum* and *tuum* ultimately requires definitive judgements ('sentences'), and these in turn require a final court of appeal. But Kant had already made this very clear in §8 of the *Doctrine of Right*, as well as later on in his discussion of the 'practical syllogism' in §45.

Kant's rejection of the right to rebellion on the part of the people therefore simply expresses his claim that no member of the people can oppose the state in the name of *right*. One can only refuse to obey the state as an individual in the name of one's own *conscience*. But this view clearly conflicts with Kant's claim that a citizen does possess *rights*, if only the 'right to emigrate' (6:338) and perhaps the right to a free press (in a narrow sense) (see *On the Common Saying*, 8:304).[6] If these are really supposed to be rights in the strict sense, it must – 'in accordance with the principle of non-contradiction' (§D) – be permissible to enforce them. But that does not seem to be the case either, for Kant claims emphatically that 'the sovereign has only rights against his subjects and no duties (that he can be coerced to fulfil)' (6:319). Thus the ruler cannot 'rightly' be compelled by the citizens to act in accordance with the very principles of right that constitute the basis for *his* legitimate capacity to coerce. To the sovereign's 'duties of right' (see 6:236) arising from these same principles there is no corresponding *juridical right to coercion* on the part of the citizens who wish to advance the republican character of their community. The 'duties of right' are simply a *moral criterion* for the internal self-reformation of sovereign power: '... it is a duty, especially for heads of state, to be concerned about how they [sc. constitutions] can be improved as soon as possible and brought into conformity with natural right, which stands before us as a model in the idea of reason, even at the cost of sacrifices to their self-seeking inclinations' (*Toward Perpetual Peace*: 8:372). The various aforementioned discussions about a possible 'right to rebellion' in Kant are ultimately expressions of the desire to glean a more than merely metaphorical sense from his talk about the '*rights*' of citizens in relation to the 'physical head of state.' Whatever solution may be found with regard to this problem, it is only the individual who could possibly enjoy such 'rights.' For Kant, there is no political subject that could assume 'rights of the people' over against the sovereign.

It is no accident that the similarity between the positions of both Kant and Hobbes with regard to an alleged right to rebellion is hardly exhausted by the line of argumentation we have already discussed. For the *Metaphysics of Morals* speaks to a political situation that in one important respect is comparable to the predicament in England that Hobbes's *Leviathan* was intended to address – namely, the problem of establishing a new government after a period of civil conflict. In both thinkers, the categorical repudiation of revolution is accompanied by the categorical demand to obey a revolutionary government once it has established itself. Hobbes expressed this basic insight in the sound practical advice he offered to the sovereign (that is, Cromwell): every attempt to justify

---

[6] Kant's critique of Hobbes in the famous passage from the essay *On the Common Saying* only really touches on *De Cive*. In the later text of the *Leviathan*, on the other hand, with which Kant was probably unfamiliar, Hobbes provides a theory of the 'Liberties of the Subject' (*Leviathan*, chapter XXI, 10) that is grounded in a very different manner, although it is also far less worked out than Kant's own theory of the 'rights of the citizen'.

the legitimacy of one's rule historically can only hasten the collapse of the state (see *Leviathan*, 'Review & Conclusion'). For his part, Kant adopts the view, explicitly attacked by Bouterwek, that only the 'idea of sovereign rule' can demand unconditional rightful obedience in relation to the actual 'supreme authority.' *All* rightful rule initially arises from the exercise of 'power' (6:318; 339) – that is, from 'the seizing of supreme power' (6:372), and can only develop towards a *true* republic, conceived as the impersonal rule of law, by means of a 'gradual reform in accordance with firm principles' (6:355). The legitimacy of the given political order cannot be justified therefore by reference to any 'historical documentation' (§52), but only by the indispensability of such an order for the realisation of right itself. In §9 of the treatment of 'Private Right,' Kant had already emphasised the 'prerogative' of the *'beati possidentes'* as the basis for our right 'to constrain everyone with whom we could have any dealings to enter with us into a constitution' (6:256; see RR: 19:602, 14). While we cannot legitimately dissolve or even destroy an unsatisfactory system of political order, it may be legitimate to *replace* it with another one: once the revolution has succeeded, the rejection of revolution implies a rejection of restoration. In relation to the political situation in France, Kant actually attempted to take the sting out of the revolution after the event by arguing that the king had already abdicated by relinquishing his right to levy taxes and transferring it to the Estates General (6:341; see Henrich 1967). Even if this argument is clearly tenuous, it seems to have concealed the stain clinging to the bloody birth of the Directory out of civil war (see *The Conflict of the Faculties*: 7:85, 19) and reconciled the heart of an engaged observer of the Revolution with the rational head of a philosopher of right.

Bibliography

Biester, J. E. 1793: 'Einige Nachrichten von den Ideen der Griechen über Staatsverfassung,' in *Berlinische Monatsschrift*, June 1793.

Henrich, D. 1967: 'Über den Sinn vernünftigen Handelns im Staat,' in Henrich, D. (ed.), *Kant – Gentz – Rehberg: Über Theorie und Praxis*, Frankfurt am Main, pp. 9–37.

Herb, K. Ludwig, B. 1994: 'Kants kritisches Staatsrecht,' in *Jahrbuch für Recht und Ethik* II, pp. 431–478.

Maus, I. 1992: *Zur Aufklärung der Demokratietheorie*, Frankfurt am Main.

Unruh, P. 1992: *Die Herrschaft der Vernunft. Zur Staatsphilosophie Immanuel Kants*, Baden-Baden.

14

Refusing Sovereign Power – The Relation between Philosophy and Politics in the Modern Age

Volker Gerhardt

There is an intrinsic contradiction in a *public* treaty containing covert or *'secret* articles.' For such provisions cancel precisely the open and public character that essentially belongs to the idea of a treaty. Kant is therefore indulging in obvious *irony* when he announces a secret article of his own in his essay *Toward Perpetual Peace* (8:368). And if we then examine the actual content of his article, we see this irony turning into an expression of the most bitter sarcasm. Firstly, this secret article must be *publicly* 'dictated,' and secondly, it demands only that *philosophers* should not be *restricted* in *the* public expression of their views. In addition, there is supposed to be only *one* such article – namely, the one that Kant is here making available by *publishing* it. It is impossible to overlook his strategy here: like the *clausula salvatoria* already mentioned in his prefatory remarks, so too the 'secret' article Kant proposes in the second supplement to the essay is his way of ridiculing the covert practices of court and cabinet politics in his own time.

This impression is amply reinforced by the justification that Kant proceeds to offer for his 'secret' article. He points out how it could only damage the standing of governments, after all, if they were ever to consult their own 'subjects' on matters concerning foreign affairs of state. It is therefore necessary to come to some strictly secret agreement before it can subsequently be made available to the public. The state thus *'tacitly invites'* its citizens to express themselves 'freely and publicly about the universal maxims of waging war and establishing peace' (8:369). And a couple of lines later, Kant expressly observes that 'no special arrangement' is required on this point since it is so clearly demanded by universal 'human reason.' The public character of these questions, here ironically described as secretly debated ones, thus essentially concerns a morally and legally self-evident matter.

Kant's 'secret article' communicates a strong impression of the philosopher's particular kind of roguish humour. He confronts the world of 'furtive politics' with its own 'duplicity' (8:386f.) and indulges in the kind of sophistries this world typically employs to deceive others (for further discussion of Kant's polemical language, see Saner 1967, pp. 215ff. and Laursen 1986). Kant's cunning use of irony is of course deployed to achieve the opposite effect, and promote general enlightenment. The entire essay is coloured by the characteristic wit and subtle polemic of a politically engaged 'Enlightener' (see Gerhardt 1995a). The resources of literary rhetoric, sharply intensified by the experience of censorship to which Kant himself was exposed from October 1794 until the end of 1797, are here enlisted for a spirited defence of human rights. The matter that Kant presents satirically could not be more serious: '*The maxims of philosophers about the conditions under which public peace is possible shall be consulted by states armed for war*' (8:368).

1. The apparent privilege of philosophy

At first, one might have the impression that Kant is here simply repeating, in slightly different form, a particular ancient *Roman institution*: the ritually established period of reflection that was demanded before any definite declaration of war. In ancient Rome, the fundamental decision concerning matters of peace and war did not lie simply with the senate, but also always involved the priestly rituals of divination. The soldiers could therefore only be sent out once another group, independent of the political class, had also expressed its assent. Even in the time of the early Roman kings, thirty days of general reflection were prescribed before taking up arms for any military campaign. A specific group of priests (the *fetiales*), who also had a say in the framing of external treaties, were expressly consulted about the declaration of any imminent war. Already in early Roman times, it was obligatory in such matters to consult the augurs who from Numa Pomplius onwards had been called upon to perform their office 'openly before the people' (*honoris ergo publicum*), as Livy relates (*Ab urbe condita* I, 18, 6). After the requisite period of reflection, the people would then express the final decision concerning war or peace. And the Roman Republic also continued to observe this practice. In the eyes of a republican thinker such as Cicero (*De re publica* II 17), the *fetiales* represented an institution that worked very much in the interests of the people. Thus he writes of Numa Pompilius as follows: he 'created the law [*ius*] concerning the declaration of war. It was established with the greatest of justice [*iustissime*] and further consecrated by the priestly law [*fetiali*] that any war not expressly pronounced and declared as such must be accounted an offence against human and divine law. And thus you may clearly see how wisely our kings were already prepared to acknowledge rights for the people'.

'To acknowledge rights for the people' – that is also, and precisely, Kant's central concern in his so-called 'secret article.' The counsel of the philosophers here replaces the role traditionally played by the *haruspices* and *augures* – but certainly not in the form of some expressly convened *consilium*, or institution, reserved exclusively for philosophers. The philosophers are called to occupy no special political office in order to deliver their counsel before any decision for war or peace is taken. For Kant, it suffices simply that they be permitted *to write and speak in public* without the state's taking offence at the fact. The article should 'tacitly' – and this expresses the last trace of secrecy – encourage a public realm of debate. And since it cannot even 'tacitly' encourage the right of free expression *solely* for philosophers, it must concede this right in principle to *all*. For here, as elsewhere for Kant, the philosopher is simply the representative of that same 'universal reason in which everyone has a voice.' Although it might initially appear that Kant is here vindicating the right to speak 'freely and publicly' only for the philosophers, he clearly indicates elsewhere that the right in question cannot properly be restricted to any particular professional group: 'This freedom [sc. concerning the employment of human reason] will carry with it the right to submit openly for discussion the thoughts and doubts with which we find ourselves unable to deal, and to do so without being decried as troublesome and dangerous citizens. This is one of the original rights of human reason, which recognises no other judge than that universal human reason in which everyone has a voice' (CPR B 780).

If Kant's article appears to be speaking only of philosophers, this itself is simply another ironical aspect of his 'secret' maxim. In fact, Kant is thinking of all those who are capable of making public use of their reason. His additional article intrinsically cancels itself out *de iure*, leaving a freedom for everyone to express his own views *de facto*. On careful examination, it is clear that what Kant vindicates for the philosopher is only something that is open in principle to all. And if it is conceded to the philosopher, it is also conceded to all. In the final analysis, one cannot properly prevent anyone from publicly expressing what seems a reasonable view of his own. But what is actually reasonable in the views we believe to be reasonable is something that can only properly be examined through public discussion. It is therefore quite clear that Kant's 'secret article' demands not some special right for philosophy to interrogate or even veto the views of others, but neither more nor less than freedom of thought for everyone capable of expressing himself publicly.

It is also obvious therefore that Kant is not recommending some special consultative role or office for philosophers in the political context. Philosophers require no special commission in order to take a public stand on political questions because they 'will do that of their own accord, if only they are not forbidden to do so' (*Toward Perpetual Peace*: 8:369). But this is not to deny that philosophers do have some kind of special responsibility here. For by making use of the 'freedom of the pen' and thereby actively defending the 'sole palladium of the people's rights' (*On the Common Saying*: 8:304), they inevitably assume a certain unique position. And in this they need neither encouragement nor censorship from the political sphere because here too, as in their own discipline, they are already subject to the strictest control there is – the control of *truth*. The public sphere is something that belongs equally to morality, politics, philosophy, and the domain of science in general. For any claim to truth, like any claim to moral or legal validity, must be capable of being defended *ad coram publico*.

Kant's frequent use of juridical metaphors in the *Critique of Pure Reason* is essentially based upon this idea. It also presupposes that the 'court of reason' is an open institution that is convened in public. Even in the absence of a final judicial ruling, there is still an exchange of methodically argued and presented ideas that appeals to rational insight. All those who come forward to 'think openly and think for themselves' thus reciprocally impose the same limits on one another 'so that they do not lose their freedom' (*On the common saying*: 8:304). But no one can be denied the right to express his own opinion. In this respect, the philosopher is in exactly the same position as everyone else.

If this is the case, we must still ask whether Kant really avoids entirely the temptation to ascribe a privileged position to the philosopher as far as open political debate is concerned. The fact that his 'secret article' bestows such prominence upon those who share his own specific academic calling only seems to strengthen the suspicion that he has fallen victim to a certain, albeit understandable, *déformation professionelle* in this respect. After all, the claim to truth that is clearly constitutive for philosophy might even provide grounds for granting the philosopher some direct access to those who actually exercise political power. If it is true that the sphere of politics cannot (or at least cannot in the long term) resist a truth that is expressly believed or acknowledged, it might appear obvious that philosophers should indeed belong amongst the privileged advisors in the political domain.

But in the essay *Toward Perpetual Peace*, there is certainly no evidence that this is what Kant actually thinks. Even when he refers in the first supplement of the essay to the kind of 'political wisdom' [*Staatsweisheit*] required of a 'moral politician,' there is no indication that he is thinking of any special relationship to the publicly expressed views of the representatives of philosophy, or of 'world wisdom' [*Weltweisheit*], as he likes to describe his discipline using a venerable traditional term. Of course 'political wisdom' is based pre-eminently upon the acknowledgement and observance of the fundamental principles of right. And while it is certainly the primary task of philosophy to set forth these principles of 'human right' (*On the Common Saying*: 8:306), this does not imply any special *political* position as far as philosophy is concerned. In the *Conflict of the Faculties*, however, there is one particular passage that does seem to ascribe certain political privileges to philosophy.

With regard to the epochal task of 'enlightening the people' – that is, of 'publicly instructing the people concerning their duties and rights with respect to the state to which they belong' the philosophers are described by Kant as the 'natural proclaimers and interpreters' of universal rights (*Conflict of the Faculties*: 7:89). That would be no cause for concern in itself if Kant did not go on to make derogatory remarks about 'professional' jurists as merely defenders of their own special interests. Insofar as they occupy their office as 'appointed by the state,' they do not, according to Kant, display the requisite freedom of judgement in these matters. For the state, which is 'always only intent on governing' (ibid.), inevitably imposes, explicitly or not, its own will upon the officials who serve it politically.

There is no doubt that Kant here, as in many other passages in his work, effectively denies that *lawyers* are really capable of forming an unprejudiced and genuinely independent judgement of the relevant issue. He regards them as an interested party in this connection, partly because they already have a duty of loyalty towards those who employ them, and partly because they are also easily corrupted by their proximity to political power (and this is clearly the decisive consideration for Kant). For even though, either in their advisory diplomatic role or as members of the faculty of law, lawyers and jurists are under no immediate compulsion to endorse the positions adopted by others, they nonetheless tend to accommodate themselves to the prevailing government view of things. This follows from the fact that they essentially regard themselves as 'representatives of the power of the state' (*Toward Perpetual Peace*: 8:369). Clearly thinking here of the Roman symbol of 'Justitia' as a Goddess with blindfolded eyes, holding a sword in her right hand and a pair of scales in her left hand, Kant suspects the lawyers of according greater respect to the demands of power than they do to the careful deliberations of reason. And things may prove even worse: 'When one side of the scale refuses to sink,' they are quite prepared to 'lay the sword on it' (ibid.). Kant's commentary has the terseness of an ancient inscription: '*vae victis.*'

This kind of unacceptable behaviour, of course, can only flourish when lawyers and jurists perform their functions in a covert or secret manner. The effective public role of philosophers must therefore be understood essentially as a counter-model here, and one that also indirectly expresses a certain challenge to the discipline of *jurisprudence* itself. The insidious process of accommodating to political power can easily lead lawyers and jurists to forget the very questions that centrally concern their own discipline: the 'scholars of the law,' as Kant says, are thus incapable of answering the question concerning what is intrinsically 'right' [*recht*]; they can only indicate what is legally 'correct' [*rechtens*] – namely, 'what the laws in a certain place at a certain time say and have said.' And they should also be required to provide the 'universal criterion through which we can recognise in general what is right and what is wrong (*iustum et iniustum*)' (*Doctrine of Right* §B:229). The philosophers therefore have to accomplish the task the jurists themselves have failed to perform – and this seems like another reason for assuming that Kant effectively claims special political rights for himself and the members of his profession as far as critical reflection and the general process of enlightenment are concerned. But this would nonetheless be a mistake. Kant is not hoping for any special privileges when he eschews a personal and popular tone for his political and philosophical critique and recommends a respectful criticism of the state instead. For this is once again simply a way of emphasising the requisite independence of the practice of critique. If it is only the rational *insight* of the critical thinker that can properly claim validity here, then the thinker must not merely maintain due distance from the powers that be, but also avoid any expression of partisanship in favour of the people.

From our own contemporary point of view, this idea may sound rather suspicious or even self-contradictory. But in fact it simply formulates a principled standard for the free and responsible exercise of critique. The philosopher who expresses himself publicly should not try and speak directly to those who would not read his writings anyway, nor should he make himself into a spokesman for any specific interests of the people. For then he would no longer be speaking as a philosopher, but merely as a representative of some particular clientele. If the philosopher wishes to make his voice heard as a 'free teacher of the law' [*freier Rechtslehrer*] (see *Conflict of the Faculties*: 8:89), and thus be treated as a defender of 'the *rights* of the people,' he can only do so by pleading the cause of reason itself. That is why he must limit himself to expounding the fundamental rights that belong to human beings as such.

2. A Government of Philosopher Kings?

The public *exposition* of rights in this sense also naturally involves the *defence* of these rights. But in defending such rights, we must also be 'respectful' towards the source that bestows and secures right in general. Kant is not reverting to some particular political position or attitude in this regard. Nor is there any indication here of any 'restorationist tendency' on Kant's part. He is simply pursuing his own project of rational critique in a consistent fashion. But this involves a clear understanding of the task in question. The philosophical critique of political arrangements must therefore recognise that it is essentially concerned with the demands intrinsically embodied in *fundamental rights*. And in addition to the demand for *objectivity* , there is also the demand for a certain *respect for right itself*. It is absurd to interpret Kant's point here as if it suggested some hidden claim to 'shared government' [*Mitregentschaft*] on the part of the philosopher.

On the contrary, it is important to see that, given the unfortunate example of the lawyers and jurists before him, Kant is insistent that no special political privilege be accorded to the philosophers. If they were directly possessed of power, or were merely close to the seat of power, they too would not be immune to lending their voice to the power they themselves now bore. In Kant's eyes, it is enough if philosophers are not impeded in their task of working to promote *enlightenment* amongst the people and thus contributing to the *universal formation of judgement* on the part of the citizens. But this means they must be permitted *simply to be philosophers* – neither more nor less than this. If they are allowed to play their role as philosophers, then they will speak publicly of their own accord and thus fulfil their 'duty through recourse to universal (morally-legislative) human reason'. In this they need no special supervision, and certainly no censorship. For they will mutually correct their own views, just as they do, or ought to do, in the usual context of scientific and philosophical debate. The search for truth and the examination of political principles are both, by virtue of their own inner logic, essentially subject to reason alone. But reason can only properly express itself in the medium of free and uncoerced judgement.

The strongest arguments for the establishment and maintenance of peace, therefore, derive from the *universal judgement of reason* as developed through *the free use of the powers of the human understanding itself*. And it is *the public domain* that promises the best and most effective insights in relation to the question of peace. Since it is the philosophers who seek explicitly to speak with the voice of reason, and since the philosophers are directly obligated through reason to defend the rights of human beings, they do enjoy a special responsibility with respect to the establishment of peace. But that certainly does not involve any special political prerogative on their part. From the political point of view, the philosophers are *citizens* just like anyone else. And anyone who believes he can understand them can also legitimately contradict and challenge them. Indeed, they should be challenged if there are indeed good rational grounds for doing so. For philosophy lives in and from the public contestation which it provokes.

Since therefore the philosopher desires no privileged position, and no exclusive right, for himself and his profession, his claims in relation to the state are also slight. Nonetheless, it is no insignificant matter when Kant demands that the philosopher 'be given a *hearing*' (8:369). If philosophy demands the observance of fundamental principles, if it insists on a proper correspondence between words and deeds, or even demands certain reforms (see section one of Kant's 'Appendix'), something must be sacrificed if the philosopher is to be allowed to speak, let alone if he is also to be heard. And philosophy inevitably courts offence if its modest contribution nonetheless reveals a claim that philosophy itself can only proclaim in ironic form, even though it is a claim that cannot be countered by any valid arguments: 'So it is said of philosophy, for example, that she is the *handmaiden* of theology (and likewise of the other two faculties [namely those of law and medicine]). But it is not clear whether "she bears the torch before her mistress or carries the train behind"' (8:369).[1]

Kant leaves open the question concerning the hierarchical ordering of the special sciences from the point of view of their historical authority or their social-practical character. Once the primacy of pure practical reason is acknowledged, there is indeed some philosophical room for recognising the particular practical advantages that accrue to medicine, law, or even theology. But it should be clear that any such assessment or hierarchical ordering can only be undertaken on the basis of a debate that, once all the important arguments are properly examined, can only be described as *philosophical* in character. Philosophy therefore rightly bears the torch wherever the relative ordering and assessment of the various other disciplines is concerned. And even if reflection upon the aims and conditions of the different disciplines is not expressly conceived under the name of philosophy, those who do reflect on such matters inevitably become philosophers if only they pursue their enquiries thoroughly enough.

Under the historical conditions of the Enlightenment, therefore, philosophy necessarily assumes a leading role, however much this discipline may seem to lag behind the other sciences in respect of reputation and achievement. And if we are no longer content simply to repeat certain hallowed values without questioning them, or merely to accept established power claims as they stand, then philosophy occupies a strong position of its own, one that also necessarily touches upon the relationship between the different disciplines. It is the same here as it is in the political domain, where philosophy may indeed be dispensable as far as public argument over particular views is concerned, but proves to be indispensable for the exposition of the fundamental principles of right. Whenever a decision concerning principles is required, the critical judgement of the philosopher cannot properly be avoided or ignored. In the public realm, therefore, even without any special office or mandate, the philosopher occupies a position that could hardly be stronger.

Hence it may well seem rather surprising when, at the end of this exemplary passage concerning the unique role of philosophy, Kant nonetheless expresses a certain *political devaluation* of the discipline. For he utterly repudiates the idea of any personal connection between philosophy and

---

[1] Kant expresses himself in the same way in the *Conflict of the Faculties* (7:28) where he adds that we should not 'drive the handmaid out, or attempt to silence her'. Since this passage predates the essay *Toward Perpetual Peace*, although censorship prevented its appearance until 1798, it looks very much as if Kant was quoting himself at this point in his essay. This would also explain the use of quotation marks here.

politics, and dismisses the venerable ideal of philosopher rule, so often invoked over the last 2,000 years, as not merely implausible but also intrinsically undesirable: 'That kings should philosophize or philosophers become kings is not to be expected, but it is also not to be wished for, since possession of power unavoidably corrupts the free judgement of reason' (8:369).

Of course, long before Kant, there have been many perceptive thinkers who have also rejected the idea that philosophers might one day come to power and govern the state, might at last succeed in shaping the political realm in accordance with those rational principles that philosophy and political thought have repeatedly attempted to identify from the very beginning. In this respect, Plato's own experience with would-be philosopher rulers hardly provided an encouraging precedent. And the fate of all those philosophically inclined kings from Marcus Aurelius to Frederick II of Prussia, not to mention the philosophers who have come all too close to real political power, can only induce the most sober of reflections. The list of the most celebrated names here would take us from Plato and Aristotle, through Cicero and Seneca, up to Machiavelli, Thomas More, and Voltaire. But no philosopher prior to Kant has so unambiguously expressed the thought that we should not even wish philosophers to occupy significant political posts and positions in the first place.

This naturally does not mean that serious doubts had never been expressed before about the possibility or even desirability of placing political rule in the hands of philosophers. Plato himself was indeed the first to express such doubts. Even in making his celebrated and notorious claim that neither the state (*polis*) nor human kind (*anthropinos*) will ever be free of evils until 'government and philosophy' (*politike kai philosophia*) are brought together, he confesses his 'fear' (*oknos*) that the very idea 'runs counter to the views of all' (*Republic* 473a). Perhaps he could have been more sanguine in this respect if he had simply contented himself with a looser connection between the spheres of politics and philosophy. It is only when he personalises the relationship between philosophy and government in the *parable of the cave* (*Republic* 520a; 535a – 540c) that his ideal model (*paradigma*), merely designed as it was to help us grasp the concept of justice itself, comes to appear in such a problematic utopian light. One should also recognise that in the Platonic dialogues that are primarily concerned with politics itself, rather than with articulating the ideal paradigm of justice, there is no longer any talk of philosophers ruling the state. In this respect, Aristotle was thus perfectly able to develop the lines of argument already presented in *The Statesman* and *The Laws* without needing to mention the idea of philosopher kings at all. There is only a single surviving fragment that allows us to claim that Aristotle regarded the prospect of philosopher rule with misgivings (Aristotle 1955, Fr. 2:62; see Bien 1973:248 and Bien 1989:585).

But the otherwise not entirely implausible claim that Kant himself follows Aristotle in 'defining the role of the philosophers as an advisor rather than as a direct political actor' (Cavallar 1992:338) appears somewhat exaggerated in this context. For Aristotle assumes a general structural correspondence between political rule and philosophy. According to his pupil Dicaearchus, 'the activity of ruling resembles that of philosophising' (Wehrli 1944, Fr. 29:18). In classical antiquity, it was the prevailing belief in this affinity that effectively prevented any fundamental criticism of Plato's identification of political rule and the philosophical life itself.

3. Practical knowledge

In the Platonic-Academic and Aristotelian-Peripatetic traditions of philosophy generally, but especially in the highly influential forms of Stoic thought, this idea of a fundamental correspondence between theoretical and practical thought was always emphatically maintained. The domains of 'physics' and 'ethics' belong in the same overall deductive context. This is why the spectacle of the later Roman emperors such as Hadrian and Marcus Aurelius could actually encourage the hope that philosophy might come at last to exercise political power. And this hope continued to inspire the idea of educating the ruler through philosophy, a notion that still survived in the tradition of modern humanism. Erasmus of Rotterdam and his *Querela pacis*, for example, can also be interpreted within this context. And although Luther expressly denies philosophy any knowledge of the living God, he defines its end and aim in relation to 'political peace and temporal goods' (*Präparationen zur Vorlesung über die Galathäerbriefe*, in *Sämtliche Werke* Bd. 40/I:20). And this too only reinforces the internal connection between political and philosophical knowledge.

Little real doubt concerning the idea of philosopher rule was ever strongly expressed up to and indeed during the early modern age, which was essentially defined by a revival of Platonic, Aristotelian, and Stoic insights (see Gerhardt 1992). Whether we are speaking of Bacon, Descartes, or Hobbes, or of Spinoza, Leibniz, or Locke, they all strive to derive practical insights from theoretical considerations in a way that involves no real repudiation of the idea of philosopher rule *in principle*. That is why Kant is the first thinker to express more than merely pragmatic reservations in this respect and thereby to develop a theoretically grounded objection to the entire conception.

But this objection does not derive, as one might perhaps expect, from Kant's attempt to provide an *a priori* foundation to the pure principles of moral practical action. For as the essay *Toward Perpetual Peace* in particular reveals, Kant's political thought essentially involves an indispensable reference to the situated and empirical context of politics. Those who wish to act successfully in the political sphere must exercise *prudence* and *judgement*. They must have some appreciation of the nature of *power* and be possessed of *sound human understanding*. Above all, they need a sense for the *appropriate moment* if political action is to achieve its immanent goal of *reform*. All of this is essentially implied by Kant's conception of politics as 'a doctrine of right put into practice' (8:370; for more on this, see Gerhardt 1995b). And here Kant is indeed closer to Aristotle than many of his interpreters care to recognise.

The significant difference between Kant and his predecessors, on the other hand, is to be found in his much stricter conception of *practical knowledge*, the very knowledge that is fundamental to politics. In Kant's philosophy, true practical consciousness acquires its effective content not from any mere description of actual states of affairs but rather from an original *awareness of obligation*. This practical consciousness – specifically in relation to the political domain itself – is a knowledge of the *responsibility* of the acting subject. It is therefore already related directly to the individual experience of *freedom* on the part of this subject.

But this has a further implication. For we can no longer simply pass from a theoretical assessment of reality to a practical conclusion by a mere act of logical inference or topical application. Action must always be mediated through the practical *self-relation* of the acting individual. And this involves the *will* of the subject as an original legitimating ground, and the will itself involves *self-legislation* through practical reason. But this simply consists in the *self-imposed obligation* of the subject to act in accordance with intelligible *reasons*. Our own specific role as individuals, the consciousness of our own responsibility, and the capacity to motivate ourselves through intelligible reasons thus acquire new weight and significance in Kant's conception of agency. However universal and necessary self-legislation through practical reason may be, it is only actualised through a *practical consciousness* that cannot be derived from any

merely theoretical premises, through a consciousness of obligation that
necessarily involves the consciousness of *freedom*.

We should simply add that this consciousness of freedom can evidently
only be an essentially *individual* consciousness, although this point
has been largely ignored by Kant's interpreters (the exceptions here are
Natorp 1924 and Simmel 1931). For this clearly reveals the real difference
between Kant and his philosophical predecessors. By distinguishing as he
does between the functions of practical and theoretical reason, Kant can
do justice to the individual, rational character of action without detriment
to the rigorous claim of reason itself. The power of reason, characterised
by the strict and compelling character of its own insights and conclusions,
can thus be consistently maintained in both its theoretical and practical
functions. But in its practical employment, reason nonetheless accomplishes its task in a specific way – namely, through *the free and conscious
responsibility of the individual who fully appreciates the significance of
his task*.

Kant is indeed therefore the first thinker to provide us with an adequate philosophical explication of the problem concerning the specific
character of practical consciousness. While his own solution certainly
binds the process of moral decision to *knowledge*, this knowledge is no
longer merely descriptive in nature. For it is now intrinsically connected
to a *concept of the self* that can only be grasped in *normative* terms. But
this normative concept of the self rules out any direct transition, through
merely logical inference, from theoretical knowledge to practical insight.
Quite apart from the adequate theoretical grasp of the specific situation
and its circumstances (which is naturally required if successful action is
to more than a matter of happy chance), political and moral action essentially involves *the individual with a will of his own*. This individual is
subject only to the demand that he act according to his *own intelligible
reasons*: he can only will to accomplish what he can acknowledge as adequately justified in the light of his own insight. It is only this that can fully
satisfy the individual's practical need in relation to reason. And it is only
here that reason itself can inspire those motivating *feelings* without which
even essentially rational action would be impossible (Gerhardt 1988).

It is this conception of practical knowledge, only roughly outlined here,
that lies behind Kant's decisive repudiation of the ancient Platonic model
of philosopher kings. In expressing this objection, formulated only in a
single clause, Kant concentrates solely on the issue of *freedom* and contents himself with vindicating this freedom for the realm of *theory*: the
'possession of power', as he puts it here, corrupts the 'free judgement of

reason' (8:369). This makes it sound as though we could simply dispense with our whole discussion of practical knowledge since there seems to be no reference here to the domain of will and action.

But in fact, Kant's brief formulation draws its force from the pathos of practical freedom, rooted in the individual consciousness, which ultimately stands behind it. Thinking itself, especially when it is publicly expressed, also represents a form of action that requires its own reasons. And the ultimate criterion of the latter, if they are indeed meant to be proper *reasons*, can only lie in the correctness and consistency of rationally formulated insight. The thinker therefore requires independence if he is to cultivate rational insight in the first place, if he is ever to convince anyone else through the exercise of his own 'free judgement.' If the thinker effectively serves strong external interests, or is even directly subjected to pressure from such interests, on the other hand, then it is highly questionable whether genuine knowledge can remain his ultimate end and aim.

In the first instance, all of this implies an intimate connection between the claim to free expression and the idea of independently verifiable truth itself. We must also insist that a 'corrupted' judgement is essentially a false judgement. The rational claim that is presupposed in all argumentation and critique would evaporate without the expectation of truth that is internal to the free and open realm of discourse itself. We cannot deny therefore that we are also essentially concerned with an issue of *knowledge* here. But it is highly significant that Kant does not make the material truth that our judgements aim to determine into the decisive criterion, but concentrates instead on the social context within which we are led to truth in the first place. He is primarily interested in the *process of discovering truth*, something that is equally essential in the context of theoretical philosophy as an open domain for mutual argument and cross-examination (CPR B 779f.). When we stand on the 'stage of conflict' (B 881) a *free relationship of individuals* is essential. The discovery of truth depends on the way in which individuals conduct themselves within a historically specific and socially organised context. It implies a 'history of pure reason' (B 880f.) through which the interest in knowledge is formed, and a '*culture* of human reason' (B 878f.) through which this interest is disciplined. This essentially *practical relationship* both to oneself and to others is thus a condition of our capacity for truth in the political domain as well. Kant's distinction between the independent philosopher and the politician involved in the exercise of power thus arises directly from the 'primacy of practical reason' (CPrR 5:119).

We have thus identified *two* criteria that allow us to distinguish between the politician and the philosopher. The *first* criterion derives from the immediate connection between an agent and the concrete situation in which he acts. Action in this sense requires particular *experience* and a practised *capacity for judgement*, and can only be accomplished through the application of *prudence*. In the *Supplements* to his essay, Kant characterises this criterion in terms of 'political prudence' [*Staatsklugheit*]. Exercising the latter does not, however, absolve us from the demands of 'political wisdom' [*Staatsweisheit*] – that is, from observing the principles of reason. On the contrary, the main task of a philosophical theory of politics lies precisely in convincing every practical agent of the unconditional validity of the fundamental principles that define the rights belonging to every human being by virtue of reason itself. But the philosopher cannot simply deduce the concrete course of action for a specific agent from these fundamental principles. Specific ways and means are required for dealing in a careful and experienced manner with both individual human beings and the interests and institutions of power. 'Reform through principles' cannot be attained simply by appealing to a set of logical inferences (on this, see Langer 1986:96 and Sassenbach 1992). Political praxis stands under quite specific conditions of its own. And these do not immediately suggest that good philosophers also make good politicians. Indeed, the reverse may prove to be the case.

The *second* criterion consists precisely in the process through which opinion itself is rationally formed. And this is intrinsically bound up with the independence of freely judging subjects. And in this regard, the essentially practical relationship that every individual must establish with himself proves to be decisive. Here too we must give due recognition to specific circumstances. For while every individual always stands under a self-imposed obligation to express his views freely and honestly, the prevailing social and historical conditions can make it easier or more difficult to assume one's own freedom. Now Kant's repudiation of the idea of philosopher rule expressly recognises the connection between our *specific situation and social position* and our *capacity for consistent moral action*! For those who regard Kant simply as a moral rigorist, this must appear as a most unlikely conclusion to draw. But the fact that Kant specifically recognises the different relation in which politicians stand to 'free judgement,' without thereby simply scorning them, clearly shows that no other interpretation is possible here.

But the independent and pragmatic sphere of political action, which we must acknowledge on the basis of these considerations, cannot simply be abandoned to its own devices. The domain of politics must remain subject to examination through 'practical theory.' But such theory can only possess any binding force in relation to the political domain inso-far as the latter is itself part of rational human praxis in general. Strictly speaking, therefore, the philosophical theorist can only draw the politi-cian's *attention* to certain issues, can only *remind* the politician of some-thing that (also always) belongs to the conditions of political action. The philosopher often therefore simply needs to take the politician at his own word, to remind him of his promises, to challenge his insincerity, and to expose his secretive dealings. Kant himself provides an example when he criticises what he calls the 'political moralist' in the 'Appendix' to his essay (8:374f.). That is why Kant's attentiveness to the specific *language of politics* is such a significant feature of the entire discussion. And the aspect of *rhetoric* also plays a correspondingly important role in Kant's criticisms of the prevailing political conditions. And the satirical form of the essay *Toward Perpetual Peace* naturally brings this aspect repeatedly to the fore. His criticisms can thereby effectively highlight the practical principles to which the philosopher and the politician alike are equally subject insofar as they understand themselves as 'rational beings' at all (for this concept, see Gerhardt 1990). And they do already understand themselves in this way whenever they defend their views and opinions publicly and thus attempt to present at least an appearance of seriousness and veracity.

4. The division of labour between politics and philosophy

There are indeed, therefore, separate and independent fields of action upon the same common ground of practical reason. There is a certain *division of labour* with respect to the domains of practical politics and philosophi-cal critique. The exercise of political rule and the practice of philosophy are complementary social activities that cannot simply be collapsed into one another without detriment to their own possible achievements in their respective domains. This is precisely what grounds the modernity of Kant's critical conception of politics *and* philosophy. In both cases, he emphasises the essentially mediating role of the public sphere. This opens up the possibility for a pluralistic conception of political unity and of inter-subjectively verifiable knowledge. The Platonic identification of politics with philosophy is therefore not merely redundant, but is also something 'not even desirable' under conditions of modernity.

It should be clear from the preceding discussion of Kant's repudiation of the Platonic model of philosopher rule that Kant would never wish to prevent the philosopher from occupying high political office. Nor, of course, would he wish in turn to deny the statesman the opportunity of engaging with philosophical questions. But whoever does either of these things does so *as* a citizen or *as* a politician, and not *as* a philosopher! The distinction between politics and philosophy should not be erased. For the domain of politics stands under different conditions than that of philosophy. The individual's proximity to political power introduces considerations that can impede the development of pure philosophical reflection. When a politician makes some philosophical claim, there is always a suspicion of some covert interest at work that is detrimental to the free exercise of judgement.

The views and opinions of the philosopher must also naturally be subjected to critical examination. This happens as a matter of course in the context of debate and the free exchange of ideas. But proximity to the influence and pressure of political power already encourages a kind of *systematic distortion* that makes it almost impossible to speak of free thought or rational legitimation. Even if a philosopher were to become king, he would no longer be able to conduct himself in the same way as before. For in assuming any such office, he would already have become a political agent, and any views he expressed would also inevitably be understood in this light.

Of course, this distinction between politics and philosophy proves to be so decisive precisely because of Kant's insistence on the *critical function* of philosophy. For the principal 'concern' of this discipline, as he puts it at the end of the first *Critique*, is with critique itself: 'The *critical* path alone is still open' (B 884). But if it is ever adequately to fulfil the task of critique there is nothing that philosophical theory more urgently needs than the exercise of *free judgement*. Philosophy must be independent of all special interests if it is truly to examine and evaluate everything in the *interest of reason* itself.

This critical conception of philosophy, that – contrary to widespread belief – does not actually exclude systematic or metaphysical concerns, is *modern* in a quite specific sense: for it trusts in a *division of labour* in questions concerning knowledge as well. The progress of culture, according to Kant, results from the ways in which human beings have learned to divide their labour and to develop very different and highly specialised skills (see *Idea for a Universal History*: 7:21f. and *Conjectural Beginning of Human History*: 8:115ff.). He could surely only have regarded the (romantic) critique of 'alienation' as a misunderstanding generated by confusing a *moral* claim concerning the worth of the human person with a *technical-practical* claim concerning the productivity of the individual. Those who look to Kant to provide further support for their critique of alienation inevitably overlook the 'never merely' in his most accurate formulation of the Categorical Imperative: 'For all rational beings stand under the law that each of them is to treat himself and all others *never merely as a means* but always *at the same time as ends in themselves*' (*Groundwork*: 4:433).

In nature, every living being can become a means for another. And human society also stands under the same law. Every mother becomes a means of life for her child insofar as she behaves as a mother. And it is not difficult to recognise the child in turn as a means that serves to realise the life plans of a mother. This reciprocal relation of ends and means is consciously shaped and developed in human society and is what we rightly describe as 'culture' in the broadest sense. When human beings share and divide their tasks in the economic, technological, and scientific fields, they consciously and reciprocally make themselves into means for each other's ends and thereby create the nexus of society in the process.

Plato had already described how the state eventually becomes indispensable with the increasing division and specification of labour (*Republic* 368b–374b). Kant elevated this thought to the methodological status of an *Idea* and made it the basis for a *Universal History from a Cosmopolitan Point of View* (8:15–31). The gradual development of economic life, of law, and of science lays a foundation for the eventual construction of a political order that human beings can freely recognise as their own. Thus, if specific and well-defined tasks are ascribed to jurisprudence and to philosophy, as well as to executive government, this too expresses a process of cultural differentiation that is advantageous to all three.

The division of labour also possesses an eminently political aspect that finds further expression in the conception of the *division of powers*. It is not only impossible for each person to do everything; it is politically undesirable as well. Kant's strict distinction between the exercise of political power and the activity of philosophical critique is analogous to the separation between executive and the judiciary. And if politicians and philosophers are to communicate meaningfully with one another without recourse to secrecy – that is publicly — then the role of the legislature must clearly also transpire in an open and public fashion. The separation between politics and philosophy thus also has *democratic implications*, for it presupposes that the actions and policies of the state must be referred back to the process of formation of the will in the public domain (specifically on this issue, see Kant's 'Appendix': 8:384f.). We must simply ask how this process of will formation can find an appropriate institutional expression, and this naturally brings us to the legislative function of parliament. It is only here that we can finally appreciate the politically progressive aspect that belongs to Kant's principled repudiation of the hopes that since Plato have repeatedly been placed in the idea of political rule by philosophers.

In this respect, we have paid dearly for the regressive position characteristic of much post-Kantian thought that essentially failed to recognise the political significance of the separation between politics and philosophy. In the eleventh of his *Theses against Feuerbach*, Marx explicitly rejected precisely this separation. It comes as no surprise, therefore, that Marx and his successors showed no understanding for the significance of positive law, or the division of powers and intrinsic human rights, and completely failed to grasp the idea that practical positions cannot be derived directly from theoretical insights.

Kant's commentators have also suggested that specific biographical and historical factors lie behind his strict distinction between the domains of politics and philosophy (see Cavallar 1992, pp. 348ff.). Such factors may indeed have played a part. But fundamentally speaking, Kant's judgement here is based upon his genuine understanding of the *systematic* difference between philosophical theory and domain of action itself. Kant presents and defends a new paradigm for conceptualising the relationship between politics and philosophy. There is no need for us simply to demonise the ancient Platonic *paradeigma*, which has certainly had its uses in this connection. But this model is fundamentally inappropriate to the specifically modern conditions of action and knowledge.

Kant's new alternative model is based upon his emphatic confidence in both the *critical* and *grounding* function of *philosophy*. But it also presupposes a new confidence in the domain of *politics*. In both cases, this confidence is sustained by the essentially mediating role of the *public sphere*, where individuals can communicate openly without forfeiting their own independence. If this process is successfully accomplished *theoretically*, we come to acquire new universally justifiable insights and thus to develop what Kant calls the 'culture of human reason.' If this process is successfully accomplished *practically*, then kings are no longer necessary and we must speak of 'royal peoples' instead (8:369). Thus Kant's greatest hope, as immediately contrasted with Plato's, is that it is the peoples themselves, rather than the philosophers, who should effectively become kings (see Schneiders 1981). And is there any real doubt that this is also a democratic hope?

And finally, Kant's distinction between politics and philosophy also sheds considerable light on the concluding 'Appendix' and the 'disagreement between morals and politics' (8:370). The first part of the 'Appendix' can easily leave the reader with the impression that Kant is unable or unwilling to distinguish between the domains of politics and morality. But if we seriously bear in mind just how decisively Kant himself has already separated the domains of politics and philosophy, then we shall approach his concluding remarks with different expectations in this respect. For we must continue to recognise the independence of politics in relation to morality. If the domain of politics is as directly connected with power as it clearly is, then it cannot simply be identified with the domain of morality.

Kant's concluding 'Appendix' should therefore not be read in abstraction from the *secret article* that we analysed at the beginning. For both discussions are concerned with a *single* theme – namely, the *humanistic function of the public sphere*, where politics and philosophy enter into an essentially reciprocal relation. In view of the important role played by a freely emerging public sphere, there can be no doubt whatsoever that Kant's revision of the Platonic idea of philosopher rule implies anything but a withdrawal of philosophy from the world of politics.

Bibliography

Aristotle 1995: *De monarchia, in: Fragmenta selecta*, ed. by David Ross (Oxford).

Bien, Günther 1973: *Die Grundlegung der politischen Philosophie bei Aristoteles* (Freiburg/München)

Bien, Günther 1989: 'Philosophie,' in *Historisches Wörterbuch der Philosophie*, ed. J. Ritter et al. vol. 7 (Basel).

Cavallar, Georg 1992: *Pax Kantiana. Systematisch-historische Untersuchung des Entwurfs 'Zum ewigen Frieden' (1795) von Immanuel Kant* (Wien/Köln/ Weimar).

Gerhardt, Volker 1988: 'Selbstbestimmung,' in *Metaphysik nach Kant?* eds. D. Henrich and R.P. Horstmann, pp. 671–688 (Stuttgart 1988).

Gerhardt, Volker 1990: 'Was ist ein vernünftiges Wesen? in *Selbstbehauptuung und Anerkennung. Spinoza–Kant–Fichte – Hegel*, ed. H. Girndt, pp. 61–77 (Bonn–St. Augustin 1990).

Gerhardt, Volker 1992: 'Moderne Zeiten. Zur philosophischen Ortsbestimmung der Gegenwart,' in *Deutsche Zeitschrift für Philosophie* 40, pp. 597–609.

Gerhardt, Volker 1995a: *Eine Theorie der Politik. Immanuel Kants Entwurf 'Zum ewigen Frieden'* (Darmstadt).

Gerhardt, Volker 1995b: 'Ausübende Rechtslehre,' in *Zur Kantinterpretation der Gegenwart*, ed. by G. Schönrich (Frankfurt).

Langer, Claudia 1986: *Reform nach Prinzipien. Untersuchungen zur politischen Philosophie Kants* (Stuttgart).

Laursen, John 1986: 'The Subversive Kant. The Vocabulary of "Public" and "Publicity," in *Political Theory* 14 pp. 584–603.

Natorp, Paul 1924: *Kant über Krieg und Frieden* (Erlangen).

Saner, Hans 1967: *Kants Weg vom Krieg zum Frieden, Band 1: Widerstreit und Einheit. Wege zu Kants politischem Denken* (München).

Schneiders, Werner 1981: 'Philosophenkönige und königliche Völker. Modelle philosophischer Politik bei Platon und Kant' in *Filosofia oggi 2*, pp. 165–175.

Sassenbach, Ulrich 1992: *Der Begriff des Politischen bei Immanuel Kant* (Würzburg).

Simmel, Georg 1931: 'Das Individuelle Gesetz,' reprinted in G. Simmel: *Das Individuelle Gesetz*, pp. 174–230 (Frankfurt 1968).

Wehrli, Fritz (ed.) 1944: *Die Schule des Aristoteles. Texte und Kommentar*, Heft 1: Dikaiarchos (Basel).

Bibliography

G. Achenwall and J.S. Pütter. *Elementa Iuris Naturae/Anfangsgründe des Naturrechts.* Latin/German, ed. and Trans. J. Schröder. Frankfurt, 1750/1995.

J.C. Adelung, ed. *Grammatisch-kritisches Wörterbuch der hochdeutschen Mundart.* Leipzig, 1793.

M. Albrecht. *Kants Antinomie der praktischen Vernunft.* Hildesheim, 1978.

H.E. Allison. *Kant's Theory of Freedom.* New York, 1990.

K. Ameriks. "Contemporary German Epistemology: The Significance of Gerold Prauss." *Inquiry* 25 (1982): 125–138.

—— "Kant on the Good Will." In *Grundlegung zur Metaphysik der Sitten: Ein kooperativer Kommentar,* ed. O. Höffe. Frankfurt, 1989, 45–65.

—— *Kant and the Fate of Autonomy.* Cambridge, 2000.

—— *Interpreting Kant's Critiques.* Oxford, 2003.

K. Ameriks. and D. Sturma, eds. *Kants Ethik.* Paderborn, 2004.

—— "Introduction." In Karl Leonhard Reinhold. *Letters on the Kantian Philosophy,* ed. K. Ameriks. Cambridge, 2005, ix–xxxv.

—— "A Commonsense Kant?" *Proceedings and Addresses of the American Philosophical Association* 79 (2005): 19–45.

Aristoteles. *Nikomachische Ethik,* ed. O. Gigon. Munich, 1972.

—— "De monarchia". In *Fragmenta selecta,* ed. W.D. Ross. Oxford, 1955.

K. Aso, M. Kurosaki, T. Otabe, and S. Yamauchi, eds. *Onomasticon philosophicum latinoteutonicum et teutonicolatinum.* Tokyo, 1989.

P. Baumann. "Zwei Seiten der Kantischen Begründung von Eigentum und Staat." *Kant-Studien* 85 (1994): 147–159.

A.G. Baumgarten. *Metaphysica.* Halle, 1739, 4th ed. 1757.

—— *Ethica philosophica.* Halle, 1740, 3rd ed. 1763 (reprinted in *Kant's Gesammelte Schriften.* Akademie-Ausgabe XXVII 871–1028).

—— *Initia philosophiae practicae primae.* Halle, 1760 (reprinted in *Kant's Gesammelte Schriften.* Akademie-Ausgabe XIX 7–91).

L.W. Beck. *A Commentary on Kant's Critique of Practical Reason.* Chicago, 1960 (German, *Kants "Kritik der praktischen Vernunft." Ein Kommentar.* Munich, 1974).

W. Betz and H. Paul, eds. *Deutsches Wörterbuch*. Tübingen, 1966.

G. Bien. "Revolution, Bürgerbegriff und Freiheit. Über die neuzeitliche Transformation der alteuropäischen Verfassungstheorie in politischer Geschichtsphilosophie." *Philosophisches Jahrbuch* 79 (1972): 1–18.

——— *Die Grundlegung der politischen Philosophie bei Aristoteles*. Freiburg and Munich, 1973.

——— "Philosophie." In *Historisches Wörterbuch der Philosophie*, ed. J. Ritter et al, vol. 7. Basel, 1989.

J. E. Biester. "Einige Nachrichten von den Ideen der Griechen über die Staatsverfassung." *Berlinische Monatsschrift*, June 1793.

R. Bittner. "Maximen." In *Akten des 4. Internationalen Kant-Kongresses, Mainz, 6.-10. April 1974*, ed. G. Funke. Berlin and New York, 1974, II.2, 485–498.

R. Bittner. and K. Cramer, eds. *Materialien zu Kants 'Kritik der praktischen Vernunft*.' Frankfurt, 1975.

——— "Das Unternehmen einer Grundlegung der Metaphysik der Sitten." In *Grundlegung zur Metaphysik der Sitten. Ein kooperativer Kommentar*, ed. O. Höffe. Frankfurt, 1989, 13–30.

——— *Doing Things for Reasons*. Oxford, 2001.

N. Bobbio. "Leibniz e Pufendorf." *Rivista di Filosofia* 38 (1947): 118–129.

S. del Boca. *Kant e i moralisti tedeschi. Wolff, Baumgarten, Crusius*. Naples, 1937.

L. E. Borowski. *Darstellung des Lebens und Charakters Immanuel Kant's*. Königsberg, 1804, and Berlin, 1912.

L. E. Borowski. and R. B. Jachmann, E. A. C. Wasianski. *Immanuel Kant. Sein Leben in Darstellungen von Zeitgenossen*. Berlin, 1912 (reprint, Darmstadt, 1968).

R. Brandt, ed. *Rechtsphilosophie der Aufklärung*. Berlin, 1982.

——— "Der Zirkel im dritten Abschnitt von Kants Grundlegung zur Metaphysik der Sitten." In *Kant. Analysen-Probleme-Kritik*, eds. H. Oberer and G. Seel. Würzburg, 1988, 169–191.

——— *Kritischer Kommentar zu Kants Anthropologie in pragmatischer Hinsicht: 1798*. Hamburg, 1999.

M. Brocker. *Kants Besitzlehre. Zur Problematik einer transzendentalphiloso-phischen Eigentumslehre*. Würzburg, 1987.

R. Bubner. *Handlung, Sprache, Vernunft. Grundbegriffe praktischer Philosophie*. Frankfurt, 1976.

R. Bubner and U. Dierse. "Maxime." In *Historisches Wörterbuch der Philosophie*, ed. J. Ritter et al, vol. 5, 943.

A. Bühler and L. C. Madonna. *Einleitung zu: Georg Friedrich Meier, Versuch einer allgemeinen Auslegungskunst*. Hamburg, 1996.

W. Busch. *Die Entstehung der kritischen Rechtsphilosophie Kants*. Berlin, 1979.

M. Campo. *Cristiano Wolff e il razionalismo precritico.* Milan, 1939 (reprint, Hildesheim and New York, 1980).

M. Casula. *La metafisica di A. G. Baumgarten.* Milan, 1973.

—— "A. G. Baumgarten entre G. W. Leibniz et Chr. Wolff." *Archives de Philosophie* 42, 1979: 547–574.

G. Cavallar. *Pax Kantiana. Systematisch-historische Untersuchung des Entwurfs Zum ewigen Frieden (1795) von Immanuel Kant.* Vienna, Cologne, and Weimar, 1992.

M. T. Cicero. *Über die Ziele des menschlichen Handelns (De finibus bonorum et malorum).* ed. and trans. O. Gigon. Darmstadt, 1988.

K. Cramer. "Metaphysik und Erfahrung in Kants Grundlegung der Ethik." In *Kant in der Diskussion der Moderne*, eds. G. Schönrich and Y. Kato. Frankfurt, 1996, 280–325.

C. A. Crusius. *Anweisung vernünftig zu leben.* Leipzig, 1744 (reprint, *Die philosophischen Hauptwerke*, eds. G. Tonelli, S. Carboncini and R. Finster, vol. 1. Hildesheim, 1969).

S. Darwall. *The British Moralists and the Internal 'Ought': 1640–1740.* Cambridge, 1995.

H.-G. Deggau. *Die Aporien der Rechtslehre Kants.* Stuttgart, 1983.

K. Deligiorgi. *Kant and the Culture of the Enlightenment.* Albany, 2005.

D. Döring. *Pufendorf-Studien. Beiträge zur Biographie Samuel von Pufendorfs und zu seiner Entwicklung als Historiker und theologischer Schriftsteller.* Berlin, 1992, 130–142.

K. Düsing. "Das Problem des höchsten Gutes in Kants praktische Philosophie." *Kant-Studien* 62 (1971): 5–42.

J. Ebbinghaus. *Gesammelte Aufsätze, Vorträge, und Reden.* Darmstadt, 1956.

R. Eisler. *Kant-Lexikon: Nachschlagewerk zu Kants sämtlichen Schriften, Briefen und handschriftlichem Nachlass.* Berlin, 1930 (reprint, Hildesheim, 1964).

B. Erdmann. *Martin Knutzen und seine Zeit. Ein Beitrag zur Geschichte der Wolfischen Schule und insbesondere zur Entwicklungsgeschichte Kants.* Leipzig, 1876 (reprint, Hildesheim, 1973).

R. Finster, G. Hunter, M. Miles, R. F. McRae, and W. E. Seager, eds. *Leibniz Lexicon. A Dual Concordance to Leibniz's 'Philosophische Schriften.'* Teil 2: Konkordanz des vollständigen Vokabulars vom *Typ Key-Word-In-Context* [on 65 microfiches]. Hildesheim, Zürich, New York, 1988.

E. Förster. "Die Wandlungen in Kants Gotteslehre." *Zeitschrift für philosophische Forschung* 52 (1998): 341–362.

F. W. Foerster. *Der Entwicklungsgang der Kantischen Ethik.* Berlin, 1893.

T. Fowler. *Shaftesbury und Hutcheson.* London, 1882.

J. Freudiger. *Kants Begründung der praktischen Philosophie. Systematische Stellung, Methode und Argumentationsstruktur der 'Grundlegung zur Metaphysik der Sitten'.* Bern, Stuttgart, Vienna, 1993.

Fr. v. Gentz. "*Über den ewigen Frieden (1800)*." In *Ewiger Friede. Friedensrufe und Friedenspläne seit der Renaissance*, ed. K. v. Raumer. Freiburg, 1953, 461–497.

C. I. Gerhart, ed. *Briefwechsel zwischen Leibniz und Christian Wolff.* Halle, 1860 (reprint, Hildesheim and New York, 1963, 2nd ed., 1971).

V. Gerhardt. "Selbstbestimmung." In *Metaphysik nach Kant?* eds. D. Henrich and R.-P. Horstmann. Stuttgart, 1988, 671–688.

—— "Was ist ein vernünftiges Wesen?" In *Selbstbehauptung und Anerkennung. Spinoza-Kant-Fichte-Hegel*, ed. H. Girndt. Bonn-St.Augustin, 1990, 61–77.

—— "Moderne Zeiten. Zur philosophischen Ortsbestimmung der Gegenwart." *Deutsche Zeitschrift für Philosophie* 40 (1992): 597–609.

—— *Eine Theorie der Politik. Immanuel Kants Entwurf 'Zum ewigen Frieden.'* Darmstadt, 1995.

—— "Ausübende Rechtslehre." In *Zur Kant-Interpretation der Gegenwart*, ed. G. Schönrich. Frankfurt, 1995.

A. Gilbert. "Must Global Politics Constrain Democracy? Realism, Regimes, and Democratic Internationalism." *Political Theory* 20 (1992): 8–37.

G. v. Gizycki. *Die Ethik David Humes.* Breslau, 1882.

J. W. Goethe. *Faust.* In *Goethes Werke*, ed. E. Trunz, vol. 3. Hamburg, 1986.

A. Götze, ed. *Trübners deutsches Wörterbuch.* Berlin, 1940.

J. C. Gottsched. *Historische Lobschrift des weiland hoch- und wohlgebohrnen Herrn Herrn Christians, des H. R. R. Freyherrn von Wolf.* Halle, 1755 (reprint, Hildesheim and New York, 1980, WW I.10).

J. Gredt. *Die aristotelisch-thomistische Philosophie*, vol. 2. Freiburg, 1935.

J. and W. Grimm, eds. *Deutsches Wörterbuch.* Leipzig, 1862.

W. Gruhn, ed. *Leben und Abenteuer des Andrej Bolotow von ihm selbst für seine Nachkommen aufgeschrieben*, vol. 1. Munich, 1990.

P. Guyer. "In praktischer Absicht: Kants Begriff der Postulate der reinen praktischen Vernunft." *Philosophisches Jahrbuch* 104 (1997): 1–18.

A. Hägerström. *Recht, Pflicht und bindende Kraft des Vertrages nach römischer und naturrechtlicher Anschauung*, ed. K. Olivecrona. Stockholm and Wiesbaden, 1965, 59–63.

J. Hare. *The Moral Gap: Kantian Ethics, Human Limits, and God's Assistance.* Oxford, 1996.

G. W. F. Hegel. "Über die wissenschaftlichen Behandlungsarten des Naturrechts, seine Stelle in der praktischen Philosophie und sein Verhältnis zu den positiven Rechtswissenschaften" (1803). In *Werke in zwanzig Bänden*, eds. E. Moldenhauer and K. M. Michael, vol. 2. Frankfurt, 1970, 434–530.

—— *Phänomenologie des Geistes* (1807). In *Werke in zwanzig Bänden*, vol. 3.

D. Henrich. *Selbstbewußtsein und Identität.* Heidelberg, 1956.

—— "Hutcheson und Kant." *Kant-Studien* 49 (1957/58): 49–69.

—— "Über Kants früheste Ethik. Versuch einer Rekonstruktion." *Kant-Studien* 54 (1963): 404–431.

—— "Über Kants Entwicklungsgeschichte." *Philosophische Rundschau* 13 (1965): 252–263.

—— "Über den Sinn vernünftigen Handelns im Staat." In *Kant-Gentz-Rehberg: Über Theorie und Praxis*. Frankfurt, 1967, 9–37.

—— "The Moral Image of the World." In *Aesthetic Judgement and the Moral Image of the World*. Stanford, 1992, 3–28.

—— *The Unity of Reason: Essays on Kant's Philosophy*. Cambridge, 1994.

—— "The Deduction of the Moral Law: The Reasons for the Obscurity of the Final Sections of the Groundwork of the Metaphysics of Morals." In *Kant's Groundwork of the Metaphysics of Morals: Critical Essays*, ed. P. Guyer. Lanham 1998, 303–341.

—— *Between Kant and Hegel: Lectures on German Idealism*. Cambridge, 2003.

B. Herman. *The Practice of Moral Judgment*. Cambridge, 1993.

M. Heyne, ed. *Deutsches Wörterbuch*. Leipzig, 1890.

—— ed. *Deutsches Wörterbuch*. Leipzig, 1905.

J. C. A. Heyse and K. W. L. Heyse, eds. *Handwörterbuch der deutschen Sprache*. Magdeburg, 1833.

F. Hinard. "La Naissance du Mythe de Sylla." *Revue des Études latines* 62 (1984): 81–94.

N. Hinske. *Kant als Herausforderung an die Gegenwart*. Freiburg and Munich, 1980.

W. Hinsch, ed. *Zur Idee des politischen Liberalismus: John Rawls in der Diskussion*, Frankfurt, 1997.

O. Höffe. "Kants kategorischer Imperativ als Kriterium des Sittlichen." *Zeitschrift für philosophische Forschung* 31 (1977): 354–384.

—— "Recht und Moral: ein Kantischer Problemaufriß." *neue hefte für philosophie* [sic] 17 (1979): 1–36.

—— "Zur vertragstheoretischen Begründung politischer Gerechtigkeit: Hobbes, Kant und Rawls im Vergleich." In *Ethik und Politik*. Frankfurt, 1979, 4th ed. 2000, 195–226.

—— "Die Menschenrechte als Legitimation und kritischer Maßstab der Demokratie." In *Menschenrechte und Demokratie*, ed. J. Schwartländer. Kehl, 1981, 241–274.

—— ed. *Grundlegung zur Metaphysik der Sitten.: Ein kooperativer Kommentar*. Frankfurt, 1989, 3rd ed. 2000.

—— "Universalistische Ethik und Urteilskraft: ein Aristotelischer Blick auf Kant." *Zeitschrift für philosophische Forschung* 44 (1990): 537–563.

—— *Immanuel Kant*. Munich, 6th ed. 2004. (English, *Immanuel Kant*. Albany, 1994.)

—— ed. *Zum Ewigen Frieden*. Berlin, 1995.

—— ed. *Metaphysische Anfangsgründe der Rechtslehre*. Berlin, 1999.

—— "Königliche Völker": zu Kants kosmopolitischer Rechts- und Friedenstheorie. Frankfurt, 2001.

—— *Kategorische Rechtsprinzipien. Ein Kontrapunkt der Moderne*, Frankfurt, 1990. (English, *Categorical Principles of Law: A Counterpoint to Modernity*. University Park, 2002.)

—— ed. *Kritik der praktischen Vernunft*. Berlin, 2002.

—— *Politische Gerechtigkeit. Grundlegung einer kritischen Philosophie von Recht und Staat*. Frankfurt, 3rd ed. 2002.

V. Hösle. *Die Krise der Gegenwart und die Verantwortung der Philosophie*. Munich, 1990.

H. Home. *Essays on the Principles of Morality and Natural Religion*. Edinburgh, 1951 (reprint, New York and London, 1976).

J. Hruschka. *Das deontologische Sechseck bei Gottfried Achenwall im Jahre 1767. Zur Geschichte der deontischen Grundbegriffe in der Universaljurisprudenz zwischen Suarez und Kant*. Hamburg, 1986.

F. Hutcheson. *Untersuchung unserer Begriffe von Schönheit und Tugend*, trans. Merk, Frankfurt and Leipzig, 1762. (English, *Inquiry concerning Beauty, Order, Harmony and Design, the Inquiry concerning Moral Good and Evil*. London, 1725.)

—— *Synopsis Metaphysicae Ontologiam et Pneumatologiam complectens*. Glasgow, 1742 (1771 ed. cited here).

—— *A System of Moral Philosophy*. 2 vols. Glasgow, 1755 (German, Leipzig, 1756.)

—— *Abhandlung über die Natur und Beherrschung der Leidenschaften*. Leipzig, 1760.

K.-H. Ilting. "Der naturalistische Fehlschluß bei Kant." In *Rehabilitierung der praktischen Philosophie*, ed. M. Riedel, vol. 1. Freiburg, 1972, 113–130.

B. Jacobs and P. Kain, eds. *Essays on Kant's Anthropology*. Cambridge, 2003.

F. Jodl. *Geschichte der Ethik*. Stuttgart, 1882–89, 2nd ed. 1906.

F. Kaulbach. *Immanuel Kants 'Grundlegung zur Metaphysik der Sitten'. Interpretation und Kommentar*. Darmstadt, 1988.

W. Kersting. *Wohlgeordnete Freiheit. Immanuel Kants Rechts- und Staatsphilosophie*. Berlin and New York, 1984.

—— "Besprechung von Kühl, 1984." *Zeitschrift für philosophische Forschung* 40 (1986): 309–313.

F. Kluge, ed. *Etymologisches Wörterbuch der deutschen Sprache*. Berlin, 1957.

J. Kneller and S. Axinn, eds. *Autonomy and Community: Readings in Contemporary Kantian Social Philosophy*. Albany, 1998.

H. Köhl. *Kants Gesinnungsethik*. Berlin and New York, 1990.

S. Körner. *Kant*. Göttingen, 1967.

C. M. Korsgaard. *Creating the Kingdom of Ends*. Cambridge, 1996.

A. Kowalewski, ed. *Die Philosophischen Hauptvorlesungen Immanuel Kants. Nach den neu aufgefundenen Kollegheften des Grafen Heinrich zu Dohna-Wundlacken*. Munich, 1924.

H. Krämer. "Antike und moderne Ethik?" *Zeitschrift für Theologie und Kirche* 80 (1983): 184–203.

P. Krausser. "Über eine unvermerkte Doppelrolle des kategorischen Imperativs in Kants Grundlegung zur Metaphysik der Sitten." *Kant-Studien* 59 (1968): 318–332.

H. Krings. *System und Freiheit: Gesammelte Aufsätze.* Freiburg, 1980.

G. Krüger. *Philosophie und Moral in der kantischen Ethik.* Tübingen, 1931, 2nd ed. 1969.

K. Kühl. *Eigentumsordnung als Freiheitsordnung. Zur Aktualität der Kantischen Rechts- und Eigentumslehre.* Freiburg and Munich, 1984.

—— "Die Bedeutung der Kantischen Unterscheidung von Legalität und Moralität sowie von Rechts- und Tugendpflichten für das Strafrecht–ein Problemaufriß." In *Recht und Moral*, eds. H. Jung et al. Baden-Baden, 1991, 139–176.

M. Kuehn. *Kant: A Biography.* New York, 2001.

—— *Scottish Common Sense in Germany, 1768–1800.* Kingston and Montreal, 1987.

M. Küenburg. *Ethische Grundfragen in der jüngst veröffentlichten Ethikvorlesung Kants. Studie zur Geschichte der Moralphilosophie.* Innsbruck, 1925.

C. Langer. *Reform nach Prinzipien. Untersuchungen zur politischen Theorie Immanuel Kants.* Stuttgart, 1986.

J. C. Laursen. "The Subversive Kant. The Vocabulary of 'Public' and 'Publicity.'" *Political Theory* 14 (1986): 584–603.

M.-H. Lee. *Das Problem des moralischen Gefühls in der Entwicklung der Kantischen Ethik.* Taiwan, 1994.

G. W. Leibniz. "Vorrede zum Codex iuris gentium diplomaticus (1693)." In *Die philosophischen Schriften*, ed. C.I. Gerhardt, vol. 3. Berlin 1887 (reprint, Hildesheim, 1960).

—— "Essais de Theodicée." In *Die philosophischen Schriften*, ed. C.I. Gerhardt, vol. 6. Berlin, 1885 (reprint, Hildesheim, 1961).

—— "Monita quaedam ad Samuelis Puffendorfii principia, Gerh. Wolth. Molano directa (1706)." In *Opera omnia*, ed. L. Dutens, vol. 4.3. Geneva, 1768 (reprint, Hildesheim, Zürich, and New York, 1989), 275–283.

M. A. Lucani *De bello civili libri X*, ed. D. R. Shackleton Bailey. Stuttgart, 2nd. ed. 1997.

B. Ludwig. "Besprechung von Kühl 1984." *Archiv für Rechts- und Sozialphilosophie* 73 (1987): 153–155.

—— *Kants Rechtslehre.* Hamburg, 1988.

B. Ludwig and K. Herb. *Kants kritisches Staatsrecht. Jahrbuch für Recht und Ethik* II. 1994: 431–478.

R. Ludwig. *Kategorischer Imperativ und Metaphysik der Sitten. Die Frage nach der Einheitlichkeit von Kants Ethik.* Frankfurt, 1992.

G. Luf. *Freiheit und Gleichheit.* Vienna and New York, 1978.

I. Maus. *Zur Aufklärung der Demokratietheorie. Rechts- und demokratietheoretische Überlegungen im Anschluß an Kant.* Frankfurt, 1992.

G. S. A. Mellin. *Encyclopädisches Wörterbuch der kritischen Philosophie,* vol. 4. Jena and Leipzig,1801 (reprint, Aalen, 1971).

M. Mendelssohn. *Gesammelte Schriften. Jubiläumsausgabe,* vol. 2. Berlin, 1931 (reprint, Stuttgart Bad-Cannstatt, 1972).

P. Menzer, ed. *Eine Vorlesung Kants über Ethik.* Berlin, 1924.

—— "Der Entwicklungsgang der Kantischen Ethik in den Jahren 1760 bis 1785," *Kant-Studien* 2 (1898), and 3 (1899), 41–104.

T. Mommsen. *Römische Geschichte,* 8 vols. Munich, 2001.

P. Müller. *Transzendentale Kritik und moralische Teleologie. Eine Auseinandersetzung mit den zeitgenössischen Transformationen der Transzendentalphilosophie im Hinblick auf Kant.* Würzburg, 1983.

G. F. Munzel. *Kant's Conception of Moral Character: The Critical Link of Morality, Anthropology and Reflective Judgment.* Chicago, 1999.

P. Natorp. *Kant über Krieg und Frieden.* Erlangen, 1924.

L. Nelson. *Critique of Practical Reason.* Scarsdale, 1957.

H. Oberer. "Zur Frühgeschichte der Kantischen Rechtslehre." *Kant-Studien* **64** (1973): 88–102.

O. O'Neill. *Acting on Principle: An Essay on Kantian Ethics.* New York, 1975.

—— *Constructions of Reason. Explorations of Kant's Practical Philosophy.* Cambridge, 1989.

F. Palladini. "Di una critica di Leibniz a Pufendorf." In *Percorsi della ricerca filosofica. Filosofie tra storia, linguaggio e politica.* Rome, 1990, 19–27.

—— *Samuel Pufendorf discepolo di Hobbes. Per una reinterpretazione del giusnaturalismo moderno.* Bologna, 1990, 33–90.

C.-G. Park. *Das moralische Gefühl in der britischen moral-sense-Schule und bei Kant.* Tübingen, 1995.

H. J. Paton. *Der kategorische Imperativ. Eine Untersuchung über Kants Moralphilosophie.* Berlin, 1962. (English, *The Categorical Imperative: A Study in Kant's Moral Philosophy,* 1947.)

L. J. Pongratz and C. Seidel. "Charakter." In *Historisches Wörterbuch der Philosophie,* eds. J. Ritter et al, vol. 1, 988.

B. Poppe. *Alexander Gottlieb Baumgarten. Seine Bedeutung und Stellung in der Leibniz-Wolffischen Philosophie und seine Beziehungen zu Kant.* Borna and Leipzig, 1907 (reprint, Ann Arbor and London, 1982).

G. Prauss. *Erscheinung bei Kant.* Berlin, 1971.

—— *Einführung in die Erkenntnistheorie.* Darmstadt, 1980.

—— *Kant über Freiheit als Autonomie.* Frankfurt, 1983.

S. Pufendorf. *De iure naturae et gentium.* (Lund, 1672) Frankfurt/Leipzig, 1759 (reprint, Frankfurt, 1967).

—— "De officio hominis et civis juxta legem naturalem." (Lund, 1673) In *Gesammelte Werke,* vol. 2. Berlin, 1997.

J. Rawls. *Lectures on the History of Moral Philosophy.* Cambridge, 2000.

H. Reiner. *Duty and Inclination: The Fundamentals of Morality Discussed and Redefined with Special Regard to Kant and Schiller.* Hingham, 1983.

E. Riedesel. *Pietismus und Orthodoxie in Ostpreußen. Auf Grund des Briefwechsels G. F. Rogalls und F. A. Schultz' mit den Halleschen Pietisten.* Königsberg and Berlin, 1937.

C. Ritter. *Der Rechtsgedanke Kants nach den frühen Quellen.* Frankfurt, 1971.

J. J. Rousseau. *Émile.* In *Œuvres complètes,* eds. B. Gagnebin and M. Raymond, vol 4. Paris, 1959–1961.

—— *La nouvelle Héloise.* In *Œuvres complètes,* eds. B. Gagnebin and M. Raymond, vol. 2. Paris, 1959–1961.

H. Saner. "Widerstreit und Einheit. Wege zu Kants politischem Denken." In *Kants Weg vom Krieg zum Frieden,* vol. 1. Munich, 1967.

J. Schapp. *Sachenrecht.* Munich, 1989.

U. Sassenbach. *Der Begriff des Politischen bei Immanuel Kant.* Würzburg, 1992.

P. A. Schilpp. "Kant's Precritical Ethics." In *Northwestern University Studies* No. 2, Evanston, 1938.

E. Schmidt-Jortzig. "Eigentum und Privatautonomie." In *Recht–Eine Information des Bundesministeriums der Justiz.* 1998.

J. Schmucker. *Die Ursprünge der Ethik Kants in seinen vorkritischen Schriften und Reflektionen.* Meisenheim am Glan, 1961.

J. Schneewind. "Pufendorf's Place in the History of Ethics." *Synthese* 72 (1987): 123–155.

—— "Kant and Natural Law Ethics." *Ethics* 104 (1993): 53–74.

—— "Barbeyrac and Leibniz on Pufendorf." In *Samuel von Pufendorf und die europäische Frühaufklärung. Werk und Einfluß eines deutschen Bürgers der Gelehrtenrepublik nach 300 Jahren (1694–1994),* eds. F. Palladini and G. Hartung. Berlin, 1996, 181–189.

—— *The Invention of Autonomy.* Cambridge, 1998.

W. Schneiders. "Philosophenkönige und königliche Völker. Modelle philosophischer Politik bei Platon und Kant." *Filosofia Oggi* 2 (1981): 165–175.

C. Schnoor. *Kants Kategorischer Imperativ als Kriterium der Richtigkeit des Handelns.* Tübingen, 1989.

C. Schwaiger. *Das Problem des Glücks im Denken Christian Wolffs. Eine quellen-, begriffs- und entwicklungsgeschichtliche Studie zu Schlüsselbegriffen seiner Ethik.* Stuttgart-Bad Cannstatt, 1995, 161–188.

J. Schwartländer. *Der Mensch ist Person. Kants Lehre vom Menschen.* Stuttgart, Berlin, Cologne and Mainz, 1968.

O. Schwemmer. *Philosophie der Praxis. Versuch zur Grundlegung einer Lehre vom moralischen Argumentieren in Verbindung mit einer Interpretation der praktischen Philosophie Kants.* Frankfurt, 1971.

W. R. Scott. *Francis Hutcheson.* Cambridge, 1900.

R. Sève. *Leibniz et l'École moderne du droit naturel*. Paris, 1989.

J.R. Silber. "Kants Conception of the Highest Good as Immanent and Transcendent." *The Philosophical Review* 68 (1959): 469–492.

—— "Die metaphysische Bedeutung des höchsten Guts als Kanon der reinen Vernunft in Kants Philosophie." *Zeitschrift für philosophische Forschung* 23 (1969): 538–549.

G. Simmel. Das individuelle Gesetz (1931). In *Das individuelle Gesetz*. Frankfurt, 1968, 174–230.

W. Stark, ed. *Immanuel Kant: Vorlesung zur Moralphilosophie*. Berlin, 2004.

F.C. Starke, ed. *Immanuel Kant's Anweisung zur Menschen- und Welterkenntniß*. Quedlinburg and Leipzig, 2nd. ed. 1838.

—— ed. *Immanuel Kant's Menschenkunde oder philosophische Anthropologie*. Quedlinburg and Leipzig, 2nd. ed. 1838 (reprint, Hildesheim, 1976).

L. Stephen. *The History of English Thought in the Eighteenth Century*, 2 vols. New York, 1876.

P.F. Strawson. "Freedom and Resentment." In *Freedom and Resentment and Other Essays*. London, 1974. (German, "Freiheit und Übelnehmen." In *Seminar: Freies Handeln und Determinismus*, ed. U. Pothast. Frankfurt, 1976, 201–233.)

M. Thomann. "Christian Wolff et le droit subjectif." *Archives de Philosophie du Droit* 9, 1964: 153–174.

U. Thurnherr. *Die Ästhetik der Existenz. Über den Begriff der Maxime und die Bildung von Maximen bei Kant*. Tübingen and Basel, 1994.

—— "Urteilskraft und Anerkennung in der Ethik Immanuel Kants." In *Anerkennung. Eine philosophische Propädeutik*, eds. M. Hofmann-Riedinger and U. Thurnherr. Freiburg and Munich, 2001, 76–92.

M. Timmons, ed. *Kant's Metaphysics of Morals: Interpretive Essays*. Oxford, 2002.

G. Tonelli. "Casula on Baumgarten's Metaphysics." *Kant-Studien* 66 (1975): 242–243.

—— "Tugend." In *Lexikon der Ethik*, ed. O. Höffe. Munich, 2nd ed. 1980, 267–270.

E. Tugendhat. "Antike und moderne Ethik (1980)." In *Probleme der Ethik*. Stuttgart, 1984, 33–56.

—— *Vorlesungen über Ethik*. Frankfurt, 1993.

P. Unruh. *Die Herrschaft der Vernunft. Zur Staatsphilosophie Immanuel Kants*. Baden-Baden, 1992.

"Verbindlichkeit." In J.H. Zedler. *Grosses vollständiges Universal-Lexicon aller Wissenschafften und Künste*, vol. 47. Leipzig and Halle, 1746 (reprint, Graz, 1962), 1555–1570.

K. Vorländer. *"Einleitung" zu Kants 'Grundlegung zur Metaphysik der Sitten'*. Hamburg, 1965.

W.H. Walsh. "Kant's Moral Theology." *Proceedings of the British Academy* 49 (1963): 263–289.

F. Wehrli, ed. "Dikaiarchos." In *Die Schule des Aristoteles. Texte und Kommentar.* Heft 1. Basel, 1944.

D. Weymann. *Beantwortung des Versuchs einiger Betrachtungen über den Optimismus.* Königsberg, 1759.

—— *De vero stabiliendo juris naturae et gentium principio. Pars prima.* [Disputation vom 12. Juni 1762] Königsberg, 1762.

—— *Bedenklichkeiten über den einzig möglichen Beweisgrund des Herrn M. Kants zu einer Demonstration des Daseyns Gottes.* Königsberg, 1763.

A. Wildt. "Zum Verhältnis von Recht und Moral bei Kant." *Archiv für Rechts- und Sozialphilosophie* 83 (1997): 159–174.

M. Willaschek. *Praktische Vernunft. Handlungstheorie und Moralbegründung bei Kant.* Stuttgart and Weimar, 1992.

—— "Was sind praktische Gesetze?" In *Proceedings of the Eighth International Kant Kongreß. Memphis 1995,* ed. H. Robinson. Milwaukee, 1995, II. 2, 533–540.

A. Winter. "Der Gotteserweis aus praktischer Vernunft." In *Der andere Kant.* Hildesheim, 2000, 257–343.

U. Wolf. *Die Philosophie und die Frage nach dem guten Leben.* Hamburg, 1999.

C. Wolff. *Gesammelte Werke,* eds. J. École, J. E. Hofmann, M. Thomann, H. W. Arndt. Hildesheim, Zürich, New York (= WW).

—— *Christian Ratio praelectionum Wolfianarum [in] mathesin et philosophiam universam.* Halle, 1718, 2nd ed. 1735 (reprint, 1972), WW II.36.

—— *Vernünfftige Gedancken von der Menschen Thun und Lassen, zu Beförderung ihrer Glückseeligkeit [=Deutsche Ethik].* Halle, 1720, 4th ed. Frankfurt and Leipzig, 1733 (reprint, 1976), WW I.4.

—— *Ausführliche Nachricht von seinen eigenen Schrifften, die er in deutscher Sprache von den verschiedenen Theilen der Welt-Weißheit heraus gegeben.* Frankfurt, 1726, 2nd ed. 1733, (reprint, 1973), WW I.9.

—— *Philosophia rationalis sive logica, methodo scientifica pertractata.* Vol. 1. Frankfurt and Leipzig 1728, 3rd ed. 1740 (reprint, 1983), WW II.1.1.

—— "De peccato in philosophum." In *Horae subsecivae Marburgenses Anni MDCCXXX, Trimestre aestivum.* Frankfurt and Leipzig, 1731 (reprint, 1983), WW II.34.2.

—— *Psychologia empirica, methodo scientifica pertractata.* Frankfurt and Leipzig, 1732, 2nd ed. 1738 (reprint, 1968), WW II.5.

—— *Theologia naturalis methodo scientifica pertractata,* vol. I.2. Frankfurt and Leipzig, 1736, 2nd ed. 1739 (reprint, 1978), WW II.7.2.

—— *Philosophia practica universalis, methodo scientifica pertractata,* vol. 1. Frankfurt and Leipzig, 1738 (reprint, 1971), WW II.10.

—— *Philosophia practica universalis, methodo scientifica pertractata,* vol. 2. Frankfurt and Leipzig 1739 (reprint, 1979) ,WW II.11.

—— *Institutiones juris naturae et gentium.* Halle, 1750 (reprint, 1969), WW II.26.

—— *Philosophia moralis sive ethica, methodo scientifica pertractata,* vol. 1. Halle. 1750 (reprint, 1970), WW II.12.

—— *Philosophia moralis sive ethica, methodo scientifica pertractata*, vol. 3. Halle. 1751 (reprint, 1970), WW II.14.

—— "Philosophia practica universalis, mathematica methodo conscripta." In *Meletemata mathematico-philosophica cum erudito orbe literarum commercio communicata*. Halle, 1755 (reprint, 1974), WW II.35.

—— "Elogium Godofredi Guilielmi Leibnitii." *Acta Eruditorum*, Juli 1717, 334 (reprinted in *Meletemata*, Sect. I, 130).

—— *Oratio de Sinarum philosophia practica. Rede über die praktische Philosophie der Chinesen*, ed. M. Albrecht. Hamburg, 1985.

R.P. Wolff. *The Autonomy of Reason. A Commentary on Kant's Groundwork of the Metaphysics of Morals*. New York, 1973.

A.W. Wood. *Kant's Moral Religion*. Ithaca, 1970.

A.W. Wood and G. di Giovanni, eds. *Religion within the Boundaries of Mere Reason, in Immanuel Kant. Religion and Rational Theology*, Cambridge, 1998.

H. Wuttke, ed. *Christian Wolffs eigene Lebensbeschreibung*. Leipzig, 1841 (reprint, 1980), WW I.10.

J.L. Zimmermann. *De actionum humanarum moralitate nec non de obligatione iuris, legibusque stricte dictis dissertatio philosophica, in qua celeberrimi Prof. Wolffii principia nonnulla moralia examinantur*. Jena, 1728.

Index